THE BEST OF FOOD&WINE

THE BEST OF
FOOD&WINE

American Express
Food & Wine Magazine
Corporation
New York

Published by American Express Food & Wine Magazine Corporation
1120 Avenue of the Americas, New York, New York 10036

Manufactured in the United States of America

Library of Congress Cataloging in Publication Data

Main entry under title:

The Best of Food & Wine.

Includes index.
1. Cookery, International. I. Food & Wine (New York, NY)

TX725.A1B482   641.5   83-26634

ISBN 0-916103-00-5

TABLE OF CONTENTS

FOREWORD

Welcome to *The Best of Food & Wine*. Those of you who know our magazine realize how highly we prize the food we present in each issue. Those who do not can rest assured that every recipe in *Food & Wine*, and therefore every recipe in this volume, has been tested and, where necessary, adapted or adjusted for use by home cooks. Two major responsibilities of our Test Kitchen cooks are to create workable recipes filled with flavor, and to simplify food preparation without robbing dishes of their fundamental integrity.

Where do these recipes come from? Some, a higher percentage than in any other American epicurean magazine, are developed by the Test Kitchen staff itself. During the period of time spanned by the contents of this book, our kitchen was directed by Jim Fobel and (since October, 1982) by Diana Sturgis. Her principal assistants are John Robert Massie and Anne Disrude. Other recipes are sent to us by readers for inclusion in our monthly "Simply Splendid" column. Most of the remainder are created by contributors to the magazine. You will find a list crediting these talented cooks and writers on pages 239-240.

It was a thrill for us at *Food & Wine* to have the opportunity to present 500 of our favorite recipes and 40 glorious photographs in this volume. Choosing from among the more than 3,000 recipes that have been published since the magazine's inaugural issue in May, 1978, was not an easy task. The recipes that have survived the winnowing process represent a balance of foods and of the various courses that make a meal. They also represent what we feel to be a superb sampling of the best of contemporary cooking, delicious and beautiful food equally suitable for your family or for entertaining the best of friends.

—William Rice
Editor-in-Chief

FOOD & WINE'S VINTAGE RATINGS
1970-1980

COMPILED BY ELIN McCOY & JOHN FREDERICK WALKER

	1970	1971	1972	1973	1974
Red Bordeaux	9 Outstanding; big & ripe. Start drinking. Will hold.	7 Uneven; can be excellent. Ready now.	3 Unripe, acid. Now or never.	5 Light, fruity, soft. Drink it up.	4 No charm. Hard & lightweight. Drink now.
Sauternes	8 Rich, fat, full. Drink now.	9 Stylish, well-balanced; ready now but will last.	2 Very poor. Avoid.	4 Lightweight & little character. Drink up.	3 Very poor. Avoid.
Red Burgundy	7 Soft, attractive, but fading. Drink now.	9 Powerful, deep, concentrated. Ready now but will keep.	8 Firm, solid, good acidity. Ready but holding well.	6 Light & pleasant; fading fast. Don't wait.	4 Light & lean; no depth. Now or never.
White Burgundy	7 Soft and fading fast. May be past it.	9 Powerful & rich. The best are at their peak.	4 Hard, lean wines. Don't wait.	6 Attractive, fruity. Most past best.	4 Thin & fading. Most past best.
Napa/Sonoma Cabernet Sauvignon	9 Classic—intense, ripe. Drink now; best holding well.	6 Variable. Most are thin and mature. Drink now.	5 Generally poor; lacks depth. Most past it.	7 Very good, well-balanced year. Drink now.	8 Fat, rich, tannic; some overripe. Most best now.
Napa/Sonoma Chardonnay	8 Full, appealing. Most past best.	7 A few excellent survivors. Drink up.	6 Ripe, rich, mature. Drink up.	7 Fragrant, fruity, fading. Drink up.	6 Full-bodied, fast-maturing. Most past best.
Piedmont Barolo & Barbaresco	8 Fragrant, rich, well-balanced. Drink now.	9½ Exceptionally rich, intense. Ready but will keep.	0 Disastrous. Barolo & Barbaresco declassified.	5 Light & fragrant. Drink now.	8 Excellent, full & round. Drink now.
Chianti	8 Flavorful & fully mature. Inconsistent; some past it.	9 Uneven; best intense, rich. Drink now.	3 Poor wines. Avoid.	5 Variable: fair to very good. Fading. Drink up.	6 Light, pleasant, fading. Drink up.
Germany	7 Soft, attractive. Most past best. Drink up.	9 Superlative balance. Drink now, but best will hold.	4 Poor, lean, acidic. Long past best. Avoid.	6 Appealing, soft wines; most past best. Drink up.	5 Uneven & fading. Drink up.
Vintage Porto	8 Well-balanced, fruity. Can start to drink. Will hold.	No vintage declared	5 Not generally declared. Light, pleasant. Enjoy now.	No vintage declared	No vintage declared

The following ratings and comments reflect a variety of opinions, including our own, on the quality and character of various categories of wines from recent vintages. The ratings—0 for the worst, 10 for the best—are averages, and better or worse wine than indicated can be found in each vintage. Assessments of the most current vintages are more predictive and hence less exact than those of older vintages.

Scores are based on a wine's quality at maturity. A lower-rated but mature wine will often be superior to a higher-rated but immature wine. When-to-drink advice is based on how such wines seemed to be developing in mid-1982, and presumes good storage. The earliest date suggested for consumption applies to the lesser wines of the vintage, which will mature faster than the finest examples of that year.

1975	1976	1977	1978	1979	1980
9½ Classic, concentrated, rich. Wait 3-10 years. Will last.	7 Soft, full, attractive. Drink now.	4 Lightweight, lacks fruit. Best now.	8½ Rich, full, good depth. Wait 2-5 years.	7½ Fruity & well-balanced. Try in 1-4 years.	5 Small-scale, lightweight, pleasant. Not for keeping.
9 Deep, rich; some classics. Start drinking; best will hold.	9 Elegant & luscious. Start drinking; will keep.	3 Very weak. Avoid.	5 Big, but lacks typical richness. Drink now.	6 Light but has character. Now.	7 Attractive, promising.
3 Thin, weak; most are poor. Avoid.	8½ Deep, full, tannic. Start drinking; best will hold.	4 Light, thin, uneven. Drink now.	9 Outstanding; excellent balance. Wait 1-2 years.	7 Soft, supple, appealing. Start sampling.	5 Light wines destined for early drinking.
4 Very light wines. Drink up.	7 Big, soft, rich wines. Enjoy now.	5 Light, lean, acidic. Drink now.	9 Superb; well-balanced. Wonderful now but will keep.	7 Attractive, fruity wines. Most best now.	5 Variable; the best should be attractive.
7 Lacks power, but best have elegance. Drink now.	7 Variable. Many heavy and tannic. Drink now.	7½ Variable. Some well-balanced wines. Drink now.	9 Full, rich, balanced. Start drinking; will keep.	8 Uneven quality; some very good. Start sampling.	8 Variable; some very promising.
8 Intense, well-balanced. Drink now.	6 Big, ripe; some too powerful. Drink now.	7 Uneven. Some attractive. Drink now.	8 Powerful, ripe wines. Drink now.	8 Rich, intense, impressive. Start drinking.	9 Many have superb balance. Start drinking.
5 Light & attractive. Drink now.	6 Light, well-balanced. Drink now.	4 Light, thin wines. Drink now.	9 Classic, concentrated & tannic. Wait 2-4 years; will last.	8 Elegant, well-balanced wines. Start sampling; will hold.	6 Uneven. Best are well-balanced, attractive. Early maturing.
9 Exceptional. Well-balanced wines. Now ready.	3 Lightweight, disappointing. Now or never.	7 Good to very good; firm, stylish. Drink now; will hold.	9 Exceptional; big, solid, tannic. Start sampling; will hold.	7 Attractive, ripe wines. Sample now; will hold.	6 Uneven; best appear small-scale, promising.
8 Excellent balance, stylish. Drink now.	9½ Super-rich wines. Enjoy; best balanced will keep.	6 Lightweight, crisp. Drink up.	6 Lightweight, crisp. Drink up.	7 Good quality & balance. Enjoy now.	5 Light & lean. Drink now.
6½ Light & stylish. Try in 2-6 years. Some wines fast-maturing.	No vintage declared	9½ Superlative; ripe & dense. Wait 10-12 years.	5 Not generally declared. Rich, soft. Try in 5-6 years.	No vintage declared	7 Light but promising. Sample in 7-10 years.

9

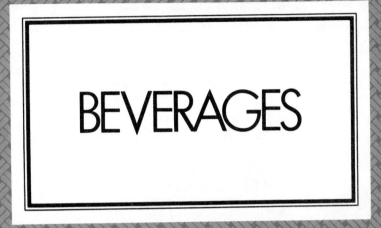

BEVERAGES

Champagne Punch

20 SERVINGS

2 packages (10 ounces each) frozen
   raspberries, thawed
2 cups brandy
2 cups raspberry brandy
½ cup orange-flavored liqueur,
   such as Cointreau, Triple Sec or
   Curaçao
1 quart club soda, chilled
2 bottles (750 ml each) champagne,
   chilled

1. About 1 hour before serving, combine the raspberries, brandy, raspberry brandy and orange-flavored liqueur in a large punch bowl.

2. Just before serving, place a block of ice in the punch bowl (or fill the bowl ⅓ full with ice cubes). Pour in the club soda and champagne and stir gently. Serve the punch in cups or tall champagne glasses

Colonel Talbott's Bourbon Punch

36 SERVINGS

1 cup sugar
10 whole cloves
2 cinnamon sticks
2 liters bourbon
2 cups apple brandy, such as
   applejack
2 cups orange liqueur, preferably
   Grand Marnier
2 tablespoons aromatic bitters
3 seedless oranges, cut in half and
   then into thin slices
1 lime, thinly sliced
2 apples, cut into 1-inch cubes
1 cup strong, hot black tea
1 quart club soda

1. In a small saucepan, combine the sugar with 1 cup of water. Bring to a boil over moderately low heat and cook, stirring to dissolve the sugar, for 5 minutes. Add the cloves and cinnamon sticks; remove the syrup from the heat and let cool.

2. In a large punch bowl, combine the bourbon, apple brandy, orange liqueur, bitters, orange slices, lime slices, apple cubes and tea. Add the syrup and let stand, covered, for 30 minutes, or until cooled to room temperature. Before serving, add ice and pour in the soda.

Cider Wassail Bowl

12 SERVINGS

1 large tart baking apple, such as
   Granny Smith or Greening—
   unpeeled, cored and cut into ½-
   inch slices
1 teaspoon lemon juice
¼ cup plus 1 tablespoon (packed)
   dark brown sugar
1 tablespoon unsalted butter
1 quart apple cider
1 tablespoon grated lemon zest
1 tablespoon grated orange zest
5 whole cardamom pods
6 allspice berries
1 cinnamon stick, broken in half
6 whole cloves
½ cup dark rum
½ cup apple brandy, such as
   Calvados or applejack
1 can (12 ounces) light ale
¼ teaspoon freshly grated nutmeg

1. Preheat the oven to 300°. Toss the apple slices in the lemon juice. Arrange them in a shallow baking pan in a single layer; sprinkle with 1 tablespoon of the brown sugar and dot with the butter.

2. Bake for about 20 minutes, or until the apples are tender; let cool slightly.

3. Bring the cider, lemon and orange zests and the remaining ¼ cup brown sugar to a boil over high heat in a large saucepan, stirring to dissolve the sugar. Tie the cardamom, allspice, cinnamon and cloves in cheesecloth and add to the cider mixture. Cover and simmer over low heat for 20 minutes.

4. Add the rum, apple brandy and ale and return to a simmer. Remove from the heat and discard the spice bag.

5. Pour the cider into a punch bowl, garnish with the apple slices and sprinkle with the nutmeg. Serve hot in punch cups or small mugs.

Orange-Coconut Drink

6 SERVINGS

1½ cups orange juice (from about 5
   juice oranges, preferably
   Valencia)
1½ teaspoons grated orange zest
½ cup sweetened, flaked coconut
½ cup heavy cream
⅓ cup dark rum
½ cup coarsely chopped ice cubes

1. Place the orange juice, orange zest and coconut in a blender or food processor. Blend or process for about 30 seconds. Strain the mixture through a fine sieve, pressing it lightly to extract the liquid. Discard the solids.

2. Return the liquid to the machine and add the cream, rum and chopped ice cubes. Blend or process for 15 seconds more. Divide among six 6-ounce glasses.

Apricot Cooler

4 SERVINGS

2 tablespoons lime juice
¼ cup plain yogurt
2 tablespoons honey
¼ teaspoon almond extract
4 ounces apricot nectar
4 ounces gin
Club soda

Combine the lime juice, yogurt, honey, almond extract, nectar and gin in a blender and mix at high speed until smooth. Pour over ice and top with club soda.

Pink Pamplemousse Cocktail

A standard blender can whip up only two or three drinks at a time to the proper slush consistency. You'll want to make three batches if you're serving six or eight.

2 TO 3 SERVINGS

¼ cup frozen grapefruit juice concentrate
1 tablespoon coarsely chopped crystallized ginger
1 tablespoon grenadine syrup
½ cup (4 ounces) gin
Thin lime slices, for garnish

Combine the grapefruit juice concentrate, crystallized ginger, grenadine and gin in a blender with 1 cup of cracked ice. Blend, adding more ice until thickened. Pour into cocktail glasses and garnish with a thin slice of lime.

Mint Julep

Here's a classic southern summertime drink. Be sure to place a glass or mug in the freezer well before serving time.

1 SERVING

6 sprigs of fresh mint
1 teaspoon superfine sugar, or more to taste
About 1½ cups crushed ice
3 ounces bourbon

1. Strip the leaves off 4 of the mint sprigs; discard the stems. Roughly chop the leaves and divide in half.

2. Place one-half of the chopped mint leaves in the bottom of a chilled 12-ounce glass or mug. Add the sugar; thoroughly mix and bruise the mint-sugar mixture with a bar muddler or the blunt end of a wooden spoon.

3. Fill the glass halfway with ice. Place the remaining chopped mint on top and fill the glass to the top with the remaining ice. Pour in the bourbon, stir and garnish with the remaining 2 mint sprigs.

Apricotrita

Inspired by the recipe for a margarita, this thick, tangy drink makes a festive frozen cocktail.

2 SERVINGS

3 tablespoons (1½ ounces) tequila
1 tablespoon (½ ounce) apricot-flavored brandy
1 tablespoon (½ ounce) honey
1 tablespoon (½ ounce) fresh lime juice
1½ cups cracked ice

In a blender, combine the tequila, brandy, honey and lime juice. Blend at medium speed. With the machine on, slowly add the ice and blend until smooth and thick. Serve in chilled wine or champagne glasses.

Margarita's Hound

2 SERVINGS

2 ounces tequila
2 ounces orange-flavored liqueur
2 ounces lime juice
2 tablespoons frozen, unsweetened grapefruit juice concentrate
Club soda

Combine the tequila, liqueur and juices in a blender and mix at high speed until smooth. Rim a highball glass with a cut lime. Holding the glass upside down, twirl the moistened edge lightly on a plate of coarse salt. Add ice, fill almost to the top with the mixture and top with club soda.

Tequila Pear

1 SERVING

3 tablespoons (1½ ounces) tequila
¼ cup (2 ounces) canned pear nectar
3 tablespoons plain yogurt
1 tablespoon honey
1 tablespoon fresh lime juice
¼ teaspoon almond extract
Thin pear slice, for garnish

Place the tequila, pear nectar, yogurt, honey, lime juice and almond extract in a blender with 1 cup of cracked ice. Starting on low speed and gradually increasing to high, blend until smooth and pour into a large glass.

Puccini

This Italian variation of a Mimosa uses freshly squeezed tangerine juice and an Italian sparkling white wine to make a refreshing drink. If tangerines are not in season, frozen concentrate may be substituted.

1 SERVING

2 ounces (¼ cup) fresh tangerine juice or ¼ cup reconstituted frozen concentrate
6 ounces (¾ cup) dry sparkling white wine, preferably Prosecco

Pour the tangerine juice over cracked ice in a champagne tulip or saucer glass. Add the sparkling wine; stir well.

The Bougainvillea

1 SERVING

4 ounces (½ cup) chilled dry champagne
4 ounces (½ cup) chilled tangerine juice
1 tablespoon Mandarine Napoléon (tangerine liqueur), Grand Marnier or Cointreau
Dash of Angostura bitters

In a tall, well-chilled glass, mix the champagne, tangerine juice, liqueur and bitters.

Orange, Lemon and Mint-Flavored Iced Tea

8 TO 10 SERVINGS

3 juice oranges
2 lemons
¼ cup loose tea or 4 to 6 tea bags
¼ cup fresh mint leaves
About 1 cup sugar
Fresh mint sprigs, for garnish

1. Squeeze the juice from the oranges and lemons and reserve both the juice and the rinds; you should have about 1¼ cups orange juice and ⅓ cup lemon juice.

2. In a large saucepan, bring 7 cups of water to a boil over high heat. Add the orange and lemon rinds and boil for 10 minutes. Add the tea and mint leaves, reduce the heat to moderate and simmer for an additional 5 minutes.

3. Strain the tea into a large pitcher. Add the reserved orange and lemon juice and 1 cup sugar; stir until dissolved. Taste and add additional sugar if desired. Let cool to room temperature; then refrigerate until chilled. Serve cold in tall glasses with ice and a sprig of mint.

Ginger Tea

For people who love the flavor of ginger, this soothing tea could easily become an addiction.

8 TO 10 SERVINGS

4 ounces fresh, unpeeled
    gingerroot
Brown sugar

Using a meat pounder or the flat side of a cleaver, smash the gingerroot. Cut into chunks with a sharp knife and place in a medium saucepan with 4 cups of water. Bring to a boil and cook over moderate heat for 45 minutes. (The tea will be quite strong at this stage. Some people will find it just right; others will want to dilute it with up to 2 additional cups of boiling water.) Serve hot in demitasse cups. Sweeten with brown sugar to taste.

Mango-Lime Spritzer

4 SERVINGS

1 large ripe mango
2 tablespoons fresh lime juice
1½ cups seltzer or club soda
Lime slices, for garnish

1. Peel and pit the mango, scraping off all the pulp from the pit. Puree the fruit in a blender.

2. Add the lime juice and seltzer and mix just to blend.

3. Strain through a sieve. Pour over ice and garnish with thin slices of lime.

Hot Honeyed Pineapple Juice

This delicious concoction fits under the heading of "a comforting drink to soothe a winter cold." Don't feel you need to wait until you catch the flu to try it.

2 SERVINGS

2 cups unsweetened pineapple
    juice
2 teaspoons honey, or to taste
Rum, to taste (optional)

Place the pineapple juice and honey in a small saucepan. Bring the mixture to a simmer over moderate heat, stirring occasionally to dissolve the honey. When the juice is piping hot, pour into mugs. Add rum, if desired.

Orange-Beet Spritzer

This is an unusual and colorful fruit and vegetable combination.

4 SERVINGS

Zest from 1 large navel orange
1 medium beet, peeled and cut
    into ½-inch dice
3 cups orange juice, preferably
    fresh
1 cup seltzer or club soda
Orange slices, for garnish

1. In a blender, combine the orange zest, beet and 1 cup of the orange juice. Puree the beet and orange zest for 1½ minutes. Add the remaining orange juice and the seltzer and mix just to blend.

2. Strain through a sieve. Pour over ice and garnish with an orange slice.

Gingery Watermelon Spritzer

4 SERVINGS

3-pound slice of ripe watermelon
8 thin slices of fresh gingerroot
¾ teaspoon fresh lemon juice
¼ teaspoon salt
¾ cup seltzer or club soda
Small triangles of watermelon with
    rind, for garnish

1. Pick the seeds out of the watermelon, remove the rind and cut the melon into 1-inch cubes.

2. In a blender, combine the watermelon, ginger, lemon juice and salt; puree until smooth, about 1 minute. Add the seltzer and mix just to blend.

3. Strain through a sieve. Pour over ice and garnish with the watermelon triangles.

Tomato Cocktail

Canned or frozen juices can be made to taste more vibrant when they are combined with their fresh counterparts: Mix approximately 2 cups canned juice with 1 cup fresh. The formula works with orange juice or lemonade, as well. The addition of vodka, gin or rum will make a tasty cocktail.

2 SERVINGS

1 large tomato, peeled and seeded
2 cups canned tomato juice
1 tablespoon fresh lemon juice, or to taste

Place the tomato in a blender or food processor and blend until thoroughly liquefied. Pour into a pitcher; add the canned tomato juice and lemon juice and stir to mix. Serve chilled.

French Coffee with Pernod

Pernod, a strong licorice-flavored spirit, is a favorite in European cafés. Made from aniseed essence and a blend of 16 other herbs, its pungent taste adds a unique flavor to this rich dessert coffee.

8 SERVINGS

4 cups freshly brewed strong coffee
2 tablespoons sweetened chocolate syrup
2½ tablespoons sugar
12 whole cloves
2 cinnamon sticks
½ teaspoon Pernod, or more to taste
8 strips lemon zest, about 1 by ½ inch
8 strips orange zest, about 1 by ¼ inch
¼ cup heavy cream, whipped

In a deep chafing dish or medium saucepan, combine the coffee, chocolate syrup, sugar, cloves, cinnamon sticks and Pernod. Steep over very low heat for 15 minutes to infuse the flavors. Ladle the hot coffee into small mugs or demitasse cups. Add a strip of lemon and orange zest to each cup and top with a spoonful of the whipped cream.

Gingered Whiskey Coffee

4 SERVINGS

2 tablespoons chopped peeled fresh gingerroot
6 ounces whiskey
About 2½ cups freshly brewed coffee
⅓ cup heavy cream, whipped

1. In a small bowl, soak the ginger in the whiskey overnight.

2. Strain out the ginger, reserving the whiskey. Divide the whiskey evenly among 4 coffee cups. Fill the cups with coffee and top with a dollop of whipped cream.

Iced Espresso

1 SERVING

1 cup brewed espresso, chilled
1½ ounces (3 tablespoons) rum
3 tablespoons heavy cream
Ground cinnamon
Sprig of fresh mint, thin orange slice and a cinnamon stick, for garnish

Pour the espresso in a tall ice-filled glass. Add the rum and cream and stir. Sprinkle some ground cinnamon over the top and garnish with the mint, orange slice and cinnamon stick.

La Mansion del Rio Hot Chocolate

Every December the River Walk in San Antonio, Texas, is lit with colorful lights and candles for a traditional Mexican Christmas festival. Many participants begin the festivities by gathering at sunset at La Mansion del Rio Hotel, where they are served this traditional hot chocolate.

10 SERVINGS

3 sticks cinnamon
½ cup Dutch cocoa powder
1 quart milk
2 cups sugar
1 quart half-and-half

1. In a small saucepan, bring the cinnamon sticks and ½ cup of water to a boil over a high heat and continue to boil until the water is reduced to 3 tablespoons, about 3 minutes. Discard the cinnamon sticks and set the water aside.

2. Dissolve the cocoa powder in 1 cup of the milk; whisk until smooth. Add the remaining 3 cups milk, the sugar and the cinnamon-flavored water and stir until smooth.

3. Place the cocoa mixture in a large saucepan. Add the half-and-half and cook over moderate heat, whisking almost constantly, until the chocolate is hot and frothy, about 5 minutes.

Berry Liquor

MAKES 1 PINT

2 cups fresh raspberries
15 whole black peppercorns
2 cups gin or vodka

1. Place the raspberries and peppercorns in a 1-quart glass or ceramic bottle. Pour in the gin or vodka. Place the cap on the bottle and let sit undisturbed at room temperature for 5 days, until the color and flavor are extracted from the berries.

2. Strain the liquid through a fine sieve; discard the raspberries and peppercorns. Serve over ice.

Firewater

Firewater, also called hot vodka, is an unusual aperitif. The first sip shocks the palate awake; then, gradually, a feeling of warmth and appetite begins to pervade the senses.

Those who cannot take the heat can dilute firewater with straight vodka, but it should never be mixed with anything else.

Firewater made with fresh green chiles has a distinctly herbal flavor and a lovely, faintly flowery fragrance. The kind made from this recipe, with dried red peppers, is hotness pure and simple—an essence, a sensation, instead of a taste. Use an inexpensive vodka for this brew since the hotness masks any subtleties of the more costly brands.

1 bottle 80-proof vodka
3 whole, small, dried hot red
**   peppers.**

Add the peppers to the bottle of vodka, replace the cap and let macerate at least overnight. The firewater will get hotter and hotter for about 2 weeks, after which it will stabilize. Remove the peppers at any point or leave them in the bottle, as I do, for the duration. The flavor will be somewhat raw for the first month or so, although the firewater is perfectly drinkable from the moment of its creation. After it has aged for a year, its heat will have rounded and mellowed. Aged firewater is more sophisticated and less aggressive but still gloriously hot.

Anisette Liqueur

MAKES 2½ QUARTS

4 cups sugar
½ cup (2 ounces) aniseed
¼ cup (1 ounce) coriander seed
1 cinnamon stick
¼ teaspoon blade mace (see Note)
2 liters 100-proof vodka

Place the sugar, aniseed, coriander seed, cinnamon stick and mace in a 3-quart jar with a tight-fitting lid. Pour in the vodka and stir with a spoon until the sugar dissolves. Cover tightly and store in a cool place for at least 2 weeks or up to 1 month. Filter the liqueur through a paper coffee filter. Serve over ice or dilute with water to taste.

NOTE: Blade mace is available at specialty food shops and spice shops. You can substitute ⅛ teaspoon ground mace.

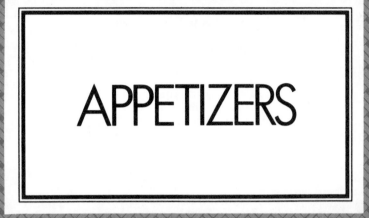

APPETIZERS

Corn Tortilla Chips

Few people know how simple it is to make corn chips. Serve fresh and crisp with guacamole or your favorite dip.

4 SERVINGS

1 dozen fresh corn tortillas, each about 5 inches in diameter
Vegetable oil, for deep-frying
Salt

1. Place the entire stack of tortillas on a cutting board. Slicing through the stack, cut each into six equal wedges.

2. Heat about 3 inches of oil in a deep-fryer to 375°. Place one-third of the tortilla wedges in a deep-frying basket and lower it into the oil. Fry the wedges, pushing them under the oil occasionally to separate and submerge them, for about 1 minute, or until crisp and golden. Remove with the basket, drain, and sprinkle lightly with salt. Fry the remaining wedges in the same manner. Serve hot or at room temperature.

Disheveled Eggs

MAKES 2 DOZEN

1½ teaspoons caraway seeds
12 eggs
¼ pound bacon (about 6 slices)
6 tablespoons mayonnaise
2 tablespoons prepared mustard
¼ teaspoon salt
¼ teaspoon pepper

1. Place the caraway seeds in a small saucepan. Add 1 cup of water and bring to a boil over high heat. Reduce the heat slightly and boil until the liquid is nearly evaporated; set aside to cool.

2. Place the eggs in a large heavy saucepan and add water to cover by 1 inch. Bring to a boil over moderate heat. Reduce the heat and simmer for 10 minutes. Rinse the eggs under cold running water until cool enough to handle; remove the shells.

3. Meanwhile, cut the bacon into ¼-inch squares, and fry them in a large skillet over moderate heat until crisp and brown. Drain on paper towels.

4. Slice the eggs in half lengthwise and remove the yolks. Mash the yolks in a medium bowl. Add the caraway seeds with their liquid, the bacon, mayonnaise, mustard, salt and pepper; blend well. Fill the egg white halves with the yolk mixture. Refrigerate until chilled.

Savory Canapés

Serve these easy-to-prepare hors d'oeuvre accompanied with ice-cold gingered vodka.

3 tablespoons unsalted butter
1 tablespoon olive oil
4 slices firm-textured white bread, each cut into 4 rounds with a 1½-inch cookie cutter
3 tablespoons minced onion
3 tablespoons minced celery
¼ teaspoon anchovy paste
1 tablespoon fresh lime juice
⅛ teaspoon freshly ground pepper
¼ cup freshly ground Parmesan cheese

1. Preheat the broiler. In a large skillet, heat 2 tablespoons of the butter with the oil until the butter foams. Add the bread rounds and sauté over moderate heat for 2 minutes on each side, or until golden brown. Drain on paper towels.

2. Melt the remaining 1 tablespoon butter in the skillet. Add the onion and celery and sauté over moderate heat for 3 minutes, until softened but not browned. Remove from the heat and stir in the anchovy paste, lime juice and pepper.

3. Dividing evenly, mound the mixture neatly on the toast circles and sprinkle generously with the cheese. Place on a cookie sheet and broil for about 1 minute, until the cheese is melted and bubbly. Serve hot.

Glazed Bacon with Walnuts

4 SERVINGS

1 pound bacon
¼ cup packed dark brown sugar
1 teaspoon all-purpose flour
½ cup chopped walnuts

Preheat the oven to 350°. Arrange the bacon slices closely together but not overlapping on a broiler pan or fine wire rack over a dripping pan. In a bowl, combine the brown sugar, flour and walnuts; sprinkle evenly over the bacon. Bake until crisp and brown, about 30 minutes. Drain on paper towels.

Easy Pâté

4 TO 6 SERVINGS

2 ounces salt pork, cut into ¼-inch dice
1 pound ground chuck
½ pound chicken livers, trimmed and coarsely chopped
2 eggs
1 medium onion, coarsely chopped
¼ cup brandy
3 tablespoons dried tarragon
1 tablespoon salt
1 tablespoon pepper
½ pound bacon

1. Preheat the oven to 375°. Plunge the salt pork cubes into a small saucepan of boiling water over high heat and cook for 5 minutes. Strain and rinse the cubes thoroughly in cold water; drain well.

2. In a medium bowl, combine the salt pork, ground chuck, chicken livers, eggs, onion, brandy, tarragon, salt and pepper; mix thoroughly. Puree the pâté mixture in a food processor or pass it through the fine blade of a meat grinder.

3. Line a 4-cup loaf pan (8 by 4 by 2½ inches) with the bacon, arranging the strips across the pan and allowing the excess to hang over both long sides. Gently pack the pâté mixture into the prepared pan, fold the ends of the bacon strips over the top of the pâté and cover the pan tightly with aluminum foil.

4. Place this pan in a larger baking pan. Transfer to the oven, then fill the larger pan with hot water until it is half way up the sides of the pâté pan. Bake for 2 hours.

5. Remove the baked pâté from the hot water and let it cool for 1 hour. Place weights (cans of food are useful) on top of the pâté and cool to room temperature, refrigerate for at least 12 hours.

6. Present the pâté in the pan or unmolded on a platter and cut it into thin slices.

Brandy Chicken Liver Pâté

MAKES ABOUT 3 CUPS

¾ pound salt pork, rind removed, cut into ½-inch cubes
½ cup (1 stick) unsalted butter
1 medium onion, minced
1 pound chicken livers—trimmed, rinsed and patted dry
2 garlic cloves, crushed
1 tablespoon ground allspice
½ cup plus 2 tablespoons brandy
1 large celery rib, minced
1 hard-cooked egg, finely chopped
Salt and freshly ground pepper
Sprigs of parsley, for garnish

1. Place the salt pork in a medium saucepan and add 1 quart of water. Bring to a boil and cook over moderate heat for 30 minutes; drain. Rinse the salt pork under cold running water, pat dry and finely chop.

2. In a large skillet, melt the butter over low heat. Add the onion and sauté, stirring, until pale gold, about 10 minutes. Add the livers, salt pork, garlic, allspice and ½ cup of the brandy. Simmer, stirring occasionally, until the livers are no longer pink, about 15 minutes.

3. Puree the mixture in a food processor or blender; strain through a sieve for finer texture, if desired. In a medium bowl, combine the liver puree with the celery and egg; stir to mix. Season with salt and pepper to taste. Stir in the remaining 2 tablespoons brandy and scrape the mixture into a crock or serving bowl.

4. Refrigerate, covered, for at least 2 hours or overnight, to chill and firm up the pâté. Garnish with sprigs of parsley and serve with whole wheat crackers or sourdough toast points.

Eggplant Caviar with Ginger

Japanese seasonings add a new twist to an eggplant dip. Make it a day before serving to allow the flavors to blend.

MAKES ABOUT 2 CUPS

1 eggplant, about 1 pound
2 tablespoons soy sauce
2 teaspoons rice or white wine vinegar
4 teaspoons grated, peeled fresh gingerroot
1 teaspoon sugar
4 teaspoons vegetable oil
1 tablespoon Oriental sesame oil
1½ tablespoons chopped fresh coriander (cilantro)
1 tablespoon minced chives or scallion green
4 drops hot pepper sauce
½ teaspoon coarse (kosher) salt

1. Preheat the oven to 400°. Place the eggplant on a baking sheet lined with foil and prick it several times with a fork. Bake for 45 to 60 minutes, or until it is very soft when pierced with a knife. Remove from the oven and let cool for about 5 minutes.

2. As soon as the eggplant is cool enough to handle, cut in half lengthwise and scoop out the flesh. Finely chop the eggplant and place it in a medium bowl; set aside.

3. In a small noncorrodible saucepan, heat the soy sauce, vinegar, 2 teaspoons of the gingerroot and the sugar over moderately high heat and bring to a boil. Cook until reduced to about 1 tablespoon, 1 to 2 minutes. Reduce the heat to low, add the vegetable oil and sesame oil and continue to cook, for about 30 seconds, scraping up any browned bits on the bottom of the pan.

4. Stir the soy mixture into the chopped eggplant. Add the remaining 2 teaspoons gingerroot, the coriander, chives, hot sauce and salt. Refrigerate, covered, for at least 2 hours before serving.

Pumpkin Seed Dip

Making a dip from ground pumpkin seeds is an old Mayan tradition, and this practice can still be found throughout Yucatán. Serve this rich, earthy dip with corn chips, fried tortillas or cold skewered shrimp.

MAKES ABOUT 1½ CUPS

1½ cups (8 ounces) hulled, unsalted pumpkin seeds (*pepitas*)*
3 tablespoons olive oil
2 garlic cloves, crushed
¾ to 1 cup chicken broth
¼ cup lime juice
1 to 2 hot chile peppers, seeded and chopped, or hot pepper sauce to taste
1 teaspoon salt
¼ teaspoon pepper
2 scallions, thinly sliced
*Available in health food stores

1. In a small ungreased skillet, cook the pumpkin seeds over moderate heat, stirring occasionally, until they begin to pop and turn golden brown, 2 to 3 minutes. Place the seeds in a blender or food processor and puree until finely ground. Reserve the ground seeds in the blender.

2. In the skillet, heat the oil over moderate heat. Add the garlic and sauté for about 30 seconds, or until fragrant. Pour the oil and garlic into the blender; add ¾ cup chicken broth, the lime juice, chile peppers or hot sauce, salt and pepper. Process, stopping occasionally to scrape down the sides, until the mixture is pureed. (If the mixture gets too thick, add a bit more chicken broth, a tablespoon at a time.) Transfer the dip to a serving bowl, cover and chill. Serve cold, garnished with the scallions.

Points of Filet Mignon

F&W Beverage Suggestion: Valpolicella from Italy, a young Rioja from Spain or a Gamay Beaujolais, slightly chilled

MAKES ABOUT 4 DOZEN

1 pound filet mignon, cut into 8 steaks, ½ inch thick
2 tablespoons unsalted butter
2 tablespoons olive oil
Salt and freshly ground pepper

1. Cut each steak into strips ½ inch thick.

2. In a large heavy skillet, warm the butter and oil over moderately high heat until very hot but not smoking. Add the strips of filet, increase the heat to high and stir-fry the meat until it is cooked, but still pink in the center, about 2 minutes. Season lightly with salt and pepper. Serve hot.

Buffalo Chicken Wings with Blue Cheese Sauce

4 TO 6 APPETIZER SERVINGS

2 tablespoons finely chopped onion
1 small garlic clove, minced
¼ cup minced fresh parsley
1 cup mayonnaise or salad dressing
½ cup sour cream
¼ cup finely crumbled blue cheese
1 tablespoon lemon juice
1 tablespoon white wine vinegar
¼ teaspoon salt
¼ teaspoon black pepper
Pinch of cayenne pepper
½ cup (1 stick) unsalted butter
¼ cup bottled hot sauce
25 chicken wings (about 4½ pounds)
About 1½ quarts vegetable oil or lard
Celery sticks, for garnish

1. In a medium bowl, combine the onion, garlic, parsley, mayonnaise, sour cream, blue cheese, lemon juice, vinegar, salt, black pepper and cayenne; whisk until blended. Cover and refrigerate the blue cheese sauce until 30 minutes before serving.

2. In a large skillet, melt the butter over moderately low heat and add the hot sauce; mix well and set aside. (This makes a medium-hot sauce. For a hotter or milder sauce, adjust the ingredients accordingly.)

3. Cut the wings into three pieces at the joints; discard the tips or reserve for stock. Pat the chicken pieces dry.

4. In a deep fryer or a heavy, deep skillet, heat the oil to 385°. Fry the chicken in batches for about 10 minutes, until brown and crisp. Drain on paper towels.

5. When all of the chicken has been fried, rewarm the hot sauce mixture in a large skillet. Add the chicken and toss to thoroughly coat each piece. Turn off the heat, cover and let stand for 5 minutes.

6. Serve the chicken accompanied with the celery and the reserved blue cheese dressing for dipping.

Prosciutto Butter

For a different flavor, substitute smoked or boiled ham in place of the prosciutto. Spread this butter on thin slices or triangles of bread or toast and top with cucumber, radishes or thinly sliced fennel.

MAKES ABOUT 1½ CUPS

¼ pound prosciutto, coarsely chopped
½ cup (1 stick) unsalted butter, at room temperature
4 ounces cream cheese, at room temperature
⅓ cup coarsely chopped shallots
2 tablespoons fresh lemon juice

Combine all the ingredients in a food processor or blender. Puree until smooth. Scrape into a bowl, cover and refrigerate for at least 2 hours.

Ham Mimosa

16 TO 20 SERVINGS

1½ tablespoons unflavored gelatin
¼ cup port or Madeira
2 cups chicken stock or canned broth
2 tablespoons unsalted butter
2 medium onions, minced
1 medium celery rib, minced
2 teaspoons minced garlic
1½ pounds boiled ham, coarsely chopped
2 tablespoons tomato paste
1 tablespoon minced fresh dill or 1½ teaspoons dried dillweed
2 tablespoons Dijon-style mustard
Salt and freshly ground pepper
1 cup heavy cream, well chilled
2 hard-cooked egg yolks

1. In a small bowl, sprinkle the gelatin over the wine and set aside until softened, about 10 minutes.

2. In a small saucepan, bring the stock to a boil. Add the softened gelatin mixture and simmer, stirring, for 2 minutes. Set aside to cool.

3. In a large skillet, melt the butter over low heat. Add the onions, celery and garlic; cover and cook until the vegetables are soft but not brown, about 10 minutes.

4. In two batches, grind the ham and cooked vegetables in a food processor until a smooth paste forms.

5. In a large bowl, combine the ham paste with the tomato paste, dill and mustard. Mix well until blended.

6. In a bowl set over ice, stir the stock until it begins to gel. Add the ham mixture and salt and pepper to taste.

7. Beat the heavy cream until soft peaks form. Fold into the ham mixture and turn into a well-oiled 6- to 8-cup mold. Refrigerate overnight.

8. To serve, unmold onto a platter. Press the egg yolk through a fine sieve, sprinkling it all over the ham mold. Serve chilled.

Ham Roulades

These bite-size roulades make an easy hors d'oeuvre for holiday entertaining.

MAKES 48 ROULADES

12 ounces cream cheese, at room temperature
¾ cup chopped brazil nuts (3 ounces)
1 teaspoon salt
½ teaspoon pepper
2½ tablespoons heavy cream
16 thin slices (6 by 4 inches) boiled ham

1. In a medium bowl, beat the cream cheese until smooth. Add the chopped nuts, salt, pepper and cream and beat until smooth. Finely chop four slices of the ham and add to the cream-cheese mixture.

2. Spread each of the 12 remaining slices of ham with 2 tablespoons of the cream-cheese mixture. Starting at the short end, roll each slice into a log. Place the roulades on a large plate or in a casserole and cover tightly. Refrigerate for at least 1 hour.

3. Just before serving, cut each roulade into 4 one-inch pieces. Serve chilled or at room temperature.

Ham and Cheese Rolls

Thin slices of ham are rolled around cheese; upon deep-frying, the cheese melts but stays within the roll. Although these rolls can be served as an entrée, they make an exceptional hors d'oeuvre.

MAKES 16 ROLLS

½ pound unsliced Swiss cheese
16 thinly sliced, 4-inch squares of ham
½ cup flour
2 eggs, lightly beaten
1 cup dry rye-bread crumbs

1. Cut the cheese into sixteen ½-by-½-by-2½-inch strips.

2. Place a slice of ham on your work surface, lay a strip of cheese horizontally on top of the ham toward the front edge, and roll the ham around the cheese, folding in and enclosing the ends as you roll. Secure the seam by piercing each end and the center with a toothpick. Repeat with the remaining ham and cheese.

3. Dip the rolls, one at a time, into the flour, then into the egg, and then into the bread crumbs.

4. In a deep-fryer with a deep-frying basket inserted, heat about 3 inches of oil to 375°. Frying two or three rolls at a time, lower them into the basket in the hot oil with a slotted spoon. Fry for 1½ to 2 minutes, or until golden brown. Remove with the basket and drain. Remove the toothpicks as soon as the rolls are cool enough to handle. Serve hot.

Crabmeat-Parmesan Balls

F&W Beverage Suggestion: California Sauvignon Blanc or a dry white Bordeaux

MAKES ABOUT 12 DOZEN

8 ounces cream cheese, at room temperature
1 pound lump crab meat, picked over to remove any cartilage or shell, and flaked
2¼ cups loosely packed minced fresh parsley
1 tablespoon fresh lemon juice
½ teaspoon salt
2 tablespoons Dijon-style mustard
⅓ cup freshly grated Parmesan cheese
¼ teaspoon freshly ground pepper

1. In a medium bowl, beat the cream cheese until fluffy. Stir in the crab meat, ¼ cup of the parsley, the lemon juice, salt, mustard, Parmesan and pepper. Cover and refrigerate for at least 2 hours, or overnight.

2. Shape the mixture into balls by rolling 2 level teaspoons at a time between the palms of your hands. Dip the bottom half into the remaining parsley and transfer the hors d'oeuvre to a platter, parsley-side down. Spear each ball with a toothpick and serve chilled. If prepared ahead of time, cover and refrigerate for up to 8 hours.

Steamed Mussels with Two Sauces

6 SERVINGS

36 mussels
½ cup cornmeal
2 tablespoons vegetable oil
1 medium onion, finely chopped (about 1 cup)
1 large carrot, thinly sliced (about ¾ cup)
1 garlic clove
1 teaspoon pepper
1⅓ cups dry white wine
Green Herb Sauce with Champagne (p. 207)
Dilled Sour-Cream Sauce (p. 210)

1. Scrub the mussels thoroughly and remove the fuzzy "beards". Place them in a large pot or sinkful of cold water, add the cornmeal and let them rest for 1 to 2 hours to remove any sand.

2. Meanwhile, in a large heatproof casserole, warm the oil over moderately high heat. Add the onion, carrot and garlic and sauté until the onion is translucent, about 5 minutes. Stir in the pepper. Add 1 cup of the wine; let the mixture simmer for 5 minutes.

3. Drain the mussels and add to the casserole. Add the remaining ⅓ cup of wine and an equal amount of water. Simmer the mussels, covered, until the shells open, 5 to 6 minutes. Using a slotted spoon, remove them from the casserole, discarding any that haven't opened.

4. Separate the two shells of each mussel by gently breaking them apart at the hinge; discard the empty portion. Decoratively arrange the halves containing the mussels on a large serving platter and chill for at least 20 minutes.

5. To serve, top half the mussels with bands of the Green Herb Sauce and the remaining half with bands of the Dilled Sour-Cream Sauce. Serve any extra sauce on the side.

Fresh Oysters in Spinach Leaves

🍷 **F&W Beverage Suggestion:**
Muscadet, such as a Marquis de Goulaine

4 SERVINGS

12 large spinach leaves
1 egg yolk, at room temperature
½ teaspoon Dijon-style mustard, at room temperature
Pinch of freshly ground white pepper
½ cup peanut oil
24 fresh oysters—shucked, with their liquor and the deeper half of each shell reserved
½ teaspoon paprika

1. In a steamer or a medium saucepan with a rack, over boiling salted water, steam the spinach leaves until tender but still bright green, about 2 minutes. Rinse under cold running water, drain and pat dry on paper towels. Cut each leaf lengthwise along both sides of the center rib to divide the leaves in half; discard the ribs.

2. In a medium bowl, whisk the egg yolk with the mustard and pepper until thickened. Gradually whisk in the oil in a thin stream to make a thick mayonnaise.

3. Strain the reserved oyster liquor through a fine sieve lined with a double thickness of dampened cheesecloth. In a medium saucepan, bring the liquor to a boil over high heat and continue to boil until reduced by half, about 4 minutes. Remove from the heat and let cool to room temperature.

4. Whisk the reduced oyster liquor into the mayonnaise, which will thin considerably.

5. Wrap each oyster in a spinach leaf and place, seam-side down, on a half-shell. Spoon 1 tablespoon of mayonnaise over the middle of each oyster, leaving some of the spinach exposed for color contrast. Sprinkle lightly with paprika.

Potted Smoked Trout

MAKES ABOUT 1 CUP

½ pound smoked trout, skinned and boned
4 tablespoons unsalted butter, cut into tablespoons and softened to room temperature
1 tablespoon half-and-half
2 hard-cooked egg yolks, sieved
2 teaspoons minced fresh dill
Salt and pepper

1. Place the trout, butter and half-and-half in a blender or food processor and puree, stopping once to scrape down the sides of the container, until smooth, about 30 seconds.

2. Transfer the trout butter to a small bowl and add the egg yolks, stirring until well blended. Mix in the dill and season with salt and pepper to taste. Spoon into a 1-cup ramekin or crock and refrigerate, covered, for up to 3 days. Remove from the refrigerator about 20 minutes before serving.

Pâté of Sole

Serve this pâté warm with a *beurre blanc* sauce or a lemony hollandaise. It is also delicious cold with a green mayonnaise.

🍷 **F&W Beverage Suggestion:**
California Chardonnay, such as Iron Horse

6 SERVINGS

1 pound sole fillets
4 egg whites, well chilled
1 cup heavy cream, well chilled
2 tablespoons tomato paste
½ teaspoon freshly grated nutmeg
1½ teaspoons salt
1 teaspoon white pepper
¼ pound boiled ham, very thinly sliced

1. Using a food processor, grind the sole fillets to a paste. Cover and refrigerate for about 30 minutes, until chilled.

2. With the machine on, gradually add the chilled egg whites to the sole paste. Cover and refrigerate for about 30 minutes, until chilled.

3. With the machine on, slowly add the cream to the sole mixture. Add the tomato paste, nutmeg, salt and white pepper; mix until well blended. Cover and refrigerate while you line the mold.

4. Preheat the oven to 350°. Line the bottom and sides of a well-buttered loaf pan (about 8½ by 4½ by 2½ inches) with the ham slices, reserving 1 or 2 for the top. Spoon the cold sole mixture into the loaf pan and cover with the remaining ham. Place a piece of buttered parchment or waxed paper loosely over the pan.

5. Place the loaf pan into a larger baking dish and fill the dish with enough hot water to reach halfway up the sides of the pan.

6. Bake for 1 hour, or until a knife plunged into the center of the loaf comes out clean. Remove from the hot water and let stand for about 20 minutes. Carefully run a knife around the sides of the pan and unmold the pâté onto a platter.

Herring with Horseradish-Apple Cream

8 SERVINGS

1 cup heavy cream
½ cup shredded, peeled tart apple
2 tablespoons prepared white horseradish, well drained
1 teaspoon sugar
2 jars (9 ounces each) *matjes* herring, plain or in wine sauce
1 tablespoon minced fresh chives

1. In a medium bowl, beat the cream until stiff. Fold in the apple, horseradish and sugar. Refrigerate, covered, until thoroughly chilled, about 1 hour.

2. Arrange the herring on a small platter and sprinkle with the chives. Serve the horseradish-apple cream on the side.

Yam Turnovers with Jalapeños and Ham

These wonderfully tasty turnovers can be filled, baked and frozen ahead. To serve, bake the frozen turnovers on an ungreased baking sheet in a 350° oven for 15 to 20 minutes, until crisp and heated through.

MAKES ABOUT 48 TURNOVERS

Pastry:

2 cups all-purpose flour
¼ teaspoon salt
⅔ cup chilled vegetable shortening, butter or lard
¼ cup ice water

Filling:

1½ tablespoons unsalted butter
1 medium onion, minced
1 cup mashed baked yams (about 2 medium)
1 whole egg
1 egg yolk
1 teaspoon ground cumin
½ teaspoon oregano
½ teaspoon salt
1 small garlic clove, crushed through a press
1 tablespoon dark rum
1 medium tomato—peeled, seeded and cut into ⅛-inch dice
¼ pound cooked ham, cut into ⅛-inch dice
4 jalapeño peppers—roasted, peeled and deveined, and cut into ⅛-inch dice

Topping:

1 egg white, lightly beaten
2½ teaspoons coarse (kosher) salt mixed with ⅛ teaspoon cayenne pepper or ¼ teaspoon ground pasilla pepper*
***Available at Latin American groceries**

1. Prepare the pastry: In a large bowl, combine the flour and salt. Cut in the shortening until the mixture resembles coarse meal. Sprinkle the ice water over the mixture, 1 tablespoon at a time, tossing with a fork until the pastry can be gathered into a ball. (Use additional drops of water if necessary.) Divide the dough in thirds, wrap each piece in waxed paper and refrigerate for at least 45 minutes.

2. Meanwhile, make the filling: In a small skillet, melt the butter over moderate heat. Add the onion and sauté until it softens and begins to brown, about 5 minutes.

3. In a small bowl, beat together the yams, whole egg and egg yolk until well blended. Add the cumin, oregano, salt, garlic, rum, tomato, ham, sautéed onion and the jalapeños; blend well. Refrigerate, covered, until you are ready to fill the turnovers.

4. Assemble the turnovers: Preheat the oven to 400°. Roll out one piece of the dough as thin as possible between sheets of waxed paper. Cut into 3-inch circles with a biscuit cutter or glass. Gather together the scraps and refrigerate.

5. Place 2 teaspoons of the filling in the center of each pastry circle and fold in half to form half-moon shapes. Press the edges together firmly to seal. Place on an ungreased cookie sheet and refrigerate while you roll out and fill the remaining pieces of dough and then the scraps.

6. Brush each turnover with the egg white and sprinkle with the seasoned salt. Bake for 15 minutes; reduce the oven temperature to 375° and bake until the turnovers are golden brown, about 20 minutes.

Avocado Tempura with Coriander and Lime

🍷 **F&W Beverage Suggestion:** California Sauvignon Blanc

6 SERVINGS

1 cup all-purpose flour
½ cup cornstarch
2 teaspoons salt
1 cup ice water
1 teaspoon baking soda
⅓ cup chopped fresh coriander
Vegetable oil, for deep-frying
2 ripe avocados, cut lengthwise into 12 slices
Lime wedges

1. Into a large bowl, sift the flour, cornstarch and 1 teaspoon of the salt. Form a well in the center and pour in the ice water all at once. Whisk briskly to form a smooth batter.

2. Cover the bowl with plastic wrap and refrigerate for at least 30 minutes. When ready to use, whisk in the baking soda and coriander.

3. Heat about 1 inch of oil in a deep-fryer or large heavy saucepan to 375°. Sprinkle the avocado slices with the remaining 1 teaspoon salt. Let sit for a minute.

4. In batches, dip the avocado slices in the batter to coat lightly; fry without crowding in the hot oil, turning once, for about 30 seconds on each side, until lightly browned. Remove and drain on paper towels. Serve hot (see Note) with wedges of lime.

NOTE: These are best served right away, but they can be held for a short time in a warm (200°) oven.

Chicken Liver, Apricot and Prune Kebabs

Serve these savory kebabs on triangles of buttered toast as a first course or an hors d'oeuvre.

MAKES 12 KEBABS

2 tablespoons ketchup
1 tablespoon Worcestershire sauce
1 tablespoon vegetable oil
2 teaspoons Dijon-style mustard
2 teaspoons anchovy paste
12 chicken livers (about ½ pound), trimmed and cut in half
12 dried apricots
12 pitted prunes
12 slices of bacon (about ¾ pound), each cut into 4 pieces
24 bay leaves

1. In a small bowl, combine the ketchup, Worcestershire, oil, mustard and anchovy paste. Add the livers, toss and allow to marinate for about 1 hour.

2. Meanwhile, place the apricots and prunes in a small saucepan with water to cover. Over high heat, bring the water to a boil; then reduce the heat to low and poach the fruit until tender but not mushy, 2 to 3 minutes. Drain, let cool and cut each piece of fruit in half.

3. Preheat the broiler. Wrap each piece of fruit in a section of bacon. Dip the bay leaves in the marinade. Onto each of twelve 7-inch skewers (see Note), thread 1 wrapped apricot, 1 bay leaf, 1 piece chicken liver and a wrapped prune, followed by another apricot, bay leaf, chicken liver and prune. Broil the kebabs 4 inches from the heat for 2 minutes on each side, or until the bacon is crisp.

NOTE: If only bamboo skewers are available, soak them in cold water for at least 30 minutes before using.

Potato Skins with Cheese and Bacon

MAKES 4 PIECES

2 baking potatoes, preferably Idaho (about 8 ounces each)
1½ tablespoons unsalted butter, melted
½ cup finely shredded Cheddar or Parmesan cheese
4 strips of cooked bacon, crumbled

1. Preheat the oven to 400°. Scrub and dry the potatoes. Pierce each one with a fork. Bake for 1 hour and 10 minutes, or until very tender when pierced with a knife. Remove the potatoes from the oven; reduce the oven temperature to 375°.

2. As soon as the potatoes can be handled, using a mitt if necessary, cut in half lengthwise. Scoop out the potatoes, leaving a ¼-inch shell. (Reserve the scooped-out potato for another use.)

3. Brush the insides of the skins generously with the melted butter. Sprinkle on the cheese and top with the crumbled bacon.

4. Return the potatoes to the oven and bake for 30 minutes, or until the tops are golden and the skins are very crisp. Serve as a side dish, or cut into strips and serve as an hors d'oeuvre.

Potatoes with Three American Caviars

The amount of caviar you buy for this recipe is flexible, depending on how extravagant you are feeling. The quantities suggested below are generous.

♦ F&W Beverage Suggestion:
Ice-cold vodka

6 SERVINGS

1 cup (8 ounces) sour cream
1 tablespoon chopped fresh chives
¼ teaspoon pepper
2 large baking potatoes
3 tablespoons butter
2 to 4 ounces golden (whitefish) caviar
2 to 4 ounces sturgeon caviar
2 to 4 ounces salmon caviar

1. In a medium bowl, combine the sour cream, chives and pepper.

2. Scrub the potatoes under cold running water until thoroughly clean. Trim off and discard the ends and cut the potatoes into 18 thin (about ¼-inch) slices.

3. In a large skillet, melt the butter over moderate heat. Add the potato slices and sauté for 3 to 4 minutes on each side, or until tender and lightly browned. Drain the potatoes briefly on paper towels.

4. Place 3 potato slices on each of 6 serving plates. Top each slice with about 2 teaspoons of the seasoned sour cream and ½ to 1 heaping tablespoon of caviar—a different type for each of the three slices. Serve while potatoes are still warm.

Soused Onions

This sweet and tangy dish is a cross between an hors d'oeuvre and a relish. It is typically served with pâté, cold sliced meats or as part of an hors d'oeuvre platter.

MAKES 2 TO 2½ CUPS

¼ cup raisins
¼ cup dark rum
3 tablespoons olive oil
1 pound small white onions, peeled, or 2 bags (8 ounces each) frozen onions, thawed
2 teaspoons brown sugar

3 large tomatoes (1½ pounds)—peeled, seeded and cut into ¼-inch dice
¼ teaspoon salt
1 large sprig of fresh thyme or ¼ teaspoon dried
8 peppercorns

1. Preheat the oven to 375°. In a small bowl, soak the raisins in the rum while you prepare the onions. In a large skillet, heat the oil over moderately high heat. Reduce the heat to moderate and add the onions. Sauté, shaking the pan, until the onions are golden brown all over, about 5 minutes. Sprinkle with the brown sugar and reduce the heat to low. Cook, shaking the pan occasionally, until the onions are caramelized on the outside, about 5 minutes. Add the tomatoes and salt, increase the heat to moderate and cook for 5 minutes.

2. Transfer the vegetables to a small casserole. Drain the raisins, reserving the rum. Add the raisins, thyme and peppercorns to the casserole. Cover and bake for about 1½ hours, or until the onions are tender but still hold their shape. Remove from the oven, and stir in the reserved rum. Taste for seasoning.

3. Let the onions cool to room temperature, then refrigerate overnight. Let them come to room temperature before serving.

Stuffed Belgian Endive

These cheese-stuffed endives make a delicious first course or hors d'oeuvre, and are simple to prepare. At serving time, they are sliced on the diagonal to reveal the layers of leaves and cheese. The endives can be made several hours ahead of time and refrigerated until just before serving.

MAKES ABOUT 24 SLICES

¼ pound Montrachet chèvre, at room temperature
3 small heads of Belgian endive (¼ pound)

1. Working with one head of endive at a time, trim away and discard about ½ inch from the stem ends. Pull off 8 to 10 of the leaves and arrange them in a row in the order in which they were removed; reserve the small center core.

2. Using a small knife, spread the smallest leaf with about ½ teaspoon of the chèvre; reattach it to the core of the endive by gently pressing it in place with your fingers—the cheese will hold it in place. Repeat the procedure with the remaining leaves in the order in which they were originally attached to the head, using ½ to 1 teaspoon of the cheese. Eventually, the endive will regain its original shape. Repeat with the remaining cheese and heads of endive. Wrap and chill for at least an hour or as long as 4 hours.

3. To serve, cut the heads on the diagonal into slices ¼ inch thick. Serve cold or at room temperature.

Brussels Sprouts Hors d'Oeuvre

<u>6 TO 8 SERVINGS</u>

2 pints (10 ounces each) Brussels sprouts
4 ounces blue cheese, at room temperature
4 ounces cream cheese, at room temperature
6 scallions (white part plus 1 inch of the green), minced
2 teaspoons salt

1. In a large pot of rapidly boiling water, cook the Brussels sprouts for about 8 minutes, until crisp-tender. Drain into a colander and rinse well under cold running water. When cool, set aside to drain.

2. Meanwhile, in a medium bowl, combine the blue cheese, cream cheese, scallions and salt; mix until well blended.

3. When the sprouts have drained, make flat bases by cutting off ⅛ inch from the stem end of each. Using a small melon baller, hollow out a deep well in the top of each sprout.

4. Pack the cheese mixture into a pastry bag fitted with a plain, ⅜-inch (#5) tube and pipe into the hollowed sprouts. Arrange the hors d'oeuvre on a platter and serve at room temperature.

Sausage-Stuffed Mushrooms

Parslied toast points make an attractive garnish for this savory first course, but the mushrooms may also be served alone, as an hors d'oeuvre.

<u>4 SERVINGS</u>

16 medium mushrooms
Fresh lemon juice
½ pound sweet Italian sausage
⅛ teaspoon salt
⅛ teaspoon pepper

Garnish:

4 slices of firm-textured white bread
3 tablespoons unsalted butter, melted
3 tablespoons finely chopped fresh parsley

1. Preheat the oven to 375°. Remove the mushroom stems and mince them. Paint the caps with lemon juice to prevent discoloration.

2. Remove the sausage meat from the casings and place the meat in a medium bowl. Add the minced mushroom stems, salt and pepper, and mix lightly to blend.

3. Spoon the sausage stuffing into the mushroom caps, smoothing the tops into a rounded shape. Arrange the stuffed mushrooms in a lightly greased small baking dish. Bake for about 15 minutes, or until the sausage meat is no longer pink.

Stuffed Mushrooms Véronique

<u>6 SERVINGS</u>

18 small mushrooms (about 1 inch in diameter)
18 seedless green grapes
1 package (5 ounces) Boursin cheese
½ cup (1 stick) unsalted butter, melted
1 cup grated Parmesan cheese (4 ounces)
Freshly ground black pepper

1. Remove the stems from the mushrooms and reserve them for another use. Place a grape in each mushroom cap.

2. Scoop up ½ tablespoon of the Boursin cheese and mound it over a mushroom, completely enclosing the grape. Repeat with the remaining mushrooms and cheese.

3. Roll each stuffed mushroom in melted butter and then in grated cheese; reserve any cheese that does not stick. Place the mushrooms on an ungreased baking sheet and refrigerate for 20 minutes.

4. Preheat the oven to 400°. Bake the mushrooms for 15 minutes. As soon as you remove them from the oven, sprinkle the hot mushrooms with the reserved cheese and a twist of freshly ground pepper. Serve warm.

Triangles with Two-Mushroom Filling

Two or three savory large triangles can be served as a luncheon dish or first course. Small triangles are a delightful hot hors d'oeuvre.

MAKES ABOUT 12 LARGE
OR 64 SMALL TRIANGLES

1 ounce dried *shiitake* mushrooms*
2 tablespoons unsalted butter
1 tablespoon vegetable oil
¼ cup chopped shallots
1 pound fresh mushrooms, chopped

½ cup dry Madeira
1 tablespoon sherry vinegar
1 teaspoon fresh lemon juice
1 teaspoon salt
½ teaspoon freshly ground pepper
2 tablespoons dry bread crumbs
1 package (1 pound) phyllo dough (see Note)
About ¼ cup clarified butter
*Available in Oriental groceries

1. Place the *shiitake* mushrooms in a small bowl. Cover with boiling water and let soak for 30 minutes.

2. Meanwhile, melt the butter in the oil in a large skillet over moderate heat. When the foam subsides, add the shallots and sauté until softened but not browned, about 2 minutes. Add the chopped mushrooms, increase the heat to moderately high and cook, stirring, until the juices evaporate and the pieces separate, about 5 minutes.

3. Preheat the oven to 375°. Drain the *shiitake* mushrooms and squeeze dry. Cut off the woody stems. Chop the caps and add to the skillet.

4. Add the Madeira and cook until reduced to a glaze, about 5 minutes. Add the vinegar, lemon juice, salt and pepper and cook for 2 minutes. Add the bread crumbs and cook, stirring frequently, for 2 minutes longer. Remove from the heat and let cool to room temperature.

5. Lay one sheet of phyllo on a flat work surface. Brush lightly with clarified butter, cover with a second sheet of phyllo and butter the top sheet. Cut the layered phyllo crosswise into 4-inch strips for large triangles, 2-inch strips for small. Working quickly with one strip at a time, spoon the filling onto the bottom of the strip; use 3 tablespoons of filling for large triangles, a heaping teaspoon (1½ teaspoons) for small. Fold up using the classic flag-folding technique. Place on a buttered baking sheet and brush the tops with clarified butter.

6. Bake in the top third of the oven for 10 minutes. Brush again with butter. Bake for 10 to 15 minutes longer, until the triangles are golden brown.

NOTE: There will be leftover phyllo dough. It can be wrapped tightly and refrigerated for another use for up to 3 days if it is not dried out.

Double Radish Rounds

The cream-cheese mixture can be prepared a day before assembling the hors d'oeuvre.

F&W Beverage Suggestion:
Vinho Verde from Portugal, a Pinot Grigio from Italy or a cold *fino* sherry

MAKES 4 DOZEN

½ cup finely shredded radishes (about 10 medium)
1 teaspoon salt
8 ounces cream cheese, at room temperature
2 tablespoons prepared white horseradish, squeezed very dry through a cheesecloth to yield 2 packed teaspoons
¼ teaspoon pepper
6 tablespoons olive oil
3 tablespoons unsalted butter
12 thin slices whole wheat or white bread, each cut into 4 rounds, 1½ inches in diameter
6 to 8 medium radishes, trimmed and sliced paper-thin

1. In a small bowl, toss the shredded radish with the salt and set aside for 15 minutes. Place the shreds in a sieve and rinse under cold running water. Transfer the shreds to a double thickness of cheesecloth and squeeze until very dry, to yield about 3 packed tablespoons.

2. In a medium bowl, beat the cream cheese until fluffy. Stir in the shredded radishes, horseradish and pepper until blended. Cover and refrigerate until firm, at least 2 hours or overnight.

3. In a large skillet, combine 2 tablespoons of the oil and 1 tablespoon of the butter over moderately high heat. When very hot but not smoking, add 16 of the bread rounds. Sauté lightly for 1 to 2 minutes on each side, or until just golden brown. Drain on paper towels. Repeat the procedure, using the remaining oil, butter and bread rounds. Allow the rounds to cool to room temperature.

4. Spread each round with 1 teaspoon of the filling, mounding it slightly in the center. Top each with three overlapping slices of radish. Although these hors d'oeuvre are best made shortly before serving, they can be prepared 1 or 2 hours ahead of time, covered with plastic wrap and refrigerated until serving time.

Two-Tomato Canapés

MAKES 10

4 tablespoons unsalted butter
1 tablespoon olive oil, preferably from the jar of sun-dried tomatoes
1 small loaf French or Italian bread, cut into 10 slices, 1½ inches thick
2 ripe plum tomatoes or other small tomatoes, cut crosswise into 5 thin slices each
Salt and freshly ground pepper
10 sun-dried tomatoes in olive oil, cut into ½-inch pieces
½ log (5½ ounces) Montrachet goat cheese, chilled

1. In a medium skillet, melt the butter in the oil over moderately low heat. Add the bread slices and sauté, turning once, for about 1½ minutes on each side, or until golden brown. Transfer to an ungreased baking sheet.

2. Preheat the broiler. Top each slice of bread with a slice of fresh tomato; season with salt and pepper to taste. Place the sun-dried tomatoes on top, dividing evenly. Cut the cheese into 10 thin rounds and place on top of each canapé. Broil for 3 to 5 minutes, until bubbling and golden brown. Serve hot.

Cheddar Cheese Triangles

🍷 **F&W Beverage Suggestion:**
Light Zinfandel from California or a young Beaujolais, lightly chilled

MAKES 5 DOZEN

½ cup (1 stick) unsalted butter, at room temperature
½ pound sharp Cheddar cheese, finely grated (about 2 cups)
1½ teaspoons baking powder
¼ teaspoon salt
⅛ teaspoon cayenne pepper
1¼ cups all-purpose flour
1 egg
1 cup (4 ounces) finely chopped walnuts

1. In a large bowl, cream the butter and cheese together until fluffy. Add the baking powder, salt, cayenne and flour and stir to form a moderately stiff dough. Gather the dough into a ball, flatten it into a round, wrap tightly and refrigerate for at least 2 hours or as long as 2 days.

2. Preheat the oven to 400°. Lightly beat the egg in a small bowl. Place the walnuts on a plate.

3. Cut the dough into quarters. Rewrap 3 of the quarters and return to the refrigerator. Lightly flour the remaining dough and place it between 2 sheets of waxed paper. Roll the dough out to a 7-inch diameter and remove the top layer of waxed paper. Invert a 6-inch round plate or bowl on it and cut out a 6-inch circle. Gather the scraps of dough, wrap them and chill until needed. Cut the circle of dough into quarters and then cut each quarter into equal thirds to make 12 triangles.

4. Using a spatula and working with one triangle at a time, dip the rounded edge first into the egg and then into the walnuts. Place on an ungreased baking sheet and continue with the remaining triangles. Bake 8 to 10 minutes, or until just slightly golden and crisp around the edges. Transfer to a rack and let cool to room temperature.

5. Using a cool baking sheet, repeat with the remaining dough, egg and nuts. After combining all the scraps, there will be enough to make an additional circle of dough. Serve the triangles at room temperature.

Chèvre Mousse

This fragrantly herbed cheese mousse is made on the same principle as *coeur à la crème*, but molded in a woven basket rather than in heart shapes. Make it the night before you plan to serve it so that the whey has a chance to drain.

12 SERVINGS

½ pound Bucheron chèvre, softened to room temperature
¼ cup sour cream
¼ cup walnut pieces (4 ounces)
½ teaspoon dried rosemary leaves, crumbled
1½ teaspoons salt
¼ teaspoon white pepper
3 teaspoons Calvados
½ pint heavy cream
Bay leaves and walnut halves, for garnish

1. In a medium-size bowl, cream the cheese with the sour cream until smooth and soft.

2. Using a rolling pin, crush the walnuts coarsely between two sheets of waxed paper. Add them to the cheese mixture along with the rosemary, salt, pepper and 2 teaspoons of the Calvados.

3. In a medium-size bowl, whisk the cream until almost stiff. Blend in the remaining Calvados. Gently stir half the whipped cream into the cheese mixture. Place the remaining whipped cream on top of the cheese mixture and gently fold it in.

4. Line a basket that will hold at least 4 cups with three layers of damp cotton cheesecloth, cutting it large enough to allow for overlapping on top of the cheese. Arrange the bay leaves and walnut halves upside down in a decorative pattern on the bottom and pour in the mousse mixture; then smooth the surface. Fold the cheesecloth over the mousse and place the basket on a rack set over a shallow bowl to catch the liquid that will drain out of the mousse. Refrigerate overnight.

5. To unmold the mousse, fold back the cheesecloth, place a serving dish over the top of the basket and carefully invert. Remove the remaining cheesecloth and serve.

Cheese Puffs

🍷 **F&W Beverage Suggestion:**
Muscadet, California Sauvignon Blanc or a *fino* sherry

MAKES 4½ DOZEN

¼ cup dry vermouth or dry white wine
3 tablespoons unsalted butter, cut into bits
1 teaspoon salt
1 teaspoon Dijon-style mustard
⅛ teaspoon cayenne pepper
½ cup all-purpose flour
2 eggs
½ cup finely shredded Swiss cheese

1. Preheat the oven to 400°. Lightly grease 2 baking sheets. In a medium saucepan, bring the vermouth, butter, salt, mustard, cayenne and ¼ cup of water to a boil over low heat, stirring to incorporate the mustard and butter with the liquid. As soon as the mixture boils, remove it from the heat and stir in the flour all at once. Beat with a wooden spoon until a smooth ball forms and pulls away from the sides of the pan.

2. One at a time, add the eggs, beating vigorously to form a smooth paste. Continue beating for 1 minute. Lightly stir in the cheese.

3. Either drop the mixture by scant teaspoonfuls onto the prepared baking sheets or pipe the mixture from a pastry bag fitted with a plain ½-inch tube into ¾-inch mounds spaced about 1½ inches apart on the sheets. Bake for 20 minutes, until puffed and golden brown. Serve warm or at room temperature.

Baked Chèvre

Serve the hot cheese rounds as a first course or with a salad course, or cut them in quarters and offer them as an hors d'oeuvre.

6 TO 8 SERVINGS

1 log Montrachet chèvre (10 to 12 ounces)
¼ cup olive oil
½ cup fresh bread crumbs, toasted

1. Preheat the oven to 400°. Slice the cheese into ½-inch-thick rounds.

2. Dip the rounds into the olive oil and then dredge in the bread crumbs, making sure to coat them completely and evenly. Place them on a baking sheet and bake for 5 to 7 minutes, or until the cheese just begins to melt and the bottom crust is golden brown.

3. Turn the cheese rounds brown-side up and serve hot.

Fresh Ricotta Cheese

The full yet delicate flavor of freshly made ricotta is a real treat, and it is easy and quick to prepare. For this delicious hors d'oeuvre, the fresh cheese is highlighted with sprinklings of salt and pepper, rosemary, green olives and a small amount of virgin olive oil.

MAKES ABOUT 1 CUP

1 quart milk
½ cup heavy cream
1 tablespoon plus 1 teaspoon fresh lemon juice
⅛ teaspoon salt
⅛ teaspoon freshly ground pepper

Pinch of finely crushed rosemary
2 brine-cured green olives, minced
2 teaspoons extra-virgin olive oil

1. In a large noncorrodible saucepan, bring the milk and cream to a boil over high heat. When the liquid is boiling vigorously, stir in the lemon juice; the mixture will separate into curds and whey in 5 to 10 seconds. Immediately remove from the heat and pour through a fine sieve lined with a double thickness of dampened cheesecloth. What collects in the cheesecloth are the curds; discard the whey. Immediately place the ricotta on a small plate and let cool, uncovered, at room temperature. (If making ahead, cover the cooled ricotta and refrigerate until ready to use.)

2. With the back of a spoon, spread the ricotta in an even layer on the plate. Sprinkle with the salt, pepper, rosemary and minced olives. Drizzle the olive oil evenly over the cheese. Serve with crackers or thinly sliced Italian bread.

Spiced Cashews

MAKES ABOUT 2 CUPS

1 egg white
2 cups (about 12 ounces) raw cashews*
1½ teaspoons salt
1 teaspoon ground coriander
½ teaspoon ground cumin
½ teaspoon allspice
½ teaspoon cayenne pepper
***Available at health food stores and in some specialty shops**

1. Preheat the oven to 300°. In a medi-

um bowl, whisk the egg white with 1 tablespoon of water until the mixture is frothy and holds a soft shape. Add the cashews and fold until they are evenly coated.

2. In a small bowl, combine the salt, coriander, cumin, allspice and cayenne. Add the spices to the nuts and toss to mix well.

3. Line a baking sheet with aluminum foil and lightly butter the foil. Scatter the nuts on the sheet in a single layer and roast them in the oven for 30 minutes. Turn the nuts over with a spatula and roast for 30 minutes longer. Cool the cashews completely and store in an airtight container.

Roasted Herbed Nuts with Sesame Seeds

F&W Beverage Suggestion:
Champagne or sparkling wine

MAKES ABOUT 6 CUPS

1 egg white
8 ounces pecan halves
8 ounces whole almonds
8 ounces whole cashews
¼ cup sesame seeds
1 teaspoon thyme, crumbled
½ teaspoon freshly ground pepper
Salt (optional)

Preheat the oven to 325°. Lightly oil a baking sheet. In a large bowl, whisk the egg white until it is frothy and begins to hold soft peaks. Add the pecans, almonds, cashews, sesame seeds, thyme and pepper. Toss the mixture until the nuts are evenly coated and place in a single layer on a baking sheet, separating them as you arrange them. Bake, turning and stirring every 10 minutes, for about 40 minutes, or until golden and crisp. Let cool on the baking sheet. Sprinkle with salt to taste before serving.

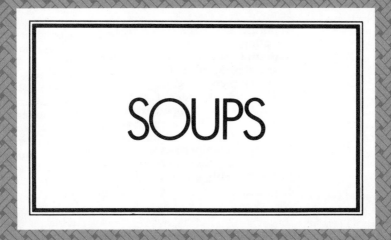

SOUPS

Oyster Stew

6 SERVINGS

2 tablespoons unsalted butter
1½ teaspoons minced shallots
1½ teaspoons lemon juice
Salt and pepper
½ cup thinly sliced celery heart
36 oysters with liquid, preferably Cotuit
½ teaspoon soy sauce
5 cups milk
1 cup heavy cream
1 tablespoon chopped fresh parsley
Celery seed, for garnish

1. In a small saucepan over low heat, melt the butter. Add the shallots, lemon juice, salt and pepper to taste and set aside in a warm place.

2. In a large, noncorrodible saucepan, combine the celery, the liquid from the oysters, the soy sauce and ½ cup water. Poach the celery over moderate heat for about 10 minutes, or until soft.

3. Add the milk, cream and oysters to the pan. Heat gently until the edges of the oysters are beginning to curl and they are just cooked, 8 to 10 minutes; do not allow the liquid to boil.

4. Stir the parsley into the butter mixture and spoon about 1 teaspoon of it into each of six bowls. Ladle the broth into the bowls and sprinkle lightly with more pepper and the celery seeds. Finally, put 6 oysters in each bowl and serve.

Connecticut Seafood Chowder

Prepare the base a day or two ahead; add the seafood of your choice and finish the soup shortly before serving.

8 TO 10 SERVINGS

Chowder Base:

3 ounces salt pork, cut into ¼-inch dice
1 medium leek (white part only), finely chopped
1 large onion, finely chopped
½ pound boiling potatoes (about 2 medium), peeled and cut into ⅜-inch dice
1 small celery rib, cut into ¼-inch dice
1 cup fish stock or bottled clam juice
2 teaspoons chopped fresh parsley
¼ teaspoon oregano
¼ teaspoon thyme
1 bay leaf, broken
¼ teaspoon freshly ground pepper

Seafood:

¼ pound bay or quartered sea scallops
¼ pound haddock, scrod or other firm-fleshed white fish, cut into ½-inch pieces
18 quahogs (chowder clams), shucked and chopped, with 3 cups of their liquor reserved
3 cups half-and-half or light cream
Dash of hot pepper sauce
1 tablespoon unsalted butter
Salt and freshly ground pepper

1. In a large kettle or flameproof casserole, sauté the salt pork over moderate heat until it is crisp and golden, about 5 minutes. Add the leek and onion and sauté until the onion begins to color, about 4 minutes.

2. Add the potatoes, celery, fish stock, parsley, oregano, thyme, bay leaf, pepper and 1 cup of water. Bring to a boil over moderate heat, reduce the heat to low and simmer the chowder base until the potatoes are barely tender, about 7 minutes. (The recipe can be prepared ahead to this point.) Let cool, then cover and refrigerate.

3. Shortly before serving, bring the chowder base to a boil over moderate heat; add the scallops, haddock and clams with their reserved liquor. Simmer until the clams are tender, about 5 minutes.

4. Stir in the half-and-half, hot pepper sauce and butter and heat to simmering over moderately low heat. Season with salt and pepper to taste before serving.

Finnish Salmon Chowder

6 SERVINGS

2 pounds salmon fillet, skinned (see Note)
Head, tail, bones and trimmings from a 7- to 10-pound salmon
8 to 10 peppercorns
1 bay leaf
1½ teaspoons salt
1½ pounds small red potatoes— peeled, halved crosswise and cut into ⅜-inch slices
2 medium onions, coarsely chopped
½ cup heavy cream
Salt and freshly ground pepper
2 tablespoons butter, cut into 6 pieces
¼ cup thinly sliced scallions

1. Cut the salmon fillet into good-sized chunks, about 3 by 2 inches. Cover and refrigerate. Rinse the salmon head, tail, bones and trimmings under cold running water and place in a large stockpot. Add 6 cups of water, the peppercorns, bay leaf and salt and bring to a boil over high heat. Reduce the heat to moderately low and simmer, covered, for 45 minutes. Strain the broth and return it to the stockpot. Discard the bones, but remove the cheek meat from the head and reserve it.

2. Add the potatoes and onions to the broth and bring to a boil over high heat. Lower the heat to moderate and simmer, uncovered, for 5 minutes, or until the potatoes are slightly tender. Place the fish fillets in the broth and simmer for 10 to 15 minutes, or until just cooked through. Add the cheek meat.

3. Ladle 1 cup of the broth into a small bowl. Whisk in the heavy cream, pour the liquid back into the pot and stir gently to mix without breaking up the fish or potatoes. Season to taste with salt and pepper. Ladle the soup into heated soup plates, top each with a pat of butter and a sprinkling of scallions.

NOTE: Any oily fish—such as sea trout, mackerel or halibut—can be substituted for the salmon.

Sweet Corn and Crab Meat Soup

This soup is sometimes made with chicken instead of crab.

4 SERVINGS

4 large ears of corn, husks removed
3 cups chicken stock or canned broth, chilled
2 teaspoons sugar
3 tablespoons cornstarch
2 eggs, lightly beaten
4 ounces crab meat, flaked and picked over to remove any bits of cartilage
1 scallion, thinly sliced, for garnish

1. Using a large sharp knife, cut the corn off the cobs and scrape the cobs with the back of the knife or a spoon to obtain as much corn and juice as possible. There will be about 3 cups.

2. Combine the corn and ½ cup of the stock in a food processor or blender and mix for about 15 seconds, until coarsely chopped.

3. In a medium saucepan, combine the corn mixture, 2 cups of the stock and the sugar. Bring to a boil over moderately high heat, then reduce the heat to moderate. Meanwhile, combine the remaining ½ cup stock with the cornstarch. Stir into the hot soup and cook, stirring constantly, until thickened, 1 to 2 minutes.

4. Just before serving, slowly stir in the beaten eggs and crab meat. Garnish with the sliced scallion, if desired.

Hebridean Mussel Soup

This soup is delicious without the puff pastry lids, though they make a spectacular presentation.

8 SERVINGS

Soup:
3½ to 4 pounds fresh mussels, scrubbed and debearded
2½ cups dry white wine
¼ cup chopped shallots
3 tablespoons vegetable oil
1 small onion, diced
1 medium leek, white part only, diced
¾ cup diced celery
¾ pound sole or bass fillets, cut into 1-inch pieces
1 cup canned, peeled tomatoes— drained, seeded and diced
1 bay leaf
2 cups heavy cream
1 teaspoon thyme
3 to 4 tablespoons lemon juice, to taste
½ teaspoon salt
¼ teaspoon freshly ground white pepper

Puff-Pastry Topping (optional):
1¼ pounds puff pastry or 1 package (1¼ pounds) frozen puff pastry (2 10-ounce squares, 10-by-10 inches each), defrosted
1 egg, beaten

1. Make the soup: Place the mussels in a large pan with the wine and shallots. Cover the pan, turn the heat to high and steam the mussels until they open, 5 to 7 minutes. As soon as they are cool enough to handle, remove the mussels from their shells and reserve the liquid. Discard any that are closed. Reserve 16 mussels for garnish and set the remainder aside. Strain the liquid through a sieve lined with a double thickness of dampened cheesecloth.

2. In a deep skillet, heat the oil over moderate heat. Add the onion, leek and celery and sauté until softened but not browned, 3 to 5 minutes. Add the fish and sauté, stirring, for 1 minute, until it begins to turn white. Add the tomatoes, bay leaf and reserved mussel liquid. Bring to a boil, reduce the heat to low and simmer, uncovered, for 20 minutes. Remove from the heat and add the mussels.

3. Puree the soup in batches in a blender or food processor and transfer to another saucepan. Stir in the cream, thyme, lemon juice, salt and pepper. Heat gently until hot (or warm, if you wish to add the puff-pastry lids) and ladle into onion soup bowls. Garnish each serving with 2 of the reserved mussels.

4. Make the puff-pastry lids: Preheat the oven to 400°. If using fresh puff pastry, roll out to ¼-inch thickness on a lightly floured surface. If using frozen, allow to defrost for just a few minutes; then unfold carefully onto the lightly floured surface. Cut the chilled pastry into 8 circles 5 inches in diameter (or 1 inch larger than the soup bowls). Allow the fresh pastry to rest in the refrigerator for 30 minutes before baking; the frozen lids may be assembled immediately.

5. Place the filled soup bowls on a baking sheet. Moisten the outer rims of the bowls with the egg and center a pastry lid on top of each. Taking care not to stretch the pastry, press very firmly around the outside of the rims to seal. Make a ½-inch steam vent in the center of each lid and brush with the remaining egg. Bake for 15 minutes, or until golden and crisp.

Assorted Meat and Vegetable Soup in a Pot

6 SERVINGS

6 cups chicken stock or canned broth
2 quarter-size slices fresh gingerroot
1½ pounds chicken parts— preferably 1 breast, 1 leg, 1 thigh and 1 wing
2 ounces cooked ham, cut into 1½-by-¼-inch strips
1 ounce dried shrimp*
6 dried black mushrooms*
2 ounces cellophane noodles*
1 pound bok choy,* coarsely chopped
8 ounces (about 2 squares) fried bean curd,* cut into 1-inch cubes
2 cups shredded Chinese cabbage*
½ teaspoon Oriental sesame oil
1 tablespoon soy sauce
2 scallions, cut on the diagonal into 1½-inch lengths
*Available at Oriental groceries

1. In a large heavy saucepan or flameproof casserole, combine the stock, ginger and chicken; bring to a simmer over low heat. Partially cover the pan and continue to simmer until the chicken is cooked through, 15 to 20 minutes. Remove the chicken and set aside. When cool enough to handle, cut into 2-inch pieces with a heavy Chinese cleaver or poultry shears.

2. To the hot stock, add the ham, shrimp and mushrooms; let the soup stand off heat for 10 minutes. Meanwhile, soak the cellophane noodles in 3 cups of boiling water for 10 minutes. Drain and set aside.

3. In a large heavy pot, bring 2 quarts of water to a boil over high heat. Add the bok choy; as soon as the water returns to the boil, drain into a colander.

4. To assemble, bring the soup to a simmer over moderate heat. Add the bean curd and cook for 3 minutes. Remove with a Chinese strainer or slotted metal spoon and arrange in a mound in a tureen. Add the Chinese cabbage to the soup and cook until just tender, about 3 minutes. Transfer to the tureen, arranging in a mound. Add the chicken to the soup and cook until just heated through, 2 to 3 minutes. Remove and arrange in another mound in the tureen. Arrange the bok choy and cellophane noodles in separate mounds in the tureen. Remove the mushrooms from the soup and set aside. Ladle the hot soup into the tureen and add the sesame oil, soy sauce and scallions. Garnish with the mushrooms.

Clear Mushroom Soup

This simple-to-make soup has a gingery sprightliness that makes it just right to begin a rich meal.

6 FIRST-COURSE SERVINGS

1 pound mushrooms, quickly rinsed
2 large shallots, sliced
1 piece ginger, about 1 inch in diameter and 2 inches long, thinly sliced
6 cups chicken or veal stock (or both), completely grease free
Soy sauce
Salt
Lime juice
Thin lime slices and fresh coriander (cilantro) sprigs, for garnish

1. Reserve about one-third of the mush-

rooms, preferably small ones. Combine the remaining mushrooms in the container of a food processor or blender with the shallots, ginger and 2 cups of the stock. Process until finely chopped, but not pureed. Transfer to a pot and add the remaining 4 cups of stock.

2. Simmer, partly covered, for 20 minutes. Strain through a sieve (you might save the chopped vegetables for a sauce). Line the sieve with cheesecloth and strain again. Slice the reserved mushrooms very thin and add to the broth. Bring to a bare simmer. Add soy sauce, salt and lime juice to taste. Cool; then refrigerate.

3. When ready to serve, reheat slowly and taste again for seasoning. Serve in small Japanese-style soup bowls, or mugs. Garnish each bowl of soup with a slice of lime and a few sprigs of coriander.

Mushroom Soup

This soup is rich with the pungent bouquet of three varieties of mushrooms.

8 TO 12 SERVINGS

4 to 6 large dried Polish mushrooms, cepes or *porcini**
12 large dried *shiitake* mushrooms**
3 quarts beef stock or broth
5 medium carrots, finely diced
5 celery ribs with leaves, finely diced
2 large onions, finely chopped
2 tablespoons finely chopped fresh parsley
1 pound fresh mushrooms, sliced
3 tablespoons chopped fresh dill or 2 teaspoons dried
1 tablespoon coarse (kosher) salt (omit if using canned broth)
½ teaspoon freshly ground pepper
½ cup very small dried pasta, such as bows, squares, alphabets or orzo
2 tablespoons unsalted butter

2 tablespoons all-purpose flour
1 cup sour cream
*Available at specialty food shops
**Available at Oriental groceries

1. Pour 2 cups of hot water over the Polish and *shiitake* mushrooms, and let them soak for 1 hour.

2. In a large pot, bring the stock to a simmer. Add the carrots, celery, onions and parsley and cook, uncovered, over low heat for 20 minutes, stirring occasionally.

3. Remove the soaked mushrooms from the water; strain the liquid through a sieve lined with a double thickness of cheesecloth and reserve. Cut the mushrooms into pieces slightly larger than the diced vegetables. Add the mushrooms and reserved liquor to the soup. Simmer for 15 minutes.

4. Add the sliced fresh mushrooms, the dill, salt (if using stock) and pepper. Simmer for 15 minutes.

5. Bring the soup to a boil. Stirring constantly, add the pasta. Reduce the heat slightly and cook, stirring occasionally, until the pasta is tender, 4 to 7 minutes.

6. Meanwhile, in a small heavy saucepan, melt the butter over moderately low heat. Add the flour, blending until smooth. Cook, stirring, for about 2 minutes without browning to make a roux. Whisk in 2 tablespoons of the sour cream until blended. Remove from the heat and stir in the remaining sour cream.

7. When the pasta is tender, add the thickened sour cream to the soup. Adjust the heat to a simmer and cook, stirring constantly, until the sour cream is completely incorporated, about 3 minutes. Serve hot or cold.

Potatoes with Three American Caviars (p. 24).

Assorted Meat and Vegetable Soup in a Pot (p. 31).

Top left, Hot Sweet-and-Sour Borscht (p. 40). Top right,
Avocado Tempura with Coriander and Lime (p. 23).
Bottom, Connecticut Seafood Chowder (p. 30).

Finnish Salmon Chowder (p. 30).

Soup Provençale with Poached Eggs

2 SERVINGS

2½ tablespoons olive oil
1 medium onion, coarsely chopped
3 garlic cloves, finely chopped
1 can (35 ounces) Italian peeled tomatoes, crushed, with their juice
1 small waxy potato, finely chopped, or ¼ cup cooked rice
½ teaspoon fennel seed, slightly crushed
¼ teaspoon thyme
1 bay leaf
2 strips of orange zest, about 2 by ½ inch
Large pinch of saffron threads
Dash of cayenne pepper
½ teaspoon salt
¼ teaspoon sugar
2 eggs
1 tablespoon chopped fresh parsley

1. Heat the oil in a medium saucepan. Add the onion and sauté over moderate heat until softened and translucent, about 3 minutes. Add the garlic and cook for 30 seconds longer.

2. Add the tomatoes and their juice, the potato, fennel, thyme, bay leaf, orange zest, saffron, cayenne, salt and sugar.

3. Bring to a boil, reduce to a simmer and cook, partially covered, for 20 minutes.

4. Remove the bay leaf and orange zest. Gently break the eggs into the soup, cover and poach until set, about 5 minutes.

5. Divide the eggs and soup between 2 bowls and garnish with the parsley.

Creamy Tomato Rice Soup

This earthy, vegetarian soup can be prepared in a little over an hour using ingredients available in most kitchens. Eaten with crusty dark bread, it will make a meal.

6 TO 8 SERVINGS

2 tablespoons olive oil
2 tablespoons butter
1 medium onion, chopped
2 medium carrots, chopped
1 celery rib, chopped
1 tablespoon minced garlic
⅔ cup long-grain brown rice
1 can (35 ounces) Italian plum tomatoes, with their liquid
¾ teaspoon dried dill weed
¾ teaspoon basil
2 teaspoons salt
¼ teaspoon pepper
1½ cups milk
½ cup heavy cream

1. In a large saucepan or stockpot, heat the olive oil and butter until the butter is melted. Add the onion and sauté over moderate heat until softened and translucent, about 3 minutes. Add the carrots, celery and garlic and sauté for 5 minutes. Add the brown rice and sauté for 1 minute longer. Add the tomatoes, mashing them with the back of a spoon to break them up. Add the dill, basil, salt, pepper and 6 cups of water. Bring to a boil, reduce the heat and simmer, uncovered, for about 45 minutes, stirring occasionally, until the rice is tender.

2. Puree half of the soup in a blender or food processor and return it to the remaining soup in the pot. Stir in the milk and cream and season with salt and pepper to taste. Heat gently just until hot.

Garlic-Tomato Soup

6 SERVINGS

1 tablespoon goose fat, duck fat or unsalted butter (see Note)
2½ tablespoons chopped garlic (7 to 8 medium cloves), or less to taste
2 tablespoons all-purpose flour
1 medium can (16 ounces) Italian peeled tomatoes, with their juice
1 teaspoon salt
½ teaspoon freshly ground pepper
2 eggs, separated

1. In a heavy medium saucepan, melt the fat over moderate heat. Add the garlic and sauté until softened but not browned, 2 to 3 minutes.

2. Stir in the flour and cook without browning for 2 minutes longer.

3. Add the tomatoes and their juice, 4 cups of water and the salt and pepper. Bring to a boil, reduce the heat and simmer for 30 minutes.

4. Pass the soup through the coarse disk of a food mill or coarsely puree in a blender or food processor. Return to the saucepan and reheat gently. With a fork, stir the egg whites to break them up. Give the soup a swirl and gradually pour in the egg whites in a thin stream, stirring the soup gently so that threads form, as in egg drop soup.

5. In a small bowl, lightly beat the egg yolks with a fork. Gradually stir in 1 cup of the hot soup to warm them. Return the mixture to the remaining soup in the saucepan. Cook, stirring, over moderate heat without boiling until the soup thickens slightly, about 2 minutes. Serve hot.

NOTE: Goose fat, which is traditionally used in this savory regional soup, will give it a most distinctive flavor.

Carrot Soup with Curry

6 TO 8 SERVINGS

2 pounds carrots, coarsely chopped
1 large leek (white part and tender green)—split lengthwise, rinsed well and coarsely chopped
2 garlic cloves, minced
2 quarts chicken stock or broth
1 cup half-and-half
1¼ teaspoons curry powder
6 tablespoons minced fresh parsley for garnish.

1. In a large saucepan, combine the carrots, leek, garlic and chicken stock. Cook, uncovered, over moderate heat, until the vegetables are tender and the stock has reduced to 5 cups, about 20 minutes.

2. Working in batches, puree the soup in a blender or food processor. Using a wooden spoon, press the puree through a fine sieve set over another clean saucepan.

3. Before serving, whisk in the half-and-half and the curry powder and simmer over moderate heat until heated through, about 3 minutes. Serve hot, garnished with the minced parsley if desired.

Snow Pea Soup

MAKES ABOUT 1 QUART

4 tablespoons unsalted butter
1 small garlic clove, minced
1 medium red onion, chopped
⅓ cup all-purpose flour
3 cups chicken stock or broth
1 pound snow peas, strings removed
1 cup milk
1 tablespoon freshly grated gingerroot
Salt and white pepper

1. In a large, heavy saucepan, melt the butter over moderate heat. Add the garlic and onion and cook until soft and translucent, about 5 minutes.

2. Off the heat, add the flour and mix thoroughly. Return to moderate heat and cook for 3 minutes, stirring, to make a roux.

3. Add the chicken stock, bring to a boil, reduce the heat and simmer, stirring, until thickened, 2 to 3 minutes. Add the snow peas and cook until the peas are puffed and bright green but not too soft, about 5 minutes. Pour in the milk and cook for 3 minutes longer.

4. Puree the mixture in a blender or food processor until very smooth. Strain through a fine sieve into a saucepan. Reheat for 5 minutes. Stir in the gingerroot and salt and pepper to taste; serve hot.

Fresh Pea Soup

6 SERVINGS

8 tablespoons clarified butter
4 shallots, chopped
2 pounds fresh peas, shelled
1 large carrot, chopped
½ head Boston lettuce, rinsed well
1 teaspoon salt
½ teaspoon white pepper
2 pints (4 cups) heavy cream
6 medium mushrooms, sliced, for garnish
18 medium fresh shrimp, for garnish
4 tablespoons cold unsalted butter
12 fresh mint leaves, for garnish

1. In a large saucepan, heat 2 tablespoons of the clarified butter. Add the shallots and cook over moderate heat until lightly colored, about 2 minutes. Add the peas, carrot, lettuce, salt, pepper and about 2 cups of water, enough to barely cover the vegetables. Bring to a boil, reduce the heat to low, cover and cook until the peas are tender, about 10 minutes.

2. Stir in the cream. Bring to a boil, reduce the heat to low and simmer, uncovered, for 5 minutes. In a blender or food processor, puree the soup, in two batches if necessary, until smooth. Return to the saucepan and season with additional salt and pepper, if necessary. (The soup can be made ahead to this point.)

3. In a medium skillet, heat 3 tablespoons of the clarified butter. Add the mushrooms and sauté over moderately high heat, stirring, until the mushrooms are tender, about 4 minutes. Season with salt and pepper to taste. Drain on paper towels.

4. In a large skillet, heat the remaining 3 tablespoons of the clarified butter. Add the shrimp in their shells and sauté over high heat, turning once, for 1 minute on each side. Reduce the heat to moderate and cook the shrimp an additional 3 minutes. Drain on paper towels. As soon as the shrimp are cool enough to handle, peel off the shells and cover the shrimp to keep warm.

5. Before serving, warm the soup over low heat. Whisk in the cold butter, 1 tablespoon at a time. Ladle the soup into 6 individual soup plates and garnish each with 3 shrimp, several mushroom slices and 2 mint leaves.

Split Pea Soup with Herbed Croutons

6 TO 8 SERVINGS

Soup:
2 tablespoons unsalted butter
½ cup chopped onion
½ cup chopped celery
½ cup chopped carrot
½ cup chopped leek (white part only)
2 cups (1 pound) split peas, rinsed and picked over
6 cups homemade chicken stock or water
1½ teaspoons salt
½ teaspoon freshly ground pepper
1 cup milk
2 cups (packed) chopped fresh spinach leaves (about 1 pound, trimmed)

Croutons:
4 slices (½ inch thick) whole-wheat or pumpernickel bread, crusts removed, cut into ½-inch cubes
2 tablespoons unsalted butter
1 garlic clove, crushed through a press
1 teaspoon oregano, crumbled
½ teaspoon rosemary, crumbled
½ teaspoon marjoram, crumbled
½ teaspoon salt

1. Begin the soup: Melt the butter in a large saucepan or Dutch oven. Add the onion, celery, carrot and leek; cover the pan and sweat the vegetables over low heat for 10 minutes, stirring occasionally. Add the split peas, stock, salt and pepper. Simmer, uncovered, for 1 hour, stirring occasionally, until the peas are tender.

2. Meanwhile, make the croutons: Preheat the oven to 350°. Place the bread cubes in a bowl. Melt the butter in a small skillet over low heat. Add the garlic and cook gently until fragrant but not browned. Add the oregano, rosemary, marjoram and salt and pour over the bread; toss to coat the bread with the herb-butter. Spread in a single layer on a baking sheet and bake in the oven for 10 to 15 minutes, or until the croutons are crunchy.

3. Complete the soup: When the peas are tender, puree them with the milk in several batches in a blender or food processor. Set aside until you are ready to serve.

4. Just before serving, add the spinach leaves to the soup and bring to a simmer over moderate heat. Season with additional salt and pepper to taste and serve hot with the croutons.

Smoky Bean and Pasta Soup

MAKES ABOUT 3½ QUARTS

2 to 3 pounds bones left over from smoked turkey, chicken, ham or pork
2 large onions, coarsely chopped
2 large carrots, coarsely chopped
2 garlic cloves, chopped
2 bay leaves
1 pound dried navy or pea beans, rinsed and picked over
1 tablespoon salt
1 can (16 ounces) whole, peeled tomatoes, chopped, juices reserved
1 teaspoon dried basil
¼ teaspoon pepper
8 ounces small pasta shells

1. Place the bones, onions, carrots, garlic and bay leaves in a large stockpot. Add 4 quarts of cold water and bring to a boil over high heat. Reduce the heat and simmer, partially covered, for 2 hours.

2. Meanwhile, place the beans with 2 quarts of cold water in a large saucepan. Bring to a boil and add the salt. Boil rapidly for 2 minutes. Remove the pot from the heat and let the beans soak for 1 hour. Reheat to boiling, reduce the heat and simmer, partially covered, for 45 minutes. Remove from the heat and set aside.

3. Strain the broth from the stockpot, reserving the liquid. If there is any meat on the bones, pick it off and reserve it. Discard the bones and vegetables.

4. In a large pot, combine the beans and their cooking liquid with the smoky broth. Simmer for 1 hour. Add the tomatoes with their juices, the basil and pepper. Simmer until the beans are tender but not falling apart, 20 to 30 minutes.

5. Meanwhile, bring 3 quarts of water to a boil, then add salt. Add the pasta and cook, stirring occasionally, until it is partially cooked, but still quite firm. Drain the pasta and add it to the soup along with any reserved meat from the bones. Simmer until the pasta is cooked to your taste. Check the seasoning and add additional salt and pepper if necessary.

Chick-Pea and Vegetable Soup

8 SERVINGS

¼ cup vegetable oil
2 cups chopped leeks (about 2 medium), white part and 2 inches of the green
¼ cup finely chopped celery
½ cup finely chopped green bell pepper
5 cups chicken stock
1¼ cups cooked or canned chick-peas
5 ounces smoked turkey or chicken breast, cut into 2-by-¼-inch julienne
1 can (35 ounces) Italian peeled tomatoes, drained and coarsely chopped
1 bay leaf
1 teaspoon salt
½ teaspoon black pepper
1 pound fresh kale or 1 package (10 ounces) frozen kale, thawed
½ pound boiling potatoes, unpeeled and cut into ½-inch cubes
1 tablespoon red wine vinegar

1. In a large saucepan, heat the oil. Add the leeks, celery and green pepper and cook, covered, over low heat for 5 minutes. Add the stock, chick-peas, smoked turkey, tomatoes, bay leaf, salt, pepper and 2 cups of water. Bring to the point of a boil, lower the heat and simmer, partially covered, for 1 hour.

2. Remove and discard the tough stems from the kale. Wash the leaves and chop them coarsely. Add the kale and potatoes to the soup and cook for 20 minutes. Remove the bay leaf and add the vinegar before serving.

Six-Onion Soup

This creamy, delicate soup uses the yellow onion and five of its relatives—leeks, shallots, garlic, scallions and chives. Long-simmered, the ingredients acquire a sweet, subtle flavor.

4 TO 6 SERVINGS

4 tablespoons unsalted butter
3 medium onions, chopped
4 large leeks (white part only), sliced crosswise
4 ounces shallots, chopped (about ½ cup)
6 medium garlic cloves, minced
4 cups chicken stock or broth
1 teaspoon thyme
1 bay leaf
1 teaspoon freshly ground pepper
1 cup heavy cream
3 scallions, cut on the diagonal into ½-inch pieces
Salt
Croutons (preferably homemade) and chopped fresh chives, for garnish

1. Melt the butter in a heavy medium saucepan. Add the onions, leeks, shallots and garlic. Cover and cook over low heat, stirring occasionally, until the vegetables are softened and translucent, about 25 minutes.

2. Add the stock, thyme, bay leaf and pepper. Bring to a boil, reduce the heat to low and simmer, partially covered, until the vegetables are very soft, about 20 minutes.

3. Strain the soup into a large bowl, reserving the solids in a sieve. Transfer these solids plus 1 cup of the liquid to the bowl of a blender or food processor. Puree until smooth.

4. Return the puree and the remaining strained liquid to the saucepan, stir in the cream and scallion pieces and simmer for 3 to 5 minutes, until the scallions are wilted. Season with salt to taste. Serve garnished with croutons and chives.

Red Cabbage Soup

The shredding, slicing, dicing and mincing of various ingredients provides texture and contributes flavor to this slightly pungent, savory soup.

6 SERVINGS

4 tablespoons (½ stick) unsalted butter
1 large red onion, very thinly sliced
1 large garlic clove, minced
1 teaspoon sugar
1 tablespoon flour
6 cups shredded red cabbage (1½- to 2-pound head)
¼ teaspoon thyme
6 cups beef broth
¼ cup red wine
2 tablespoons red wine vinegar
1 teaspoon salt
¼ teaspoon white pepper
Garnish:
½ pound kielbasa (Polish sausage), sliced ¼ inch thick
8 ounces sour cream
1 tart apple—peeled, cored and coarsely shredded (optional)

1. In a large pot, melt the butter over low heat; add the onion and sauté for 5 minutes. Stir in the garlic, cover and cook gently for 3 minutes.

2. Stir in the sugar and flour; cook for 1 minute. Add the cabbage, thyme, broth, wine, 1 tablespoon of the vinegar, salt and pepper; cook, stirring occasionally, over moderate heat for 2 minutes.

3. Increase the heat slightly and bring the soup to a boil. Reduce the heat so that the soup is simmering, and cook for 20 minutes.

4. In the meantime, sauté the kielbasa in a heavy skillet over medium heat until cooked through and crisp, about 5 minutes.

5. Stir the remaining tablespoon of vinegar into the soup and remove from the heat. Ladle into six shallow bowls and garnish each with five or six slices of kielbasa, a dollop of sour cream, and some of the optional shredded apple.

Hot Sweet-and-Sour Borscht

Many people express surprise to learn there is a borscht other than summer's cold, pinky-magenta beet soup with the inevitable boiled potato. This other borscht is not a heated-up version of the summer favorite, but a stewlike affair that contains cabbage and meat, or at least is made with meat stock. Very practical in a country of severe winters and limited food resources, it is served all over Russia in countless variations and permutations. The beef from which the stock is made can be served sliced or diced in the soup, as in this recipe, or dished up as a separate course, to be eaten with horseradish and pickles, along with buttered slabs of black or rye bread.

6 TO 8 SERVINGS

Stock:
3 to 4 pounds beef knuckle and/or marrow bones, cracked
1½ pounds shin beef or brisket (see Note)
2 ribs celery
1 onion, quartered
1 carrot, quartered
1 parsley root—trimmed, peeled and quartered (optional, see Note)
Bouquet garni: celery leaves, several parsley stems and 2 bay leaves tied in a double thickness of cheesecloth
1 tablespoon salt
8 to 10 peppercorns

Soup:
3 tablespoons vegetable oil
1 medium onion, chopped

2 garlic cloves, minced
4 to 5 large, fresh beets (about 1½ pounds after trimming), peeled and coarsely grated
1 pound (2 large) boiling potatoes, peeled and cut into 1-inch cubes
1 can (8 ounces) tomato puree
¼ cup red wine vinegar, or more to taste
1 teaspoon sugar, or more to taste
½ small cabbage (about 1 pound), cored and coarsely shredded
Salt and freshly ground pepper
Minced fresh dill (optional)
1 cup sour cream (optional)

1. Prepare the stock: Wash the bones in several changes of cold water. Place them in a large heavy stockpot, add the shin beef or brisket and 4 quarts of cold water and bring to a boil over high heat. Cook for about 10 minutes, skimming to remove the foam. Add the celery, onion, carrot, parsley root, bouquet garni, salt and peppercorns. Reduce the heat to moderately low and simmer, partially covered, for 3 hours, adding water as needed if more than half boils away. If using brisket, remove when the meat is tender, after about 1½ hours, and set aside to serve as a separate course. If using shin beef, allow to cook the full 3 hours. Remove the meat and set aside until you finish the soup.

2. Strain the stock through a sieve set over a large bowl. There will be about 8 cups of liquid. Let the stock cool and skim off as much fat as possible from the surface. (The recipe can be prepared ahead to this point the day before or early in the day. Reserve the stock and refrigerate the meat, wrapped in foil, until ready to use.)

3. Make the soup: In a large, heavy stockpot, heat the oil over moderate heat. Add the onion and cook until just softened, about three minutes. Add the garlic and cook, stirring, until the onions are lightly browned, about 2 minutes longer.

4. Add the beets, potatoes, tomato puree, vinegar, sugar and 4 cups of the reserved beef stock. Bring to a boil, lower the heat slightly and simmer, partially covered, for 20 minutes.

5. Add the cabbage and the remaining beef stock. Cut the reserved shin beef into 1-inch cubes or larger chunks, if you prefer, and add to the soup. Continue to simmer until the potatoes and the cabbage are tender, 15 to 20 minutes. Correct the seasoning with salt and pepper and add more sugar or vinegar if the sweet-sour balance is not to your liking. Serve very hot from the pot or a heated tureen, sprinkled with the dill. Pass sour cream separately, if you wish.

NOTE: Shin beef, from the shank, is the traditional cut used in borscht. It is extremely tasty, but not particularly attractive. **Brisket,** while almost too elegant for this dish, is preferable if you are going to serve the meat as a separate course.

Parsley root is not to be confused with parsnip or the tiny roots that normally appear on leaf parsley. This is the Hamburg or turnip-rooted parsley widely used in Russian soups and stews. It is often found in packages of combination vegetables labeled "soup greens" and has a flavor somewhat like celery root. Russians often add it, grated, to the borscht along with beets.

Tennessee Corncob Soup

8 TO 10 SERVINGS

10 ears of yellow corn
2 tablespoons unsalted butter
1 cup heavy cream
1½ teaspoons salt
½ teaspoon freshly ground pepper

1. Using a corn grater or a sharp knife, scrape the kernels off each ear and set aside; there will be about 5 cups. Reserve the cobs.

2. Put the cobs in a large saucepan and add 6 cups of cold water. Bring to a boil, reduce the heat to a simmer and cook, covered, for 1 hour.

3. Remove the cobs, reserving the cooking liquid. Scrape any remaining corn left on the cobs into the cooking liquids.

4. Add the reserved corn kernels, the butter, cream, salt and pepper to the saucepan. Cook, covered, over low heat for 15 minutes.

Wild Wind's Cream of Pumpkin Soup

If fresh pumpkin is not available, butternut squash may be substituted.

4 SERVINGS

2 cups fresh pumpkin cubes (1 inch)
4 cups chicken stock or canned broth
½ cup heavy cream
½ teaspoon freshly grated nutmeg
¼ teaspoon salt
Dash of cayenne pepper
Chopped fresh chives, for garnish

1. In a large saucepan, combine the pumpkin and stock. Bring to a boil, reduce the heat to low and simmer until the pumpkin is tender, 8 to 10 minutes. Remove from the heat and let cool slightly.

2. In a blender or food processor, puree the soup in batches until smooth. Return to the saucepan and place over low heat. Add the cream, nutmeg, salt and cayenne. Heat through and serve warm or refrigerate and serve chilled. Garnish with chopped chives or additional nutmeg.

Squash Soup Spiked with Apple

12 SERVINGS

1 large butternut squash (2 pounds)—peeled, seeded and cut into 1-inch cubes
5 cups chicken stock or broth
2 tart apples (such as Greening or Granny Smith), cored and quartered (do not peel)
2 tablespoons fresh lemon juice
Pinch of ground mace
Salt and freshly ground pepper
1 cup heavy cream
12 freshly cut thin apple wedges, for garnish

1. In a large saucepan, simmer the squash in 4 cups of the stock until the squash is tender, about 10 minutes. Puree, in batches if necessary, in a blender or food processor; pass through a fine sieve. Return to the saucepan.

2. In a blender or food processor, puree the quartered apples with the remaining 1 cup stock. Pass through a fine sieve to remove any bits of peel. Add the apple puree to the squash mixture. Bring to a boil, reduce the heat, add the lemon juice and mace and season with salt and pepper to taste. (The soup can be made ahead to this point, cooled and refrigerated or frozen. Just before serving, reheat the soup and proceed to Step 3.)

3. Beat the cream until soft peaks form. Fold two-thirds of the whipped cream into the soup. Heat through, but do not allow to boil. Serve hot, garnished with the apple wedges and a dollop of the remaining whipped cream.

Pea, Pear and Watercress Soup

10 SERVINGS

½ cup (1 stick) unsalted butter
1 small onion, roughly chopped
2 pounds fresh peas, shelled (to yield 1 pound peas) or 1 pound frozen peas
1 pound pears—peeled, cored and sliced
½ cup dry sherry
½ teaspoon salt
¼ teaspoon mace
⅛ teaspoon pepper
4 cups hot chicken stock

Garnish:
Toasted croutons
Thin slices of pear sautéed in butter
Heavy cream
Sprigs of watercress

1. In a large saucepan, melt the butter. Add the onion and sauté gently, stirring occasionally, over moderate heat, until the onion is soft and translucent, about 5 minutes. Add the peas, pears, sherry, salt, mace and pepper. Place a piece of waxed paper on top of the vegetables and pears and cover the pan. Simmer over very low heat, stirring once or twice, for 1 hour.

2. Gradually stir the hot stock into the vegetables. In a blender or food processor with a metal blade, add equal amounts of liquids and solids and process until smooth. (To avoid a mess, never fill the container more than halfway and keep your hand on the blender top.)

3. Pour the pureed soup through a fine sieve: using the round side of a ladle, gently stir and press the soup through the sieve into a clean saucepan. Gently warm the soup until just heated through. Serve with one or more of the suggested garnishes.

Curried Papaya Soup

Slices of papaya and pieces of fresh mint, added at serving time, enhance the flavor as well as the appearance of this lovely soup.

4 SERVINGS

1 teaspoon vegetable oil
½ to ¾ teaspoon curry powder, to taste
½ teaspoon minced, peeled fresh gingerroot
¼ teaspoon chopped garlic
3 cups chicken stock or canned broth
2 teaspoons fresh lime juice
Salt
1 small firm papaya—peeled, halved, seeded and sliced
1 tablespoon chopped fresh mint

1. In a medium saucepan, heat the oil. Add the curry powder, ginger and garlic and stir fry over high heat for 10 seconds. Stir in the chicken stock. Just before the mixture boils, reduce the heat to low, cover and simmer for 20 minutes.

2. Strain through a fine mesh sieve. Season with the lime juice and salt to taste.

3. Just before serving, reheat if necessary. Stir in the papaya slices and the mint.

Watercress-Pork Soup

6 SERVINGS

4 slices (quarter-sized) peeled fresh gingerroot
3 large slivers orange zest
1 tablespoon soy sauce
1 teaspoon salt
¾ pound pork butt, cut into thin strips (1 by ¼ inch)
1 large bunch watercress, tough stems removed
¼ teaspoon Oriental sesame oil

1. Place the gingerroot, orange zest, soy sauce and salt in a medium saucepan. Add 6 cups of water and bring to a boil over moderate heat. Reduce the heat to low and simmer, partially covered, for 10 minutes.

2. Add the pork to the broth and simmer, partially covered, for 5 to 7 minutes.

3. Coarsely chop the watercress. Add it to the soup and cook for 3 minutes; remove from the heat. Taste for additional seasoning. Stir in the sesame oil and serve.

Cream of Fennel Soup

4 TO 6 SERVINGS

½ cup (1 stick) unsalted butter
1 medium onion, chopped
4 medium fennel bulbs (about 3 pounds), chopped, green fronds removed
5 cups chicken stock or broth
1 cup heavy cream
Salt and white pepper

1. Melt the butter in a large saucepan over moderate heat. Add the onion and sauté until soft and translucent, about 4 minutes. Add the fennel and stock and bring to a boil. Reduce the heat to low and simmer, partially covered, for about 45 minutes, or until the fennel is soft.

2. Puree the soup in batches in a blender or food processor and return to saucepan. Just before serving, reheat the soup until it is hot, add the cream and season with salt and pepper to taste.

Cream of Celery Soup

4 SERVINGS

5 tablespoons unsalted butter
4 cups chopped celery (7 or 8 ribs), including some of the inner leaves
1½ cups chopped onions (2 medium)
1 large garlic clove
1 bay leaf
¾ cup dry white wine
4 cups degreased chicken stock or broth
2 teaspoons salt
¼ teaspoon white pepper
½ teaspoon basil
1 cup half-and-half
2 tablespoons flour
Inner celery leaves, for garnish

1. In a heavy, medium saucepan, melt 3 tablespoons of the butter over moderate heat. Add the celery, onion and garlic; sauté, stirring occasionally, until the onion is translucent, about 10 minutes. Add the bay leaf, ½ cup of the wine and the chicken stock. Bring the mixture to a boil, reduce the heat slightly and simmer for 20 minutes. Remove and discard the bay leaf.

2. Force the mixture through a food mill fitted with a medium disk and set over a heavy, medium saucepan, or puree in a food processor and then force it through a sieve into the pan. Stir in the remaining white wine, salt, pepper, basil and the half-and-half. Place the soup over low heat.

3. In a small skillet, melt the remaining butter over moderate heat. Stir in the flour and cook, stirring constantly, for about 1 minute. Remove from the heat. Stirring constantly, blend in about 1 cup of the soup. Transfer the mixture to the pot of soup, increase the heat slightly and cook, stirring, until the soup simmers and thickens slightly. Serve hot garnished with celery leaves.

Cauliflower and Cheese Soup

10 SERVINGS

½ cup (1 stick) unsalted butter
1 small onion, chopped
2 pounds cauliflower, broken into florets
½ cup dry sherry
½ tablespoon sugar
¾ teaspoon dry mustard
½ teaspoon freshly grated nutmeg
½ teaspoon salt
⅛ teaspoon pepper
4 cups hot chicken stock
4 ounces Cheddar cheese, grated (about 1 cup)

Garnish:

Small cauliflower florets, sautéed until just tender in vegetable oil
Grated Cheddar cheese
Sprigs of deep-fried parsley

1. In a large saucepan, melt the butter. Add the onion and sauté gently, stirring occasionally, over moderate heat, until the onion is soft and translucent, about 5 minutes. Add the cauliflower, sherry, sugar, mustard, nutmeg, salt and pepper. Place a piece of waxed paper on top of the vegetables and cover the pan. Simmer over very low heat, stirring once or twice, for 45 minutes.

2. Gradually stir the hot stock into the vegetables. In a blender or food processor with a metal blade, add equal amounts of liquids and solids and process until smooth.

3. Pour the pureed soup through a fine sieve: using the round side of a ladle, gently stir and press the soup through the sieve into a clean saucepan. Gently warm the soup until just heated through. Just before serving, stir in the cheese and garnish as desired.

New England Cheese Soup

The full flavor of aged, sharp Cheddar gives this light-bodied soup a pleasantly rich taste.

4 SERVINGS

1 cup canned chicken broth
2 cups milk
2 tablespoons vegetable oil
¼ cup diced onion
¼ cup diced carrot
¼ cup diced green bell pepper
¼ cup diced celery, including the leafy tops
1 tablespoon whole wheat flour
½ cup nonfat dry milk
1½ cups (6 ounces) grated sharp Cheddar
2 teaspoons prepared mustard
4 tablespoons toasted slivered almonds

1. In two small saucepans, warm the broth and the milk separately until hot; keep warm over low heat.

2. In a large saucepan, warm the oil over moderate heat. Add the onion and sauté, stirring, for 30 seconds, or until barely softened. Add the carrots and sauté, stirring, for 1 minute. Add the bell pepper and celery and sauté for 2 minutes longer.

3. Sprinkle the flour and the dry milk over the vegetables. Cook, stirring, for 30 seconds. Pour in the hot broth and whisk until smooth. Whisk in the hot milk. Add the cheese gradually, whisking until the cheese is completely melted. Whisk in the mustard.

4. To serve, divide the soup evenly among 4 bowls. Sprinkle each serving with 1 tablespoon of the almonds.

Cream of Pistachio Soup

Although this unusual soup was created to be served piping hot, we discovered that it is equally good chilled.

4 TO 6 SERVINGS

4 slices bacon, cut into ¼-inch squares
1 celery rib, finely chopped (about ½ cup)
1 small onion, finely minced (about ½ cup)
1 medium garlic clove, minced
1 bay leaf
¾ cup dry sherry
6 cups chicken stock or broth
¼ cup rice
¾ cup shelled pistachios
1 tablespoon vegetable oil
¼ cup chopped parsley
About 1 cup heavy cream
Salt and white pepper

1. In a skillet, sauté the bacon over moderately high heat until the pieces are crisp and brown. Remove with a slotted spoon and drain on paper towels. Add the celery, onion and garlic; reduce the heat slightly and cook until the onion is translucent, about 5 minutes. Remove with a slotted spoon and drain on paper towels, blotting with additional towels to remove excess fat. Discard the bacon fat in the skillet.

2. In a 3-quart saucepan, combine the bacon with the vegetable mixture. Add the bay leaf and the sherry; simmer over moderate heat until the wine has evaporated, about 5 minutes. Stir in the chicken stock and the rice; bring the mixture to a boil, reduce the heat and simmer until the rice is very soft, about 30 minutes. Discard the bay leaf.

3. Meanwhile, place the pistachios in a sieve and rinse away the salt under cool running water; pat dry with paper towels. In a small skillet, warm the oil over moderate heat. Add the nuts and stir-fry until they are lightly browned, about 2 minutes. Drain on paper towels and finely grind in a blender or food processor. Remove 1 tablespoon of nuts and set aside.

4. To the nuts in the blender or food processor add the stock mixture and parsley (working in batches if necessary) and puree. Stir in the cream, adding more if a thinner consistency is desired. Stir in salt and pepper to taste. To serve hot, reheat the soup, stirring over low heat. Ladle into shallow bowls and garnish with the reserved ground pistachios.

Cold Beet Soup with Scallops

6 TO 8 SERVINGS

6 medium beets
2 quarts chicken stock or canned broth, at room temperature
1½ pounds sea scallops
1 cup sour cream
¾ pound boiled ham, cut into fine julienne strips
1½ cups thinly sliced scallions
2 tablespoons red wine vinegar
2 large cucumbers—peeled, seeded and chopped
¼ cup fresh lemon juice
¼ cup minced fresh dill

1. Preheat the oven to 350°. Wrap the beets together tightly in aluminum foil and bake on a cookie sheet for 1 hour. Unwrap and let cool.

2. Meanwhile, bring 1 cup of the stock to a simmer. Add the scallops and poach for 5 minutes. Remove the scallops with a slotted spoon and let cool. Thinly slice the scallops and return them to their cooled poaching stock; set aside.

3. In a small bowl, blend the sour cream with 1 cup of the remaining stock; set aside.

4. Slip the skins off the beets and cut them into thin julienne strips.

5. In a large bowl, combine the beets, ham, scallions, vinegar, cucumbers, lemon juice and dill. Add the sour cream-stock mixture, the scallops with their stock and the remaining 6 cups stock. Refrigerate until chilled, about 2 hours.

Iced Buttermilk Soup

6 SERVINGS

¼ cup finely chopped walnuts
3 large scallions
¾ cup finely chopped fresh parsley
1 quart buttermilk
2 cups degreased chicken broth
⅛ teaspoon nutmeg

1. In a medium skillet, toast the nuts over low heat, stirring once or twice, until lightly browned. Remove from the heat. Reserving the greens for garnish, cut the scallions in half lengthwise and slice them into thin half-rounds. Stir into the nuts with the parsley. Cool to room temperature.

2. Combine the buttermilk and broth in a large bowl. Blend in the nut mixture with a fork and chill until ice-cold. Cut the reserved scallion greens into 1½-by-⅛-inch julienne strips. Ladle the soup into chilled bowls and garnish with the scallion greens and nutmeg.

Arugula Gazpacho

This soup may be prepared a day ahead.

4 TO 6 SERVINGS

1½ pounds tomatoes, peeled
1½ cups packed arugula, finely chopped
1 medium onion, finely chopped
1 small cucumber, peeled and finely chopped
1 small green bell pepper, finely chopped
2 medium garlic cloves, finely chopped
¼ cup olive oil
3 tablespoons fresh lime juice
¾ teaspoon salt
Pinch of cayenne pepper, or more to taste
Freshly ground black pepper
Croutons and small arugula leaves, for garnish

1. Cut the tomatoes in half. Squeeze into a strainer set over a small bowl; discard the seeds and reserve the juice. Chop the tomatoes.

2. In a large stainless steel or glass bowl, combine the arugula, tomatoes, onion, cucumber, green pepper and garlic. Add the reserved tomato juice, the oil, lime juice, salt, cayenne, black pepper and 1 cup of water. Refrigerate, covered, for 2 hours or overnight.

3. Serve chilled, garnished with croutons and small whole arugula leaves. Pass a cruet of olive oil at the table for extra flavor if desired.

Chilled Cherry Soup

4 TO 6 SERVINGS

½ cup sugar
1 pound Bing cherries, quartered and pits discarded
1 bay leaf
¼ teaspoon cardamom seeds
1 tablespoon arrowroot
1 teaspoon red wine vinegar
⅓ cup heavy cream
½ cup dry red wine, chilled
Whole cherries, for garnish

1. In a medium saucepan, combine the sugar with 3 cups of water. Cook over moderate heat, stirring once or twice, until the sugar dissolves. Add the quartered cherries, bay leaf and cardamom seeds. Bring to a boil, reduce the heat to low and simmer until the cherries are tender, about 10 minutes.

2. Mix the arrowroot with 2 tablespoons of water and stir into the pan. Bring just to the boil and cook, stirring constantly, until the soup thickens slightly and becomes clear, about 3 minutes. Stir in the vinegar. Remove from the heat and let cool to room temperature; cover and refrigerate until chilled.

3. Just before serving, remove the bay leaf. Stir in the cream and wine. Serve the soup in chilled bowls or large wine goblets. Garnish each serving with a whole cherry.

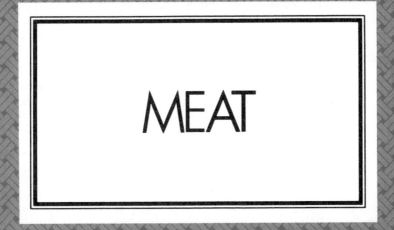

MEAT

Gingered Veal with Three Mushrooms

F&W Beverage Suggestion:
Alsace Gewürztraminer, such as Trimbach or Hugel

6 TO 8 SERVINGS

8 large dried black Chinese mushrooms
1 cup boiling water
1-inch piece of peeled fresh gingerroot
2 large garlic cloves
1 small dried hot red pepper
3 scallions (white part only), finely chopped; reserve the green tops
3 pounds boneless veal stew meat, cut into 2-inch cubes
¼ cup all-purpose flour
1¼ teaspoons coarse (kosher) salt
⅜ teaspoon black pepper
About 6 tablespoons vegetable oil
1 cup chicken stock or broth
¾ cup dry white wine
8 ounces fresh mushrooms, sliced
1 can (15 ounces) whole, peeled straw mushrooms, drained and rinsed
⅓ cup heavy cream
2 tablespoons fresh lemon juice
1 teaspoon grated, peeled fresh gingerroot

Garnish:

3 scallions (green part only, reserved from above), thinly sliced
3 tablespoons slivered red bell pepper
1 tablespoon minced, peeled fresh gingerroot

1. In a small bowl, pour the boiling water over the dried mushrooms. Soak until softened, about 30 minutes; strain, reserving the liquid. Squeeze the mushrooms over the bowl to extract excess water; trim off the stems. Cut the caps into thin strips.

2. In a food processor or with a large knife, mince the piece of ginger, the gar-lic and hot pepper. Mix with the chopped white of the scallion and set aside.

3. Pat the veal dry with paper towels. Combine the flour, ½ teaspoon of the salt and ⅛ teaspoon of the black pepper in a pie plate or shallow dish. Dredge the veal in the seasoned flour, shake off any excess and reserve the flour. In a large Dutch oven, heat 3 tablespoons of the oil. Working in batches and adding more oil as necessary, sauté the veal over high heat, turning, for about 3 minutes, until browned. As the veal browns, remove and set aside.

4. Reduce the heat to moderate and add 1 tablespoon additional oil to the pan. Stir in the minced gingerroot mixture and any reserved seasoned flour. Cook for about 30 seconds, stirring constantly, to cook the flour without browning. Add the chicken stock, wine, reserved mushroom liquid and ½ teaspoon salt. Scrape up any browned bits from the bottom of the pan.

5. Return the veal to the Dutch oven. Bring the stew to a boil; reduce the heat to low, and simmer, covered, for 45 minutes, occasionally skimming fat from the surface.

6. Add the reserved black mushroom strips and cook until the meat is tender when pierced with a fork, 15 to 20 minutes longer. Stir in the fresh mushrooms and straw mushrooms and simmer, stirring occasionally, until the fresh mushrooms are cooked, about 5 minutes longer.

7. Carefully pour the stew into a colander placed over a medium saucepan. Return the veal and mushrooms to the Dutch oven and cover to keep warm.

8. Boil the sauce over high heat, skimming occasionally, until reduced to 2 cups, about 10 minutes. Add the cream and continue to boil for another 5 minutes, until the sauce measures about 1⅔ cups. Stir in the lemon juice, grated gingerroot and remaining ¼ teaspoon salt and ¼ teaspoon black pepper. Pour the sauce over the veal and mushrooms and stir to coat.

9. Before serving, warm the stew over low heat. Mix together the scallions, red pepper and minced gingerroot and serve as a garnish beside each portion.

Veal Cutlets with Lime

F&W Beverage Suggestion:
Italian Red, such as Barbera or Dolcetto

4 SERVINGS

2 tablespoons minced fresh parsley
1 tablespoon minced pine nuts
1½ teaspoons grated lime zest
½ teaspoon minced garlic
¼ cup all-purpose flour
1 teaspoon tarragon
Salt and white pepper
8 veal cutlets (about 1¼ pounds total), cut from the leg ¼ inch thick and pounded to ⅛ inch or less
3 tablespoons unsalted butter
1½ tablespoons olive oil
¾ cup dry white wine
1 tablespoon fresh lime juice
1 lime, thinly sliced, for garnish

1. In a small bowl, combine the parsley, pine nuts, ½ teaspoon of the lime zest and the garlic.

2. On a sheet of waxed paper, mix the flour with the remaining lime zest, the tarragon and salt and pepper to taste. Dust the veal in the seasoned flour; shake off the excess and place the cutlets on a clean sheet of waxed paper.

3. In a large heavy skillet, warm the butter and oil over moderately high heat until it sizzles. When the butter stops sizzling, reduce the heat to moderate and add 2 of the cutlets to the skillet. Sauté the veal for about 30 seconds on each side, or until lightly browned. Transfer the veal cutlets to a heatproof dish as they are finished and keep warm in a 200° oven. Sauté the remaining cutlets in the same manner.

4. Pour the wine into the skillet. Cook, scraping up any brown bits clinging to the pan, until the wine is reduced to ½ cup, about 2 minutes. Stir in the lime juice and the parsley mixture.

5. Remove the veal from the oven and with tongs, dip each cutlet in the sauce in the skillet. Arrange the cutlets on dinner plates or a platter. Spoon the remaining sauce in the skillet over the veal and garnish with lime slices.

NOTE: Thin slices of turkey breast may be substituted for the veal in this recipe.

Veal Scallops with Basil

6 SERVINGS

12 veal scallops, about 1½ pounds
½ cup loosely packed fresh basil
    leaves
1½ cups demi-sec white or rosé
    wine
1½ cups heavy cream
¾ cup coarsely chopped shallots
About 5 tablespoons unsalted
    butter
½ cup slivered basil leaves, for
    garnish

1. Lightly pound the veal between sheets of waxed paper. Place in noncorrodible bowl with the basil and wine; cover and marinate for 1 hour.

2. Remove the veal from the marinade, pat dry and set aside. Strain the liquid into a small saucepan, stir in the cream and shallots and cook over moderate heat until reduced by half, about 15 minutes.

3. Meanwhile, melt 1½ tablespoons of the butter in a skillet and, working in batches, sauté the veal for about 1 minute on each side, or until lightly browned; cover and set aside while you sauté the remaining veal, adding more butter as necessary.

4. Puree the sauce in a blender and strain through a fine sieve. Divide among six individual plates, top each portion with two of the scallops and garnish with the basil.

Stuffed Breast of Veal

Cutting a slit through the membrane over each rib bone in a breast of veal before baking encourages the bones to slip out easily after cooking.

6 TO 8 SERVINGS

1 portion breast of veal, 7 to 8
    pounds, cut from the wide plate
    end
6 ounces baked ham, thinly sliced
4 ounces Gruyère cheese, thinly
    sliced
4 ounces smoked provolone or
    other smoked cheese, thinly
    sliced

2 carrots, coarsely chopped
2 celery ribs, coarsely chopped
1 medium onion, coarsely
    chopped
1 tablespoon minced fresh parsley
½ teaspoon grated lemon zest
1½ cups dry white wine
1 teaspoon salt
½ teaspoon pepper

1. Preheat the oven to 350°. Wipe the veal with a damp cloth and place it, bone side up, on a work surface. Using a boning knife, cut through the center of the membrane covering each rib bone, working along the entire length of each rib.

2. Turn the meat over so that the widest end of the breast (the longest rib) faces you. Using a boning knife, make a lateral slit into the natural pocket occuring in the wide end between the two main layers of muscle. Keeping the long outside edges of the meat intact, carefully enlarge this natural pocket with the tip of the knife until you have cut through the opposite end.

3. Cover the bottom of the opening with a layer of ham, overlapping the slices if necessary. Top with a layer of Gruyère and then a layer of provolone.

4. Close the ends of the opening by sewing them with a trussing needle and string or by vertically inserting a row of round toothpicks through each end.

5. Tear off a 1-yard-long sheet of wide aluminum foil and center it in a large roasting pan. Lay the veal, bone side down, on the foil. Spoon the carrots, celery and onion around the meat and sprinkle them with the parsley and lemon zest. Fold up the edges of the foil and pour 1 cup of the wine over the meat and vegetables. Sprinkle the meat with the salt and pepper and fold the foil over the meat.

6. Bake in the center of the oven for 1½ hours. Turn back the foil and pour the remaining wine over the meat and vegetables. Continue to bake, uncovered, for 1 hour more, allowing the meat to brown.

7. Remove the pan from the oven and set it aside for 15 minutes to allow the juices in the veal to settle. Then remove the bones by gripping one end of each firmly with a towel and twisting it slightly to one side while steadily pulling. Place the meat on a carving platter; remove the string or toothpicks.

8. Pour the contents of the foil through a sieve into a saucepan, discarding the solids; heat briefly. To serve, thinly slice the veal and top with the pan juices.

Butterflied Leg of Lamb

8 TO 12 SERVINGS

Lamb:

1 tablespoon plus 1 teaspoon olive
    oil
1 teaspoon soy sauce
1 tablespoon finely chopped fresh
    rosemary or tarragon or 1
    teaspoon dried, crumbled
1 leg of lamb (about 7 pounds),
    trimmed of fat, boned and
    butterflied
2 large garlic cloves, each cut into
    12 slivers
3 tablespoons lemon juice

Sauce:

1 large garlic clove, crushed and
    chopped
1 tablespoon lemon juice
¾ teaspoon fresh thyme or ¼
    teaspoon dried, crumbled
1 tablespoon finely chopped fresh
    parsley

1. Prepare the lamb: Preheat the oven to 400°. In a small bowl, combine 1 tablespoon of the olive oil with the soy sauce and 2 teaspoons of the fresh rosemary or tarragon or ¾ teaspoon of the dried. Rub the lamb all over with the mixture.

2. With a small sharp knife, make 24 slits in the boned side of the lamb and insert a garlic sliver in each. Rub the lamb with the remaining olive oil and rosemary or tarragon and pour the lemon juice over all.

3. Place the lamb, boned-side down, on a broiler rack with a broiler pan underneath to catch the drippings. Roast in the oven for about 20 minutes, or until the internal temperature reaches 120°. Turn the oven temperature to broil and place the lamb in the broiler about 5 inches from the heat. Broil 2 to 3 minutes, or until the meat starts to brown. Transfer the lamb to a carving board and let it rest for about 10 minutes.

4. Meanwhile, prepare the sauce: Stir the garlic, lemon juice and thyme into the pan juices, cover and keep warm.

5. To serve: Carve the lamb and transfer the slices to a serving platter. Stir the parsley into the sauce and pour it over the lamb or pass separately.

Medallions of Lamb with Parsley Puree

6 SERVINGS

Lamb and Sauce:

2 racks of spring lamb, each about 3 pounds
2 medium onions, chopped
3 garlic cloves, minced
¼ cup freshly brewed tea
2 tablespoons dry white wine
1 tablespoon dry mustard
3 tablespoons tomato paste
4 tablespoons (½ stick) unsalted butter
¼ teaspoon sugar
Salt and pepper

Parsley Puree:

6 cups firmly packed parsley leaves
1½ teaspoons salt
¼ teaspoon pepper

Garnish:

6 tablespoons heavy cream, warmed slightly
Sprigs of flat-leaf parsley

1. Prepare the lamb and sauce: Preheat the oven to 400°. Using a boning knife, carefully remove the fillets from the racks of lamb (or have the butcher do it for you); you should have two fil-

lets, each of which is about 7 inches long and 1½ inches in diameter and weighs about ½ pound; reserve the bones. Wrap the fillets in aluminum foil and refrigerate until needed.

2. Place the bones in a large, noncorrosive, flameproof roasting pan and bake for 1 hour. Pour off and discard the fat. Using tongs, remove the bones and set aside. Reduce the oven temperature to 375°. Scatter the onion and garlic over the bottom of the pan and place the bones on top. Add 3 quarts of water and return the pan to the oven. Bake for 2 hours.

3. Again using tongs, remove the bones and reserve them for another use. Reserving the roasting pan for deglazing, pour the stock through a sieve into a bowl; discard the solids. Allow the stock to rest for 15 minutes. Pour off and discard the fat that has risen to the top. Measure and reserve 1 cup; refrigerate the rest for another use.

4. Pour the tea into the roasting pan, place it over moderate heat and deglaze the pan, scraping up the bits that cling to the bottom. Stir in the reserved stock. Remove the pan from heat. Add the white wine to the mustard and blend; stir the mixture into the deglazed pan. Whisk in the tomato paste, butter, sugar and salt and pepper to taste. If the butter does not melt completely, place the pan over moderate heat for a minute, stirring constantly. Transfer the sauce to a small pan, cover and set aside.

5. Prepare the parsley puree: Preheat the oven to 400°. Cook the parsley in a large pot of boiling water for 1 minute, pushing it down into the water occasionally. Rinse under cold running water and drain thoroughly in a colander or strainer, pressing with a spoon to extract as much liquid as possible. Puree

the parsley in a food processor or food mill. Transfer the puree to a small saucepan, stir in the salt and pepper and set aside.

6. Roast the fillets: Place the fillets on a rack set over a small roasting pan (or directly in the pan if you don't have a rack). For rare lamb, roast for 10 minutes. If you prefer lamb less rare, cook it for up to 2 minutes more—longer cooking will dry out the meat. Set aside.

7. Assemble the dish: Heat six ovenproof plates in a 300° oven. Meanwhile, place the parsley puree over low heat; cook, stirring occasionally, until hot. Place the sauce over moderate heat and bring it to a simmer, stirring occasionally; remove from the heat.

8. Place the fillets on a board and cut them across the grain into slices about ⅜ inch thick. Ladle a little of the sauce over each of the heated plates, fan 5 medallions around the edge of each and add a large dollop of the pureed parsley. Using a spoon, make an indentation in each puree mound and pour 1 tablespoon of the heavy cream into it. Garnish the top of each medallion with a single leaf of parsley and serve.

Roast Rack of Lamb

F&W Beverage Suggestion: Beaujolais-Villages

4 SERVINGS

2 racks of spring lamb, trimmed (about 1½ pounds each)
1 teaspoon thyme
Salt and pepper
1 teaspoon vegetable oil
½ cup dry white wine

1. Preheat the oven to 450°. Season the lamb with the thyme and salt and pepper to taste. Place in a roasting pan and sprinkle the oil over the meat. Roast for 30 to 40 minutes, according to taste (rack of lamb is best when quite pink). The lamb should be rare after 30 minutes, medium after 35 minutes and well-done after 40 minutes.

2. Transfer the roasted lamb to a serving platter. Discard all but 1 tablespoon of the drippings from the pan. Deglaze the pan with the white wine. Pour the juices over the lamb, carve and serve.

Lamb Vindaloo

This dish is best made a day ahead of time so that the flavors have a chance to blend.

6 SERVINGS

Vindaloo Paste:

2 teaspoons cumin seed
1 teaspoon black cumin seed
2 or 3 dried, hot red chile peppers
1 teaspoon black peppercorns
1 teaspoon cardamom seed
1 piece (1½ inches long) cinnamon stick
1½ teaspoons black mustard seed
1 teaspoon fenugreek seed
¼ cup red wine vinegar
1 tablespoon tamarind paste (see Note)
1½ to 2 teaspoons salt
1 teaspoon sugar
½ cup plus 2 tablespoons vegetable oil
2 medium onions, halved lengthwise and thinly sliced

Lamb:

2 pounds lean, boneless shoulder of lamb, cut into 1-inch cubes
1 tablespoon coarsely chopped fresh gingerroot
1 whole bulb (about 6 ounces) garlic, separated into cloves and peeled
1 tablespoon ground coriander
½ teaspoon ground turmeric

1. Prepare the vindaloo paste: In a blender or spice grinder, grind the two types of cumin, chile peppers, peppercorns, cardamom, cinnamon, black mustard and fenugreek seeds. Put the ground spices in a bowl and add the vinegar, tamarind paste, salt and sugar. Mix well and set aside.

2. In a large skillet, heat the oil, add the onions and sauté over moderate heat, stirring frequently, until they turn brown and crisp. Remove the onions with a slotted spoon and place them in the con-tainer of a blender or food processor; reserve the pan and oil for use in Step 4. Add 3 tablespoons of water to the onions and puree; add the puree to the ground spice mixture.

3. Prepare the lamb: Using paper towels, pat the meat cubes dry. Place the ginger and garlic in the container of a blender or food processor. Add 3 tablespoons water and blend to make a smooth paste.

4. Heat the oil remaining in the skillet over moderately high heat. When almost smoking, add one-third of the lamb cubes and brown them lightly on all sides. Transfer them with a slotted spoon to a plate and set aside. Repeat with the remaining lamb.

5. Reduce the heat to moderate and add the ginger-garlic paste. Stir for a few seconds, and add the coriander and turmeric. Stir for a few seconds. Add the lamb, along with any juices that may have accumulated on the plate, and the vindaloo paste. Add 1 cup water and bring to a boil. Cover the pan, lower the heat and simmer gently, stirring occasionally, for 45 to 60 minutes, or until the lamb is tender. Transfer to a platter and serve.

NOTE: If you cannot get tamarind paste, which is sold in Indian and Mexican specialty food shops, place a 1-inch cube of dried tamarind in a medium saucepan with 1 cup water, bring to a boil, cover the pan and simmer for 15 minutes. Push the mixture through a sieve.

Grilled Lamb Patties with Lemon, Garlic and Mint

Charcoal grilling gives a smoky, succulent quality to lamb; and when combined with lemon, garlic and fresh mint, the flavor is memorable.

F&W Beverage Suggestion:
California Zinfandel

5 SERVINGS

1¾ pounds lean ground lamb
½ cup chopped fresh mint
3 large garlic cloves, crushed through a press or very finely minced
Grated zest from 1 lemon
¼ cup fresh lemon juice
1 teaspoon salt
Freshly ground pepper
Fresh mint sprigs and lemon wedges for garnish

1. Pat the lamb dry with paper towels. Using your hands, mix the mint, garlic and lemon zest with the ground lamb, and then add the lemon juice. When the lemon juice has been absorbed, the mixture will be loose and wet but will hold together. Season with the salt and pepper to taste.

2. Form the meat into 10 thin patties. Store, covered, in the refrigerator until ready to grill.

3. Light the charcoal or preheat the broiler. Grill the patties 4 to 6 inches above hot coals (or broil 4 to 5 inches from the heat), turning once, until browned on the outside and slightly pink on the inside, about 5 to 8 minutes. Serve garnished with fresh mint sprigs and lemon wedges.

Pork Chops Creole

This easy one-pot recipe is a good use for thin, family-pack chops.

3 TO 4 SERVINGS

3 tablespoons peanut or corn oil
6 to 8 center-cut pork chops, cut ⅜ to ½ inch thick, trimmed of excess fat
2 medium onions, sliced
1 green bell pepper, sliced
2 large garlic cloves, finely chopped
½ cup dry white wine
1 can (16 ounces) Italian peeled tomatoes, with their juice

3 tablespoons lemon juice
1½ tablespoons Worcestershire sauce
⅛ teaspoon hot pepper sauce
1 teaspoon salt
¼ teaspoon freshly ground black pepper
1 bay leaf

1. In a large deep skillet or flameproof casserole, heat 1½ tablespoons of the oil. Add the pork chops (in batches if necessary) and fry over moderately high heat, turning once, until browned on both sides, about 10 minutes. Remove the chops and set aside. Discard the fat from the skillet.

2. Heat the remaining 1½ tablespoons oil in the skillet. Add the onions and sauté over moderately high heat, stirring occasionally, until lightly browned, 3 to 5 minutes. Add the green pepper and garlic and sauté until the garlic is fragrant, about 1 minute.

3. Add the wine and bring to a boil, stirring to scrape up any browned bits from the bottom of the pan. Reduce the heat to moderate. Return the chops to the skillet and spoon some of the onions and peppers over them. Add the tomatoes and their juice, lemon juice, Worcestershire sauce, hot pepper sauce, salt, black pepper and bay leaf. Add enough water to cover.

4. Partially cover the pan and simmer, turning the chops occasionally, until they are very tender, about 1 hour.

5. If the sauce is watery, increase the heat to high and boil to thicken slightly. Serve over white rice.

Braised Pork Chops with Fresh Tomato Sauce

Plump, ripe tomatoes make a rich, naturally sweet sauce. The pork chops are braised in the sauce for added flavor. Vermicelli, thin spaghetti or orzo can be a delicious accompaniment. This dish may be prepared several hours ahead of time.

F&W Beverage Suggestion:
A white Rhône, such as Château Beaucastel

6 SERVINGS

6 pork chops, cut 1 inch thick (about 2½ to 3 pounds)
About ¼ cup all-purpose flour, for dredging
¼ cup olive oil
7 medium onions, chopped
5 garlic cloves, crushed and minced
4 pounds ripe tomatoes (about 10 medium)—peeled, seeded and coarsely chopped
1 tablespoon basil
2 teaspoons oregano
2 cups dry red wine or chicken broth
1 tablespoon sugar
1 tablespoon salt
½ teaspoon freshly ground pepper

1. Dredge the pork chops in the flour; shake off any excess. In a large, heavy noncorrodible skillet, heat the oil until almost smoking. Working in batches if necessary, add the pork chops and cook over moderately high heat, turning once, until crisp and golden brown, about 5 minutes on each side. Remove and set aside.

2. Add the onions to the pan drippings in the skillet, reduce the heat to moderate and sauté, stirring occasionally, until golden brown, about 20 minutes. Add the garlic and cook for 5 minutes longer. Add the tomatoes, basil, oregano, wine, sugar, salt and pepper. Bring to a boil, reduce the heat to low and simmer, stirring occasionally for 30 minutes.

3. Return the pork chops to the skillet. Cover them with the sauce, cover and simmer, basting occasionally, for 2 hours. Watch carefully during the last 30 minutes and stir to prevent the sauce from sticking or scorching.

Fennel Pork Roast Sonoma

6 TO 8 SERVINGS

1 rolled, boneless pork loin, 2½ to 3 pounds
1 teaspoon coarse (kosher) salt
½ teaspoon pepper
1 can (16 ounces) whole tomatoes in puree
½ cup honey
½ cup Cabernet Sauvignon or other dry red wine
2 tablespoons red wine vinegar
2 large garlic cloves, crushed and minced
1 teaspoon crushed fennel seed

1. Preheat the oven to 350°. Rub the roast with the salt and pepper. Place it on a rack in a shallow roasting pan and cook for 1 hour.

2. Meanwhile, simmer the remaining ingredients in a small saucepan, uncovered, for 20 minutes, stirring occasionally. Press the sauce through a fine sieve, discarding the solids. Measure the liquid. If there is more than 1½ cups, return it to the pan and boil gently until it is reduced to that amount. Remove the pan from the heat.

3. When the meat has roasted for 1 hour, remove it from the oven and baste with 2 to 3 tablespoons of the sauce. Repeat the basting procedure twice, at 10 minute intervals, turning the roast each time to coat it evenly. After a total cooking time of 1½ to 1¾ hours (or when the internal temperature of the thickest part of the meat registers 150°), remove the roast from the oven and allow it to rest in a warm place for 10 minutes.

4. To serve, carve into slices. Reheat the remaining sauce and serve it with the pork.

Pork Chop Pockets

Cutting slits, or pockets, into thick pork chops makes it possible to fill them with a diced mushroom stuffing, which imparts a rich flavor to the meat as it cooks.

8 SERVINGS

Stuffing:

2 tablespoons unsalted butter
2 garlic cloves, minced
1 pound mushrooms, cut into ¼-inch dice (about 4 cups)
½ cup dry white wine
2 tablespoons dry bread crumbs
1 tablespoon grated Parmesan cheese
1 egg yolk
1 teaspoon coarse (kosher) salt
¼ teaspoon pepper

Pork:

8 center-cut pork chops, each 1 inch thick
1 tablespoon unsalted butter, melted
1 teaspoon coarse (kosher) salt
¼ teaspoon pepper

Sauce:

1 cup heavy cream

1. Prepare the stuffing: In a medium skillet, melt the butter over low heat, add the garlic and sauté for a few seconds. Add the mushrooms and cook, stirring, over moderate heat, for about 3 minutes. Add the wine and cook until all the liquid has evaporated, about 15 minutes.

2. Remove the pan from the heat and blend in the bread crumbs, cheese, egg yolk, salt and pepper.

3. Prepare the pork chops: Preheat the oven to 425°. With a boning knife, cut a lateral slit into the edge of each pork chop. Work the knife through the meat all the way to the bone and almost to the side edges. The result should be a pocket about 2 by 2 inches.

4. Stuff about 2 tablespoons of the mushroom mixture into each pocket. Close the pockets with toothpicks inserted at right angles to the chops.

5. Brush some of the melted butter over a shallow, flameproof roasting pan large enough to hold the chops in a single layer. Place the chops in the pan and brush the tops with the remaining melted butter. Sprinkle with the salt and pepper and bake for 35 to 40 minutes, or until slightly browned. Transfer to a warm platter; discard the toothpicks.

6. Prepare the sauce: Pour off and discard the fat from the roasting pan. Place the pan over moderate heat and add ⅓ cup of water. Stir to incorporate the pan drippings and boil for 1 minute. Add the cream and boil, stirring, for 1 minute. Serve this sauce over the chops.

Pork Casserole with Cashews and Stir-fried Vegetables

The pork in this dish is marinated in an apricot sauce and then baked in a casserole. The stir-fried vegetables are added at the last moment. Accompany the completed dish with steamed rice if desired.

6 TO 8 SERVINGS

Pork:

1 ounce dried Chinese mushrooms* (about 12)
3 pounds lean pork, cut into ½-by-½-by-1½-inch strips
1 two-inch length of fresh gingerroot, peeled and cut into ⅛-inch julienne strips

Marinade:

1½ cups (one 12-ounce can) apricot nectar
½ cup soy sauce
2 tablespoons dry sherry
2 teaspoons oyster sauce*
1½ tablespoons honey

Vegetable Topping:

3 tablespoons peanut oil
½ cup coarsely chopped unsalted cashews
¾ pound fresh snow peas, cut into ⅛-inch julienne strips (about 3 cups)
8 scallions, cut into quarters lengthwise and then into 2-inch lengths
1 can (8 ounces) water chestnuts—drained, rinsed and cut into ⅛-inch julienne strips
½ cup (one 4-ounce can) bamboo shoots—drained, rinsed and cut into ⅛-inch julienne strips
½ teaspoon Oriental sesame oil

*Available at Oriental groceries

1. Prepare the pork: Place the mushrooms in a medium mixing bowl and pour 1 cup hot water over them; let them rest for 15 minutes. Drain and discard the juice or reserve it for another use.

2. In a shallow 4-quart casserole, combine the pork with the mushrooms and ginger.

3. Prepare the marinade: In a medium mixing bowl, combine all the marinade ingredients with ½ cup of water. Pour the marinade over the meat and mushrooms, tossing them well. Marinate 1 hour.

4. Preheat the oven to 350°. Cover the casserole tightly and bake for 2 to 2½ hours, or until the meat is tender and easily pierced with a fork. Remove from the oven and set aside.

5. Stir-fry the vegetables: In a wok or large heavy skillet, warm the peanut oil over moderate heat. Add the cashews and stir-fry for about 30 seconds. Stir in the snow peas, scallions, water chestnuts and bamboo shoots; stir-fry until the vegetables are heated through but still crisp, 2 to 3 minutes. Stir in the sesame oil for flavoring.

6. Transfer the pork and mushrooms to a platter and arrange the sitr-fried vegetables in a crescent shape over half the dish.

Red Cabbage Braised Pork

Once this casserole is in the oven, your work is almost done. The roux in Step 8 can be made before company arrives; just remove the pan from the heat and set it aside until the casserole is done. Then, just before serving, reheat the roux over moderately low heat and make the sauce.

6 SERVINGS

½ pound lean bacon strips
2 pounds boneless pork loin, rolled and tied
4 red onions, sliced
2 garlic cloves, crushed
1 head of red cabbage (about 3 pounds)
2 tablespoons fennel seed
1 teaspoon salt
¼ teaspoon pepper
1 cup dry red wine
About 1 cup beef broth
½ cup Aquavit
2 tablespoons red wine vinegar
2 tablespoons unsalted butter
2 tablespoons all-purpose flour

1. Cut the bacon crosswise into ½-inch pieces and place them in a 5-quart flameproof casserole or Dutch oven. Cook over low heat until the bacon is golden. Remove the bacon with a slotted spoon and set aside in a medium bowl.

2. Increase the heat to high. Cook the pork loin in the bacon drippings, turning frequently, until it is browned all over, about 5 minutes. Remove to a rack to cool slightly.

3. Reduce the heat to moderate and add the onions and garlic to the casserole. Cook, covered, until the onions are softened, about 10 minutes. Remove from the heat and, with a slotted spoon, transfer the onions and garlic to the bowl with the bacon.

4. Blanch the whole head of cabbage in boiling water for 15 minutes. Drain and let it cool for a few minutes. Core the cabbage and carefully remove enough outer leaves, pulling from the core end, to line the bottom, sides and top of the casserole; set the leaves aside. Coarsely chop the rest of the cabbage.

5. Pound the fennel seeds with a mortar and pestle to a rough powder. Rub half of the powder, ½ teaspoon of the salt and ⅛ teaspoon of the pepper into the pork loin.

6. Preheat the oven to 400°. Line the bottom and sides of the casserole with outer cabbage leaves. Place half of the reserved onions, garlic and bacon and half the chopped cabbage onto the leaves. Arrange the pork loin on top and smother it with the rest of the onions, garlic, bacon and chopped cabbage. Pour on the wine, 1 cup of broth, the Aquavit, vinegar and remaining powdered fennel seeds, salt and pepper. Cover the top completely with overlapping cabbage leaves. Place a sheet of buttered waxed paper on top of the cabbage and cover the casserole. (The recipe can be prepared ahead to this point and refrigerated until the next day. Bring to room temperature before proceeding.)

7. Cook the covered casserole in the preheated oven for 2 hours, or until a meat thermometer reads 150°. Remove the pork and cover with foil to keep warm. Reserving the vegetables, strain the liquid from the casserole into a small bowl. You should have about 1½ cups; if not, add additional broth.

8. In a small heavy saucepan, melt the butter over moderately low heat. Whisk

in the flour. Cook, stirring frequently, for 2 minutes to make a roux.

9. Whisk in the cooking liquid and cook over moderate heat, whisking frequently, until the sauce boils and thickens.

10. Line a large, heated platter with the whole cabbage leaves. Spoon the chopped cabbage and the onions onto the center. Cut the pork into ¼-inch slices and arrange decoratively on the vegetables. Coat the pork with several spoonfuls of the sauce; pass the rest separately.

Skewered Pork and Sausages

🍷 **F&W Beverage Suggestion:**
Chianti Riserva, such as Ruffino

6 SERVINGS

1 loaf of day-old Italian bread, cut into 24 1½-inch cubes
6 sweet or hot Italian sausages (1 pound), each cut into thirds
18 imported bay leaves, fresh if possible
1 pound trimmed boneless pork, cut into 1½-inch cubes
6 thin slices of prosciutto (3 to 4 ounces) cut into thirds and folded into quarters
¼ cup olive oil, preferably extra-virgin
Freshly ground pepper

1. Preheat the oven to 400°. On 6 metal skewers about 12 inches long, alternate a bread cube, then a chunk of sausage, a bay leaf, a cube of pork and a piece of prosciutto 3 times; end each with a bread cube.

2. Pour the olive oil into a baking dish large enough to hold the skewers comfortably with space between. Place the skewers in the oil and rotate to coat lightly. Grind the pepper over the skewers.

3. Place the baking dish in the oven and bake for 12 minutes. Turn the skewers and continue to cook until the pork is cooked through and no longer pink, 12 to 15 minutes longer.

Anise Beef with Vegetables Vinaigrette (p. 69).

Above, Sausage-Stuffed Mushrooms (p. 25).
Left, Double-Wrapped Cabbage (p. 62).

55

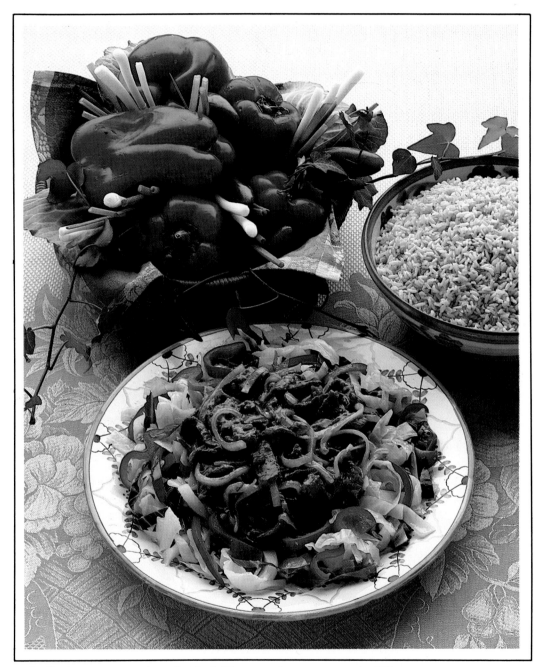

Garlic-Lime Marinated Beef with Cabbage and Peppercorns (p. 67).

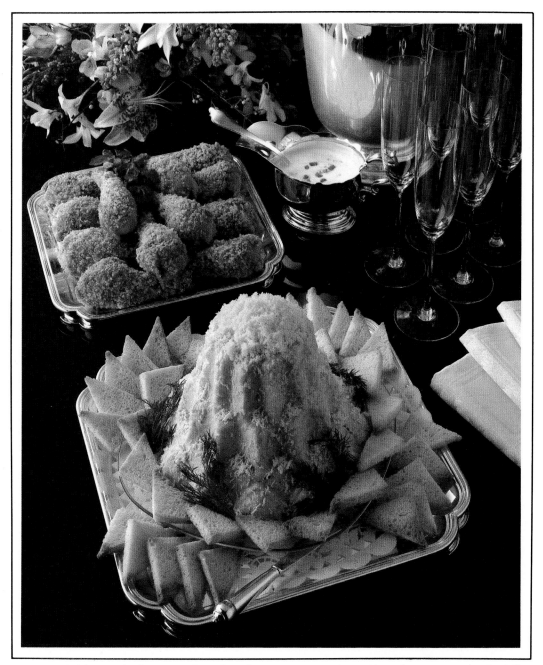

Cold-Hot Chicken Legs (p. 80) with Yogurt Sauce (p. 210) and Ham Mimosa (p. 20).

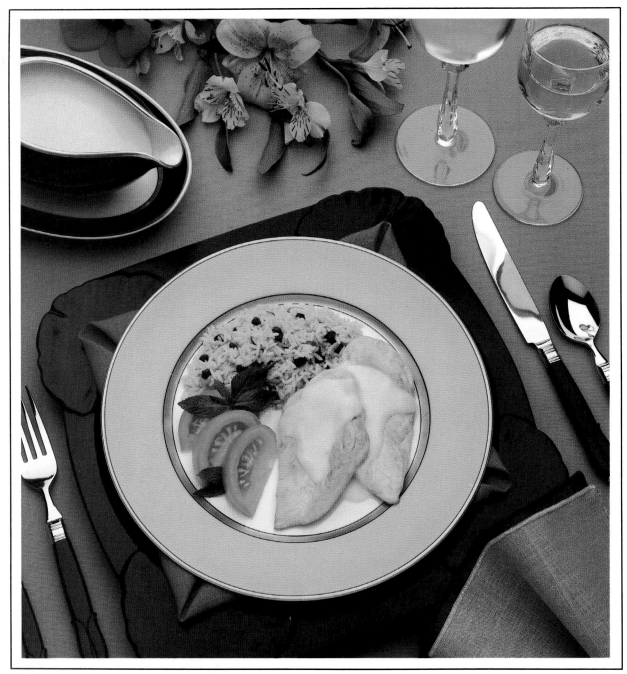

Chicken Breasts Avgolemono (p. 86).

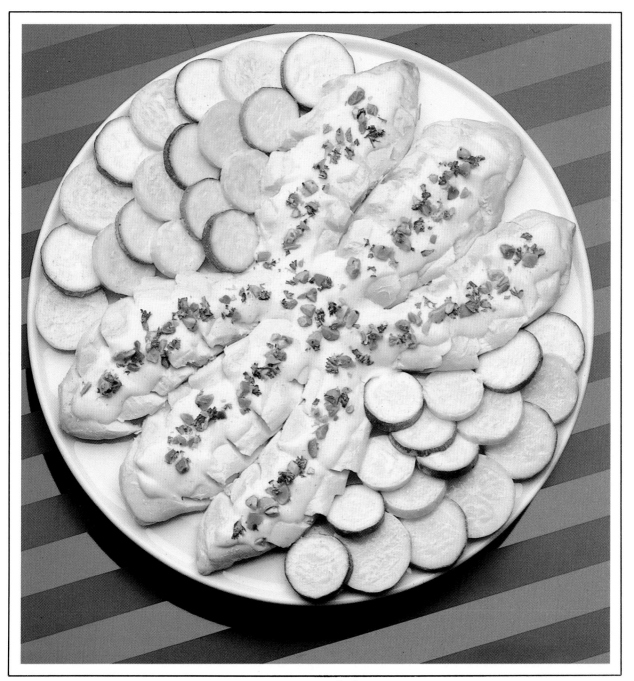

Chicken Breasts with Orange-Almond Sauce (p. 85).

Ham-and-Leek Casserole

8 SERVINGS

3 pounds yams, peeled and halved
7 carrots, thinly sliced (about 3 cups)
5 white turnips, peeled and thinly sliced (about 3 cups)
4 tablespoons unsalted butter, softened
5 leeks, white parts only, thinly sliced (about 3 cups)
2 garlic cloves, minced
3 tablespoons all-purpose flour
3 cups unfiltered apple juice
½ cup grainy mustard, such as Pommery
2 pounds baked ham, cut into ¼-inch cubes
¼ cup heavy cream
1 teaspoon freshly ground white pepper
1 teaspoon salt
3 egg yolks

1. Cook the yams in a large pot of boiling water until tender, about 25 minutes. After the yams have cooked for 10 minutes, steam the carrots and turnips until tender, 12 to 15 minutes. Grease a 9-by-13-by-2½-inch baking pan.

2. Meanwhile, preheat the oven to 350°. In a large saucepan, warm the butter; add the leeks and garlic and sauté until they are soft, 3 to 4 minutes. Stir in the flour and cook, stirring, over moderate heat for 2 minutes. Add the apple juice and mustard and boil gently, stirring, for 3 more minutes. Remove the pan from the heat and mix in the ham.

3. When the vegetables have cooked, spread the turnips and carrots over the bottom of the prepared pan. Top with the ham mixture.

4. Beat the yams with the cream, pepper and salt until smooth; add the egg yolks and beat until smooth. (This step may be done in a food processor.) Spread the yam mixture evenly over the top of the casserole or, to give a more decorative finish, pipe it through a pastry bag with a ½-inch tip. Bake for 15 minutes, increase the heat to 400°, and bake for 10 more minutes.

Easy Cassoulet (p. 75).

Baked Ham with Cider Glaze

🍷 **F&W Beverage Suggestion:**
California Pinot Noir Blanc

14 TO 18 SERVINGS

1 smoked ham with bone, about 12 pounds
2 large garlic cloves, thinly slivered
4 cups unfiltered apple cider or juice

1. Preheat the oven to 325°. Place the ham, fat-side up, on a rack in a roasting pan. Score the fat in a diamond pattern, cutting at 1-inch intervals. Using the tip of a paring knife, make a slit about ½ inch deep in the center of each diamond. Insert a sliver of garlic into each slit. Bake the ham in the lower third of the oven for 2 hours.

2. Pour 2 cups of the apple cider over the ham and bake for 15 minutes. Baste the ham with some of the pan drippings and bake for 15 minutes. Pour the remaining apple cider over the ham and continue baking for an additional 45 minutes (for a total of 3¼ hours), basting the ham with the pan drippings every 10 minutes.

3. Transfer the ham to a serving platter or cutting board and allow it to rest for at least 20 minutes before slicing. Serve hot, at room temperature or cold.

World's Best Hamburger

After extensive testing in our kitchen, *F&W* found that the best hamburger is made by grinding lean chuck at home, either in a meat grinder or food processor, then cooking the burgers in a hot cast-iron skillet over high heat.

3 SERVINGS

1 pound lean chuck, well-chilled and cut into 1-inch cubes
1 teaspoon coarse (kosher) salt
Freshly ground pepper

1. If using a meat grinder: Using the fine blade (⅛-inch holes), put the meat through the grinder once. Do not pack the meat tightly once it is ground. **If using a food processor:** Partially freeze the beef cubes until they are very firm and offer slight resistance to a knife. Place them in a food processor fitted with the metal blade and, using an on-and-off motion, process the meat just until it has a coarse texture; do not over-process or the texture will be too smooth.

2. Gather the ground beef into a ball, pressing it gently until it holds together. Handle the meat as little as possible. Divide the meat into thirds and quickly shape each portion into a patty about 3½ inches in diameter and ¾ inch thick.

3. Place a large heavy skillet, preferably cast iron, over high heat and sprinkle it with the salt. Heat the pan for 3 to 5 minutes, or until the salt begins to smoke. Add the hamburger patties, leaving at least 1 inch of space between them. Press them gently with a spatula and fry over high heat for 2 minutes. Reduce the heat to moderate and continue cooking for 3 minutes. Turn the burgers carefully with the spatula, so that the browned crust is not left behind. Sprinkle with pepper to taste and cook 2 minutes for rare or 3 minutes for medium rare (our preference), or slightly longer for medium or well done.

Chili and Beans for a Crowd

30 SERVINGS

Chili:

¼ cup vegetable oil
6 cups chopped onions (about 6 large)
2 tablespoons coarse (kosher) salt
6 pounds coarsely ground beef
2 tablespoons whole cumin seed
1 tablespoon whole fennel seed
3 tablespoons chopped garlic (about 9 cloves)
½ cup powdered *chile ancho** or commercial chili powder
½ cup powdered *chile pasilla** or commercial chili powder
2 tablespoons unsweetened cocoa powder
1 tablespoon sugar
1 can (35 ounces) peeled tomatoes, chopped
3 cans (8 ounces each) tomato sauce

Beans:

½ pound bacon, cut into ½-inch squares
2 pounds dried pinto beans, rinsed and picked over
4 garlic cloves, crushed and chopped
Salt

Accompaniments:

2 cups thinly sliced scallions
2 cups sour cream, at room temperature
2 cups shredded Monterey Jack cheese (8 ounces)
2 cups shredded Cheddar cheese (8 ounces)

*Available at Latin American groceries

1. Prepare the chili: In a large skillet, heat the oil over moderate heat. Add the onions and sauté, stirring occasionally until the onions are translucent, about 20 minutes.

2. Sprinkle the salt into a large, heavy stockpot or Dutch oven. Crumble the ground beef into the pot and brown it, stirring occasionally, over moderately high heat.

3. Pulverize the cumin and fennel seeds with a mortar and pestle or a spice grinder. Add to the meat along with the sautéed onion and the garlic. Add the chili powders, cocoa and sugar. Stir in the tomatoes, tomato sauce and 4 cups of water. Bring to a boil; reduce the heat and simmer, stirring occasionally, for 3½ hours. If the chili becomes too thick or sticks to the bottom, add water as needed.

4. Meanwhile, prepare the beans: In a large, heavy pot, cook the bacon over moderately high heat, stirring occasionally, until it is crisp and golden brown. Add the beans, garlic, salt to taste and 3 quarts of water. Bring to a boil over moderate heat, reduce the heat to low and simmer, stirring occasionally, until the beans are tender but not falling apart, about 1½ hours. Using a slotted spoon or a sieve, transfer the beans to the chili; reserve the liquid.

5. Simmer the chili and beans for 30 minutes. The thickness is to taste; if you want thin chili, add some of the reserved bean liquid; if you want a thicker chili, cook it a little longer. Taste for seasoning; if desired, add additional chili powder, ground cumin, salt and pepper.

6. To serve, place the accompaniments in separate bowls and allow each guest to top the chili as desired.

Double-Wrapped Cabbage

Since the flavor of this casserole improves when it rests overnight, you may want to prepare it the day before you serve it.

8 SERVINGS

Cabbage:

1 large, firm head of cabbage (about 3½ pounds)

Filling:

6 slices bacon, cut into ¼-inch squares
¼ cup long-grain rice
1 pound lean ground beef
½ pound lean ground pork
½ pound lean ground veal
1½ cups finely chopped onion
2 large garlic cloves, minced
½ cup minced fresh parsley
1 egg
¾ cup dry bread crumbs
¾ cup chicken broth
1½ teaspoons caraway seed, ground
1 teaspoon fennel seed, ground
½ cup dry white wine
2 teaspoons salt
½ teaspoon pepper

Casserole:

4 ounces Canadian bacon, cut into ¼-by-1-inch julienne strips
4 garlic cloves, thinly sliced
4 sprigs of dill, each 3 inches long (optional)
Salt and pepper
¼ cup tomato paste
2 cups chicken broth
2 cups dry white wine

1. Prepare the cabbage: Core the cabbage. Leaving all outer leaves intact, add the cabbage to a large pot of boiling salted water and cook until the outer leaves are tender, 5 to 8 minutes. Carefully transfer the cabbage to a colander and remove as many leaves as are tender, cutting them away from the head if necessary and set them aside. Return the remaining cabbage head to the boiling water and again cook until the outer leaves are tender; remove them and set them aside. Continue with this procedure until 26 leaves have been cooked and removed. Chop and set aside 2 cups of the inner cabbage head (reserve any remaining for another use). Using a paring knife, and slicing across the top of each leaf, remove and discard the raised portion of the vein.

2. Choose a 4-quart casserole, ideally one with a lid, that is about 8 by 12 by 4 inches deep. Place two of the greenest outer leaves over the bottom and six around the sides—they should overlap slightly and the side leaves extend at least 1 inch above the top of the casserole. Reserve two of the remaining greenest leaves to cover the casserole while it is baking. You should have 16 leaves remaining to be stuffed; set them aside.

3. Prepare the filling: In a small skillet, cook the bacon over moderately high heat until crisp and golden brown, 3 to 5 minutes. Using a slotted spoon, transfer the bacon to a large bowl and set aside.

4. In a small saucepan, bring 3 cups of water to a boil over high heat. Add the rice and, when the boiling resumes, boil for 8 minutes, reducing the heat slightly if necessary to prevent the water from boiling over. Drain the rice in a strainer and add it to the reserved bacon. Blend in the beef, pork, veal, onion, garlic, parsley, egg, bread crumbs, broth, caraway, fennel, wine, salt and pepper.

5. Stuff the cabbage leaves: Place one of the leaves reserved for stuffing, concave side up, on a work surface and, depending on the size of the leaf, place ⅓ to ½ cup of the filling in the center. Roll up the leaf, eggroll fashion, tucking in the ends, to enclose the filling. Repeat with the remaining leaves.

6. Assemble the casserole: Preheat the oven to 350°. Scatter the reserved chopped cabbage over the leaf-lined casserole. Arrange 8 of the cabbage rolls on top; sprinkle with half the Canadian bacon and half the garlic. Top with two sprigs of the dill and sprinkle with salt

and pepper to taste. Top with the remaining rolls and cover with remaining Canadian bacon, garlic and dill and salt and pepper. Place the tomato paste in a medium bowl and slowly stir in the broth and then the wine. Pour enough of it over the cabbage so that it is about ½ inch from the top of the casserole. Top with the reserved cabbage leaves and fold the extended portions of the leaves around the sides over the rolls.

7. Bake the casserole: Place the casserole on a baking sheet and cover it tightly with a lid or several layers of aluminum foil. Bake for 2 hours, carefully uncovering and basting the top with a bulb baster several times. Let the casserole rest for 30 minutes before serving, or cool to room temperature and then refrigerate overnight. To reheat, bring the casserole back to room temperature and place in a preheated 350° oven to bake for 1 hour, basting once or twice. Serve hot.

Mosaic Meat Loaf

Displaying a pattern of hard-cooked eggs and blanched carrot strips between the meat layers, this meat loaf slices neatly and attractively.

MAKES 2 LOAVES/
4 TO 6 SERVINGS EACH

4 carrots
11 eggs
3 pounds lean ground chuck
½ pound fresh spinach leaves,
    washed and coarsely chopped
8 large garlic cloves, finely minced
1 large onion, chopped
2 cups soft bread crumbs
1 to 1½ teaspoons ground cumin

1 tablespoon salt
1½ to 2 teaspoons thyme
½ to 1 tablespoon rosemary,
    crumbled
1½ teaspoons freshly ground
    pepper

1. Cut the carrots into quarters lengthwise so that you have 16 strips. Place them in a saucepan and cover them with cold water. Bring the water to a boil and cook the carrots until they are just tender, about 6 minutes. Cool completely under cold running water, drain and set aside.

2. Place 8 of the eggs in a saucepan, cover them with cold water, and bring it rapidly to a boil. Boil the eggs uncovered for exactly 12 minutes. Rinse them under cold running water and then let them rest in cold water for 10 minutes or more. Peel the eggs under cold running water and set them aside.

3. Preheat the oven to 350°. Crumble the ground chuck into a large mixing bowl. Add the spinach, garlic, onion, bread crumbs, cumin, salt, thyme, rosemary and pepper. Beat the remaining 3 eggs lightly and add them. Lightly toss everything together.

4. To assemble: Choose two 6-cup loaf pans or molds. Use about one-eighth of the meat mixture to line the bottom of each loaf pan and lay 4 strips of carrot in two rows down the length of each pan, each row about an inch from the side of the pan. Smooth another layer of meat over the carrots. Lay a row of 4 hard-cooked eggs down the center of each loaf. Add about half the remaining meat, smoothing it, and repeat the carrot layer. Top the loaves with the remaining meat, smoothing the tops of the loaves.

5. Place the loaf pans on a baking sheet and bake the meat loaves for 1½ hours in the center of the oven.

6. Allow the loaves to rest about 10 minutes in the pan before turning them out to serve; or let one or both loaves cool in the pan, chill and serve.

Stifado

This classic Greek casserole is usually made with wine, but our version calls for beer, which adds an interesting variation to an already-delicious blend of flavors.

8 SERVINGS

1½ pounds small white onions (about 30)
¼ cup olive oil
3 pounds stewing beef, preferably bottom round, cut into 1-inch cubes
2 tablespoons coarse (kosher) salt
1 tablespoon freshly ground pepper
4 garlic cloves, minced
1 tablespoon light brown sugar
1 tablespoon red wine vinegar
3 tablespoons tomato paste
1 bay leaf, crumbled
1 three-inch-long cinnamon stick, broken in two pieces
5 whole cloves
¼ teaspoon ground cumin
¼ teaspoon rosemary
1½ cups dark beer

1. Place the onions in a large pot of boiling water for 1 minute to facilitate peeling. Drain them in a colander and immediately cool under cold running water. Using a paring knife, peel the onions and trim the ends; also cut a ¼-inch-deep X into each stem end to prevent the onions from bursting when cooked.

2. In a large heavy skillet, heat the oil over moderately high heat; add the beef cubes and brown them on all sides, working in batches if necessary. Remove the meat with a slotted spoon, reserving any oil that remains in the pan, and place the beef in a 4-quart casserole. Sprinkle the meat with the salt and pepper.

3. Preheat the oven to 350°. In the oil remaining in the skillet, quickly sauté the onions and garlic over moderate heat until fragrant, 2 to 3 minutes, and add to the casserole.

4. Combine the remaining ingredients in a bowl. When the beer has stopped foaming, add the mixture to the casserole. Toss gently until the meat and onions are coated. Cover the casserole lightly.

5. Bake for 2½ hours, or until the beef is tender when pierced with a fork and the sauce has thickened slightly and turned a rich brown color.

Steak Diane

F&W Beverage Suggestion: Spanish Red, such as Torres Coronas

2 SERVINGS

1-pound boneless sirloin steak, cut about ½-inch thick
4 tablespoons unsalted butter
¼ cup brandy
2 tablespoons Madeira
1 tablespoon Worcestershire sauce
1 teaspoon Dijon-style mustard
Salt and pepper
1 teaspoon minced fresh parsley

1. Cut the steak lengthwise in half. Pound each piece between 2 sheets of waxed paper until ⅛ inch thick.

2. In a large heavy skillet, heat 2½ tablespoons of the butter. Add one of the steaks and sauté over moderate heat for 30 seconds on each side. Remove from the pan and quickly sauté the second steak.

3. Return both steaks to the pan and pour the brandy over them. Remove the skillet from the heat and ignite. Shake the pan over the heat until the flame dies out, then remove the steaks to a warm platter.

4. Whisk the Madeira, Worcestershire sauce, mustard and salt and pepper to taste into the skillet and heat to simmering. Cook for 1 minute, remove from the heat and swirl in the remaining 1½ tablespoons butter. Dip the steaks in the sauce to coat. Sprinkle with parsley and serve.

Skillet Steak in Scotch and Tarragon Sauce

Here is a skillet version of *côte de boeuf,* quick and easy to prepare for a few people. The result of the top-of-the-stove cooking is a wonderfully tender piece of meat covered by a tasty brown crust. The piquant tarragon and green pepper sauce, flavored with Scotch, complements the steak beautifully.

3 OR 4 GENEROUS SERVINGS

8 tablespoons (1 stick) unsalted butter
1½-pound shell or strip steak, cut 2 to 2¼ inches thick
1½ teaspoons coarse (kosher) salt
¼ teaspoon freshly ground black pepper
½ cup Scotch whisky
1 cup Brown Chicken Stock (p. 204) or beef broth
1 teaspoon green peppercorns (packed in brine), drained
2 teaspoons potato starch or 1 tablespoon arrowroot
2 to 3 tablespoons minced fresh tarragon or 1 to 2 teaspoons dried, to taste
Sprigs of watercress, for garnish

1. In a small saucepan, melt 6 tablespoons of the butter over low heat. Carefully skim off and discard the milky foam on top. Spoon out 3 tablespoons of the clarified butter into a heavy 10-inch skillet (preferably cast iron). (If there is extra, reserve it for another use.) Discard the milky solids at the bottom of the pan.

2. Wipe the steak dry and season on both sides with the salt and pepper.

3. Heat the clarified butter in the skillet over high heat. Add the steak and sauté on one side for 3 minutes, until well browned. Turn and sear the second side for 3 minutes. Reduce the heat to moderately high and continue cooking for 10 minutes. Carefully tilt the pan and spoon out all but about 2 tablespoons of the fat.

Turn the steak and cook for another 10 minutes for rare, 14 minutes for medium. The steak is done to rare when there is slight resistance to pressure (the meat will seem to "spring back" when touched). Remove the steak to a cutting board and let it rest while you prepare the sauce.

4. Discard all the fat in the skillet. Add the remaining 2 tablespoons butter and melt over moderately high heat. Add the Scotch and boil until reduced to a glaze, about 2 minutes. Add all but 1 tablespoon of the stock and bring to a boil; then add the green peppercorns.

5. Stir the potato starch into the reserved tablespoon stock until dissolved. Whisk this mixture into the sauce and cook, stirring, until thickened. Season with the tarragon and salt and pepper to taste. Remove the sauce from the heat.

6. Slice the steak crosswise into ¼-inch slices and arrange them on individual plates or a platter. Spoon the sauce over the steak and garnish with sprigs of fresh watercress.

Carpaccio Gold

Here is an unusual and delicious luncheon dish. Paper-thin slices of prime shell steak are spread with a mushroom and cheese salad and rolled into a crescent-shaped pillow. As a luncheon dish, accompany this with potato or rice salad. As an appetizer, serve mushroom salad without the meat on a bed of lettuce.

4 SERVINGS

1 pound fresh medium mushrooms, stemmed
5 ounces Emmenthaler cheese, sliced ⅛ inch thick, cut into ⅜-inch squares

4 scallions, sliced ¼ inch thick
2 tablespoons capers
2 teaspoons Dijon-style mustard
3 tablespoons tarragon vinegar
1 teaspoon freshly ground pepper
¼ teaspoon salt
6 tablespoons peanut oil
16 paper-thin slices of prime shell steak (about 8 ounces; see Note)
Olive oil

1. With a small sharp knife, cut the mushroom caps vertically into ⅛-inch-thick slices. Cut the slices crosswise in half.

2. In a medium bowl, combine the mushrooms, cheese, scallions and capers.

3. In a small bowl, whisk together the mustard, vinegar, pepper and salt. Gradually whisk in the oil in a thin stream. Pour the vinaigrette over the salad and toss.

4. Slightly overlap the long sides of 4 slices of the meat to make a rectangular shape. Spoon about ½ cup of the salad along one long end of the rectangle. Roll up and transfer to a plate. Tuck the short ends under and curve the ends of the roll slightly to form a crescent. Brush the meat lightly with olive oil. Repeat with the remaining meat and salad to make 3 more rolls. There will be extra salad; spoon this decoratively around the meat.

NOTE: Order ahead from your butcher and have it sliced for you.

Carpetbagger Steak

F&W Beverage Suggestion: California Cabernet Sauvignon

4 SERVINGS

4 center-cut tenderloin steaks, about 2 inches thick
8 raw oysters
2 tablespoons olive oil
2 tablespoons unsalted butter
Salt and pepper
Béarnaise Sauce (optional; p. 209)

1. Make a pocket in each steak by cutting a slit deep into the side. Tuck 2 oysters into each steak and skewer the pockets shut with toothpicks.

2. In a large skillet, heat the olive oil and butter over high heat until almost smoking. Add the steaks and brown all

over, including the edges, about 1 minute. Reduce the heat to low and cook the steaks 5 minutes on each side for medium-rare. Season with salt and pepper to taste and serve with Béarnaise Sauce, if desired.

Flank Steak with Whiskey Butter Sauce

F&W Beverage Suggestion: American beer, such as Anchor Steam

6 TO 8 SERVINGS

Marinade:
2 flank steaks, 1¼ to 1½ pounds each
2 cups vegetable oil
2 cups dry red wine
½ cup soy sauce
½ teaspoon hot pepper sauce
2 tablespoons Worcestershire sauce
5 garlic cloves, mashed
1 tablespoon rosemary
5 bay leaves, crumbled
2 teaspoons thyme
2 teaspoons coarsely ground pepper
1 large onion, quartered and thinly sliced

Sauce:
1 small onion, minced
2 garlic cloves, minced
½ cup plus 1 tablespoon whiskey
¼ cup Worcestershire sauce
1½ teaspoons dry mustard
¼ teaspoon hot pepper sauce
¼ cup white wine vinegar
1 teaspoon salt
1 tablespoon freshly ground pepper
1½ cups (3 sticks) unsalted butter, softened

1. Marinate the steaks: In a noncorrodible container large enough to hold the two flank steaks, combine all the marinade ingredients; mix well. Add the two steaks, making sure they are covered with the liquid. Marinate at room temperature, turning occasionally, for 2 hours.

2. Begin the sauce: In a medium, noncorrodible saucepan, combine the onion, garlic, ½ cup of the whiskey, the Worcestershire sauce, mustard, hot pepper sauce, vinegar, salt and pepper. Bring to a boil over high heat and cook until reduced to about ¾ cup, 8 to 10 minutes. (The recipe can be prepared ahead up to this point.)

3. Grill the steaks: Preheat the broiler with the broiler pan in place about 4 inches from the heat. Remove the steaks from the marinade; scrape off any pieces of herbs or vegetables sticking to the meat and pat dry with paper towels. Place on the preheated broiler pan and cook, turning once, for 10 to 12 minutes, until medium rare. Let sit for 5 minutes before carving.

4. Meanwhile, finish the sauce: Reduce the heat to low and whisk in ½ cup (1 stick) of butter, 1 tablespoon at a time. Continue whisking in the remaining 2 sticks of butter several tablespoons at a time. Whisk in the remaining 1 tablespoon whiskey; the sauce will be thin.

5. Assemble the dish: Cut the steak against the grain on the diagonal into thin slices. Coat lightly with the sauce. Serve the remaining sauce on the side.

London Broil Marinated in Lemon and Pepper

4 SERVINGS

1½-pound top round or flank steak about 1¼ inches thick
¼ cup lemon juice
⅓ cup vegetable oil
½ teaspoon pepper
Salt

1. Using a fork, prick the meat deeply all over. In a small glass or ceramic baking dish just large enough to hold the meat, combine the lemon juice, oil and pepper. Allow the meat to marinate for 2 hours, turning every 30 minutes.

2. Preheat the broiler about 10 minutes before cooking the meat. Remove the meat from the marinade. Broil 3 inches from the heat for about 4½ minutes on each side for a medium-rare top round, or about 3 minutes per side for flank steak.

3. Let the meat rest 5 minutes before thinly slicing it across the grain, on the diagonal. Salt to taste and serve immediately.

Japanese-Style Marinated Flank Steak

This marinade is used to make a steak sauce; it has an intense, pungent flavor and should be used sparingly.

F&W Beverage Suggestion:
British Ale

4 SERVINGS

1½-pound flank steak
¾ cup sake
½ cup mirin* (sweet rice wine)
½ cup soy sauce, preferably Japanese
2 tablespoons shredded fresh gingerroot
1 medium garlic clove, minced
1 teaspoon sugar
2 teaspoons cornstarch
*Available at Oriental groceries

1. Lightly score one side of the steak, on the diagonal and at 1-inch intervals. In a glass or ceramic baking dish large enough to hold the meat, combine the sake, mirin, soy sauce, gingerroot, garlic and sugar. Marinate the steak at room temperature for 30 minutes, turning the meat once or twice.

2. Preheat the broiler about 10 minutes before you plan to cook the steak. Remove the meat from the marinade, reserving the marinade. Broil the steak 3 inches from the heat for about 3½ minutes on each side for a medium-rare steak. Let the steak rest for 5 to 10 minutes before thinly slicing it across the grain, on the diagonal.

3. Meanwhile, make the sauce: Strain the marinade and measure out 1 cup; discard the remainder. Place the 1 cup of marinade in a small saucepan and whisk in the cornstarch until smooth. Bring the mixture to a boil over moderate heat and cook, stirring constantly, for about 1 minute. Spoon 2 to 3 tablespoons of the sauce over the meat and serve the remainder separately.

Grilled Flank Steak with Dill

F&W Beverage Suggestion:
California Petite Sirah or French Côtes-du-Rhône

4 SERVINGS

1 flank steak, about 1½ pounds
Salt and pepper
1 tablespoon unsalted butter
1½ tablespoons chopped dill
¼ lemon
Hot pepper sauce

1. Rub the steak with salt and pepper to taste and, in a preheated broiler or on an outdoor grill, broil about 4 inches from the heat for 4 to 5 minutes on each side.

2. Transfer to a warm platter and dot with the butter, sprinkle with the dill, squeeze the lemon over and add a dash or two of the pepper sauce. Carve on the diagonal into thin slices and serve.

Flank Steak with Tomato-Olive Sauce

F&W Beverage Suggestion:
Sturdy red wine, such as California Petite Sirah or Côtes-du-Rhône

8 FIRST-COURSE OR 4 MAIN-COURSE SERVINGS

1½-pound flank steak, trimmed of fat, at room temperature
8 canned Italian plum tomatoes—seeded, coarsely chopped and well drained
1 small garlic clove, mashed
8 oil-cured olives—halved, pitted and cut into thin strips
1 large shallot, finely diced
1 teaspoon white wine vinegar
3 tablespoons extra-virgin olive oil
½ teaspoon coarsely ground pepper
Salt
2 tablespoons finely chopped parsley

1. In a pan that will hold the steak comfortably, bring enough water to cover it by about ½ inch to 140°.

2. Add the steak. Poach for 7 minutes. Turn the steak over and poach for 7 to 8 minutes longer, until rare. The steak is rare when it is springy to the touch in

the center and the internal temperature is 135° to 140°. (If unsure, remove the steak and cut a small slit in the center to check.)

3. Remove the steak to a platter, cover loosely and let cool to room temperature. Then slice and serve or wrap well and refrigerate overnight.

4. In a medium bowl, combine the tomatoes, garlic, olives, shallot, vinegar, oil, pepper and salt to taste. Let stand for 1 hour or overnight to let the flavors blend. Just before serving, stir in the parsley.

5. To serve, slice the steak very thin on the diagonal for maximum tenderness. Arrange on a platter and spoon the sauce over the meat.

Steak Pizzaioli

F&W Beverage Suggestion:
Chianti Classico Riserva

4 SERVINGS

¼ cup olive oil
2½-pound chuck steak, about 1 inch thick, bone in
1 tablespoon minced garlic
1 can (35 ounces) peeled Italian tomatoes, with the juice
1 teaspoon salt
1 teaspoon basil
1 teaspoon oregano
½ teaspoon crushed hot red pepper

1. Preheat the oven to 350°. In a large skillet, warm the oil over high heat. Add the steak and sear for 2 minutes on each side; transfer to a large, shallow baking dish.

2. Reduce the heat to moderate; add the garlic and sauté until it begins to turn golden, about 45 seconds. Remove from the heat. Add the tomatoes with their juices, breaking them up with a wooden spoon. Stir in the salt, basil, oregano and red pepper and pour the sauce over the steak in the baking dish.

3. Bake, covered, for 2 hours, basting 4 or 5 times. Uncover and bake for an additional 30 minutes.

Garlic-Lime Marinated Beef with Cabbage and Peppers

Lime, garlic, hot pepper and allspice are the dominant seasonings in the Creole cuisine of the French West Indies; they work well in this melting pot of techniques and ingredients. The sauce that results from the combination of flavors is both peppery-hot and citrusy-sour—but not very garlicky, as the lime cuts the impact of the volatile oil.

When choosing beef for this recipe, ask for a relatively tender cut, which, although expensive, should not bother the budget in the quantity required. You can use any part of the sirloin, first-cut top round or top blade section of the chuck. You could also vary the possibilities by substituting pork, lamb, chicken, turkey or any kind of liver.

2 SERVINGS

Scant ½ teaspoon ground allspice
2 large garlic cloves, minced
4 teaspoons cornstarch
3 tablespoons fresh lime juice (see Note)
3 teaspoons corn or peanut oil
6 ounces well-trimmed boneless steak
1 small head of cabbage, 1 to 1¼ pounds
1 large red bell pepper, cut into very thin strips about 2 inches long
1 large onion, halved and sliced crosswise
1 cup beef stock, well skimmed
1 small, very hot green pepper, such as jalapeño—seeded, deribbed and minced

1. In a small bowl, combine the allspice, half the minced garlic and the cornstarch. Gradually stir in the lime juice. Add 1 teaspoon of the oil. Slice the meat into very thin strips about 2 inches long and ½ inch wide and combine with the marinade. Set aside.

2. Remove any heavy outer leaves from the cabbage, then quarter and core it. Cut into slices ¼ to ½ inch wide. Separate the cabbage layers into strips. Place the cabbage and red pepper strips in a steamer. Cover and steam until crisp-

tender, about 15 minutes. Turn into a hot serving dish and place in a warm oven.

3. Heat 1 teaspoon of the oil in a large heavy skillet. Add the onion and cook over moderate heat, stirring often, until well browned, about 10 minutes.

4. Drain the meat well, reserving the marinade. Add the beef stock to the marinade.

5. Add the remaining 1 teaspoon oil to the onions in the skillet. Stir in the beef, remaining garlic and the minced hot pepper. Sauté briefly, tossing, to lightly brown the meat.

6. Add the stock-marinade mixture and stir vigorously over moderate heat, scraping up the browned bits in the pan, until the sauce boils. Pour the meat and sauce over the steamed vegetables and serve at once.

NOTE: Substitute 1 tablespoon of beef stock for 1 of the lime juice if you don't enjoy a very tart dish.

Filet Mignons in Cognac Cream Sauce

F&W Beverage Suggestion:
Red Burgundy, such as Cuvée Latour

2 SERVINGS

4 filet mignons, cut 1 inch thick
Freshly ground pepper
½ cup Cognac
1 teaspoon salt
4 tablespoons unsalted butter
1 tablespoon vegetable oil
2 shallots, minced
½ cup heavy cream
½ teaspoon fresh lemon juice

1. Season the steaks liberally with pepper. Marinate in ¼ cup of the Cognac at room temperature, turning occasionally, for 30 minutes. Remove the steaks and reserve the marinade. Pat the steaks dry and season with the salt.

2. In a large heavy skillet, melt 2 tablespoons of the butter in the oil over moderately high heat. Sear the steaks, turning once, until well browned, about 2 minutes on each side. Lower the heat to moderate and cook, turning occasionally, until rare, about 6 minutes, or medium-rare, about 8 minutes.

3. Remove the steaks to a platter and cover loosely with foil to keep warm. Pour off the fat in the skillet. Melt the remaining 2 tablespoons butter and add the shallots. Cook over low heat until softened, about 1 minute.

4. Pour in the reserved marinade and the remaining ¼ cup Cognac. Increase the heat to moderately high and bring to a boil, scraping up the browned bits clinging to the bottom of the skillet. Cook until reduced by half. Add the cream and boil until reduced by half again. Season with the lemon juice and salt and pepper to taste. Spoon the sauce over the steaks.

Standing Rib Roast

If, for your holiday dinner this year, you plan to feast on roast beef, why not try this method? It will produce a perfectly cooked standing rib roast.

8 TO 10 SERVINGS

4-rib roast (about 9 pounds), trimmed and tied (see Note)
5 large garlic cloves, cut into 10 slivers each
2 tablespoons all-purpose flour
1 teaspoon pepper

1. Preheat the oven to 500°. With the tip of a small knife, cut 50 slits ½ inch deep all over the meat. Insert a sliver of garlic into each cut.

2. Mix the flour and pepper and rub the mixture all over the surface of the roast.

3. Place the meat, rib-side down, in a roasting pan. Roast the beef for 1 hour (15 minutes for each rib) for a rare roast or 1 hour 12 minutes (18 minutes per rib) for a medium-rare roast. Turn off the heat but do not open the oven door. Let the roast sit in the oven for 1 hour longer to finish cooking. Remove from the oven and let rest for 15 minutes before carving.

NOTE: Ask your butcher to remove the thick chine bone, trim off any excess fat and tie the roast.

Panfried Tournedos

F&W Beverage Suggestion: California Zinfandel

2 SERVINGS

1 tablespoon unsalted butter
1 tablespoon olive oil
2 tournedos (center-cut fillet steaks), about 2 inches thick (about 8 ounces each)
⅓ cup beef stock or broth
⅛ teaspoon pepper

1. In a small skillet, heat the butter and olive oil over high heat until very hot but not smoking. Sear the tournedos for 1 minute on each side, and holding the steaks with tongs, quickly brown the sides. Reduce the heat to low and cook the steaks for 5 minutes on each side for medium-rare. Transfer to warm plates and set aside.

2. Pour the grease out of the skillet. Increase the heat to high and add the beef stock, stirring and scraping up the browned bits on the bottom. Cook until the broth is reduced by half, 2 to 3 minutes. Season with the pepper. Pour over the tournedos and serve.

Pot-Roasted Brisket of Beef

8 TO 10 SERVINGS

1 brisket of beef (about 4 pounds)
Salt and freshly ground pepper
2 large onions, coarsely chopped
8 to 10 garlic cloves
1 tablespoon thyme
1 bottle (12 ounces) light beer or ¾ cup beef stock mixed with ¾ cup water

Optional Accompaniments:
Prepared horseradish
Dijon-style mustard

1. Pat the brisket dry with paper towels and rub the meat with salt and pepper to taste. Place the meat, fat-side down, in a heavy flameproof casserole or Dutch oven into which it fits snugly. Over medium heat, brown the meat thoroughly on all sides, using only the fat rendered from the brisket. When the meat is uniformly colored, about 15 min-

utes, remove the brisket from the pot and set it aside.

2. Pour off and discard all but 1 tablespoon of the cooking fat. Add the onions and garlic to the pot, and cook over medium heat, stirring, until the onions are slightly translucent, about 10 minutes.

3. Add the thyme, beer and 2 cups of water. Return the brisket to the pot, cover, and simmer very gently on top of the stove for 3½ to 4 hours. Turn the brisket occasionally to ensure uniform cooking. Add water as necessary to keep the onions barely submerged in liquid. When the meat is easily pierced with a fork, transfer the brisket to a cutting board. Pour the cooking juices into a bowl and allow them to stand until the fat rises to the top.

4. With a long, sharp knife, cut the brisket across the grain into thin slices, holding the knife at an angle to the board to produce a bias cut. Arrange the slices on a warmed platter. With a spoon, skim off the fat from the pan juices and discard, or blot the surface with paper towels. Taste the degreased juices, add seasoning and reheat if necessary. Pour into a serving boat and pass with the meat. If you wish, offer the horseradish and Dijon-style mustard as accompaniments.

Beef Vinaigrette

An unusual combination in which a spicy vinaigrette makes a lovely sauce for *hot* pot roast.

12 SERVINGS

Beef:

1 beef brisket, about 6 pounds
1 onion, halved
1 carrot, halved lengthwise
2 celery ribs
1 garlic clove
2 bay leaves
1 teaspoon salt

Sauce Vinaigrette:

½ cup vegetable oil
½ cup olive oil
½ cup mild white wine vinegar
2 tablespoons finely chopped red onions
1 tablespoon finely chopped shallots

2 tablespoons finely chopped fresh
 parsley
1 tablespoon finely chopped chives
1½ tablespoons chopped pimiento
2 tablespoons chopped capers
1 teaspoon white pepper
1 teaspoon salt
1½ teaspoons dry mustard
1 teaspoon garlic powder
2 dashes hot pepper sauce
3 hard-cooked eggs, chopped

1. Cook the beef: Heat the oven to 325°. Trim as much surface fat as possible from the beef. Put it in a baking pan and surround it with the vegetables, garlic and bay leaves and sprinkle with the salt. Pour in enough water to cover. Cover the pan and bake it for 3 to 4 hours, or until the brisket is tender.

2. Meanwhile, make the vinaigrette: Beat the oils and the vinegar together until smooth. Stir in the remaining ingredients.

3. Drain the beef. Slice it thinly and arrange the slices on a serving platter. While the beef is still hot, cover with the Sauce Vinaigrette.

Roast Beef Hash

The key to this classic dish is to cut its main ingredients—roast beef, potato and onion—to a uniform size so that all cook at the same rate.

6 SERVINGS

6 tablespoons vegetable oil or
 unsalted butter
1 large onion, cut into ¼-inch dice
 (about 1 cup)
1 pound cold roast beef, cut into
 ¼-inch dice (about 3 cups)
2 medium potatoes, cooked and cut
 into ¼-inch dice (about 2 cups)
½ teaspoon thyme
2 tablespoons finely minced fresh
 parsley
1 teaspoon salt
½ teaspoon pepper

1. In a large skillet, warm 2 tablespoons of the oil over low heat. Add the onion and sauté until translucent, about 10 minutes.

2. Transfer the onion to a medium mixing bowl and add the roast beef, potatoes, thyme, 1 tablespoon of the parsley, salt and pepper. Cover and refrigerate for at least 3 hours, or overnight.

3. In a large skillet, preferably nonstick, warm 2 tablespoons of the oil over moderate heat. Add the hash to the pan, and cook over low heat, occasionally pressing down firmly with a spatula, until the underside is brown and crusty, about 10 to 12 minutes.

4. To remove the hash, loosen the bottom with a spatula. Invert a plate slightly larger than the skillet over the hash. Then carefully invert the skillet over the plate.

5. Add the remaining oil to the skillet and warm it over moderate heat for a minute. Carefully slide the hash back into the pan, pressing it down with a spatula, and cook over low heat until the bottom is golden brown and crusty.

6. Loosen the hash and turn it out as described in Step 4. Garnish with the remaining tablespoon parsley and serve hot.

Anise Beef with Vegetables Vinaigrette

F&W Beverage Suggestion: Flavorful white wine, such as Hermitage Blanc or Vernaccia di San Gimignano

10 TO 12 SERVINGS

1 whole beef tenderloin (4½ to 5
 pounds), trimmed of fat and cut
 in half, at room temperature
2 cups soy sauce, preferably
 mushroom soy*
¼ cup whole star anise* plus 1
 tablespoon finely ground star
 anise
⅛ cup whole Szechuan
 peppercorns* plus 1 tablespoon
 coarsely ground Szechuan
 peppercorns
2 tablespoons dry white wine
2 tablespoons rice wine vinegar
1 cup safflower oil
½ teaspoon salt
¼ teaspoon freshly ground pepper
1½ pounds small red potatoes,
 skins on, sliced ⅜ inch thick

3 scallions, coarsely chopped, plus
 20 to 25 whole scallions,
 trimmed to 6 inches
1 small garlic clove, minced to a
 paste
20 medium carrots with green tops
1 tablespoon grated fresh
 gingerroot
3½ pounds asparagus, trimmed and
 peeled
1 tablespoon coarse (kosher) salt
1 teaspoon Oriental hot oil, or a
 few drops hot pepper sauce
1 teaspoon Oriental sesame oil

*Available in Oriental groceries

1. Select a deep pan large enough to comfortably hold both pieces of beef in a single layer. Add the soy sauce, whole star anise, whole Szechuan peppercorns and 1 quart of water. Bring to a boil, reduce the heat and simmer for 5 minutes. Using an instant-reading thermometer as your guide, add enough cold water to lower the temperature of the poaching liquid to 140°.

2. Add the beef. Add hot tap water, if necessary, to cover by about ½ inch. Poach over low heat, turning occasionally, for about 35 minutes for rare. The beef is rare when it is springy to the touch at the narrower end of the fillet and the internal temperature is 135° to 140°. (If unsure, remove the beef and cut a small slit in the center to check.)

3. Remove the beef to a platter, cover loosely and let cool to room temperature. Strain the poaching liquid. Reserve 1 cup; cool, then freeze the remainder for another use if desired. Then slice the meat and serve (see Step 9) or wrap well and refrigerate overnight. (Let return to room temperature before serving.)

4. In a small bowl, whisk together the wine, vinegar, safflower oil, salt and pepper. There will be 1¼ cups vinaigrette.

5. Cook the potato slices in a large saucepan of boiling salted water until tender, about 10 minutes; drain. Combine ½ cup of the vinaigrette with the chopped scallions and garlic. Add the warm potatoes and toss to coat. Let stand until cool, tossing occasionally.

6. Trim the tops of the carrots, leaving 1 inch of green. Cut off the narrow tips so that the carrots measure about 2½ inches and trim to resemble baby carrots;

reserve the tips for another use. Cook the carrots in a large saucepan of lightly salted boiling water until tender, about 15 minutes; drain. Combine ¼ cup of the vinaigrette with the ginger. Add the warm carrots and toss to coat. Let stand until cool, tossing occasionally.

7. Blanch the whole scallions in a skillet of simmering lightly salted water until softened but still bright green, 4 to 5 minutes. Drain and rinse under cold running water until cool; pat dry with paper towels. Set aside.

8. Blanch the asparagus in a large skillet of lightly salted boiling water until crisp-tender, 2 to 3 minutes. Drain and rinse under running water until cool; pat dry with paper towels. Set aside.

9. To serve, cut the beef into ½- to ¾-inch-thick slices. Combine the ground star anise, ground Szechuan peppercorns and coarse salt in a small bowl; sprinkle on both sides of the fillet slices. Arrange overlapping slices of beef on a large platter.

10. Combine the hot oil with ¼ cup of the vinaigrette. Toss with the whole scallions until coated. Combine the sesame oil with the remaining ¼ cup vinaigrette and toss with the asparagus until coated.

11. Arrange the vegetables around the beef. Pour a small ladleful of the reserved poaching liquid over the beef and pass the remainder separately.

Fillet of Beef on a String

This classic technique gently poaches a fillet by suspending it in a stockpot. This gentle cooking method yields an extremely moist, tender beef best served rare.

F&W Beverage Suggestion:
Côte Rôtie or California Petite Sirah

8 TO 10 SERVINGS

5½ to 6½ quarts brown stock or 3 quarts canned beef broth diluted with 2½ to 3½ quarts of water (see Note)
2 tablespoons unsalted butter
2 tablespoons peanut oil

1 whole fillet of beef, trimmed (4 to 4½ pounds) and tied at 2-inch intervals, at room temperature

Garnish:
2 leeks (white part only)
2 carrots
2 celery ribs
Horseradish Sauce (p. 210)

1. Place a round wire rack in a large casserole or stockpot 12 or 14 inches in diameter and at least 5 inches deep. Add 5½ quarts of the stock and bring to a boil over high heat.

2. Meanwhile, in a large skillet, heat the butter and oil. When the foam subsides, add the fillet and sauté over moderately high heat, turning occasionally, until browned on all sides, about 6 minutes. Remove the fillet from the pan and loop it around in a horseshoe shape so that it will fit in your pot. Tie the two ends together, leaving at least ½-inch slack so that the beef is not touching itself at any point. Leave a length of string at the end of the knot. Holding the beef by the string, lower it onto the rack in the boiling stock. If the beef is not completely covered with liquid, add additional stock to cover. As soon as the stock begins to simmer, reduce the heat and simmer gently for 20 to 25 minutes (5 to 6 minutes per pound) for rare beef. (Do not let the liquid boil at any time.)

3. Meanwhile, prepare the garnish: Cut the leeks, carrots and celery into julienne strips. Steam the vegetables until just tender, about 2 minutes.

4. When the meat is done, let rest for 10 minutes before carving. Cut the beef into ¾-inch slices and arrange on a platter garnished with the julienne vegetables. Serve hot or at room temperature with the Horseradish Sauce.

NOTE: After poaching the beef, the stock can be strained through a double thickness of dampened cheesecloth and reused.

Roast Rabbit in Orange Barbecue Sauce

In our test kitchen, we found that this recipe works beautifully with chicken as well.

F&W Beverage Suggestion:
Gewürztraminer from California or Alsace

4 SERVINGS

Sauce:
1 cup (8 ounces) frozen orange juice concentrate
1 cup (8 ounces) Southern Comfort
1 cup ketchup
¼ cup Dijon-style mustard
¼ cup maple syrup
¼ cup red wine vinegar
3 tablespoons fresh lemon juice
4 garlic cloves, halved
1 small onion, quartered
1½ teaspoons cinnamon
1 teaspoon allspice
½ teaspoon ground cloves
½ teaspoon pepper

Rabbit:
1½ tablespoons vegetable oil
1 rabbit (2½ to 3 pounds), cut into 8 pieces
1 tablespoon paprika
½ teaspoon thyme
Salt and pepper
⅔ cup dry white wine

1. Make the sauce: Place all sauce ingredients into a food processor or blender and puree until smooth and thick, about 40 seconds. Tranfer to a medium saucepan, heat to simmering and cook, uncovered, over low heat until the sauce is reduced to 3 cups, about 30 minutes.

2. Prepare the rabbit: Preheat the oven to 500°. Lightly oil a baking dish large enough to hold the rabbit pieces in a single layer. Rub the remaining oil over the rabbit pieces and season with the paprika, thyme and salt and pepper to taste. Bake, uncovered, for 20 minutes. Add the wine, cover with foil and continue to bake until the juices run clear, about 15 minutes.

3. Pour the sauce over the rabbit and bake, uncovered, for 20 minutes longer.

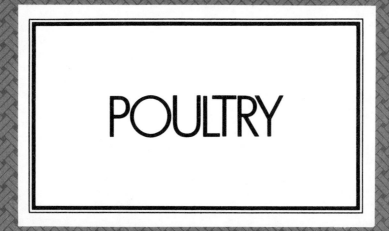

POULTRY

Aromatic Duck

This manner of flavoring and roasting duck produces meat that is so succulent and rich tasting that it is possible to feed four with an amount that is usually suggested for two or three. The precooking seasoning (which takes two days, so plan accordingly) and slow, fat-melting roasting make for a successful presentation at room temperature—unusual for such a fat bird. At this temperature, the flesh is more compact and juicy and the flavor more complex than when hot. This also enables the cook to be with his or her guests, a boon for those who have never been able to coordinate the roasting of a duck with the arrival of guests.

Beverage Suggestion:
Zinfandel, such as Ridge, Fetzer or Clos du Val

<u>4 SERVINGS</u>

1 duckling, about 5 pounds
2 teaspoons peppercorns
1 teaspoon thyme
2 bay leaves, crumbled
6 cloves
1 tablespoon coarse (kosher) salt
1 tablespoon brown sugar
1 tablespoon gin, vodka or brandy
1 garlic clove
5 or 6 large, neat red cabbage leaves

1. Cut off the wing tips of the duckling and wrap them up with the giblets for future stock-making. Pull out and discard any loose interior fat. Rinse the duckling inside and out and pat dry, inside and out.

2. Mix together in a spice mill or mortar the peppercorns, thyme, bay leaves, cloves and salt. Grind to a fine texture. Combine in a small dish with the brown sugar and liquor. Place the duck in a heavy plastic bag that fits snugly. Rub half the spice mixture inside the duck and the remaining half over the outside. Place the garlic in the duck's cavity. Close the bag tightly and refrigerate for 24 hours, rubbing the surface and squeezing in the spices whenever you think of it.

3. Remove the duck from the bag and gently pat it dry. Set it on a cake rack over a plate and return it, uncovered, to the refrigerator for another 24 hours or so, turning once.

4. Pat the duck to dry it thoroughly (if it is not already dry) and let it come to room temperature (at least 2 hours). Preheat the oven to 300°. Using a large needle and white cotton thread, sew closed the neck and tail openings. Place the duck on its side on a rack set in a roasting pan.

5. Roast the duck for 45 minutes. With the needle, prick the fatty parts on the upper side; do not prick deeply enough to pierce the flesh. Grab the duck by the legs (using paper towels to protect your hands) and turn it onto the other side. Increase the oven temperature to 350° and roast 30 minutes. Prick the fatty parts on the upturned side and then turn the duck onto its breast. Roast 25 minutes longer. Prick the upturned side. Turn the duck breast upward. Increase the heat to 400° and roast about 30 minutes longer, or until the duck is deeply browned and most of the fat has melted away. Remove from the oven and let cool 1 to 3 hours before serving.

6. To serve: Using a heavy cleaver or poultry shears, carefully cut through the flesh and bone of the duck to make about 12 to 14 serving pieces, keeping the skin neatly intact on each piece. Spread the cabbage leaves over a platter, shallow basket or wooden bowl and arrange the duck on them.

NOTE: If you prefer duck sizzling hot, you can easily heat the pieces. Arrange them in a pan in a single layer, cut side down, and roast in a preheated 350° oven for 15 minutes, or until hot.

Minted Duck

F&W Beverage Suggestion:
Bordeaux, such as Château Greysac

<u>6 TO 8 SERVINGS</u>

3 ducks (4½ to 5 pounds each)
Coarse (kosher) salt and freshly ground pepper
½ cup red currant jelly
¼ cup white crème de menthe
3 small onions
9 whole cloves
3 bunches of fresh mint

1. Preheat the oven to 350°. Rinse and dry the ducks thoroughly. Generously rub the inside of each duck with salt and pepper.

2. In a small saucepan, warm the jelly with the crème de menthe over low heat until melted; set aside in a warm place.

3. Stick each of the onions with 3 of the cloves. Place 1 onion in the cavity of each duck. Divide the mint into 6 equal bunches. Place a bunch in each duck and close the cavities with skewers or thread. Reserve the remaining mint.

4. Prick the ducks all over and place on a rack in a large roasting pan and roast, breast-side down, for 30 minutes. Turn the birds onto one side and roast for 15 minutes; turn onto the other side and roast for 15 minutes longer. Turn the birds breast-side up, prick all over again and roast for an additional hour, brushing with the currant glaze twice. Remove the ducks from the oven and let rest until cool enough to handle.

5. Remove and discard the onions and mint. Carve the ducks into serving pieces. Serve at room temperature, garnished lavishly with the remaining mint.

Suprèmes of Duck Glazed with Molasses and Black Pepper

This elegant dish uses only the boned breasts of the duck. The rest of the bird is used to make the dark, savory sauce. If you wish, the legs and thighs may be set aside after the sauce is completed and eaten separately or cut up and made into a salad.

F&W Beverage Suggestions:
French Rhône, such as Côte-Rôtie, or California Petite Sirah

2 MAIN-COURSE OR 4 LUNCHEON SERVINGS

Garnishes:

1 large or 2 small sweet potatoes or yams
3 tablespoons clarified butter
1 red or yellow Delicious apple
1 tablespoon fresh lemon juice
1 tablespoon unsalted butter
1 teaspoon sugar
12 snow peas (about 1½ ounces)

Ducks:

2 mallard* or Long Island ducks, about 5 pounds each
⅓ cup dark, unsulphured molasses
3 teaspoons salt
1½ tablespoons peanut oil
½ teaspoon freshly ground pepper
1 large onion, coarsely chopped
1 large carrot, cut into 1-inch lengths
1 garlic clove, cut in half
1 red or yellow Delicious apple, cut into ¼-inch slices
1 sprig fresh thyme or ¼ teaspoon dried
½ cup apple cider vinegar
½ cup dry white wine
3 cups chicken stock or brown duck stock (see Note)
½ cup heavy cream
2 tablespoons grainy mustard, such as Pommery
4 tablespoons unsalted butter
2 teaspoons fresh coarsely ground black pepper

*Mallard ducks may be ordered at many specialty butcher shops

1. Prepare the garnishes: Preheat the oven to 400°. Bake the sweet potatoes for 20 to 30 minutes, or until partially cooked but still resistant to the tip of a knife. Let cool until they can be handled easily; then cut in half lengthwise. With the small end of melon-ball cutter, scoop out 12 balls.

2. In a small saucepan, warm the clarified butter over high heat until hot. Add the sweet potato balls and sauté, shaking the pan frequently, until golden brown; 3 to 4 minutes. Remove with a slotted spoon and drain on paper towels.

3. Peel the apple and scoop out 12 balls with the small end of the melon-ball cutter.

4. In a small skillet, place the lemon juice, 1 tablespoon butter, sugar and ¼ cup of water over high heat. When the butter melts, add the apples and cook, stirring gently once or twice, until the water has evaporated and the apples are golden brown and caramelized. Transfer the apples to a plate and sprinkle them with 2 tablespoons of cold water to prevent sticking.

5. String the snow peas and cook them in a medium saucepan of boiling salted water until bright green and slightly tender, about 30 seconds. Remove with a slotted spoon and transfer to a bowl of ice water. Cut on the diagonal into ½-inch-wide strips. Set aside.

6. Cut up the ducks: Remove the leg and thigh sections from each duck. Cut along the breast bone of each duck, scraping the knife down against the side of the bone to free each breast in one piece. If using Long Island ducks, which are fatter than the mallards, remove the skin and underlying fat from each breast. Chop the carcasses into small pieces and set aside.

7. Marinate the duck breasts: Spoon about 3 tablespoons of the molasses

onto a large plate. Season the duck breasts with 1 teaspoon of the salt. Place flesh-side down in the molasses. Spoon the remaining molasses over the top and spread to cover the breasts. Let marinate in the molasses for at least 30 minutes at room temperature, turning several times.

8. Prepare the sauce: In a large heavy skillet, warm the oil over high heat until it is almost smoking. Add the duck legs and thighs and sauté, turning once, until well browned, about 3 minutes on each side. Add the carcass pieces, season with the remaining 2 teaspoons salt and the pepper and continue to cook, stirring occasionally, until well browned. Add the onion and carrot and sauté until the vegetables begin to brown, 3 to 5 minutes.

9. Drain the bones and vegetables in a colander to remove excess fat. Return the bones and vegetables to the skillet and add the garlic, apple and thyme. Pour in the vingear and boil over high heat, scraping up any browned bits from the bottom, for about 1 minute, to deglaze the pan. Add the wine and stock and return to a boil. Reduce the heat to moderate and cook until the sauce is reduced to 1 cup, about 25 minutes; occasionally skim off any fat that has risen to the surface.

10. Add the cream and simmer for 3 to 4 minutes, or until the sauce thickens slightly. Strain through a fine sieve into a small saucepan. Whisk in the mustard and season with salt and pepper to taste. Swirl in 2½ tablespoons of the butter. Keep the sauce warm over low heat.

11. Assemble the final dish: Preheat the broiler. Sprinkle each duck breast with ½ teaspoon of the coarsely ground pepper. Transfer the breasts to a broiler pan lined with aluminum foil. Broil 4 inches from the heat for about 2½ minutes on each side, or until medium-rare; the meat should remain pink in the center. Remove to a plate and cover with aluminum foil to keep warm.

12. In a medium skillet, melt the remaining 1½ tablespoons butter over moderately low heat. Add the sweet potato balls, snow peas and apples, keeping each separate. Cover and cook, shaking the pan to prevent sticking, until heated through, about 2 minutes.

13. Cut each duck breast crosswise on the diagonal into thin slices. Spoon about ¼ cup of the sauce onto each plate. Decoratively arrange the duck on top of the sauce. Alternate the apple balls and sweet potato balls in a ring around each serving of duck. Place the snow peas down the center of the duck slices.

NOTE: You can make a brown duck stock, like a veal stock, by browning a duck carcass with some chopped onion, garlic, celery, carrots, tomato puree and white wine. Once browned, water, bay leaf and parsley are added and boiled until a rich stock is obtained.

Duck with Port and Rosemary Sauce

6 SERVINGS

3 ducks, about 5 pounds each
Salt and freshly ground pepper
1½ cups imported ruby port
6 sprigs of fresh rosemary or 1½
teaspoons dried
1 medium onion, thinly sliced
1 carrot, thinly sliced
Bouquet garni: 4 sprigs of parsley,
¼ teaspoon thyme and 1 bay leaf
tied in a double thickness of
cheesecloth
1½ teaspoons arrowroot dissolved
in 2 tablespoons cold water
2 tablespoons vegetable oil
Fresh sprigs of rosemary, for
garnish

1. Trim the neck skin off the duck and reserve it. Cut up each duck by removing the breast meat with skin in one piece from each side. Remove the legs with thighs attached. Cut away any large pieces of skin from the carcasses, reserving the skin and the carcasses; wrap the skin and bones separately and refrigerate.

2. Season the pieces of duck lightly with salt and pepper. Place in a large bowl and add the port and rosemary. Cover and let marinate at room temperature for at least 3 hours, or overnight in the refrigerator, turning occasionally.

3. Meanwhile, make a stock with the re-

served carcasses: Preheat the oven to 400°. With a large chef's knife or heavy cleaver, chop the bones into small pieces. Spread out on a baking sheet and roast in the oven, stirring once or twice, until browned, about 30 minutes.

4. Use the reserved pieces of duck skin to line the bottom of a large Dutch oven. Add the browned bones, the onion, carrot and bouquet garni. Cover and cook over low heat for 15 minutes, or until the fat begins to render and the vegetables to soften. Add 6 cups of water and simmer, partially covered, for 3 hours, skimming occasionally. Strain the stock and skim off the fat. Alternately, chill the stock for several hours and lift the congealed fat from the surface. (The recipe may be made a day ahead up to this point.)

5. In a large saucepan, boil the stock over high heat until reduced to 1 cup.

6. Meanwhile, remove the duck from the marinade; strain the marinade into a small saucepan. Boil, skimming once or twice if necessary, until reduced to ½ cup, about 20 minutes.

7. Preheat the oven to 400°. In a small saucepan, combine the reduced stock and marinade; bring to a boil. Whisk in the arrowroot mixture and return to a boil, whisking until thickened and smooth. Remove the sauce from the heat. Season with salt and pepper to taste.

8. In a large, heavy skillet, heat the oil. Working in batches, sauté the duck breasts and legs over moderately high

heat, turning once, until browned on the outside to seal in the juices, for only 2 to 3 minutes.

9. Place the duck pieces, skin-side up, on a rack in a roasting pan and roast for 15 minutes. Remove the breasts from the pan and cover loosely to keep warm. Roast the legs and thighs for another 5 to 10 minutes, until medium-rare. Meanwhile, gently reheat the sauce.

10. Slice the breasts thinly and fan out, one on each of 6 warmed plates. Place a leg on each plate and spoon the sauce over the meat. Garnish with rosemary.

Skillet Roast Duck in Honey and Lime Sauce

3 SERVINGS

1 duck, 4½ to 5 pounds (see Note)
Salt and freshly ground pepper
2 tablespoons unsalted butter
1 teaspoon olive oil
2 medium onions, quartered
2 cups Brown Chicken Stock
(p. 204) or chicken broth
¼ cup honey mixed with ¼ cup
fresh orange juice
2 teaspoons arrowroot
3 tablespoons apricot preserves
3 tablespoons fresh lime juice
Sprigs of watercress, for garnish

1. Preheat the oven to 400°. Remove the neck and giblets from the duck and include them in the Brown Chicken Stock, if you are preparing it. Dry the duck thoroughly with paper towels. Season inside and out with salt and pepper and truss with string.

2. In a heavy 12-inch skillet (preferably cast iron) with an ovenproof handle, heat the butter and oil. Place the duck on its side in the hot fat and sauté over moderate heat until lightly browned, about 3 minutes. Turn the duck over and cook until the other side is nicely browned. Add the onions to the skillet and place in the oven.

3. Roast the duck on its side, uncovered, for 15 minutes. Carefully spoon most of the fat out of the skillet. Reduce the heat to 350°. Add ⅓ cup of the stock to the pan and continue roasting the duck, turning it once halfway through, for 2½ hours. Remove excess fat from the pan with a bulb baster and baste the duck with some of the stock every 15 minutes. During the last 30 minutes of cooking, baste the duck twice with the honey-orange juice mixture. The duck is done when the juices run clear and the meat in the thickest part of the thigh registers 170°. Transfer the duck to a baking sheet and keep it warm in the turned-off oven while you make the sauce.

4. Remove and discard the onions in the skillet. Degrease the pan juices. Add all but 1 tablespoon of the remaining stock to the skillet and boil until reduced to ¾ cup, about 5 minutes. Reduce the heat to low.

5. Stir the arrowroot into the reserved 1 tablespoon stock until smooth. Stir into the sauce, heat to simmering and cook until thickened. Whisk in the preserves and lime juice. Taste and correct the seasoning with salt and pepper.

6. Carve the duck and arrange on a large platter. Spoon the sauce over the duck and garnish with the watercress.

NOTE: If using a frozen duck, defrost it in the refrigerator. Then wrap it well in paper towels and let it remain in the refrigerator for 12 to 24 hours before using. This removes excess moisture and produces a crisp cooked duck.

Easy Cassoulet

4 TO 6 SERVINGS

1 cup dried navy beans, rinsed and picked over
½ pound salt pork
1 large onion, sliced
1 large bouquet garni: 6 sprigs of parsley, 1 tablespoon thyme, 3 whole cloves, 2 garlic cloves and 1 bay leaf tied in a double thickness of cheesecloth
2 cups coarsely chopped smoked duck (about ¾ pound)
1 apple, cored and cut into ½-inch cubes
¾ cup dry red wine
¼ cup Armagnac or other brandy
1 teaspoon salt
¼ teaspoon pepper

1 cup fresh bread crumbs
3 tablespoons finely chopped fresh parsley
3 tablespoons unsalted butter, melted

1. Bring 6 cups of water to a boil in a Dutch oven. Add the beans and cook for 1 minute. Remove from the heat and let stand, covered, for 1 hour.

2. Meanwhile, boil the salt pork in 4 cups of water for 20 minutes. Drain, reserving the cooking liquid. Skim off the fat and boil the liquid until it is reduced by half. Remove the rind from the salt pork and cut the pork into ¼-inch dice.

3. Add the onion and bouquet garni to the beans. Bring to a boil. Reduce the heat and simmer, partially covered, for 1 hour. Drain the beans; remove and discard the bouquet garni.

4. Preheat the oven to 400°. Return the beans to the pot. Add the duck, the reduced cooking liquid, the salt pork, apple, wine, Armagnac, salt and pepper. Sprinkle the bread crumbs and parsley over the top and drizzle with the butter. Bake uncovered for 20 minutes. Reduce the heat to 350° and bake uncovered for 1 hour more.

Boned Broiled Quail

Beverage Suggestion: Cabernet Sauvignon

6 SERVINGS

12 quail, backbone removed and birds deboned, leaving the wings intact (ask your butcher to do this if you wish)
⅓ cup Dijon-style mustard
3 tablespoons gin
1 tablespoon olive oil

1. Skewer a plain toothpick through the top of each bird to pin the wings to the breast meat; with another toothpick, skewer the two legs together.

2. Preheat the broiler. In a small bowl, stir the mustard, gin and olive oil until blended. Brush the quail all over with about one-third of the mixture. Place the birds, breast-side up, on a rack over a broiler pan.

3. Broil the quail 4 inches from the heat for 4 minutes, basting once with half of

the remaining mustard mixture. Using tongs, turn the birds over, brush with the remaining mustard mixture and broil for an additional 2 minutes, or until the breast meat is a light pink color. Remove the toothpicks before serving.

Panfried Squabs with Squab Liver Butter

F&W Beverage Suggestion: California Cabernet Sauvignon, such as Robert Mondavi

4 SERVINGS

Squabs:
4 squabs (about 12 ounces each), cleaned and split in half lengthwise, livers reserved
1 quart milk

Squab Liver Butter:
3 tablespoons unsalted butter, at room temperature
1 tablespoon minced shallot
⅛ teaspoon minced fresh rosemary
2 tablespoons Cognac or brandy
⅛ teaspoon salt
Pinch of freshly ground pepper

Cooking the Squabs:
8 small sprigs of fresh rosemary
5 tablespoons clarified butter
½ teaspoon salt
¼ teaspoon freshly ground pepper

1. Prepare the squabs: Place the halved squabs in a bowl and pour in the milk to cover. Cover and let stand at room temperature for 3 hours.

2. Meanwhile, make the squab liver butter: In a small skillet, melt 1 tablespoon of the butter over moderately high heat. Add the reserved squab livers, the shallot and rosemary and cook until the livers have lost all traces of pink, about 3 minutes. Add the Cognac and ignite, shaking the pan until the flames subside.

3. Pass the livers and any liquids in the pan through a fine sieve. Blend in the remaining 2 tablespoons butter and the salt and pepper. Cover and refrigerate until chilled but not firm, about 1 hour.

4. Cook the squabs: Remove the squabs from the milk and pat dry with paper towels; discard the milk.

5. Use your finger to gently separate the skin from the flesh of the breast without removing or tearing the skin. Stuff a small sprig of rosemary under the skin of each breast. Season with the salt and pepper.

6. In a 14-inch cast-iron skillet, warm the butter over moderately high heat. When hot enough to evaporate a droplet of water on contact, add 4 squab halves, skin-side down. Cook until golden brown on the bottom, 4 to 5 minutes; remove and set aside. Repeat with the remaining squabs.

7. Pull out and discard the rosemary sprigs. Return all the squabs to the skillet, skin-side up; reduce the heat to moderate, cover and cook until the juices from the thigh run clear when pierced, about 20 minutes. Serve 2 halves per plate, with a dollop of the squab liver butter on top of each half.

Pigeon with Foie Gras and Apples in Black Currant Sauce

2 SERVINGS

Apples:

1 tablespoon butter
1 red or yellow Delicious apple, peeled and sliced thin
2 tablespoons fresh lemon juice

Pigeons:

2 baby pigeons (squabs), 8 to 9 ounces each*
½ teaspoon salt
¼ teaspoon pepper
1 tablespoon peanut oil

Black Currant Sauce:

½ cup Brown Chicken Stock (p. 204)

2 tablespoons black currants in light syrup**
1 tablespoon crème de cassis or port (optional)
1½ tablespoons unsalted butter

Foie Gras:

2 to 3 ounces foie gras, sliced thin
½ teaspoon salt
¼ teaspoon freshly ground pepper

Garnish:

1 teaspoon pine nuts
*Available at specialty butcher shops
**Available at specialty food shops

1. Prepare the apples: In a medium skillet, melt the butter over moderate heat. Add the apple and lemon juice and cook, stirring gently, until the apples are just tender but still hold their shape, 3 to 4 minutes. Remove from the heat and set aside.

2. Prepare the pigeon: Preheat the oven to 400°. Using a small boning knife, cut along the center of each pigeon breast, scraping the knife down against one side of the breast bone to separate the meat from the bone in one piece. Repeat with the other side of each breast. (Save the rest of the carcass and use it the next time you make stock.)

3. Season the pigeon breasts with the salt and pepper. In a large ovenproof skillet, heat the oil over moderate heat. Add the breasts, skin-side down, and sauté, turning once, for 2 to 3 minutes on each side, until lightly browned. Place the skillet in the oven for 4 to 5 minutes, or until the meat is medium-rare (still pink in the center) and sizzling.

4. Remove the skillet from the oven and transfer the pigeon breasts to a cutting board. Thinly slice the meat against the grain and cover with aluminum foil to keep warm.

5. Make the sauce: Add the Brown Chicken Stock, currants, with their syrup, and cassis to the skillet and heat to boiling over moderate heat. Remove from the heat and whisk in the butter until just incorporated.

6. Prepare the foie gras: Gently reheat the apples over moderately low heat until warm while you prepare the foie gras. Season the foie gras with the salt and pepper. Place a small, heavy, ungreased skillet over moderate heat and add the foie gras. Let it sizzle, off heat, for about 15 seconds on each side, until it is heated through, browned on the outside and rare inside. Too much heat (or direct heat) will melt the foie gras.

7. Assemble the dish: Place the cooked apple slices on the side of each of two plates and arrange the foie gras on top of the apples, dividing the slices evenly. Arrange the slices of pigeon breast on each plate, fanning them out around the foie gras and apples. Spoon the currant sauce over the pigeon and garnish with the pine nuts.

Cornish Hens with Apricot Stuffing

F&W Beverage Suggestion: California Cabernet Sauvignon, such as Fetzer

4 SERVINGS

5 tablespoons unsalted butter
½ cup brown rice
1¾ cups chicken stock or canned broth
2½ teaspoons salt
1 large onion, chopped
1 teaspoon sugar
2 teaspoons minced garlic
¾ cup diced fresh apricots (about 3 medium)
½ cup chopped parsley
½ cup diced water chestnuts
½ teaspoon curry powder
½ plus ⅛ teaspoon freshly ground pepper
4 Cornish game hens, about 1 pound each
1 tablespoon olive oil

1. In a medium saucepan, melt 2 tablespoons of the butter over moderately low heat. Add the rice and cook, stirring once or twice, for 5 minutes. Add the chicken stock and ½ teaspoon of the salt. Bring to a boil, cover and simmer over moderately low heat until the rice has absorbed the stock, about 30 minutes. Transfer to a bowl.

2. Meanwhile, melt the remaining 3 tablespoons butter in a medium skillet over moderately low heat. Add the onion and sugar and cook, stirring occasionally, until the onion is golden, about 10 minutes. Add the garlic and cook for 1 minute longer. Add to the bowl of rice.

3. Add the apricots, parsley, water chestnuts, curry powder and ⅛ teaspoon of the pepper and mix thoroughly.

4. Preheat the oven to 450°. Rub the hens inside and out with the olive oil; season with the remaining 2 teaspoons salt and ½ teaspoon pepper. Loosely fill the cavities of the hens with the stuffing; sew or skewer closed. Place the stuffed hens, breast-side up, on a rack in a roasting pan and roast for 20 minutes. Reduce the heat to 350° and cook for another 30 to 40 minutes, or until the juices run clear when the thigh joint is pierced with a fork. Remove the hens from the roasting pan and let rest 10 minutes before serving.

Egyptian Stuffed Game Hens

In Egypt, this traditional recipe is made with squab or baby chickens, but we recommend game hens because they are readily available in this country.

4 SERVINGS

Hens:

2 medium onions, grated
½ cup fresh lemon juice
2 teaspoons salt
4 Cornish game hens (1 to 1¼ pounds each), livers reserved

Stuffing:

4 tablespoons unsalted butter
1 small onion, finely chopped
Reserved livers from hens, chopped
½ cup finely chopped walnuts

2 cups *fireek* (Egyptian cracked wheat) or bulgur wheat*
2 tablespoons dried mint
Salt and freshly ground pepper
1½ cups chicken stock or broth
2 tablespoons olive oil
*Available at Middle Eastern groceries and health food stores

1. Prepare the hens: In a large bowl, combine the onions, lemon juice and salt. Rinse the hens inside and out and pat them dry. Place them in the onion marinade and turn to coat well all over. Cover and let marinate at room temperature, turning the hens every 20 minutes, for 2 hours (or up to 4 hours in the refrigerator; let return to room temperature before grilling).

2. Make the stuffing: In a medium skillet, melt the butter over moderate heat. Add the onion, livers and walnuts and cook, stirring frequently, until the onion is lightly browned, 5 to 7 minutes. Add the bulgur, mint and salt and pepper to taste; cook, stirring, for 3 minutes. Add the broth, bring to a boil, reduce the heat and simmer, stirring often, for 5 minutes. Remove from the heat and let cool for 5 minutes.

3. Remove the hens from the marinade, scraping any excess marinade back into the bowl; reserve the marinade. Loosely fill the hens with stuffing. (Reserve extra stuffing to reheat and serve as a side dish.) Truss the hens, closing the body cavity securely.

4. Light the charcoal. Rub the hens all over with the oil. Place them breast-side up on the grill 4 to 6 inches above hot coals and cook for 5 minutes. Turn onto one side and grill for 5 minutes; turn onto the other side and grill for another 5 minutes. Turn the hens breast-side down and grill for 5 minutes longer. Baste with the reserved marinade. Repeat the entire procedure, basting with the marinade each time you turn the birds, about 3 more times, until they are cooked through and the thigh juices run clear, a total of 1 to 1½ hours, depending on whether you are using a covered-kettle or open grill.

NOTE: The birds may also be cooked in a 375° oven, turning and basting as described above, for 1 hour to 1 hour 15 minutes.

Chicken Quenelles with Mushroom Duxelles

F&W Beverage Suggestion: Vouvray Sec or California Dry Chenin Blanc

8 SERVINGS

4 tablespoons unsalted butter
¼ cup minced shallots
2 cups (6 ounces) finely chopped mushrooms
¼ cup all-purpose flour
½ cup chicken stock or canned broth
1 pound skinless, boneless chicken breast, cut into 1-inch pieces and chilled
¾ teaspoon salt
Pinch of white pepper
Pinch of cayenne pepper
5 egg whites, chilled
1 cup heavy cream, chilled
Beurre Blanc (p. 209)

1. In a medium skillet, melt 2 tablespoons of the butter over moderate heat. Add the shallots and mushrooms and sauté, stirring, until the mushrooms have given up their juice and are reduced in volume by half, about 5 minutes. Set aside the mushroom duxelles.

2. In a medium saucepan over moderately low heat, melt the remaining 2 tablespoons butter. Add the flour and cook, stirring, for 5 minutes without browning to make a roux. Whisk in the stock, bring to a boil and cook, stirring, until thickened and smooth, about 1 minute. Remove the thickened flour base from the heat and let cool to room temperature.

3. In a food processor, grind the chicken to a smooth paste, 3 to 4 minutes. Scrape down the sides of the bowl and add the salt, white pepper and cayenne. Mix to blend well, about 30 seconds. Add the cooled flour base and mix until well blended, about 30 seconds.

4. Scrape the mixture into a large bowl set over ice. With a wooden spoon, beat in the egg whites, one at a time. Gradually beat in the heavy cream, about 1 tablespoon at a time. Continue to beat over ice for 1 to 2 minutes to lighten the mixture. Cover and refrigerate for at least 15 minutes to chill well. (The recipe may be prepared ahead to this point and refrigerated overnight.)

5. Spread 4 sheets of parchment paper (12 by 9 inches) on a flat surface. Spoon one-quarter of the chicken mixture (about 1 cup) in a 6-by-2-inch strip down the middle of one sheet of parchment. Make a deep groove down the center of the chicken and neatly fill with one-quarter (about ¼ cup) of the duxelles. With a rubber spatula, gently lift the long edges of the chicken mixture up and over the filling to completely enclose it and form a filled roll. Wrap the roll in the parchment paper by folding over the two long sides and pinching and tying the two short ends with string to form a sausage shape. Do not wrap too tightly; allow some room for expansion as the mixture cooks. Repeat to form 3 more rolls with the remaining ingredients.

6. Fill a large deep skillet with 3 inches of water; bring to a simmer. Gently lower the rolls into the simmering water and poach, turning after 10 minutes, for about 20 minutes, or until firm.

7. Remove the rolls, unwrap and drain on paper towels. Slice each roll crosswise on the diagonal into 10 slices. Arrange 5 overlapping slices on each plate and coat lightly with Beurre Blanc.

Palmiers of Chicken with Oranges and Leeks

Inspired by the classic *palmiers,* which are small Parisian cookies made with puff pastry, our version uses chicken breasts and orange segments. It makes an elegant first course or appetizer.

6 SERVINGS

5 tablespoons olive oil, or 2 tablespoons olive oil and 3 tablespoons walnut oil
1½ cups chopped leeks (white portions only)
2½ tablespoons Chinese salted black beans*, rinsed and coarsely chopped
3 whole chicken breasts (about 3 pounds), skinned and boned to yield 1½ pounds meat
2 navel oranges, peeled and segmented
Orange segments, watercress leaves and chutney, for garnish
*Available at Oriental groceries

1. Heat 3 tablespoons of the olive oil (or 2 tablespoons olive oil and 1 tablespoon walnut oil) in a skillet. Add the leeks, and sauté for 1 minute over moderate heat. Add the beans and sauté until the leeks are soft, 2 to 3 minutes.

2. Split the chicken breasts in half and, between sheets of waxed paper, pound them until they are about ¼ inch thick (or slightly less) and oval-shaped; carefully peel off the waxed paper. Brush one side of each fillet with some of the remaining oil and then spread it with about ¼ cup of the leek mixture, leaving a ¼-inch border all around. Place an orange segment near each end of each chicken oval and turn the ends of the chicken over the oranges to meet in the center. Then fold the chicken in half to enclose the oranges. Tie the roll closed at each end with string and place in a steamer. Cover and steam the palmiers 10 minutes.

3. Cool the palmiers to room temperature, cover and then chill. Just before serving, remove the string and cut them crosswise into ½-inch-thick slices. Serve cold or at room temperature garnished with the orange segments, watercress leaves and chutney.

Stir-Fried Chicken with Shiitake Mushrooms and Jicama

4 SERVINGS

2 pounds chicken breasts, skinned and boned to yield 1 pound meat
1 tablespoon cornstarch
1 tablespoon sake or dry sherry
½ teaspoon sugar
2½ tablespoons peanut oil
2 ounces cooked ham, cut into 1-by-⅛-inch julienne strips
1 teaspoon minced fresh gingerroot
1 garlic clove, minced
¼ pound well-rinsed, fresh shiitake mushrooms* or 12 dried (see Note), cut into ⅛-inch slivers
3 tablespoons chicken broth or water
1 cup julienne (⅛ by 1 inch) of jicama*
1 tablespoon Chinese oyster sauce*
1 tablespoon Chinese mushroom soy, light soy or imported Japanese soy sauce
1 teaspoon Oriental sesame oil
⅓ cup thinly sliced scallions
*Available at specialty food stores or Oriental groceries

1. Prepare the chicken: Trim away and discard any fat and tendons from the chicken breasts, wrap and partially freeze to facilitate slicing; the chicken should be firm but not frozen solid. Then, cut the chicken on the bias into thin slices. Toss them in a bowl with the cornstarch, sake and sugar. Marinate at room temperature for 20 minutes.

2. In a wok or large heavy skillet, warm 2 tablespoons of the oil over moderately high heat. Add the ham and stir-fry until it begins to curl, 1½ to 2 minutes. Add the chicken and any remaining marinade and stir-fry until the chicken turns opaque, 2 to 3 minutes. Remove the ham and chicken from the wok and reserve.

3. Add the remaining peanut oil to the wok along with the ginger and garlic; stir-fry for 15 seconds. Stir in the mushrooms and the broth. Reduce the heat to low, cover and cook until the mushrooms wilt, 2 to 3 minutes. Uncover, add the jicama and cook, stirring, for 30 seconds.

4. Raise the heat to moderately high and stir in the reserved chicken and ham. Add the oyster sauce, soy, sesame oil and scallions. Stir for 30 seconds and serve.

NOTE: If using dried shiitake mushrooms, first soak them in warm water for 30 minutes; then drain and squeeze out excess water.

Chicken Pot Pies

A good addition to a cook's chicken repertoire is this version of an American classic. In most pot-pie recipes, the chicken is cooked twice: It is usually boiled before making the pie filling and then baked within the pie. We have found this double-cooking unnecessary; when uncooked chicken is added to the filling, the result is meat that is tender as well as tasty. To make the recipe, you will need eight 5-inch tart pans.

8 SERVINGS

Pastry:
4 cups all-purpose flour
1 teaspoon salt
6 tablespoons lard, chilled
8 tablespoons (1 stick) unsalted
  butter, chilled and cut into
  pieces
8 tablespoons vegetable shortening
10 to 12 tablespoons ice water

Chicken Filling:
2 pounds chicken breasts, skinned
  and boned to yield 1 pound meat
3 cups chicken stock
2 medium carrots, cut into ⅛-inch
  slices (about 1 cup)
1 medium boiling potato, cut into
  ⅜-inch dice (about 1 cup)
1 cup peas
1 small to medium white turnip,
  peeled and cut into ⅜-inch dice
  (about 1 cup)
7 tablespoons unsalted butter
1 medium onion, finely diced
  (about ¾ cup)
7 tablespoons all-purpose flour
½ cup dry sherry

Glaze: 1 egg

1. Prepare the pastry: In a large mixing bowl, combine the flour and salt. Using a pastry blender or two knives, cut in the lard, butter and vegetable shortening until the mixture resembles coarse meal.

2. Sprinkle 10 tablespoons of the ice water over the mixture and stir rapidly with a fork to blend. If the pastry will not gather into a ball, stir in up to 2 additional tablespoons. Do not overmix or the pastry will be tough. Divide the dough into two portions, flatten them and wrap separately in waxed paper. Chill for 30 minutes.

3. Meanwhile, prepare the chicken filling: Remove and discard any fat or tendons from the breast halves. Cut the halves lengthwise into thirds. Cut the strips across the grain into ½-inch pieces. Cover and refrigerate.

4. In a 3-quart saucepan, bring the chicken stock to a boil over high heat. Add the carrots and potato. When the boiling resumes, cook for 3 minutes. With a slotted spoon, transfer the vegetables to a large bowl; set aside. Return the broth to a boil, add the peas and turnip and cook for 3 minutes. Transfer the vegetables to the bowl with the carrots and potato. Measure the chicken stock; you should have 2 cups. If you have less, add broth or water; reserve.

5. In a medium, heavy skillet, melt the butter over moderate heat. Add the onion and sauté until translucent, about 5 minutes. Stir in the flour and cook, stirring for 2 minutes.

6. Combine the sherry with the reserved stock and add it all at once to the skillet. Stirring constantly with a wire whisk or a fork, cook the sauce over

moderate heat until it thickens, 3 to 4 minutes. Remove the skillet from the heat, cover the sauce with a round of waxed paper and cool it to room temperature (this can be done in the refrigerator if desired).

7. Prepare the pie pans: Have ready eight 5-inch tart pans. On a lightly floured surface and using a lightly floured rolling pin, roll out half the pastry to a ⅛-inch thickness. For each pie, you will need one 7-inch round to line the pan and one 6-inch round for the top crust. Cut out as many 7-inch rounds as possible and carefully fit them into the pie pans without stretching the dough. Stack the prepared pie pans, wrap them in foil and chill until needed. Gather the scraps and refrigerate them. Roll out the remaining half of the dough in the same manner and cut as many 6-inch rounds as possible. Stack these between sheets of waxed paper and refrigerate. Gather the scraps and combine them with the chilled scraps. Roll out the dough and cut as many 6- and 7-inch rounds as needed to complete the pies. Again gather the scraps, roll them ⅛ inch thick, place between sheets of waxed paper and chill.

8. Preheat the oven to 400°. Combine the chicken with the reserved vegetables, add the sauce and gently toss the mixture to blend the ingredients evenly. Remove the pastry-lined pie pans, the 6-inch pastry rounds and the rolled scraps from the refrigerator. Using the small end of a funnel or a ¼-inch cutter, cut a steam hole in the center of each 6-inch round. As optional garnish, use the reserved rolled-out scraps of pastry and a small petal-shaped cutter or a paring knife to cut out 72 petal shapes.

9. Assemble the pies: In a small bowl, beat the egg with 1 tablespoon cold water. Using a small pastry brush, paint a ½-inch circle of the egg wash around each steam hole; attach nine petals around each hole to form a flower.

10. Place about ¾ cup of the chicken filling in each prepared pie pan. Working with one pie at a time, moisten the top surface of the pastry in the pans all around. Then center a 6-inch round of pastry over the top and press the seam together to seal in the filling. Tuck the excess pastry under all around and crimp to make a fluted edge.

11. Brush the top of each pie with some of the remaining egg wash and place on a heavy cookie sheet. Bake for about 40 minutes, or until the crust is crisp and golden brown. Serve hot accompanied with a tossed green salad if desired.

Cold-Hot Chicken Legs

F&W Beverage Suggestion:
Rosé of Cabernet Sauvignon, such as Firestone

6 SERVINGS

8 tablespoons (1 stick) unsalted butter
2 tablespoons olive oil
12 chicken drumsticks
6 tablespoons hot Dijon-style mustard
3 canned hot green chiles, about 2 inches long
3 tablespoons fresh lime juice
2 teaspoons ground cumin
4 cups fresh bread crumbs
Yogurt Sauce (p. 210)

1. In a large skillet, melt 4 tablespoons of the butter in the oil over moderately high heat. Add the drumsticks and sauté, turning, until browned on all sides, about 5 minutes. Remove from the pan; reserve the fat.

2. In a blender or food processor, combine the mustard, chiles, lime juice and cumin. Mix until smooth. With the machine on, slowly drizzle in enough of the reserved fat until the mixture is the consistency of mayonnaise.

3. Paint the drumsticks with the mustard mixture and let stand at room temperature for at least 2 hours.

4. Preheat the oven to 350°. Roll the drumsticks in the bread crumbs to coat all over. Place on a rack in a baking pan. Bake for 15 minutes.

5. Meanwhile, melt the remaining 4 tablespoons butter. Drizzle over the drumsticks. Bake for another 15 minutes. Remove from the oven and let cool. Serve at room temperature or refrigerate and serve cold. Serve with the Yogurt Sauce.

Chicken Roasted with Rosemary and Carrots

Beverage Suggestion:
Pinot Noir, such as Robert Mondavi

4 SERVINGS

2 tablespoons unsalted butter
3-pound broiling chicken, at room temperature
1 teaspoon salt
½ teaspoon freshly ground pepper
5 sprigs of fresh rosemary or 2 teaspoons dried
10 medium carrots, peeled and cut diagonally into 3-inch lengths
Sprigs of fresh rosemary or parsley, for garnish

1. Preheat the oven to 400°. Grease a large ovenproof skillet or baking pan with 1 tablespoon of the butter.

2. Rub the chicken inside and out with the salt and pepper. Put the 5 sprigs of rosemary into the cavity. Close the neck and lower cavities with small skewers. Tuck the wings behind the body.

3. Place the chicken, breast-side down, in the pan. Arrange the carrots around the chicken and dot them with the remaining 1 tablespoon butter.

4. Bake for 15 minutes. Turn the chicken breast-side up. Turn the carrots. Return to the oven and bake until the juices of the thigh run clear when the meat is pierced with a knife, 30 to 45 minutes longer.

5. Remove the chicken from the pan and let rest for 5 minutes. Remove the skewers and cut the chicken into quarters. Discard the rosemary from the cavity. Arrange the chicken and the carrots on warmed plates. Spoon the pan juices over the chicken. Garnish with sprigs of rosemary.

Aromatic Roast Chicken

The stuffing for this roast chicken has been placed under the skin rather than in the cavity, which makes for more succulent breast meat and shortens the cooking time.

F&W Beverage Suggestion:
Red Rioja

6 TO 8 SERVINGS

1 chicken, about 5 pounds
2 teaspoons salt
¾ teaspoon pepper
1 cup dry bread crumbs
½ teaspoon grated lemon zest
2 tablespoons minced fresh parsley
1 large garlic clove, minced
2 tablespoons olive oil
1 lemon, cut in half
3 tablespoons unsalted butter, melted

1. Preheat the oven to 450°. Rinse the chicken under cold running water and pat it dry with paper towels.

2. Place the chicken, breast-side up, on a work surface. Using your fingers and working from the cavity toward the neck, carefully loosen the skin covering the breast to make a pocket. Rub the interior and exterior of the chicken with 1½ teaspoons of the salt and ½ teaspoon of the pepper.

3. In a small bowl, combine the bread crumbs with the lemon zest, parsley, garlic and remaining salt and pepper. Stir in the olive oil. Using your fingers, insert this stuffing under the skin of the entire breast. Place the lemon halves in the cavity of the chicken and truss the bird.

4. Place the chicken, breast-side up, on a rack in a shallow roasting pan and brush it with 1 tablespoon of the melted butter. Roast for 10 minutes. Reduce the temperature to 375° and turn the chicken on its side. Baste with ½ tablespoon more of the butter, roast for another 20 minutes, turn it on its other side and baste with another ½ tablespoon butter. Cook another 20 minutes, turn the chicken breast-side down, baste with another ½ tablespoon butter and cook another 20 minutes. Turn the chicken breast-side up, baste with the remaining butter and cook a final 30 minutes, or until the juices run clear when the thigh is pierced with a fork or a meat thermometer inserted into the thickest part of a thigh registers 165°.

5. Reserving the pan juices, transfer the chicken to a serving platter and allow it to rest for 10 to 15 minutes. In the meantime, pour the pan juices into a small bowl and allow the fat to rise to the top. Skim or pour off most of the fat. Carve the bird and serve with the degreased pan juices.

Caraway Chickens with Light Gravy

Savory and succulent, these buttery roast chickens taste of the caraway seeds that are tucked under their skins before roasting. The seeds enhance the light, flavorful gravy, too. Make the caraway butter several hours or even a day ahead of time so it can chill before you prepare the chickens.

12 SERVINGS

1 tablespoon plus 2 teaspoons whole caraway seeds
½ cup (1 stick) unsalted butter, at room temperature
2 large roasting chickens (about 6 pounds each)
About 1 cup chicken stock, canned broth or water
3 tablespoons all-purpose flour
¼ cup dry white wine
Salt and freshly ground pepper

1. Place 1 tablespoon of the caraway seeds in a mortar, spice grinder or blender and pulverize. In a small bowl, beat the butter until fluffy. Stir the caraway powder into the butter to blend. On a square of aluminum foil, form the caraway butter into a log about the size of a stick of butter. Wrap tightly, twisting the ends of the foil, and refrigerate until solid, at least 1 hour.

2. Preheat the oven to 350°. Place the chickens, breast-side up, on a work surface. Beginning near the main cavity, carefully slip your fingers between the skin and breast meat and gently work apart to separate almost to the neck area of each bird; be careful not to tear the skin. Cut three-quarters of the chilled caraway butter into thin slices and, divid-

ing equally, slide it under the skin of each breast half. Toss 1 teaspoon of the remaining 2 teaspoons whole caraway seeds into the cavity of each chicken. Truss the chickens with string and place them breast-side up on a rack in a large shallow roasting pan.

3. Melt the remaining caraway butter in a small saucepan over low heat. Lightly brush the chickens with half of the melted caraway butter.

4. Roast the chickens in the center of the oven for 30 minutes. Brush with the remaining caraway butter and continue to roast, basting with the pan drippings every 20 minutes, for about 1½ hours longer, or until the internal temperature reaches 165° to 170°. Transfer to a large platter to rest for 10 minutes while the juices settle.

5. Meanwhile, pour the drippings from the roasting pan into a heatproof bowl or large measuring cup. Carefully pour the juices from the cavities of the birds and any that have accumulated on the platter into the bowl. Spoon 3 tablespoons of fat from the surface of the drippings into a medium, noncorrodible skillet; skim off and discard any remaining fat. There will be about 1 cup of juice remaining. Add enough stock or water to make a total of 2 cups; reserve.

6. Add the flour to the chicken fat in the skillet and stir over moderate heat until bubbling; cook for 2 minutes without coloring to make a roux. Pour in the reserved chicken juices and the wine. Whisk constantly over moderate heat until the gravy boils and thickens slightly. Simmer, stirring constantly, for 3 minutes; remove from the heat. Season with salt and pepper to taste.

7. To serve, carve the chickens; arrange on a platter and accompany with the hot gravy.

Mustard Chicken

Although this chicken dish is delicious served hot, it is even better at room temperature and can be eaten cold. If made the day before, the flavors will develop and the chicken can be reheated. Salt-free bread is available at most health food stores. Use commercially available salt-free mustard or make the Low-Sodium Mustard a day or two ahead.

🍷 **F&W Beverage Suggestion:**
Pouilly-Fumé, such as Ladoucette, or California Fumé Blanc, such as Chateau St. Jean

4 SERVINGS

1 chicken (about 3 pounds), cut into 8 serving pieces
½ cup commercially prepared or homemade Low-Sodium Mustard (p. 218)
2 eggs, lightly beaten
2½ cups fresh salt-free bread crumbs
1 tablespoon paprika
1 teaspoon tarragon
1 teaspoon freshly ground pepper
3 tablespoons unsalted butter
3 tablespoons olive oil
⅓ cup fresh lemon juice

1. Make a slit at the main joint of each wing and remove the skin from the larger portion of the wing. Remove and discard the skin from the remaining chicken pieces. In a large bowl, toss the chicken with the mustard to coat. Cover and marinate at room temperature, tossing occasionally, for 30 minutes.

2. Preheat the oven to 375°. Place the eggs in a shallow bowl. In a pie pan or shallow dish, combine the bread crumbs with the paprika, tarragon and pepper.

3. One at a time, dip the mustard-coated chicken pieces into the egg and then roll in the crumb mixture to coat evenly; place in a shallow baking dish large enough to hold the chicken in a single layer.

4. In a small saucepan, melt the butter in the olive oil over low heat. Remove from the heat and stir in the lemon juice. Spoon half of the lemon butter over the chicken pieces. Bake for 30 minutes. Spoon the remaining lemon butter over the chicken and bake for about 30 minutes longer, until the chicken is cooked through and the juices run clear when the thickest part of a thigh is pierced with a fork. Let rest for at least 15 minutes before serving.

Chicken Cutlets in Tarragon Crumbs with Lime Juice

6 SERVINGS

**3 whole chicken breasts (about 3
  pounds), skinned and boned to
  yield 1½ pounds
2 eggs
1½ cups dry bread crumbs
1 tablespoon tarragon
1 teaspoon salt
½ teaspoon pepper
4 tablespoons olive oil
4 tablespoons unsalted butter
2 limes, cut into wedges**

1. Split the chicken breasts in half lengthwise. Remove and discard any tendons fat and gristle. Have ready twelve 12-inch squares of waxed paper. Place each of the 6 half-breasts between sheets of waxed paper. Using a mallet or meat pounder, work each into a thin fillet about 6 by 8 inches. Carefully peel off the waxed paper.

2. In a shallow bowl or pie plate, beat the eggs. In another shallow bowl or pie plate, combine the bread crumbs, tarragon, salt and pepper.

3. Dip each cutlet first in egg and then in the crumbs, tapping the meat on each side so that the crumbs adhere. Place them on a wire rack and refrigerate, uncovered, for 1 hour.

4. In a large heavy skillet, warm the oil over moderate heat; stir in the butter until melted. Increase the heat to moderately high. When the fat is almost smoking, add 2 or 3 of the cutlets, depending on the size of the skillet, and sauté them for about 1 minute on each side, or until they are crisp and golden brown. Do not overcook. Drain on paper towels, and sauté the remaining cutlets in the same manner. Serve hot with the wedges of lime, to be squeezed over the cutlets.

Spontaneous Chicken in Mustard Sauce

4 SERVINGS

**4 tablespoons unsalted butter
1 tablespoon vegetable oil
4 Spontaneous Chicken Cutlets
  (recipe follows)
1 bunch of scallions (white part
  and about 2 inches of the green),
  thinly sliced (about 1 cup)
1 cup heavy cream
½ cup dry white wine
2 teaspoons mustard seed
1 tablespoon strong, Dijon-style
  mustard
Salt and pepper**

1. In a large skillet set over moderate heat, melt the butter with the oil until foamy. Working in batches, as necessary, sauté the chicken cutlets for 1 minute on each side (the chicken will finish cooking in the sauce). Remove from the skillet and set aside. Reserve the drippings in the skillet.

2. In the same skillet, stir-fry the scallions over moderate heat, until soft, about 2 minutes. Add the cream, wine and mustard seed and cook, stirring frequently, for 5 minutes.

3. Stir the mustard into the sauce; season with salt and pepper to taste. Return the four chicken cutlets to the skillet and turn to coat them with the sauce. Reduce the heat to low and simmer gently for 2 to 3 minutes, or until the chicken is just cooked through. Serve with the sauce spooned over the top.

Spontaneous Chicken Cutlets

A perfect solution to last-minute dinners. These thinly pounded chicken cutlets—which are individually wrapped and stacked neatly in the freezer—can be sautéed from the frozen state. With the addition of a simply made sauce and a side serving of rice or noodles, they make splendid entrées.

FOR 4 SERVINGS

2 whole chicken breasts, boned

1. Cut the chicken breasts in half lengthwise; remove the skin and trim off any excess fat.

2. Place each chicken-breast half between two sheets of waxed paper and pound to about a ¼-inch thickness. Carefully remove the paper and place the chicken cutlets on a cookie sheet, or any flat surface, and place in the freezer for 1 hour.

3. Wrap the cutlets very tightly in foil and stack them flat in the freezer until ready to use. They will keep well for up to 2 months.

Dilled Chicken and Vegetables in Pita Bread

MAKES 3 SANDWICHES

**3 tablespoons peanut oil
8 ounces skinless, boneless
  chicken breast, cut into ½-inch
  dice
½ medium onion, thinly sliced
1 celery rib, thinly sliced
1 small garlic clove, minced
8 medium mushrooms, quartered
3 tablespoons minced fresh dill
½ teaspoon lemon juice
4 drops of hot pepper sauce, or to
  taste
½ teaspoon salt
¼ teaspoon freshly ground pepper
1 medium tomato—peeled, seeded
  and coarsely chopped
3 pita bread rounds, warmed**

1. In a medium skillet, heat 1 tablespoon of the oil until almost smoking.

Add the chicken and toss over high heat to coat with oil; reduce the heat to moderate. Cook, stirring, until lightly browned, about 2 minutes. Remove the chicken to a medium bowl.

2. Add the onion to the skillet and sauté, stirring, over moderate heat until soft, about 3 minutes. Add the celery and garlic and cook for 30 seconds longer. Add to the chicken.

3. Add the remaining 2 tablespoons oil to the skillet and heat until almost smoking. Add the mushrooms and sauté over moderately high heat until well browned, about 3 minutes.

4. Add the mushrooms to the vegetables and chicken and toss with 2 tablespoons of the dill, the lemon juice, hot pepper sauce, salt and pepper.

5. In a separate bowl, toss the remaining 1 tablespoon dill with the chopped tomato and a pinch of salt.

6. To assemble, fill the pita breads with the chicken mixture, then top with the dilled tomato.

Chicken Teriyaki

4 SERVINGS

Marinade:

½ cup mirin (sweet rice wine)*
¾ cup sake
½ cup Japanese soy sauce
2 tablespoons shredded fresh
    gingerroot
1 medium garlic clove, minced
1 teaspoon sugar

Chicken:

12 chicken thighs (3 pounds),
    skinned and boned to yield 1½
    pounds
½ cup peanut oil
¼ cup cornstarch
¼ cup all-purpose flour

Teriyaki Sauce:

2 teaspoons cornstarch
*Available at Oriental groceries

1. Prepare the marinade: Combine all the marinade ingredients in the con-

tainer of a blender or food processor and blend for about 1 minute, or until the ginger and garlic are pulverized. Place a wire sieve over a bowl and strain the sauce through it, pushing on the solids with a wooden spoon to extract as much liquid as possible.

2. Prepare the chicken: Cut the chicken meat into pieces about ¾ by ¾ by 1 inch and soak them in the marinade for 10 minutes.

3. Preheat the broiler. In a large heavy skillet, warm the peanut oil over moderately high heat until almost smoking.

4. Meanwhile, combine the cornstarch and flour in a paper bag. Drain the chicken in a strainer or colander set over a bowl; reserve 1 cup of the marinade. Place the chicken pieces in the bag and shake to coat them. Place about half the pieces in the hot oil and fry them for 1 to 1½ minutes, or until crisp and golden on one side. Quickly turn them over with tongs and fry for 30 seconds more. Transfer the pieces to paper towels to drain and fry the remaining chicken in the same manner.

5. Prepare the teriyaki sauce: Place the reserved marinade in a small saucepan. Whisk in the 2 teaspoons of cornstarch, stirring until dissolved. Place the pan over moderate heat and, stirring constantly, cook the sauce until it is smooth and has thickened.

6. Broil and serve: Place the chicken pieces on a broiling pan. Drizzle the top of the chicken with about ⅓ cup of the teriyaki sauce. Broil 4 to 5 inches from the heat for 1 to 2 minutes, or until the sauce is bubbling. Serve with the remaining sauce and accompany with boiled rice and a salad, if desired.

Mediterranean Chicken with Lemons and Olives

4 SERVINGS

2 cups boiling water
1 pound green Greek or Italian
    olives
1 lemon, thinly sliced
2 teaspoons salt
½ cup all-purpose flour
1 teaspoon pepper
1 chicken (3½ pounds), cut into 10
    serving pieces
3 tablespoons olive oil
2 medium onions, finely chopped
    (about 1½ cups)
2 garlic cloves, chopped
1 tablespoon coriander seed,
    crushed
½ cup chopped fresh parsley
¼ teaspoon ground saffron
1½ cups chicken stock
2 tablespoons lemon juice

1. In a medium bowl, pour 1½ cups of boiling water over the olives and let them steep for 20 minutes. Drain, cover and set aside.

2. Place the lemon slices in a small bowl, sprinkle them with ½ teaspoon of the salt, pour ½ cup boiling water over them and let them steep for 2 to 3 minutes. Drain, cover and set aside.

3. In a paper bag, combine the flour with ½ teaspoon of the salt and ½ teaspoon of the pepper. Shake the chicken pieces in the bag of flour until lightly coated.

4. In a large noncorrodible skillet, warm the oil for a minute or two over moderate heat. Add the chicken, a few pieces at a time, and brown lightly on both sides. Remove the chicken pieces with a slotted spoon and set aside.

5. Add to the skillet the onions, garlic, coriander, parsley, saffron and the remaining salt and pepper. Sauté over low heat for 4 to 5 minutes. Return the chicken to the skillet, add the chicken stock and bring it to a boil over moderately high heat. Lower the heat, cover and simmer the chicken until the juices run clear when a thigh is pierced with a fork, 15 to 20 minutes.

6. Remove the skillet from the heat and stir in the reserved sliced lemon and olives. Blend in the lemon juice. Transfer to a serving dish and serve hot.

Chicken Fricassee with Cherries and Sherry Vinegar

8 SERVINGS

6 medium carrots, cut into 1½-inch lengths
5 small white turnips, peeled and quartered lengthwise
Salt
½ pound green beans, halved crosswise if long
8 chicken breast halves or 8 chicken legs with thighs, or a mixture of both (about 8 ounces each)
¼ cup all-purpose flour
¼ cup olive oil
Freshly ground pepper
1 shallot, minced
¾ cup sherry vinegar
¾ cup Brown Chicken Stock (p. 204)
1 tablespoon butter kneaded with 1½ tablespoons flour until smooth
1 jar (5 ounces) cherries preserved in sherry vinegar *(see Note), drained
1 teaspoon tarragon
2 tablespoons unsalted butter
***Available at specialty food stores**

1. With a small paring knife or vegetable peeler, carve the carrots and turnips into ovals about 1½ inches long and 1 inch in diameter. Put the two vegetables into separate small saucepans, add water to cover and ½ teaspoon salt to each and bring to a boil over moderate heat. Reduce the heat and simmer until just tender, allowing 5 to 10 minutes of cooking time for each. Drain thoroughly

2. Cook the beans in a small saucepan of boiling water with ½ teaspoon salt until tender but still slightly crunchy, 4 to 6 minutes. Rinse under cold running water and drain thoroughly; set aside.

3. Preheat the oven to 450°. If using chicken legs, separate the thighs and drumsticks. Lightly flour the chicken pieces. Heat the oil in a large, noncorrodible, ovenproof skillet. Add enough of the chicken to fit in a single layer, sprinkle with salt and pepper and sauté over high heat, turning often, until browned all over, about 5 minutes. Drain on paper towels. Repeat with the remaining chicken. When all the pieces are browned, return them to the skillet and place it in the oven. Bake, turning once or twice, for 20 to 25 minutes, or until the juices run clear when pierced with a fork. Transfer the chicken to a platter and cover with aluminum foil to keep warm.

4. Reheat the vegetables in a steamer or in the oven while you finish the sauce. Discard the fat from the skillet. Add the shallot and vinegar and bring to a boil over moderately high heat. Pour in the stock and whisk in enough of the kneaded butter, 1 or 2 teaspoons at a time, to thicken the sauce so it coats a spoon lightly. Lower the heat, add the cherries and tarragon and simmer for 2 to 3 minutes. Season with salt and pepper to taste. Remove from the heat and stir in the butter, in small pieces.

5. To serve, arrange some carrot and turnip ovals and a small serving of beans on each plate with the chicken. Spoon the sauce and cherries over the chicken.

NOTE: If cherries preserved in sherry vinegar are not available, substitute 1 can (17 ounces) dark, sweet, pitted cherries marinated in sherry vinegar to cover (about ¾ cup) for 12 to 24 hours. Drain before using.

Chicken Sauté with Raspberries and Garlic

Garlic with raspberries may seem an unlikely pairing, but braised until mellow, and laced together in a delicate sweet-sour sauce tinged with raspberry vinegar, they combine in a spectacular manner.

F&W Beverage Suggestion:
California Cabernet Sauvignon Rosé

2 SERVINGS

16 medium garlic cloves, peeled
1 tablespoon sugar
¼ cup plus 1 teaspoon Raspberry Vinegar (p. 218)
2 chicken breast halves, boned, with skin attached (about 12 ounces)
2 tablespoons plus 1 teaspoon cold unsalted butter
1 teaspoon vegetable oil
¼ teaspoon salt
¼ teaspoon freshly ground pepper
¼ cup fresh raspberries

1. In a small saucepan, combine the garlic cloves, sugar, 1 teaspoon of the vinegar and ½ cup of water. Bring to a boil over high heat. Reduce the heat to low and simmer, uncovered, until the sugar dissolves, about 3 minutes. Increase the heat to moderate, cover and cook until the garlic is tender enough to pierce with a fork, about 10 minutes.

2. Uncover the saucepan, increase the heat to high and cook until the liquid is reduced to a thick syrup and the garlic is caramelized, about 10 minutes.

3. Add the remaining ¼ cup vinegar and cook for 30 seconds to dissolve any sugar clinging to the pan. Set the sauce aside.

4. Cut each chicken breast half crosswise into 5 slices; leave the skin on. Pat dry.

5. In a large, heavy, noncorrodible skillet, melt 1 teaspoon of the butter in the oil over high heat until sizzling. Add the chicken pieces, skin-side down. Reduce the heat to moderate and sauté until the skin is well browned, about 3 minutes. Turn and cook until browned on the second side, about 3 minutes. Remove to a plate and cover loosely to keep warm. Pour off any fat in the pan.

6. Add the reserved sauce with garlic cloves to the skillet. Bring to a boil over high heat, scraping up any browned bits from the bottom of the pan. Continue to boil for 1 to 2 minutes, until the sauce is thick and syrupy. Remove from the heat. Season with the salt and pepper. Whisk in the remaining 2 tablespoons cold butter, 1 tablespoon at a time.

7. Return the chicken with any accumulated juices to the skillet. Toss gently to coat with the sauce. Add the raspberries and toss gently again. Serve hot.

Marinated Chicken Breasts Alexandre

Here is a unique chicken-based hors d'oeuvre, excellent for stimulating the appetite.

Beverage Suggestion:
Beaujolais Nouveau

4 TO 6 SERVINGS

2 pounds veal bones
3 cups chicken stock or canned broth
4 skinless, boneless chicken breast halves (about 1 pound)
2 tablespoons sherry wine vinegar
2 tablespoons white wine vinegar
¼ cup olive oil
2 tablespoons corn or peanut oil
2 teaspoons Dijon-style mustard
1 tablespoon fresh lemon juice
1 teaspoon Cognac or brandy
2 whole cloves
1 medium shallot, finely minced
2 tablespoons minced fresh chives
2 tablespoons minced fresh tarragon or 2 teaspoons dried
Salt and freshly ground pepper
1 cup green beans, cut into 2-inch lengths, for garnish
1 large ripe tomato, quartered and seeded, for garnish
12 very thin slices black truffle (optional)

1. In a large saucepan, simmer the veal bones, 1 cup of the chicken stock and water to cover for 1 hour, skimming the foam from the top occasionally. Strain and skim off the fat. Measure out 1 cup of the stock to use in the marinade in Step 3; reserve the remainder for another use.

2. In a large deep skillet or heatproof casserole, arrange the chicken breasts in a single layer. Add the remaining 2 cups chicken stock and enough water, if necessary, just to cover. Heat to a bare simmer, cover and poach gently until the breasts are barely pink in the center, 8 to 10 minutes. Remove, drain and pat dry.

3. Meanwhile, make the marinade: In a small bowl, whisk the reserved 1 cup of stock, the sherry wine vinegar, white wine, olive oil, corn oil, mustard, lemon juice and Cognac until blended. Stir in the cloves, shallot, chives and tarragon. Season with salt and pepper to taste.

4. With a very sharp knife, cut each chicken breast horizontally into 3 thin slices. Arrange the slices in a single layer in a large noncorrodible pan or baking dish. Pour the marinade over the chicken; turn to coat both sides. Marinate, turning the slices every 30 minutes, for at least 1 and up to 3 hours.

5. Serve the chicken at room temperature, sauced with a little of the marinade. Garnish each plate with some green beans and a tomato quarter, dressed with the marinade. Decorate each piece of chicken with a truffle slice, if desired.

Chicken Breasts with Orange-Almond Sauce

F&W Beverage Suggestion:
California Chardonnay, such as Sebastiani

4 TO 6 SERVINGS

6 skinless, boneless chicken breast halves, trimmed of fat and sinew, at room temperature
2 large oranges
1 egg yolk
1 tablespoon plus 1 teaspoon white wine vinegar
½ teaspoon Dijon-style mustard
½ teaspoon salt
Pinch of sugar
Pinch of white pepper
1¼ cups safflower oil
2 or 3 small zucchini, sliced into ¼-inch rounds and blanched for 30 seconds
2 or 3 small yellow squash, sliced into ¼-inch rounds and blanched for 30 seconds
⅓ cup toasted slivered almonds, coarsely chopped
2 tablespoons finely chopped parsley

1. Lightly pound the thicker end of the chicken breasts to allow more even cooking.

2. In a pan that will hold the breasts comfortably in a single layer, bring enough water to cover them by about ½ inch to 140°.

3. Add the chicken breasts. Poach for 20 to 25 minutes, until the flesh is springy to the touch and the internal temperature is 140°. (If unsure, remove a breast, cut a small slit in the thickest end on the underside and check to see that the flesh has lost its translucency and has just the barest hint of pink color.)

4. Remove the breasts to a platter, cover loosely and let cool to room temperature. Then slice and serve or wrap well and refrigerate overnight.

5. Grate the zest from the oranges; there will be about 1½ tablespoons. Squeeze ¼ cup juice. In a medium bowl, whisk together 1 tablespoon of the zest, the egg yolk, orange juice, vinegar, mustard, salt, sugar and pepper.

6. Gradually whisk in the oil, beginning with a few drops at a time; when the sauce thickens and becomes emulsified, whisk in the remaining oil in a thin stream. Cover and refrigerate the sauce overnight or until ready to use.

7. To serve, cut each chicken breast crosswise on the diagonal into 5 or 6 slices. Fan them out on the platter and sprinkle with salt.

8. In separate small bowls, toss the zucchini and squash slices in 1 to 2 table-spoons each of the sauce to coat. Taste and add salt and pepper if needed. Arrange alternating green and yellow slices in rows around the chicken.

9. Spoon some sauce down the length of each chicken breast. Toss together the almonds, parsley and remaining orange zest and sprinkle over the sauce. Serve the remaining sauce on the side.

Poached Breast of Chicken with Autumn Vegetables

🍷 **F&W Beverage Suggestion:**
Côtes-du-Rhône

4 SERVINGS

2 whole chicken breasts (about ¾ pound each)
4 small red potatoes (about 2 inches in diameter), peeled
4 medium carrots, peeled and quartered lengthwise
4 small turnips, peeled and halved
4 small white onions (about 1 inch in diameter), peeled
4 medium celery ribs, cut into 3-inch lengths
Bouquet garni: 6 sprigs of parsley, ½ teaspoon thyme, 4 peppercorns and 1 bay leaf tied in a double thickness of cheesecloth
½ teaspoon salt

1. Place the chicken breasts in a large deep pot. Add enough water to cover by 1 inch. Bring to a boil over moderate heat; skim off the foam.

2. Add the potatoes, carrots, turnips, onions, celery, bouquet garni and salt; return to a boil. Reduce the heat to moderately low, cover the pot and simmer until the chicken is no longer pink and the vegetables are tender, about 25 minutes.

3. Remove the chicken with a slotted spoon. Peel off the skin and pull the meat from the bone in one piece. Cut the chicken into thin slices. Arrange on a large platter and surround with the vegetables.

Chicken Breasts with Lime

🍷 **F&W Beverage Suggestion:**
A chilled Provençal rosé, such as Domaines Ott

4 SERVINGS

4 large skinless, boneless chicken breast halves (about 6 ounces each)
¼ cup clarified butter
2 shallots, minced
¾ cup chicken stock or broth
⅔ cup crème fraîche
3 tablespoons fresh lime juice
Salt and pepper
4 tablespoons cold, unsalted butter
2 limes, thinly sliced, for garnish

1. Trim off all excess fat and remove the tendons from each chicken breast.

2. In a large noncorrodible skillet, heat the clarified butter. Add the chicken breasts and sauté over moderate heat, turning once, until cooked through, firm and springy to the touch and light golden in color, 8 to 10 minutes. Transfer the chicken to a warm plate and cover to keep warm.

3. Add the shallots to the skillet. Cook over moderately low heat until softened but not browned, about 1 minute. Add the chicken stock, increase the heat to high and boil until reduced to ¼ cup. Add the crème fraîche and continue to boil gently until reduced by half, about 5 minutes. Add the lime juice. Season with

salt and pepper to taste. Remove from the heat and whisk in the cold butter, 1 tablespoon at a time.

4. Cut each chicken breast crosswise on the diagonal into 5 or 6 slices. Arrange the chicken slices on 4 warm plates, coat lightly with the sauce and garnish each plate with several slices of lime.

Chicken Breasts Avgolemono

🍷 **F&W Beverage Suggestion:**
Chilled Soave

8 SERVINGS

16 small skinless, boneless chicken breast halves (about 4 ounces each)
½ teaspoon salt
2 to 3 tablespoons unsalted butter
4 cups chicken stock or broth
Avgolemono Sauce (recipe follows)
Fresh mint leaves, for garnish

1. Trim and discard any fat from the chicken breasts; pat dry and sprinkle with the salt.

2. In a large heavy skillet, melt 2 tablespoons of the butter over moderately high heat. When the foam subsides add as many breasts as fit in a single layer and sauté for 2 minutes on each side, until very lightly browned. Repeat with the remaining chicken, adding more butter as necessary. As they are sautéed, transfer the chicken breasts to a Dutch oven.

3. Pour 1 cup of the stock into the skillet and bring to a boil, scraping up the brown bits that cling to the bottom of the pan. Pour the mixture into the Dutch oven and add the remaining 3 cups stock. Bring to a boil over high heat, reduce the heat to low and simmer, covered, until the meat is springy to the touch, 8 to 10 minutes. If not serving immediately, remove from the heat and keep the chicken moist in the stock.

4. To serve warm, arrange the chicken breasts on a warmed platter and spoon some of the Avgolemono Sauce over the center of each breast. Pass the remaining sauce separately. If you want to serve the dish cold, refrigerate the chicken in the stock until chilled. Arrange on a platter and coat with chilled or slightly warmed sauce and garnish the platter with mint leaves.

Avgolemono Sauce

MAKES ABOUT 2½ CUPS

6 egg yolks, at room temperature
1 tablespoon plus 1 teaspoon all-purpose flour
2 cups chicken stock or broth
¼ cup fresh lemon juice
Salt and white pepper

In a double boiler, whisk the yolks until blended. Whisk in the flour and then the stock. Cook over simmering water, stirring constantly, until the sauce thickens, 10 to 12 minutes. Continue to cook, stirring, for 2 to 3 minutes longer, to remove any raw taste of the flour. Pour in the lemon juice and season to taste with salt and pepper. If not serving immediately, keep warm over gently simmering water; or cover and refrigerate until cold.

Poached Chicken Breasts with Green Sauce

A lovely picnic or light supper dish.

F&W Beverage Suggestion: Pinot Grigio

6 SERVINGS

6 whole chicken breasts—boned, skinned and split in half
2 medium leeks (white and tender green)—trimmed, washed and cut into ½-inch slices
1 imported bay leaf
1 teaspoon salt
4 peppercorns
3 tablespoons fresh lemon juice
Green Sauce (recipe follows)
Tomato slices, radishes or roasted red bell pepper strips, for garnish

1. In a large noncorrodible saucepan, put the chicken breasts. Cover with the leeks, bay leaf, salt, peppercorns and lemon juice; add enough cold water to cover. Bring the water to a boil over high heat. Immediately reduce the heat to moderate and poach for 10 to 15 minutes, until the chicken has just lost its pink in the center. Remove from the heat and let cool in the poaching liquid.

2. With a slotted spoon, remove the chicken and leeks from the poaching liquid and arrange on a platter. (Save the liquid to use as a stock.) Pour the Green Sauce over the chicken. Garnish with tomatoes, radishes or roasted peppers if desired. Serve at room temperature.

Green Sauce

MAKES ABOUT 1½ CUPS

1 cup flat-leaf Italian parsley
½ cup fresh basil
1 medium garlic clove
1 tablespoon drained capers
3 cornichons (French gherkin pickles)
1 celery rib, cut up
½ cup extra-virgin olive oil
1 tablespoon red wine vinegar
1 to 2 tablespoons fresh lemon juice
2 to 4 tablespoons chicken stock or water (optional)
Salt and freshly ground pepper

In a food processor, combine the parsley, basil, garlic, capers, cornichons, celery, olive oil and vinegar. Chop but do not puree. Stir in the lemon juice to taste. If the sauce seems too thick, add a few tablespoons of stock (the poaching liquid from the chicken breasts will do nicely). Season with salt and pepper to taste.

Turkey Breast with Anchovy-Celery Sauce

6 SERVINGS

2- to 2½-pound whole turkey breast, skinned and boned, at room temperature
5 anchovy fillets, rinsed and finely chopped (1½ tablespoons)
½ cup minced celery
½ cup minced green bell pepper
1 tablespoon minced fresh hot green pepper
1 small garlic clove, minced
¼ cup plus 1 tablespoon olive oil
2 tablespoons white wine vinegar
¼ teaspoon freshly ground black pepper
2 tablespoons finely chopped parsley
Salt
4 or 5 plum tomatoes, thinly sliced

1. Split the turkey breast in half and trim off any excess fat. Remove the fillet piece from each of the breast halves. Lightly pound the thicker ends of the two remaining pieces.

2. In a deep pan that will hold both the turkey breast halves and the fillets comfortably in a single layer, bring enough water to cover them by about ½ inch to 140°.

3. Add the turkey and poach for about 20 minutes for the fillets, and 40 to 50 minutes for the larger pieces, until the flesh is springy to the touch and the internal temperature is 140°. (If unsure, remove the meat and cut a small slit in the thickest end on the underside. Check to see that the flesh has lost its translucency and has only the barest hint of pink color.)

4. Remove the turkey pieces to a platter, cover loosely and let cool to room temperature. Then, slice and serve or wrap well and refrigerate overnight.

5. In a medium bowl, combine the anchovies, celery, bell and hot peppers, garlic, oil, vinegar and black pepper. Let stand for 1 hour or overnight to allow the flavors to blend. Just before serving, stir in the parsley and salt to taste.

6. To serve, thinly slice the turkey. Arrange alternating slices of turkey and tomato on plates or a platter. Lightly salt, then spoon the sauce in a band over the top.

Braised Turkey Breast with Cider Sauce

F&W Beverage Suggestion:
Chenin Blanc

20 SERVINGS

Turkey:

3 tablespoons unsalted butter

2 tablespoons vegetable oil

6 medium carrots, cut into ½-inch slices (about 3 cups)

3 medium onions, coarsely chopped (about 3 cups)

2 garlic cloves, crushed

1 whole turkey breast, bone in (about 10 pounds)

2 bottles (6 cups) hard apple cider, preferably French

2 tablespoons salt

1 large bouquet garni: 8 sprigs of parsley, 1 tablespoon dried thyme, 1 tablespoon dried rosemary, 1 bay leaf and 6 peppercorns tied in a double thickness of cheesecloth

Sauce:

2½ cups mayonnaise, preferably homemade

¼ cup dry white wine

2 tablespoons brandy

2 tablespoons Dijon-style mustard

3 tablespoons minced parsley, for garnish

1. Make the turkey: Preheat the oven to 375°. In a large skillet, heat the butter and oil. Add the carrots, onions and garlic; cover the skillet and cook over low heat until the vegetables soften, about 10 minutes. Transfer the vegetables to a casserole or deep roasting pan that will hold the turkey breast snugly. Place the turkey on top of the vegetables.

2. Add the cider, salt and bouquet garni to the casserole. Cover with aluminum foil or a tight lid and bake for 2 to 2½ hours, or until a thermometer inserted in the thickest part of the breast registers 160°. Remove from the oven, uncover and let rest until the turkey is cool enough to handle.

3. Remove and discard the turkey skin. Using a long, sharp knife and working close to the breast bone, remove the meat in 2 solid pieces (one from each side of the breast) and place in a deep bowl. Strain the broth from the casserole over the turkey; cover and let cool to room temperature. Discard the breast bone and the solids in the sieve.

4. Remove the turkey from the broth and reserve the broth for the sauce. Slice the turkey thinly across the grain. Arrange the slices on a large platter. Cover tightly with plastic wrap and refrigerate until chilled.

5. Prepare the sauce and assemble the dish: Degrease the reserved broth; there will be about 8 cups. Pour the broth into a medium saucepan, heat to boiling and cook over moderately high heat until reduced to 1 cup, about 45 minutes. (The broth will reduce to a thick syrup; watch carefully during the last 15 minutes to prevent scorching.) Remove from the heat and let cool to room temperature, stirring occasionally.

6. Place the mayonnaise in a medium bowl and whisk in the reduced broth, wine, brandy and mustard until blended. Spoon the sauce over the turkey and garnish with the parsley. If not serving immediately, cover and refrigerate. Let stand at room temperature for ½ hour before serving.

Stuffed Venetian Turkey

F&W Beverage Suggestion:
Barolo, such as Fontanafredda, Vieti or Conterno

12 SERVINGS

Stuffed Turkey:

12-pound turkey, thawed if frozen

1½ pounds chestnuts

3 cups beef stock

3 cups cubed (½-inch) firm-textured white bread

½ cup milk

6 tablespoons unsalted butter

4 celery ribs, chopped

1 medium onion, chopped

½ pound ground veal

½ pound ground pork

2 tablespoons minced fresh parsley

1 teaspoon thyme

3 tablespoons white or tawny port

1 cup quartered prunes

½ cup freshly grated Parmesan cheese

4 eggs, lightly beaten

1 tablespoon salt

½ teaspoon pepper

4 to 6 slices *pancetta* or a thin sheet of fatback

1½ cups unsweetened pomegranate juice*

Sauce:

12 cups chicken stock

1 cup white or tawny port

4 tablespoons unsalted butter

Garnish: Fresh pomegranate seeds

*Available in health food stores

1. Preheat the oven to 400°. Remove the giblets and neck from the turkey and reserve them for the sauce.

2. Prepare the stuffing: Cut an X in the flat side of each chestnut with the tip of a small knife and place them in an ungreased baking pan. Bake for 20 minutes, or until the shells begin to curl. Let stand until cool enough to handle, then remove the shells.

3. Simmer the chestnuts in the beef stock, uncovered, until all the liquid is absorbed, about 40 minutes. Puree the chestnuts through the medium disk of a food mill.

4. Preheat the oven to 350°. Place the bread in a large bowl. Pour on the milk and let the bread soak for 10 minutes, stirring once or twice.

5. In a large skillet, melt 3 tablespoons of the butter over moderate heat, Add the celery and onion and sauté until softened, about 10 minutes. Add to the bowl with the bread. Add the pureed chestnuts, the veal, pork, parsley, thyme, port, prunes, cheese, eggs, salt and pepper and mix well. This should yield about 8 cups of stuffing.

6. Turn the turkey breast-side down. Lightly pack about 1 cup of the stuffing into the neck. Pull the neck skin over to seal and fasten it to the turkey with metal skewers or wooden picks. Turn the turkey breast-side up and lightly fill the main cavity with about 4 cups of the stuffing. Fold the wing tips under and truss the turkey. Rub it with the remaining 3 tablespoons butter and cover the breast with the slices of *pancetta*, securing them with toothpicks. Place the remaining stuffing in a buttered baking dish and set it aside until 45 minutes before the turkey is done.

7. Roast the turkey in the oven for 1½ hours. At the end of that time, baste it generously with pomegranate juice. Roast the turkey about 2 hours longer, basting every 30 minutes with pomegranate juice and the drippings in the bottom of the pan. The turkey is done when the breast meat registers 160° and the thigh meat 170° and the juices run clear. During the last 45 minutes of cooking, bake the extra stuffing, uncovered.

8. Meanwhile, begin preparing the sauce: Boil the chicken stock with the reserved turkey giblets and neck until the liquid is reduced by half. Strain the stock and discard the giblets and neck. Add the port and set the sauce aside until the turkey is done.

9. Remove the turkey from the roasting pan; remove the toothpicks and peel off the *pancetta*. Pour the drippings out of the pan. Add the sauce to the roasting pan and heat to boiling, scraping up any brown bits that cling to the pan. Cook until reduced by half, about 15 minutes. Strain into a small saucepan, heat to boiling and whisk in the butter, 1 tablespoon at a time.

10. Serve the turkey and stuffing with the sauce. Garnish each serving with the fresh pomegranate seeds, if you wish.

Roast Turkey with Lemon-Cornbread Stuffing

🍷 **F&W Beverage Suggestion:** Fresh Hard Cider or California Zinfandel, such as Louis M. Martini or Ridge

16 SERVINGS

1 turkey (16 pounds), thawed if frozen
6 cups hot Lemon-Cornbread Stuffing (recipe follows)
1 tablespoon olive oil
1 large onion, sliced
2 carrots, sliced
2 bay leaves
1 sprig of parsley
2 garlic cloves, sliced
5 or 6 peppercorns, cracked
¼ cup all-purpose flour
¾ cup dry white wine, chicken broth or water
Salt and freshly ground pepper

1. Preheat the oven to 475°. Remove the neck and giblets from the turkey and reserve them. Rinse the turkey inside and out under cold running water and pat dry.

2. Place the turkey breast-side down. Loosely fill the neck with 1 cup of the *hot* stuffing. Pull the neck skin over the cavity to seal it and fasten to the back of the turkey with skewers or wooden picks. Turn the turkey breast-side up and fold the wings under the turkey.

3. Lightly pack the remaining 5 cups stuffing into the main cavity. Tie the drumsticks together with kitchen string or, if your turkey has a metal clamp, arrange the drumsticks so that the clamp will hold them in place. Rub the turkey with the oil.

4. Place the turkey breast-side up, on a rack in a roasting pan and roast in the lower third of the oven for 45 minutes. The initial 45 minutes will begin to brown the turkey very quickly, so be sure your oven temperature is not higher than 475°.

5. Meanwhile, make the stock for the gravy (let it simmer while the turkey roasts): Place the reserved neck and giblets in a medium saucepan. Add the onion, carrots, bay leaves, parsley, garlic, peppercorns and 2 quarts of water. Bring to a boil and reduce the heat to low. If the liquid reduces to less than 2 cups at any time, add additional water. Just before the turkey is done, strain the stock and discard the solids; you should have 2 cups of liquid.

6. Lower the oven temperature to 400° and loosely cover the turkey with an aluminum foil tent. Continue to roast, basting with the pan juices every 30 minutes or so, for about 2¼ hours, or until the internal temperature of the breast registers 160° and the thigh meat 170° (the juices will run clear when pierced with a fork).

7. Remove the turkey from the oven and lift it on the rack from the roasting pan; allow it to rest for 20 minutes before carving. Meanwhile, prepare the gravy: Pour the drippings from the roasting pan into a measuring cup and let the fat rise to the top. Spoon off most of the fat but keep 1 cup drippings. Pour these drippings back into the roasting pan and add the flour. Place the pan over 2 burners adjusted to moderate heat and cook, stirring constantly, until the mixture is bubbling, about 3 minutes. Add the wine and reserved stock and cook, stirring constantly, until the gravy thickens and boils, about 2 minutes. Season with salt and pepper to taste.

Lemon-Cornbread Stuffing

Be sure to make the cornbread for this recipe a day ahead so it can dry overnight.

MAKES 6 CUPS,
ENOUGH FOR A 16-POUND TURKEY

1 recipe Cornbread (p. 197)
¼ cup olive oil
½ cup (1 stick) unsalted butter
2 cups finely chopped onion
1½ cups chopped celery
1 tablespoon minced garlic
1 cup minced parsley leaves
1 tablespoon grated lemon zest
½ cup fresh lemon juice (from 3 or 4 lemons)
1 tablespoon salt
1 teaspoon pepper
4 eggs
½ cup chicken or turkey stock

1. Cut the cornbread into rectangles about 3 by 4 inches, place them on a rack and let dry overnight.

2. Preheat the oven to 350°. Cut the cornbread into ¼-inch croutons; you should have about 7 cups. Place the croutons on a baking sheet and bake for 35 to 40 minutes, until dry, golden brown and crisp.

3. In a large heavy skillet, heat the olive oil and butter over moderate heat until the butter melts. Add the onion and celery and sauté until the onion is softened and translucent, about 10 minutes. Add the garlic and sauté for 2 minutes. Stir in the cornbread croutons and cook, stirring until they are heated through, 2 to 3 minutes. Remove the skillet from the heat and stir in the parsley, lemon zest, lemon juice, salt and pepper.

4. In a medium bowl, whisk the eggs with the stock until blended. Stir the egg mixture into the stuffing and mix well.

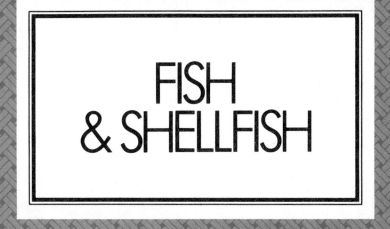

FISH
& SHELLFISH

Swordfish with Horseradish Butter

F&W Beverage Suggestion:
Napa Valley Chardonnay

2 OR 3 SERVINGS

1 pound swordfish steak, cut about
  1 inch thick
½ cup milk
2½ tablespoons unsalted butter
1½ tablespoons prepared white
  horseradish
1 tablespoon fresh lemon juice
2 sprigs fresh thyme or ¼ teaspoon
  dried
1 lemon, cut into wedges

1. Place the swordfish in a small baking pan. Pour the milk over the fish. Refrigerate, covered, for 1 hour.

2. Preheat the oven to 350°. In a small saucepan, melt the butter over moderate heat. Add the horseradish, lemon juice and thyme. Cook, stirring, until slightly thickened, about 3 minutes. Spoon the horseradish butter over the swordfish and bake for about 15 minutes, or until just tender when tested with a fork. Place under the broiler until golden brown, bubbling and opaque throughout, 4 to 5 minutes. Serve with lemon wedges.

Stuffed Bass

The bass in this recipe has been boned so that the head, tail and fillets are kept intact and the finished dish has the appearance of a whole fish.

6 TO 8 SERVINGS

Stuffed Bass:
1 whole striped bass, 6 pounds—
  cleaned, fins removed, head and
  tail intact
5 tablespoons peanut oil
¾ pound medium shrimp—shelled,
  deveined and cut into ½-inch
  pieces
3 small carrots, cut into 2-inch
  julienne strips
3 small zucchini, cut into 2-inch
  julienne strips
1 tablespoon finely chopped fresh
  gingerroot
1 tablespoon light soy sauce

Ginger Sauce:
⅓ cup light soy sauce
⅓ cup dry white wine
1 tablespoon finely chopped fresh
  gingerroot
¼ cup thinly sliced scallions

1. Prepare the bass: With a boning knife, make a slit along the top of the backbone extending from the base of the head to the tail. With the tip of the knife inserted in the slit at the base of the head, begin to cut the flesh away from the backbone, working the knife somewhat diagonally across the width of the fish toward its belly before moving toward the tail and lifting up the flesh as you cut deeper. The head and tail should be attached to the fillet. Now, turn the fish over and loosen the fillet on the other side in the same way. At this point, you should have two loose fillets joined by the head and tail.

2. With the fish on its side, lift up the top fillet and, working between the two fillets, sever the backbone at the head and tail ends; remove and discard the backbone. Also pull out any bones that may have remained in the flesh of the fillets. Rinse the fish under cold water and pat it dry with paper towels.

3. Preheat the oven to 375°. Rejoin the two fillets along the back by sewing them together or by pinning the two edges together with bamboo shish-kebab skewers.

4. Place a large, heavy skillet or wok over moderately high heat and add 4 tablespoons of the oil. Add the shrimp, carrots, zucchini and ginger, and sauté for 3 minutes; set aside.

5. Line a roasting pan with a large piece of foil and lay the fish on it. Stuff the cavity with the vegetables and shrimp and sprinkle the soy sauce over the stuffing. Close the opening by sewing or pinning. Brush the fish with the remaining oil and bake for 35 to 40 minutes, or until the flesh is firm, opaque and will flake easily when pierced with a fork.

6. Prepare the ginger sauce: While the fish is baking, place the soy sauce, ⅓ cup water and the wine in a small saucepan set over moderate heat and bring the mixture to a boil. Remove from the heat and pour into a heatproof bowl; add the ginger. When the mixture has reached room temperature, add the scallions.

7. Place the fish on a platter. To serve, slice it crosswise into 2-inch-wide pieces. Transfer the slices to individual plates, making sure that each contains some of the stuffing. Spoon a little of the sauce over each serving.

Broiled Bass with Endive Vinaigrette

4 SERVINGS

1½ pounds striped bass fillets,
  skinned
¼ cup walnut oil
½ cup olive oil
¼ cup sherry wine vinegar
Salt and pepper
2 tablespoons minced shallots
3 tablespoons finely chopped fresh
  parsley
4 small heads of Belgian endive
1 tablespoon unsalted butter,
  softened
1 teaspoon coarse (kosher) salt

1. Using a sharp slicing knife and working at a 45-degree angle, cut the fish into 2½-inch-square slices, ¼ inch thick.

2. In a small mixing bowl, whisk together the walnut oil and olive oil; continue beating while you add the vinegar and salt and pepper to taste. Stir in the shallots and parsley. Set the vinaigrette aside.

3. Preheat the broiler. Cut the endive in half lengthwise; remove and discard the cores at the stem ends. Cut the endive lengthwise into shreds and arrange over a serving plate.

4. Lightly grease a shallow baking pan or jelly-roll pan with the butter and sprinkle with the salt. Arrange the pieces of bass in a single layer over the salt and broil, 4 to 5 inches from the heat, for 2 minutes, or until opaque and flaky.

5. While the fish is broiling, heat the reserved vinaigrette in a small saucepan until warm but not hot.

6. Arrange the bass over the endive and spoon the vinaigrette over the fish. Serve immediately.

Top left, Papaya Golden Sole (p. 103); bottom right, Crab-Pecan Salad (p. 162).

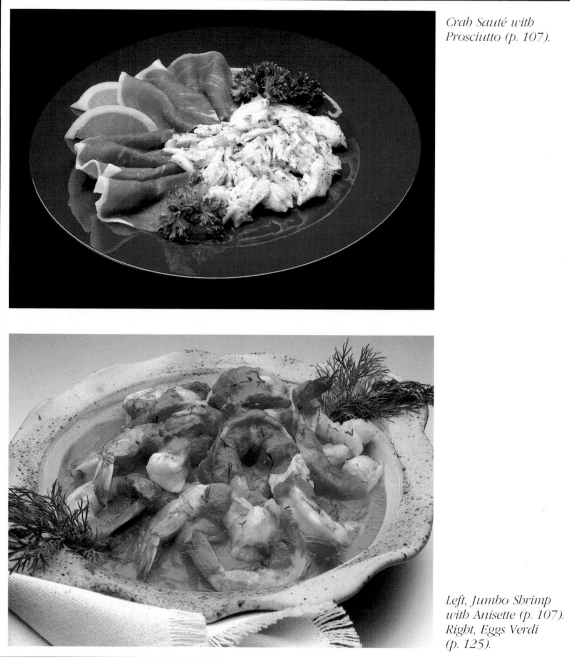

Crab Sauté with Prosciutto (p. 107).

Left, Jumbo Shrimp with Anisette (p. 107). Right, Eggs Verdi (p. 125).

Baked Bass with Fresh Spinach and Fennel

F&W Beverage Suggestion:
California dry Chenin Blanc, such as Chappellet

6 SERVINGS

3-pound striped bass, filleted, bones and head reserved
6 tablespoons unsalted butter
1 medium onion, coarsely chopped
1 celery rib, coarsely chopped
8 parsley stems
½ small bay leaf
Pinch of thyme
4 white peppercorns
1 teaspoon salt
½ cup dry white wine
1 large fennel bulb—base trimmed, top stalks removed, green sprigs chopped and reserved for garnish
1 pound fresh spinach, stemmed and well-rinsed
2 shallots, finely chopped
1 cup heavy cream
Pinch of freshly ground white pepper
2 tablespoons fresh lemon juice

1. Remove and discard the gills from the fish head. Rinse any blood off the fish bones and head. In a heavy, medium, noncorrodible saucepan, melt 1 tablespoon of the butter. Add the fish trimmings and cook over moderately high heat, stirring occasionally, until the fish has lost its translucency, about 5 minutes. Cover, reduce the heat to low and cook for 5 minutes longer.

2. Add the onion, celery, parsley, bay leaf, thyme, peppercorns, ½ teaspoon of the salt and ¼ cup of the wine. Add enough cold water to cover (about 1 quart) and slowly bring to a simmer, skimming off any scum that accumulates. Simmer uncovered for 20 minutes. Strain and reserve ¾ cup of the stock for the sauce. (The remainder can be cooled, then frozen for another use.)

3. Preheat the oven to 425°. Quarter the fennel bulb and cook in a small pan of boiling salted water until very soft, about 15 minutes. Drain and rinse under cold

Panfried Fish Dumplings with Baby Bok Choy (p. 100).

running water until cool enough to handle. Gently squeeze out excess moisture and puree in a food processor until very smooth.

4. Cook the spinach in a pan of boiling salted water just until limp, 30 seconds to 1 minute. Drain and rinse under cold running water until cool. Squeeze out excess moisture with your hands; finely chop. Melt 2 tablespoons of the butter in a small saucepan. Add the chopped spinach and sauté for 2 minutes, tossing to coat with the butter. Remove from the heat.

5. To make the sauce, place the ¾ cup fish stock, remaining ¼ cup wine and the shallots in a small, noncorrodible saucepan. Boil over moderately high heat until reduced to ¼ cup, about 10 minutes. Add the cream and fennel puree and boil until the sauce coats the back of a spoon, about 10 minutes. Add the spinach and simmer for 2 minutes. Season with the remaining ½ teaspoon salt, the white pepper and lemon juice. Dot with 1 tablespoon of butter to prevent a skin from forming. (The recipe can be prepared 2 or 3 hours ahead to this point.)

6. Use about 1 tablespoon of the remaining butter to grease a large gratin dish. Divide the fish fillets into 6 equal portions and arrange in a single layer. Dot with the remaining 1 tablespoon butter. Cover with waxed paper or parchment and bake for 8 to 10 minutes, until the fillets are almost opaque.

7. To serve, reheat the sauce if necessary. Ladle the sauce onto 6 heated plates, dividing evenly. Arrange the fish fillets on top. Garnish with the fennel greens.

Orange Butter Bass

Beverage Suggestion:
California Chardonnay, such as Chateau St. Jean, Trefethen or Chateau Montelena

4 SERVINGS

2 pounds sea bass fillet, skinned and cut into 4 equal pieces
Salt and freshly ground pepper
2 tablespoons grated orange zest
2 tablespoons grated lemon zest
2 tablespoons minced scallions (white part only)
1½ tablespoons minced fresh parsley
6 tablespoons unsalted butter
Parsley sprigs, for garnish

1. Preheat the oven to 350°. Butter a shallow baking dish large enough to hold the fish in a single layer.

2. Season the fish on both sides, generously with salt and lightly with pepper; arrange in the baking dish. Sprinkle the orange zest, lemon zest, scallions and minced parsley evenly over the fish. Dot with the butter.

3. Bake for 15 to 18 minutes, basting twice, until the fish barely separates when tested with a spoon. Serve with the pan juices spooned over the fish. Garnish with parsley sprigs.

Red Snapper with Walnut-Garlic Sauce

Beverage Suggestion:
Vins Gris of Pinot Noir of Edna Valley Vineyard or Bandol Rosé of Domaine Tempier

4 SERVINGS

2 egg yolks
2 tablespoons white wine vinegar
1 tablespoon fresh lemon juice
1 to 2 garlic cloves, or more to taste
¾ teaspoon salt
1 cup plus 1½ tablespoons olive oil
½ cup (about 3 ounces) ground walnuts
⅓ cup minced fresh parsley
4 skinless fillets of red snapper, rockfish or striped bass, about 8 ounces each
Lemon wedges, for garnish

1. Place the egg yolks, vinegar, lemon juice, garlic and salt in a blender or food processor; blend until smooth. With the machine on, gradually pour in 1 cup of the olive oil in a thin, steady stream until all the oil is thoroughly incorporated and the sauce thickens. Scrape into a small mixing bowl and stir in the nuts and parsley. Set aside.

2. Preheat the broiler. Brush the fillets lightly on both sides with the remaining 1½ tablespoons oil and broil 4 inches from the heat, without turning, for about 4½ minutes, or until the fish separates easily when tested with a spoon.

3. Transfer the fillets to 4 plates and salt lightly. Spoon several tablespoons of the sauce over each fillet, garnish with lemon wedges and serve immediately. Pass the remaining sauce separately.

Red Snapper Provencal

The sauce for this dish can be prepared ahead of time and reheated before serving.

<u>4 SERVINGS</u>

Court-Bouillon and Fish:
2 carrots, peeled and thinly sliced (about 1 cup)
3 large onions, thinly sliced (about 3 cups)
2 celery ribs, finely chopped (about 1 cup)
2 large or 6 small shallots
3 garlic cloves
3 bay leaves
15 peppercorns
2½ teaspoons salt
5 sprigs of parsley
4 to 5 sprigs of thyme or 2 teaspoons dried
2 cups dry white wine
1 red snapper or striped bass (about 4 pounds), cleaned

Provençal Sauce:
1 medium fennel bulb
3 medium tomatoes
3 garlic cloves, crushed
3½ tablespoons minced parsley
3 to 4 tablespoons chopped basil leaves or 2 teaspoons dried
Salt and pepper
½ cup olive oil

Garnish:
2 lemons, thinly sliced
Fennel greens

1. Prepare the court-bouillon: Place all the ingredients for the court-bouillon in a fish poacher and add 1½ cups water. Bring the mixture to a boil over moderate heat, lower the heat, cover and simmer gently until the vegetables are tender, 10 to 15 minutes.

2. Meanwhile, prepare the Provençal sauce: In a large saucepan of boiling salted water, blanch the fennel until it is barely tender when pierced with the tip of a knife, 7 to 10 minutes. Drain and cool. Blanch the tomatoes in the boiling water for 3 minutes; drain and cool. Cut the fennel into ¼-inch dice and place in a heatproof serving bowl. Peel and seed the tomatoes; cut into ¼-inch dice and add to the serving bowl. Add the garlic, parsley, basil, and salt and pepper to taste. Slowly mix in the oil. Place the bowl in a pan of simmering water over low heat to keep the sauce warm.

3. Cook the fish: Set two small ramekins or custard cups on the bottom of the poacher. Place the fish on the poaching rack and gently lower it into the pan of simmering court-bouillon, resting it on the ramekins so that the fish doesn't touch the liquid. Place a piece of waxed paper over the fish and cover the poacher (use aluminum foil to cover the poacher if the lid will not fit over the rack handles). Simmer over moderately low heat until the fish flakes easily, 25 to 35 minutes. Check occasionally to make sure the liquid hasn't simmered away, adding additional wine or water as necessary.

4. Transfer the fish to a large serving platter. With a slotted spoon, remove some of the vegetables from the court-bouillon and arrange them around the fish. Strain the court-bouillon and add ½ cup to the sauce (reserve the remainder for another use); mix well. Garnish the fish with the lemon slices and fennel greens. Serve warm with the sauce on the side.

Rich Salt-Cod Pie

The salt cod must be soaked for 24 hours, so plan your time accordingly.

<u>8 TO 10 SERVINGS</u>

1 pound salt cod
7 tablespoons unsalted butter, cut into ¼-inch slices and softened
White pepper
1 cup heavy cream
4 large eggs

1. Place the cod in a bowl of cold water to cover and refrigerate for 24 hours, changing the water several times.

2. Preheat the oven to 400°. Drain the cod, rinse thoroughly under cold water and place in a medium saucepan. Add enough water to cover, bring it to a boil, lower the heat and poach the cod until it flakes easily with a fork, about 2 minutes.

3. This step can be done in a food processor or blender. If using a processor, puree the cod with the butter and white pepper to taste for 30 seconds, or until the mixture is smooth and light, scraping down the sides once. With the motor still running, add the cream in a steady stream. If using a blender, puree the cod with the butter, cream and pepper in three batches on low speed. Transfer the puree to a medium bowl.

4. Beat the eggs until they are light and fluffy and almost double in volume. Fold them into the cod puree.

5. Spread the cod mixture evenly into a lightly buttered, shallow 6- to 8-cup baking dish. Bake in the upper third of the oven for 15 minutes, or until lightly browned. Cut into squares and serve warm.

Trout Rolls with Ginger-Duxelles Filling

4 SERVINGS

2 trout (1 pound each), filleted and skinned
Cornstarch
6½ tablespoons peanut oil
1½ tablespoons minced fresh gingerroot
2 garlic cloves, minced
5 medium mushrooms, minced (about ¾ cup)
3 scallions, minced (about ½ cup)
1 tablespoon dry sherry
2 tablespoons soy sauce
1 package (8 ounces) cellophane noodles (also called bean thread or transparent noodles)*
3 tablespoons mushroom soy sauce* or regular soy sauce
3 tablespoons Oriental sesame oil
Hot pepper sauce
2 scallions, thinly sliced
5 fresh asparagus spears, cut on the diagonal into ½-inch slivers
Finely chopped fresh coriander (optional)
***Available at Oriental groceries**

1. Cut each fillet in half crosswise. Place each piece between 2 sheets of waxed paper and sprinkle with a little cornstarch to prevent sticking. Using a meat pounder or the flat side of a cleaver, gently pound the fillets until they are about ⅛ inch thick. Check to make sure they are not sticking; add additional cornstarch if necessary. Refrigerate until needed.

2. In a medium skillet, warm 2½ tablespoons of the oil over high heat. Add the gingerroot and stir for about 1 minute. Add the garlic, mushrooms and minced scallions and cook until all the liquid from the mushrooms is absorbed, 2 to 3 minutes. Turn off the heat, stir in the sherry and 1 tablespoon of soy sauce; let cool to room temperature.

3. Place the noodles in a large bowl and pour 4 cups of boiling water over them. Leave until tender, about 5 minutes. Drain and place in a bowl of ice-cold water for about 10 minutes (this keeps them from sticking together). Drain the noodles and separate the strands with

your hands. Place in a large bowl and add the 3 tablespoons of mushroom soy sauce, the sesame oil and hot sauce to taste. Add the sliced scallions and toss.

4. Place about 1 heaping tablespoon of the filling along a long side of a pounded fillet. Starting at the filled side, roll tightly into a cigarette shape. (If the fillet doesn't stick together, use equal amounts of cornstarch and water to make a paste; dab a little along the edges to help the ends stick together.) Repeat with the additional fillets.

5. In a medium skillet, warm 1 tablespoon of oil over high heat. When the oil is sizzling, add the asparagus and stir-fry until slightly cooked but still crunchy, about 30 seconds.

6. In a large skillet, warm the remaining 3 tablespoons oil over moderately high heat until hot. Add the fillets, seam-side down, and sauté, turning gently, for 2 to 3 minutes on each side, or until cooked through. Add 1 tablespoon soy sauce during the last minute of cooking.

7. Place the seasoned noodles on a serving plate and arrange the trout rolls on top. Scatter the sautéed asparagus around the sides of the fish and sprinkle with the chopped coriander. Serve warm or cold.

Petits Poissons au Jardin

🍷 **F&W Beverage Suggestion:**
Sauvignon Blanc, such as Sancerre

4 SERVINGS

4 small rainbow trout, each about 1 pound, or any other small fish, such as porgie or whiting—cleaned but with head and tail intact
¼ cup all-purpose flour
Salt and pepper
½ cup olive oil
¼ pound spinach, washed and trimmed
¼ pound sorrel, washed and trimmed
2 to 3 lettuce leaves
8 to 10 scallions
1 cup mixed herbs, such as chives, thyme, tarragon, basil and oregano
1 or 2 lemons, quartered, for garnish

1. Rinse the fish, pat dry with paper towels and lightly score the skins to prevent curling; dust with the flour and season with salt and pepper to taste.

2. Heat the oil in a large skillet until almost smoking. Meanwhile, roughly chop the greens.

3. Add the fish to the skillet and, over moderately high heat, brown for 2 minutes on each side. Push the fish to the side and add the greens and herbs. Tossing, cook until they just begin to wilt, about 1 minute. Season the fish with more salt and pepper, garnish with the lemon and serve from the skillet.

Panfried Brook Trout with New Potatoes

🍷 **F&W Beverage Suggestion:**
California or Alsace Riesling

2 SERVINGS

6 or 8 small new potatoes (about ½ pound)
2 trout (about 10 ounces each)
4 sprigs of fresh thyme or ½ teaspoon dried
4 tablespoons clarified butter
¼ teaspoon salt
⅛ teaspoon freshly ground pepper
1 tablespoon minced fresh chervil or parsley

1. Steam the potatoes until tender, about 15 minutes. Cut each in half and set aside.

2. Stuff each trout with 2 sprigs of the fresh thyme or sprinkle the inside of each with ¼ teaspoon of the dried.

3. In a 12-inch cast-iron skillet, warm the butter over moderately high heat. When hot enough to evaporate a drop of water on contact, add the trout. Cook for 5 minutes. Turn and add the halved potatoes to the skillet. Cook, turning the potatoes occasionally, until they are lightly browned and the trout is just opaque near the bone, about 5 minutes. Season with the salt and pepper and garnish with the chervil.

Panfried Fish Dumplings with Baby Bok Choy

This is a refreshing dish, appealing to many tastes. Use a fine-textured fish with a neutral taste; pike is the best choice. Pork fat gives the dumplings a discernible lightness; buy it fresh from your butcher.

F&W Beverage Suggestion:
California Chenin Blanc, such as a Charles Krug

3 TO 4 SERVINGS

2 walnut-size nuggets of fresh gingerroot
3 medium scallions, cut into 1-inch lengths
¾ pound skinned and boned pike fillets, cut into cubes
2 tablespoons minced Smithfield or Westphalian ham
1 teaspoon coarse (kosher) salt
1 tablespoon plus 2 teaspoons Chinese rice wine or dry sherry
1 tablespoon minced fresh white pork fat
1 egg white
6 tablespoons ice water
1 pound baby bok choy (see Note) or fresh broccoli
6 tablespoons corn or peanut oil
⅛ teaspoon sugar
1 cup plus 2 tablespoons rich, unsalted chicken stock or canned broth
Salt and freshly ground pepper
2½ teaspoons cornstarch
Hakka Chili Sauce (p. 211)

1. In a food processor or blender, chop the ginger and scallions. Add the fish and process until minced. Add the ham, ¾ teaspoon of the salt, 1 tablespoon of the wine, the pork fat, egg white and ice water. Grind to a smooth, thick paste.

2. To check the seasoning, poach about 1 teaspoon of the fish paste in a small saucepan of simmering unsalted water for 30 seconds. Taste and add additional salt if necessary. (The fish paste can be made ahead to this point, covered and refrigerated overnight. The flavors will develop.)

3. Shape the fish paste into walnut-size balls by scooping the mixture out with a tablespoon dipped in ice water; or, using your hand as a pastry bag, squeeze the paste in your fist so that it emerges in a ball between the circle of your thumb and first finger. As the fish balls are formed, transfer them to a stockpot two-thirds filled with ice water.

4. When all the balls are made, bring the water to a simmer over moderately high heat. Simmer until the balls rise to the surface. With a skimmer or slotted spoon, transfer the balls to a platter, arranging them in a single layer. (The poached fish balls can be refrigerated, covered, for 1 to 2 days before completing the recipe. Let return to room temperature before proceeding.) As an optional garnish, with a small knife, cut a tic-tac-toe pattern of lines about three-quarters of the way through each poached fish ball to make them resemble flowers (see photo, p. 96).

5. Cut a thin slice, about ¼ inch thick, off the base of each bok choy to create a flowerlike disk. Cut the remainder of the ribs crosswise into 1-inch pieces. Cut the leaves into 2- to 3-inch-wide bands, leaving the small leaves intact. If using broccoli, cut the florets into acorn-size pieces. Peel the stems and cut on the diagonal into ⅛-inch slices.

6. About 10 minutes before serving, heat a large heavy skillet over high heat until hot enough to evaporate a bead of water on contact. Add 3 tablespoons of the oil to the pan and reduce the heat to moderately high. Add the bok choy and toss briskly to coat with the oil; adjust the heat if necessary so that the vegetable sizzles without scorching. Sprinkle with the remaining ¼ teaspoon salt and the sugar and toss to mix. Sprinkle on the remaining 2 teaspoons wine and toss several times more. Transfer to a heated bowl and cover to keep warm.

7. Carefully wipe the pan clean with damp paper towels. Return to moderately high heat and add the remaining 3 tablespoons oil. When the oil is sizzling hot, add the fish balls to the pan. Cook, shaking the pan gently to turn and sear the balls on all sides, until they are hot to the touch; adjust the heat if necessary so they sizzle without scorching.

8. Add 1 cup of the chicken stock to the pan. Bring to a simmer, reduce the heat to low, cover and simmer for 3 minutes. (If you are using broccoli, return it to the pan and simmer with the fish balls just until tender.) Season the sauce with salt and pepper to taste.

9. Dissolve the cornstarch in the remaining 2 tablespoons stock and add it to the pan. Stir gently over low heat until the sauce is glossy and slightly thickened, 10 to 15 seconds. Arrange with the bok choy on a heated platter. Serve accompanied with Hakka Chili Sauce.

NOTE: Baby bok choy is an especially tender young cabbage that is harvested when about 5 inches long. It is called *ching-gong tsai* in Mandarin and *ching-gong-choy* in Cantonese and is available in well-stocked Chinese markets.

Panfried Catfish with Walnuts and Bacon

Skinning catfish is painstaking work. Ask your fishmonger to prepare the fish for cooking.

F&W Beverage Suggestion:
California French Colombard, such as Parducci

4 SERVINGS

8 thick slices hickory-smoked bacon
½ cup coarsely chopped walnuts
1 egg
½ cup milk
1 cup all-purpose flour
1 cup yellow cornmeal
4 catfish (about 1 pound each)— skinned, cleaned and head removed
½ teaspoon salt
½ teaspoon freshly ground pepper
4 tablespoons fresh lemon juice
½ cup (1 stick) unsalted butter
¼ cup vegetable oil
Lemon halves, for garnish

1. Preheat the oven to 350°. Cook the bacon slices on a baking sheet with sides until crisp, about 20 minutes. (Drain off grease midway in cooking.) Drain on paper towels, then cut into ½-inch pieces.

2. Meanwhile, roast the walnuts on a cookie sheet in the oven until lightly browned, about 15 minutes. Set aside. Leave the oven on.

3. In a medium bowl, beat the egg and milk until blended.

4. In a shallow pan or dish long enough to hold one fish, mix together the flour and cornmeal.

5. Rinse the catfish under cold running water; pat dry. Sprinkle the fish inside and out with the salt, pepper and 2 tablespoons of the lemon juice.

6. In a large skillet, melt 4 tablespoons of the butter in the oil over moderately high heat. Dip the fish into the egg-milk mixture and then into the cornmeal-flour mixture to coat lightly. When the butter and oil are sizzling, add the fish and cook, turning once, until golden brown on each side, about 5 minutes total.

7. Transfer the fish to a baking pan large enough to hold them in a single layer. Bake for 8 to 10 minutes, until the fish has lost its pink color next to the bone.

8. Place on a warmed platter or plates. Sprinkle the bacon pieces and walnuts over the fish.

9. Place the remaining 4 tablespoons butter in a small saucepan and cook over high heat until it foams and turns nut brown. Add the remaining 2 tablespoons lemon juice, then pour over the fish. Garnish with lemon halves.

Fish Fillets in Red Wine Sauce

F&W Beverage Suggestion: Chilled Bardolino, such as Scamperle

4 SERVINGS

12 small white boiling onions (about 1 inch in diameter)
3 tablespoons unsalted butter
3 tablespoons vegetable oil
½ cup diced (¼ inch) carrots

½ cup diced (¼ inch) celery
1½ pounds firm, white fish fillets, such as red snapper or striped bass, or 1½-inch-thick halibut or tilefish steaks
½ cup all-purpose flour
1 teaspoon salt
½ teaspoon freshly ground pepper
1 cup robust red wine (Barbera, Chianti Classico or California Zinfandel)

1. Using the tip of a paring knife, trim the unpeeled onions and cut a cross in the root end of each. Drop the onions into a small saucepan of boiling water. Blanch for 5 minutes; drain and rinse under cold running water to stop the cooking. When cool enough to handle, remove the skins.

2. In a large noncorrodible skillet, melt 2 tablespoons of the butter in the oil over moderate heat. Add the onions and cook, turning occasionally, until browned, about 5 minutes.

3. Add the carrots and celery to the pan, cover and cook over moderate heat, stirring occasionally, until the vegetables are tender and lightly browned, about 10 minutes. With a slotted spoon, transfer the vegetables to a plate, leaving all the fat and cooking juices in the pan.

4. Pat the fish fillets dry with paper towels. Dredge lightly in the flour and shake off the excess.

5. Add the remaining 1 tablespoon butter to the skillet and increase the heat to high. When the foam subsides, put the fish in a single layer without overlapping. Brown the fish on both sides (you may want to sauté in batches), turning carefully, with two spatulas if necessary, about 2 minutes on each side. Season with the salt and pepper and transfer to a warmed platter.

6. Return the vegetables to the skillet. Add the wine and boil over high heat, scraping the bottom of the pan with a wooden spoon to loosen any cooking residues, until the wine is reduced by half.

7. Return the fish to the skillet, reduce the heat to moderate and cook, uncovered, until the fish is barely opaque in the center, 5 to 7 minutes, depending on the thickness of the fillets.

8. Arrange the fillets on a platter and spoon the vegetables over the fish. If the juices in the skillet are thin, rapidly boil until reduced to a coating consistency. Pour over the fish and serve hot.

Fish Fricassee with Lime and Ginger

4 TO 6 SERVINGS

2-pound piece of monkfish with bones in, skinned (see Note)
1 teaspoon salt
⅛ teaspoon white pepper
½ teaspoon thyme
¼ cup fresh lemon juice
1 tablespoon olive oil
½ medium onion, sliced
16 tablespoons (2 sticks) plus 2 teaspoons unsalted butter
1 cup dry white wine
Bouquet garni: 4 sprigs of parsley, ½ teaspoon thyme, ½ bay leaf and 5 black peppercorns tied in a double thickness of cheesecloth
Zest of 2 lemons, finely minced (about 3 tablespoons)
4 scallions, thinly sliced
2 tablespoons heavy cream
3 limes—peel and outer membrane removed, halved lengthwise and thinly sliced
½ teaspoon grated fresh gingerroot or a pinch of powdered ginger
2 tablespoons chopped parsley

1. Fillet the monkfish: Place the fish bellyside down on a cutting board. Using a small boning knife, cut along one side of the backbone, which runs vertically through the fish. Gently scrape the knife against one side of the bone to separate the flesh. Repeat on the other side of the backbone. There will be two whole fillets; reserve the bones for the stock. Remove the membrane that covers the outside. Cut the fish into 2-inch chunks.

2. Place the fish, salt, white pepper, thyme, lemon juice and oil in a bowl. Toss lightly and marinate at room temperature, stirring once or twice, for 1 hour.

3. Meanwhile, make the stock: Place the fish bones, onion, 2 teaspoons of the butter, ½ cup of the wine and the bouquet garni in a medium saucepan. Add 2 cups of water, bring to a boil over moderate heat and simmer for 15 minutes. Strain the stock into a bowl and set aside.

4. Place the lemon zest in a small saucepan and add 1 cup of cold water. Bring to a boil over high heat and cook for 3 minutes. Drain and refresh under cold running water. Set aside.

5. Drain the fish and discard the marinade. In a large, heavy skillet, melt 2 tablespoons of the butter. Add the scallions and sauté over low heat until soft but not brown, about 5 minutes. Add the fish and cook, stirring several times, for 2 to 3 minutes. Add the remaining ½ cup wine and enough of the reserved fish stock to cover the fish. Bring to a boil, reduce the heat and simmer, partially covered, until the fish is just tender, about 10 minutes. Remove the fish and set aside. (The fish can be cooked up to 24 hours ahead and refrigerated, covered, in its cooking liquid. If prepared ahead, undercook slightly to allow for reheating.)

6. To assemble the dish: Reheat the fish if necessary. Remove to a warm heatproof platter, cover with foil and keep warm in a very low oven. Boil the cooking liquid over high heat until it is reduced to about 3 tablespoons, 15 to 20 minutes.

7. Add the cream and reduce the liquid again to about 3 tablespoons, 1 to 2 minutes. Gradually whisk in the remaining butter, 1 tablespoon at a time, adding each piece just as the previous one is almost incorporated. If necessary, return to low heat briefly, whisking, to produce a creamy emulsion, but do not allow the butter to melt completely or the sauce will become liquid.

8. Add the lemon zest, lime slices and gingerroot. Season to taste with salt and white pepper. Arrange the fish on a platter or individual plates. Add the chopped parsley to the sauce and spoon it over the fish.

NOTE: This fricassee can also be prepared with eel, sea bass, turbot, or another firm-fleshed white fish.

Fish Fillets with Rosemary

4 SERVINGS

¼ cup all-purpose flour
1 teaspoon sweet Hungarian paprika
¾ teaspoon dried rosemary, crumbled
Salt and white pepper
4 sole fillets (about 7 ounces each)
2 eggs
2 cups fresh bread crumbs (from 5 slices firm-textured white bread)
About ¼ cup peanut oil
2 tablespoons minced fresh parsley
2 lemons, quartered, for garnish

1. Mix the flour, paprika, rosemary and salt and pepper to taste on a sheet of waxed paper. Dredge the fish fillets in the seasoned flour; shake off any excess and place them on a clean sheet of waxed paper.

2. Lightly beat the eggs in a shallow dish. Place the bread crumbs on a sheet of waxed paper or on a large plate. One by one, dip the fish fillets in the beaten egg and then coat both sides with the bread crumbs, pressing the crumbs with your hand to make sure they adhere. As they are breaded, place the fillets on a clean sheet of waxed paper.

3. In a large heavy skillet, warm 3 tablespoons of the oil over moderate heat until the oil begins to shimmer. Fry the fish fillets one or two at a time, for about 30 seconds on each side, or until golden brown, regulating the heat if they seem to be browning too quickly. Add the remaining tablespoon of oil if they start to stick to the pan.

4. Drain the cooked fillets on paper towels. Arrange them on dinner plates or a platter. Sprinkle with parsley and garnish with lemon wedges.

Sole and Salmon in Lettuce Leaves

6 SERVINGS

6 fillets of sole, about 6½ ounces each
6 slices salmon fillet, about 4 ounces each
6 tablespoons chopped, toasted almonds
2 tablespoons chopped dill
2 tablespoons finely chopped scallions
2 large heads of Boston lettuce
1½ cups fish stock or ¾ cup clam juice diluted with ¾ cup water
¾ cup dry white wine
3 tablespoons chopped shallots
Cucumber Beurre Blanc (p. 209)

1. Preheat the oven to 375°. Place a sole fillet between sheets of waxed paper and, using a mallet, gently pound it to a thickness of ¼ inch. Remove the top sheet of waxed paper and place a salmon fillet on top of the sole. Cover with waxed paper and continue to pound gently until the salmon has spread out ½ inch less than the sole. Remove the paper. Sprinkle with 1 tablespoon of the almonds and 1 teaspoon of the dill and scallions. Repeat with the remaining fillets. Starting at the narrow ends, roll up the fillets and set them aside, seam-sides down.

2. Separate the heads of lettuce and, using the 12 largest leaves, dip them into boiling water for 5 to 10 seconds; rinse immediately in cold water and blot dry with paper towels. Wrap each fish roll in two or three of the leaves, tucking the ends under the rolls and placing them in a shallow baking pan just large enough to hold them. Add the stock, wine and shallots.

3. Lay a sheet of buttered waxed paper directly over the surface of the rolls and poach in the oven for 20 to 30 minutes, or until the fish is opaque. (To test, slice one roll crosswise through the center.) Using a slotted spoon, transfer the rolls to a rack and cool for 5 to 10 minutes.

4. To serve, cut each roll into four slices and arrange cut side up on individual plates. Sauce with Cucumber Beurre Blanc.

Anise-Coated Goujonettes of Sole

F&W Beverage Suggestion:
A dry Italian white, such as a Gavi

2 SERVINGS

2 cups all-purpose flour
½ cup cornstarch
2 teaspoons salt
1½ cups ice water
10 ounces sole fillets
¼ cup aniseed, lightly crushed
1½ to 2 quarts vegetable oil, for deep-frying
1 teaspoon baking soda
Lemon wedges, for garnish

1. Into a large bowl, sift together 1 cup of the flour, the cornstarch and salt. Form a well in the center and add the ice water. Mix thoroughly, then cover and let rest in the refrigerator for 30 to 60 minutes.

2. In the meantime, cut the sole into long, narrow strips about 3 by ⅜ inch. Toss with the aniseed.

3. Preheat the oven to 250°. Heat 1 to 2 inches of oil in a deep-fat fryer or large heavy saucepan.

4. Just before cooking, sprinkle the baking soda over the batter and stir until blended. Place the remaining cup of flour in a bowl next to the batter.

5. Dust the fish strips with flour. Dip in the batter to coat; then draw both sides of the strips across the lip of the bowl to remove excess batter. Carefully slide into the hot oil. Cook as many at a time as your fryer will hold without crowding.

6. Fry until well-browned and crisp, about 4 minutes. Remove to a paper towel-lined ovenproof platter and keep warm in the oven while cooking remaining batches.

7. Serve hot on a napkin-covered plate with wedges of lemon.

Sole Fillets Stuffed with Shrimp Quenelle

F&W Beverage Suggestion:
Puligny-Montrachet, such as Joseph Drouhin, or California Chardonnay, such as Simi

8 SERVINGS

8 sole fillets, preferably Dover (about 6 ounces each), cut lengthwise in half
Salt and white pepper
½ recipe Shrimp Quenelles (p. 106), prepared with 3 egg whites, through Step 4
Sauce Américaine (p. 207)

1. Place the halved fillets, skinned-side down, on a work surface. Season lightly with salt and white pepper. Spoon about 2 tablespoons of the quenelle mixture onto the smaller end of each fillet and roll up. Secure with a toothpick.

2. In each of 2 large deep skillets or flameproof casseroles, bring 4 quarts of salted water to a boil over moderately high heat. Reduce the heat to maintain a gentle simmer. Divide the stuffed fillets between the two pans and poach for about 15 minutes, turning once, until firm and opaque throughout.

3. Remove from the poaching liquid with a slotted spoon and drain on paper towels. Place 2 stuffed fillets on each of 8 warmed plates. Coat lightly with Sauce Américaine.

Steamed Sole with Orange-Soy Sauce

2 TO 3 SERVINGS

½ pound snow peas
2 small carrots, cut into 2½-by-¼-inch sticks
¼ teaspoon salt
Pinch of white pepper
4 sole fillets (3 to 4 ounces each), cut in half lengthwise
8 thin slices plus 1 teaspoon minced fresh gingerroot
4 scallions (white and light green), cut in half crosswise
1 teaspoon peanut oil

Zest of 1 orange, cut into fine shreds
1 teaspoon minced garlic
2 tablespoons soy sauce

1. In a steamer, arrange the snow peas and carrots in a layer. Sprinkle with the salt and pepper.

2. Starting at the narrow tail end, roll up each piece of fish loosely. Arrange 1 inch apart on top of the vegetables. Top each piece of fish with a slice of ginger and a scallion section.

3. Set the steamer over at least 2 inches of boiling water; cover and steam for 8 minutes, until the fish is just opaque throughout.

4. Meanwhile, make the sauce. In a small skillet, warm the oil over moderate heat. Add the orange zest and fry until it begins to curl, about 30 seconds. Add the minced ginger and garlic and cook just until fragrant, about 30 seconds longer. Add the soy sauce and 1 tablespoon of water; bring just to a boil, then remove from the heat.

5. Transfer the fish to a heated platter and surround with the vegetables. Pour the sauce over the fish, evenly distributing the orange zest.

Papaya Golden Sole

Beverage Suggestion:
Dry, crisp Riesling, such as Heitz Cellars

4 SERVINGS

4 sole fillets, about 6 ounces each
1 small papaya, at room temperature, peeled and cut into ½-inch slices
¼ teaspoon salt
7½ tablespoons unsalted butter
⅓ cup minced fresh parsley
½ cup (about 3 ounces) hazelnuts (filberts)—toasted, loose skins rubbed off and the nuts finely chopped
2 tablespoons fresh lemon juice
Lemon wedges, for garnish

1. Preheat the oven to 400°. Pat the fish dry. Arrange the fillets and papaya slices in a single layer in a shallow, lightly buttered baking dish. Season the fish evenly with the salt. Melt 1½ tablespoons of the butter and drizzle over the fillets and papaya slices.

2. Bake in the middle of the oven just until the fish almost separates when tested with a spoon, about 5 minutes, depending upon the thickness of the fillets.

3. Immediately transfer the fillets onto 4 warmed plates; divide the papaya slices among the dishes, placing them on the sides. Sprinkle the parsley and hazelnuts evenly over the fish.

4. In a medium skillet, over moderately high heat, brown the remaining 6 tablespoons of butter until it reaches a hazelnut color; do not allow to burn. Immediately remove from the heat, add the lemon juice and pour over the fillets. Garnish each plate with lemon wedges.

Salmon with Red Radish-Dill Sauce

F&W Beverage Suggestion: California Chardonnay, such as Beringer

4 SERVINGS

½ cup dry white wine
½ cup heavy cream
1 shallot, finely chopped
1 cup (2 sticks) plus 1 tablespoon unsalted butter
¾ teaspoon salt
¼ teaspoon white pepper
8 large red radishes, trimmed
3 tablespoons chopped fresh dill
1 tablespoon drained prepared white horseradish
1 cup milk
½ cup all-purpose flour
1 tablespoon vegetable oil
4 salmon fillets, about 8 ounces each
4 sprigs of fresh dill, for garnish

1. In a medium, noncorrodible saucepan, combine the white wine, cream and shallot. Bring to a boil and cook over moderately high heat until reduced to ½ cup, about 10 minutes.

2. Reduce the heat to low and whisk in 1 cup of the butter, 1 or 2 tablespoons at a time. Season with ½ teaspoon of the salt and the white pepper. Remove from the heat and set aside.

3. Cut 12 thin slices from the radishes for garnish; set aside in a small bowl of cold water. Finely chop the remaining radishes and add to the sauce. Stir in the chopped dill and horseradish.

4. Place the milk in a shallow bowl. Sprinkle the flour on a sheet of waxed paper. In a large skillet, melt the remaining 1 tablespoon butter in the oil over moderately high heat. When it begins to sizzle, dip each salmon piece in the milk; dust with flour, shake off any excess and add to the skillet.

5. Sauté, turning once, until lightly browned, about 3 minutes on each side. Reduce the heat to moderate and continue cooking, turning once or twice, until the fish has almost lost its translucency in the thickest part, 1 or 2 minutes longer, depending on the thickness of the fish. Season with the remaining ¼ teaspoon salt.

6. Warm the sauce over low heat; divide among 4 heated plates. Place the salmon on top and garnish with the reserved radish slices and sprigs of dill.

Salmon and Sorrel Soufflé

This soufflé is served with a Maltaise Sauce—an orange-flavored hollandaise.

Beverage Suggestion: California Fumé (Sauvignon) Blanc or Chardonnay

6 TO 8 SERVINGS

2-pound center-cut piece of salmon, skinned and boned to yield 2 fillets (ask your fishmonger to do this)
¼ teaspoon freshly ground pepper
6 tablespoons unsalted butter
5 tablespoons all-purpose flour
3 cups fish stock
1 teaspoon grated lemon zest
2 tablespoons fresh lemon juice
1 teaspoon salt
6 whole eggs, separated
½ cup finely chopped shallots
1 cup bottled pureed sorrel (see Note)
1 cup lightly packed, chopped fresh spinach
2 egg whites
Sauce Maltaise (p. 209)

1. Preheat the oven to 425°. Butter and flour a large (about 15 inches by 10 inches), shallow glass casserole.

2. Cut each salmon fillet horizontally to yield 4 slices about ½ inch thick. Arrange the salmon in a single layer in the prepared casserole. Season with the pepper.

3. In a medium saucepan, melt 4 tablespoons of the butter over moderately low heat. Whisk in 4 tablespoons of the flour and cook, stirring, for 2 minutes without coloring to make a roux. Stir in 2 cups of the fish stock, the lemon zest, lemon juice and ½ teaspoon of the salt. Bring to a boil, whisking, until thickened and smooth. Reduce the heat and simmer for 10 minutes. Remove from the heat and whisk in the egg yolks, 1 at a time. Set aside.

4. In a medium saucepan, melt the remaining 2 tablespoons butter over moderately low heat. Add the shallots and sauté, stirring frequently, until softened but not browned, about 5 minutes. Stir in the remaining 1 tablespoon flour and the pureed sorrel. Whisk in the remaining 1 cup fish stock and simmer, stirring frequently, until slightly thickened, about 8 minutes. Let cool slightly.

5. Pour the sorrel mixture over the salmon, spreading it evenly with a spatula. Scatter the chopped spinach over the sorrel.

6. In a large bowl, beat the 8 egg whites until frothy. Add the remaining ½ teaspoon salt and beat until soft peaks form. Using a spatula, fold the egg yolk mixture into the whites. Spoon over the salmon spreading to the edges of the dish. Bake for about 15 minutes, or until firm and golden brown on top. Spoon some Maltaise Sauce onto each plate and top with a portion of soufflé. Serve immediately.

NOTE: If fresh sorrel is available, 4 cups chopped leaves can be substituted for the sorrel puree and the chopped spinach.

One-Minute Salmon with Sauce Aigrelette

The slices of the fish are so delicate and thin that once they are baked, they simply cannot be lifted from a serving platter to the plates. So they have to be actually cooked on the dinner plates. You should not, therefore, use your best and thinnest china in a 550° oven, even though it's only in for a few seconds. Serve small amounts as an hors d'oeuvre; larger portions as a light main dish or the dramatic fish course of a grand dinner party.

F&W Beverage Suggestion: Savennières or dry Vouvray

4 MAIN-COURSE OR 6 APPETIZER SERVINGS

1 egg yolk
1 teaspoon Dijon-style mustard
3 teaspoons fresh lemon juice
½ cup peanut oil
¼ cup olive oil
¼ cup soybean oil
3 tablespoons dry white wine
2 tablespoons canned chicken broth
1 tablespoon white wine vinegar
1 tablespoon minced fresh chives
1 tablespoon minced fresh tarragon or 1 teaspoon dried
½ teaspoon coarse (kosher) salt
⅛ teaspoon freshly ground pepper
2 pounds fresh salmon—boned and cut on the diagonal into about 20 very thin slices (see Note)

1. In a medium bowl, whisk the egg yolk, mustard and 1 teaspoon of the lemon juice. Gradually begin to whisk in the peanut, olive and soybean oils, drop by drop, until the mayonnaise begins to thicken. Then continue to whisk in the oils in a thin stream until they are all incorporated. (If the sauce becomes too thick, beat in 1 or 2 teaspoons of the wine, then add the rest of the oil.) Beat in the wine, broth, vinegar and remaining 2 teaspoons lemon juice. Stir in the chives, tarragon, salt and pepper. (The recipe may be prepared ahead to this point. Cover and refrigerate the sauce.)

2. If the sauce has been refrigerated, take it out and let return to room temperature. Preheat the oven to 550°. Lightly butter 4 or 6 heatproof plates or a platter. Sprinkle lightly with salt and pepper. Arrange the salmon slices on the plates and let come to room temperature.

3. Slide the plates into the oven and bake for about 1½ minutes, until the fish is pale but still rose-colored at its center. Immediately remove from the oven; the heat of the plate will continue to cook the fish.

4. Spoon about 1 tablespoon of the sauce over each slice of salmon and serve immediately, warning guests of the hot plates.

NOTE: Ask your fishmonger to do this. Or if you prefer to slice the salmon at home, put it in the freezer for 10 minutes to firm the fish and make it easier to slice.

Fresh Salmon Steak Tartare

Here's a variation on the classic steak tartare. Though the salmon isn't cooked, there is no raw or fishy taste once the fish is coated in its velvety sauce. This dish can be served either as a first course (with thin slices of black bread, sliced tomatoes and sprigs of fresh dill) or as a luncheon dish (mounded in avocado shells with chunks of avocado on the side).

4 FIRST-COURSE SERVINGS

1 egg yolk
2 tablespoons Dijon-style mustard
2 tablespoons olive oil
1 small onion, minced
2 tablespoons minced fresh dill
3 tablespoons fresh lemon juice
½ teaspoon A-1 steak sauce
¼ teaspoon salt
¼ teaspoon freshly ground pepper
1 pound fresh salmon steak—skinned, boned and cut into ¼-inch dice

In a medium bowl, whisk the egg yolk, mustard and oil until blended. Add the onion, dill, lemon juice, steak sauce, salt and pepper and mix well. Stir the diced salmon into the sauce until just coated. Serve chilled.

Smoked Salmon Soufflé

4 TO 6 SERVINGS

3 tablespoons unsalted butter
5 tablespoons grated Gruyère cheese
¾ cup milk
2 bay leaves
2 tablespoons all-purpose flour
3 egg yolks
2 ounces smoked salmon, shredded with a fork (see Note)
¼ teaspoon salt
Pinch of pepper
4 egg whites, at room temperature

1. Grease a 1-quart soufflé dish with 1 tablespoon of the butter; coat with 3 tablespoons of the cheese. Refrigerate the dish while you prepare the soufflé mixture.

2. In a small saucepan, bring the milk and bay leaves to a simmer over low heat. Remove from the heat and discard the bay leaves.

3. In a medium saucepan, melt the remaining 2 tablespoons of butter over low heat. Whisk in the flour until smooth. Cook, stirring, for 1 minute. Gradually add the hot milk, whisking until smooth. Increase the heat to moderate and bring to a boil. Cook, whisking constantly, until the mixture thickens; simmer for 2 minutes. Remove the pan from the heat. Whisk in the egg yolks, one at a time, then stir in the remaining cheese, the smoked salmon, salt and pepper.

4. Preheat the oven to 400°. Beat the egg whites with a pinch of salt until stiff but not dry. Stir ¼ of the egg whites into the sauce to lighten it. Pour the sauce over the egg whites and fold gently until just blended.

5. Pour the soufflé mixture into the prepared dish and place on the middle rack of the oven. Immediately reduce the heat to 375° and bake 25 to 30 minutes, or until the soufflé is puffed and golden.

NOTE: Use a relatively less salty variety, such as Nova Scotia, Scottish or Irish.

Seviche of Sole

Gray sole is the best choice here, as lemon sole tends to break down and lose its flavor more rapidly.

6 SERVINGS

2 pounds sole fillets, cut into 1-inch squares
¾ cup fresh lime juice (from 8 to 10 limes)
1 medium onion, coarsely chopped
1 medium green bell pepper, coarsely chopped
1 medium celery rib, coarsely chopped
1 tablespoon finely minced garlic
1 jar (14 ounces) pimientos, drained and coarsely chopped
1 teaspoon thyme leaf
1 teaspoon ground cumin
¼ cup olive oil
¼ cup finely minced hot green peppers
2 teaspoons coarse (kosher) salt
¼ cup finely chopped flat Italian parsley or fresh coriander (cilantro)

Combine all the ingredients in a large bowl and refrigerate, covered, for at least 24 hours, stirring occasionally. Serve chilled on a bed of lettuce or in individual bowls with endive spears.

Pickled Shrimp

8 TO 10 SERVINGS

¾ cup olive oil
3 garlic cloves, finely minced
2 medium onions, 1 coarsely chopped and 1 sliced into thin rings
2 pounds medium shrimp, shelled and deveined
½ cup vinegar
1½ teaspoons salt
½ teaspoon pepper
¼ teaspoon dry mustard
2 pickled hot peppers (such as jalapeños), cut into strips, or ¼ teaspoon ground dried chile peppers

1. In a large saucepan, heat ¼ cup of the oil. Add the garlic and chopped onion and cook over moderately low heat, stirring frequently, for 10 minutes. Increase the heat to moderate; add the shrimp and cook, stirring occasionally, for 5 minutes. Remove from the heat and let cool for 15 minutes.

2. Transfer the shrimp to a mixing bowl and combine with the remaining oil, the onion rings, vinegar, salt, pepper, mustard and pickled hot peppers. Marinate in the refrigerator for 24 hours, turning the mixture several times. Serve on a bed of lettuce.

Crevettes Esmontese

4 SERVINGS

⅓ cup clarified butter
2 garlic cloves, thinly sliced
16 jumbo shrimp, shelled and deveined (about 1¼ pounds)
1 tablespoon lemon juice
1 tablespoon tomato paste
½ cup heavy cream
⅓ cup snipped chives

1. Preheat the oven to 275°. Heat the clarified butter in a skillet set over moderate heat until hot but not bubbling. Add the garlic and sauté for about 1 minute; do not brown. Add the shrimp and cook just until they are still moist and slightly raw in the center, 25 to 30 seconds on each side. Transfer four shrimp to each of four ovenproof dishes and keep warm in the oven.

2. Discard the butter and garlic in the skillet. Place the skillet over moderate heat and add the lemon juice, tomato paste and cream. Cook, stirring occasionally, for 1 minute. Stir in the chives. Remove the shrimp from the oven and top each portion with one-fourth of the sauce. Serve hot.

Shrimp Quenelles

Wonderfully adaptable, these mousselike quenelles are particularly good with Sauce Américaine (p. 207).

8 SERVINGS

2 tablespoons unsalted butter
¼ cup all-purpose flour
½ cup fish stock or bottled clam juice
1 pound medium shrimp, shelled and deveined
¾ teaspoon salt
Pinch of white pepper
Pinch of cayenne pepper
Pinch of nutmeg
5 egg whites, chilled
1 cup heavy cream, chilled

1. Melt the butter in a small heavy saucepan over moderately low heat. Add the flour, blend thoroughly and cook, stirring, for about 5 minutes without browning to make a roux.

2. Whisk in the stock, bring to a boil and cook, stirring, until thick and smooth, about 1 minute. Remove the thickened flour base from the heat and let cool to room temperature.

3. In a food processor, purée the shrimp until it forms a smooth paste, 2 to 3 minutes. Add the salt, white pepper, cayenne and nutmeg. Mix until well blended, about 30 seconds. Scrape down the sides of the bowl. Add the cooled flour base and mix until well blended, about 30 seconds longer.

4. Turn the shrimp mixture into a large bowl set over ice. With a large sturdy whisk or wooden spoon, beat in the egg whites, 1 at a time. Gradually beat in the cream. Continue to beat over ice for 1 to 2 minutes to lighten the mixture. Cover and refrigerate for at least 15 minutes, until well chilled. (The recipe may be prepared ahead to this point and refrigerated overnight.) After chilling, the quenelle mixture will be stiff enough to mass together and drop from a spoon without roping.

5. In a large deep skillet or flameproof casserole, bring 3 inches of salted water to a simmer. To shape the quenelles, scoop up about 2 tablespoons of the mixture in an oval serving spoon or tablespoon dipped in hot water. Use a second spoon to form the mixture into classic, oval, egg-shaped dumplings. As they are formed, slip them into the simmering water. Cook, turning once, until they float to the top and are firm to the touch, 10 to 12 minutes. With a slotted spoon, remove the quenelles and drain on paper towels.

NOTE: The quenelles can be served at once, or they may be cooked ahead and refrigerated in a pan of cold water for one day.

Jumbo Shrimp with Anisette

Beverage Suggestion:
Chardonnay

4 SERVINGS

3 tablespoons unsalted butter
1 tablespoon vegetable oil
20 jumbo shrimp, shelled and deveined
2 medium shallots, minced
1 garlic clove, crushed
1 teaspoon finely chopped fresh chervil or ½ teaspoon dried
1 teaspoon minced fresh chives
⅛ teaspoon fennel seeds, finely crushed
2 tablespoons anisette liqueur
½ cup fish stock or bottled clam juice
½ cup dry white wine
3 medium tomatoes—peeled, seeded and pureed, or 1 can (8 ounces) Italian peeled tomatoes—drained, seeded and pureed
¼ cup heavy cream
Salt
1 teaspoon chopped fresh dill, for garnish

1. In a large skillet, melt the butter in the oil over moderately high heat. Add the shrimp and sauté, shaking the pan frequently, until they are evenly cooked and opaque throughout, 2 to 3 minutes.

2. Stir in the shallots, garlic, chervil, chives and fennel. Sprinkle the anisette over the mixture and ignite. When the flames subside, transfer the shrimp with a slotted spoon to a heated platter and cover to keep warm.

3. Add the fish stock, wine, tomato pulp and cream to the skillet. Bring to a boil over high heat and boil until reduced by half, about 10 minutes. Season with salt to taste and strain the sauce over the shrimp. Garnish with the dill.

Shrimp and Crab with Orange-Thyme Cream

F&W Beverage Suggestion:
Fetzer Mendocino Gewürztraminer

4 SERVINGS

1 large navel orange
2 cups heavy cream
2 teaspoons fresh thyme or ½ teaspoon dried
5 garlic cloves, halved
¾ pound small fresh shrimp, shelled, with shells reserved
¾ pound fresh lump crabmeat, picked over to remove cartilage
1 teaspoon salt
¼ teaspoon freshly ground pepper
2½ cups freshly cooked rice
Snipped fresh chives, for garnish

1. Finely grate the zest from the orange; set aside. With a paring knife, remove the white pith covering the orange. Cut the orange crosswise into thin slices; quarter each slice.

2. In a large saucepan, combine the cream, orange zest, thyme, garlic and shrimp shells. Bring to a boil over moderately high heat, reduce the heat to moderately low and simmer, stirring occasionally, until the cream is thickened and reduced to 1½ cups, about 15 minutes.

3. Pour the sauce through a fine sieve into a large, heavy skillet, pressing gently with a wooden spoon to extract all the juices.

4. Add the shrimp and crabmeat to the skillet. Cook, stirring, over moderately high heat until the shrimp turn pink, about 4 minutes. Season with the salt and pepper. Stir in the cooked rice until thoroughly mixed. Spoon onto a serving platter. Arrange orange quarters around the edge and sprinkle with the chives. Serve hot.

Crab Sauté with Prosciutto

Serve with thinly sliced, lightly toasted French or Italian bread.

Beverage Suggestion:
California Chardonnay, such as Heitz Cellars; Pinot Grigio, such as S. Margherita; or light Valpolicella, such as Antinori

4 SERVINGS

2½ tablespoons unsalted butter
3 tablespoons minced shallots
½ pound flaked, fresh lump crabmeat, picked over to remove cartilage
2 teaspoons minced fresh parsley
⅛ teaspoon freshly ground pepper
8 thin slices prosciutto
Thin lemon wedges and sprigs of parsley, for garnish

1. In a heavy medium skillet, melt the butter over moderately high heat. When it foams, add the shallots and sauté until softened, about 1 minute.

2. Add the crab and sauté, stirring, just until heated through, about 1 minute. Remove from the heat and stir in the minced parsley and the pepper.

3. Arrange 2 slices of prosciutto on each of 4 warmed plates. Spoon one-fourth of the crab mixture onto each plate. Garnish with lemon wedges and parsley sprigs. Pass a pepper grinder at the table.

Sea Scallops in Sauternes Sauce

F&W Beverage Suggestion:
Rich, dry white wine, such as Puligny-Montrachet or Laville Haut-Brion

4 SERVINGS

12 large sea scallops
4 tablespoons unsalted butter
2 shallots, minced
1 cup Sauternes
2 cups heavy cream, reduced by half (see Note)
½ teaspoon salt
¼ teaspoon freshly ground pepper
½ teaspoon curry powder
1 tablespoon fresh lemon juice

¼ cup green pistachio nuts—shelled, skinned and coarsely chopped
1 tablespoon minced fresh chives

1. Preheat the oven to 500°. Cut each scallop horizontally in half. Arrange them on a lightly buttered cookie sheet.

2. In a heavy, medium, noncorrodible saucepan, melt 1 tablespoon of the butter. Add the shallots and cook over low heat until wilted, about 2 minutes. Add the Sauternes, increase the heat to moderate and boil until reduced by half, about 3 minutes. Add the reduced cream. Boil for 2 minutes longer. Whisk in the remaining 3 tablespoons butter, the salt, pepper, curry powder and lemon juice. Strain through a fine sieve and keep the sauce warm over low heat.

3. Bake the scallops for 1 minute. Turn them over and cook for 1 to 2 minutes longer, until just opaque throughout.

4. Divide the scallops among 4 warmed plates and coat each serving with about ¼ cup of the sauce. Sprinkle the top with the pistachios and chives.

NOTE: Simmer the cream until reduced by half, about 45 minutes.

Sautéed Scallops in Cream and Leek Sauce

F&W Beverage Suggestion: California Sauvignon Blanc, such as Sterling

4 TO 6 SERVINGS

3 cups fish stock
½ cup dry vermouth, preferably Noilly Prat
1 cup crème fraîche
3 large leeks (white part only)
About 8 tablespoons unsalted butter
1 teaspoon salt
¼ teaspoon freshly ground white pepper
1½ pounds sea scallops, of uniform size, cut crosswise in half if large
About ⅓ cup all-purpose flour
2 tablespoons minced fresh parsley

1. In a heavy, noncorrodible medium skillet, boil the fish stock over moderately high heat until it is reduced to ¾ cup, about 30 minutes. Add the vermouth and

boil for 5 minutes longer. Add the crème fraîche, reduce the heat to low and simmer until the sauce is reduced to 1 cup, about 15 minutes. Cover and keep warm over very low heat.

2. Meanwhile, split the leeks lengthwise and wash very well in cold water. Drain and cut into fine julienne strips.

3. In a 10-inch skillet, melt 2 tablespoons of the butter. Add the leeks and season them with the salt and pepper. Add 3 tablespoons of water, cover the skillet and cook over low heat until the leeks are just tender, about 5 minutes. Transfer the leeks with a slotted spoon to the sauce, folding them in gently. Keep warm while you sauté the scallops.

4. Dredge the scallops lightly in the flour; shake off any excess. In a heavy 10-inch skillet, melt 3 tablespoons of the butter over moderate heat. Sauté the scallops in batches in a single layer without crowding. Cook for about 30 seconds on each side, until just opaque (do not overcook). Remove with a slotted spoon; cover with aluminum foil to keep warm while sautéing the remaining scallops. Add butter to the skillet as needed.

5. To serve, spoon some of the sauce onto individual plates and top with the scallops. Garnish with the parsley and serve at once.

Toasted Scallops

F&W Beverage Suggestion: Chateau Ste. Michelle Chenin Blanc

4 TO 6 SERVINGS

3 cups fresh bread crumbs, made from half a 10-ounce loaf Italian or French bread
⅓ cup minced fresh dill or 1 tablespoon dried dillweed
1 tablespoon minced fresh thyme or 1 teaspoon dried
1 teaspoon salt
¼ teaspoon pepper
2 eggs
2 pounds sea scallops
5 tablespoons unsalted butter, melted

1. Preheat the oven to 400°. Mix the bread crumbs, dill, thyme, salt and pepper until blended. Spread these seasoned bread crumbs on a baking sheet and bake until crisp and golden, about 8 minutes. Transfer to a shallow bowl. Increase the oven temperature to 450°.

2. In a small bowl, beat the eggs until blended. Pat the scallops dry. One at a time dip the scallops into the eggs and then coat with the toasted bread crumbs.

3. Brush the bottom of a large baking pan with 1½ tablespoons of the butter. Arrange the breaded scallops in a single layer without crowding and drizzle on the remaining butter.

4. Bake until the scallops are opaque throughout, about 10 minutes. Serve with tartar sauce and lemon wedges.

Shellfish Casserole with Champagne

6 SERVINGS

Shellfish:
12 large mussels (about 1 pound)
½ cup cornmeal
1 pound sea scallops
4 lobster tails (about 1 pound)
1½ pounds large shrimp

Stock:
¾ cup finely chopped carrots (2 medium)
¾ cup finely chopped celery (2 ribs)
¾ cup finely chopped shallots (6 large)
2 garlic cloves, chopped
2 tablespoons olive oil
1 teaspoon tarragon
1 bay leaf
6 peppercorns
2 cups clam juice

Sauce:

2 cups heavy cream
2 cups champagne
4 tablespoons (½ stick) unsalted butter
4 tablespoons all-purpose flour
1½ teaspoons sugar
½ teaspoon salt
¾ teaspoon freshly ground white pepper
1 tablespoon chopped fresh parsley

1. Prepare the shellfish: Scrub the mussels and remove the "beard." Rinse them in several changes of cold water in a large bowl, allowing them to soak for 10 minutes or so between changes. Add the cornmeal to the final bowl of rinsing water and soak the mussels for 1 hour in this mixture. This will encourage the mussels to expel any sand.

2. Cut each scallop in half across the grain. Place in a bowl, cover, and refrigerate.

3. Trim the fanlike ends and tiny feathered parts from the lobster tails and, with scissors, snip and pull away the clear membrane that holds the flesh inside the shell. Reserve these scraps for the stock. Cut the lobster tails, still cradled in their shells, into 1½-inch pieces. Refrigerate with the scallops.

4. Remove the shells from the shrimp and reserve them, with the lobster trimmings, to flavor the stock. Devein the shrimp. Refrigerate the shrimp with the lobsters and scallops.

5. Prepare the stock: In a medium-size, heavy pan, sauté the carrots, celery, shallots and garlic in the olive oil for 3 minutes.

6. Add the tarragon, bay leaf, peppercorns, shellfish trimmings, clam juice and 2 cups of water. Stir and simmer, uncovered, for about 30 minutes.

7. Strain the liquid through a sieve, pressing lightly with a spoon; discard the solids. Reserve the stock for the sauce.

8. Prepare the sauce: Preheat the oven to 375°. In a medium-size, heavy saucepan, heat 1 cup of the prepared stock, the cream and champagne over moderate heat until it comes to a boil. Adjust the heat to keep the liquid at a gentle simmer.

9. Blend the butter and flour to form a *beurre manié* and, stirring rapidly with a whisk, add it a little at a time to the liquid.

10. Stir in the sugar, salt, pepper and parsley, and simmer, uncovered, for 5 minutes.

11. Place the lobster pieces in a 3½-quart casserole. Pour the sauce over them and bake the casserole, covered, for 15 minutes.

12. Remove the casserole from the oven and stir in the shrimp, scallops and mussels. Re-cover and bake for an additional 10 minutes. Uncover and stir gently. Bake for an additional 10 minutes, or until the shrimp are cooked. (Discard any mussels that do not open.) Serve hot.

F&W Cioppino

This exciting mixture of fish and shellfish, simmered in a hearty sauce of tomatoes, wine and herbs, is San Francisco's answer to Marseilles's bouillabaisse. It can be made with almost any assortment of fish though crabs are a must in a true cioppino. Serve with a crusty loaf of San Francisco sourdough or with garlic bread.

8 SERVINGS

⅓ cup olive oil
2 medium onions, chopped
1 cup (about 10) thinly sliced scallions (white part only)
½ cup chopped green bell pepper
3 garlic cloves, minced
¼ pound mushrooms, sliced
½ cup plus 2 tablespoons minced parsley
1 can (35 ounces) Italian peeled tomatoes, roughly chopped, with their liquid
1 can (16 ounces) tomato sauce
2 cups dry red wine
1 bay leaf
1 teaspoon basil
½ teaspoon oregano
½ teaspoon salt
½ teaspoon freshly ground black pepper
2 medium Dungeness crabs, cleaned and quartered, or 4 Alaskan King crab legs, cut into 4 pieces each and cracked
1 pound firm white fish fillets, such as sea bass, striped bass or scrod, cut into 2½-by-2-inch pieces
1 pound medium shrimp, shelled and deveined, with the tail intact
24 littleneck or cherrystone clams, well scrubbed

1. In a large, heavy casserole, heat the oil. Add the onions, scallions, green pepper and garlic and sauté over moderate heat until the vegetables are almost tender, about 3 minutes. Add the mushrooms and sauté for 1 to 2 minutes. Add ½ cup of the parsley, the tomatoes and their liquid, tomato sauce, wine, bay leaf, basil, oregano, salt and pepper. Bring to a boil, reduce the heat and simmer, uncovered, for 25 minutes.

2. Add the crabs, fish fillets and shrimp to the casserole. Place the clams on top in a single layer; cover and simmer until the fish is cooked and the clams have opened, 10 to 12 minutes. Serve hot, sprinkled with the remaining parsley.

Lobster Pot au Feu

F&W Beverage Suggestion: Puligny Montrachet or Napa Valley Chardonnay

6 SERVINGS

3 tablespoons clarified butter
3 fresh lobsters (2 pounds each), cut in half lengthwise
1 carrot, finely chopped
1 leek (white part only), finely chopped
1 celery rib, finely chopped
4 shallots, finely chopped
Bouquet garni: 6 sprigs of parsley, ½ teaspoon thyme and 1 bay leaf tied in a double thickness of cheesecloth

¼ cup Armagnac or brandy
2 cups dry white wine
6 medium carrots, cut into 3-by-½-
by-¼-inch sticks
3 medium leeks (white part only),
trimmed at the root so the base
remains attached, and quartered
lengthwise
6 large white turnips (3½ to 4
inches in diameter), peeled and
cut into 3-by-½-by-¼-inch sticks
24 tiny pearl onions
6 tablespoons cold, unsalted butter

1. In a large deep skillet or Dutch oven, heat the clarified butter. Working in batches, add the lobsters in a single layer, cut-side down, and cook over moderately high heat for 5 minutes.

2. Return all the lobsters to the skillet and reduce the heat to moderately low. Add the chopped carrot, leek, celery, shallots, the bouquet garni and the Armagnac to the skillet. Ignite the Armagnac and when the flames subside, add the white wine. Cover and simmer until the lobster meat is opaque throughout, about 10 minutes.

3. Remove the lobsters from the skillet. Pick the meat out of the tails and claws, keeping the large pieces intact; place the meat on a warm plate and cover with aluminum foil to keep warm. Return the shells to the skillet and simmer, covered, for 10 minutes. Uncover, increase the heat to moderately high and boil until the liquid is reduced to about 1 cup. Strain into a small saucepan.

4. Steam the carrot sticks, whole leeks, turnip sticks and pearl onions separately for 2 to 3 minutes, until just tender when pierced with a knife.

5. Bring the sauce to a boil, remove from the heat and whisk in the cold butter, 1 tablespoon at a time. Return to low heat briefly, if necessary, to create a smooth emulsion, but do not let boil or the sauce will separate.

6. On each of six large, warm plates, place the meat from half a lobster tail and one claw. Arrange a small portion of each vegetable decoratively about the lobster. Spoon the sauce over the vegetables; serve at once.

Lobster Custard

6 SERVINGS

Lobster:
1 fresh lobster (1½ to 1¾ pounds)
or 2 frozen lobster or crawfish
tails in the shell (about 7 ounces
each), thawed

Sauce:
2 tablespoons vegetable oil
1 medium, unpeeled onion,
chopped
1 medium carrot, chopped
1 cup dry white wine
2 tablespoons dry sherry
2 tablespoons tomato paste
1 tablespoon chopped fresh parsley
1 small bay leaf
4 peppercorns
¼ cup heavy cream

Custard:
1½ tablespoons chopped fresh
parsley
¼ cup thinly sliced scallions
8 eggs
1¾ cups chicken broth
¾ cup heavy cream
2 tablespoons dry sherry

Garnish:
Watercress or parsley
Pieces of lobster shell or
medallions of lobster tail
(optional)

1. Prepare the lobster: In a large saucepan, bring 3 cups of water to a boil over moderately high heat. Add the lobster or lobster tails, cover and boil for 1 minute. Remove from the heat and let stand for 10 minutes without removing the lid. Remove the shellfish and reserve the poaching liquid. Remove the meat from the shell and cut it into ½-inch cubes. Reserve the pieces of shell for the sauce.

2. Make the sauce: In a medium saucepan, heat the oil. Add the reserved lobster shells, the onion and carrot and sauté over moderate heat until the vegetables are softened but not browned, about 4 minutes. Add the wine, sherry, tomato paste, parsley, bay leaf and peppercorns. Stir in the reserved poaching liquid and bring to a boil. Reduce the heat to low, cover and simmer for 1 hour.

3. Strain the liquid and discard the solids. (Some pieces of lobster shell can be set aside for garnish if you wish.) Boil the liquid until it is reduced to ¾ cup; set aside.

4. Prepare the custard: Generously butter six 1-cup custard cups. Line the bottom of each cup with a circle of well-buttered waxed paper, buttered-side up. Divide the parsley, scallions and cubes of lobster meat equally among the cups.

5. In a medium bowl, beat the eggs, chicken broth, ¾ cup of cream and the sherry until blended. Pour about ⅔ cup of the custard mixture into each cup. Cover the top of each cup with aluminum foil, folding tightly around the rim to seal.

6. Place the cups on a rack in a steamer or large, deep pot. Pour in boiling water to reach halfway up the sides of the cups. Cover and gently cook the custards over very low heat (see Note) for 30 minutes. To check for doneness, remove the foil from one of the puddings. The custard should be set to within 1 inch of the center, which will still be slightly soft (the custard becomes firm as it stands). If too soft, return to the steamer and cook a bit longer. Remove the cups from the steamer and let them rest, covered, for 5 minutes.

7. Meanwhile, reheat the sauce and stir in the ¼ cup of cream.

8. Remove the foil from the cups, loosen the custard from the sides with a blunt knife and invert the puddings onto individual plates; shake sharply to unmold. Remove waxed paper. Spoon 2 tablespoons of the sauce around each pudding and garnish with a sprig or two of watercress and a bit of lobster shell or lobster medallions, if desired.

NOTE: It is important to steam custards gently over very low heat to prevent them from becoming tough and pitted.

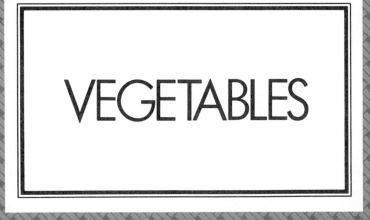

VEGETABLES

Lacy Artichoke Pancakes

These German-style pancakes are made without flour and are notable for the delicious and unusual flavor of the knobby, tuberous vegetable known commercially as the sunchoke. Grate the Jerusalem artichokes just before you make the pancakes and serve the pancakes immediately, since they begin to lose flavor and texture shortly after cooking.

MAKES 8 PANCAKES

½ pound Jerusalem artichokes
1 tablespoon fresh lemon juice
2 eggs
½ teaspoon salt
⅛ teaspoon freshly ground pepper
1 small onion (optional)
1 tablespoon unsalted butter
1 tablespoon vegetable oil

Optional Accompaniments:
1 cup sour cream
1 cup applesauce

1. Wash and peel the artichokes and place them in a quart of water to which the lemon juice has been added

2. Beat the eggs with the salt and pepper. Drain and dry the artichokes, and using a fine grater (not a shredder), grate them directly into the egg mixture, incorporating the grating juices as well (they make the pancakes thinner and more delicate). Grate in the onion if desired. Stir to blend well.

3. Preheat the oven to 200°. In a large skillet, preferably one with a nonstick surface, heat the butter and oil over moderate heat until almost smoking. Spoon four rounds of batter into the skillet, using about 2 tablespoons of batter for each round and using the spoon to spread the rounds to a 3-inch diameter. Cook until browned on each side, about 6 to 8 minutes in all. (If desired, you can use two large skillets and cook all the pancakes at once.) Transfer the cooked pancakes to a heatproof platter and keep them warm in the oven while you cook the remaining four. Serve the pancakes immediately with sour cream and/or applesauce.

Artichoke Hearts with Mushrooms

6 SERVINGS

6 large globe artichokes
½ cup fresh lemon juice
2 tablespoons vegetable oil
⅔ cup green olive oil
2 tablespoons dry vermouth
1 teaspoon oregano
½ teaspoon basil
¼ teaspoon thyme
½ teaspoon salt
6 ounces mushrooms, thinly sliced
3 tablespoons freshly grated
   Parmesan cheese

1. To trim the artichokes: One at a time, using a stainless-steel knife, cut off the stems. Snap off all of the outer leaves by bending them back. With a knife, slice off the inner leaves about two-thirds of the way down, flush with the top of the choke. Trim away the dark, fibrous leaf ends to form a smooth, neat artichoke heart. To prevent discoloration, immediately place each heart in a large noncorrodible saucepan filled with 1 quart of water, ¼ cup of the lemon juice, and the vegetable oil. Cover with a piece of cheesecloth to keep the artichokes moist and submerged.

2. When all the artichokes are trimmed, place the saucepan over moderate heat, bring to a boil and cook the artichokes (still covered with cheesecloth) until tender when pierced with a knife, 30 to 40 minutes.

3. Meanwhile, in a medium bowl, whisk the remaining ¼ cup lemon juice, olive oil, vermouth, oregano, basil, thyme and salt until blended. Add the mushrooms and stir to coat well. Let marinate at room temperature, stirring occasionally, while the artichokes cook.

4. When the artichokes are tender, remove them with a slotted spoon and drain, inverted, on paper towels, until cool enough to handle. Scoop out the hairy chokes with a spoon.

5. Stir the cheese into the mushrooms and their marinade. Spoon half the mixture into a shallow dish. Arrange the artichoke hearts on top and fill them with the remaining mushrooms and marinade. Let marinate at room temperature for at least 1 and up to 6 hours.

Asparagus Bundles

4 FIRST-COURSE OR SIDE-DISH SERVINGS

2 sheets of phyllo dough, cut
   lengthwise in half
About ¼ cup clarified butter
20 thin asparagus tips, 3 inches
   long
4 scallions (white and green parts)
   trimmed to 3 inches
Salt and freshly ground pepper

1. Preheat the oven to 375°. Lightly brush both sides of half a sheet of phyllo with butter. Arrange 5 of the asparagus tips and 1 scallion in a bundle along one short edge of the dough; there will be a 1-inch margin on either side.

2. Season the asparagus with salt and pepper. Fold in the edges of the phyllo and roll up. Place the bundle on a cookie sheet and brush with butter. Repeat with the remaining ingredients to make 3 more bundles.

3. Bake for 12 to 15 minutes, until golden brown. Serve hot.

Flan of Asparagus with Gazpacho Sauce

6 SERVINGS

Asparagus Flan:

2 tablespoons unsalted butter,
   softened
1 pound asparagus (24 small to
   medium stalks)
2½ cups milk
2 whole eggs
4 egg yolks
Salt and white pepper

Gazpacho Sauce:

1 medium, ripe tomato, chopped
1 medium green bell pepper,
   seeded and diced
1 small onion, chopped (½ cup)
1 garlic clove, minced
½ medium cucumber—peeled,
   seeded and chopped
1 cup tomato juice
Dash of hot pepper sauce
Dash of Worcestershire sauce
3 tablespoons heavy cream
Salt and white pepper

Garnish: Lemon wedges

1. Prepare the flan: Coat six 1-cup custard cups with the softened butter and set aside. Break off the top 2½ inches of the asparagus spears and set them aside. Using a swivel-bladed vegetable peeler, remove any tough, stringy fiber from the bottom portions of the stalks; set aside.

2. Cook the asparagus tips in boiling lightly salted water for 3 minutes after the water returns to a boil. Drain them in a colander under cold running water and set aside.

3. Dice the reserved asparagus stalks and combine them with the milk in a medium saucepan. Place the pan over *very* low heat and let the milk come to a simmer, 20 to 25 minutes. Puree the mixture in a food processor or blender, then put it through a food mill set over a bowl. Cool to room temperature

4. Preheat the oven to 325°. In a bowl, beat the whole eggs and egg yolks until they are light-colored. Add the asparagus-flavored milk and beat until well-blended; stir in salt and pepper to taste.

5. Divide the asparagus heads among the custard cups, arranging them so that the points are downward. Pour the flan mixture over the asparagus, dividing it equally among the cups. Cover the cups with foil, place them in a baking pan and add 1 inch of hot water to the pan. Bake for 50 to 60 minutes, or until a knife inserted in the center of the flan comes out clean. Remove the foil and cool the flan to room temperature. Run the tip of a paring knife around the edge of the flan to loosen it and unmold the cups on six individual plates. Refrigerate until cool.

6. Meanwhile, prepare the gazpacho sauce: Puree the tomato, bell pepper, onion, garlic, cucumber and tomato juice in a blender or food processor, then put it through a food mill set over a bowl. Stir in the hot pepper and Worcestershire sauces, the cream and salt and pepper to taste. Cover and refrigerate until cool but not thoroughly chilled.

7. To serve, spoon the sauce around the flan and garnish each plate with a lemon wedge.

Avocado Frittata

1 SERVING

½ avocado, cut into 1-inch chunks
½ teaspoon lemon juice
¼ teaspoon salt
1 ounce goat cheese, such as Montrachet or Bucheron, crumbled (about ¼ cup)
¼ teaspoon rosemary, crushed
4 oil-cured black olives, pitted and cut into slivers
3 eggs
¼ teaspoon coarsely ground black pepper
1½ teaspoons olive oil

1. Preheat the broiler. In a small bowl, toss the avocado with the lemon juice and salt. Add the goat cheese, rosemary and olives; toss gently.

2. Beat the eggs with the pepper and a pinch of salt.

3. Set an ovenproof omelette pan or heavy medium skillet over moderately high heat and add the oil. When the oil is hot but not smoking, add the eggs. Cook for about 1½ minutes, stirring once or twice, until the bottom is set and the top is still slightly runny. Remove from the heat and sprinkle the avocado mixture evenly over the eggs.

4. Broil about 4 inches from the heat until the top of the frittata is set and the edges slightly browned, about 2 minutes.

Sesame Green Beans

4 SERVINGS

1 pound green beans
2 tablespoons Oriental sesame oil
1 tablespoon sesame seeds
¼ teaspoon salt
1 tablespoon lemon juice

1. Cut the beans in half crosswise. Steam for 5 minutes, or until crisp-tender.

2. In a large skillet or wok, heat the sesame oil. Add the beans, sesame seeds and salt and stir-fry over moderate heat for 1 minute. Remove from the heat and sprinkle the lemon juice over the beans.

Stir-Fried Green Beans with Beef Sauce

4 TO 6 SERVINGS

1 cup peanut oil
1 pound green beans
¼ cup chicken broth or stock
1 tablespoon soy sauce
1 tablespoon brown bean sauce*
1 tablespoon dry sherry
1 teaspoon red wine vinegar
2 teaspoons minced fresh gingerroot
1 teaspoon minced garlic
½ pound ground chuck
½ teaspoon cornstarch

*Available at Oriental groceries

1. Preheat a wok or large skillet over moderately high heat. Add the oil and, when it is hot, the green beans. Stir-fry until they start to wrinkle, about 3 minutes. Remove the beans with a slotted spoon and pour off all but 1 tablespoon oil.

2. In a small bowl, combine the chicken broth, soy sauce, bean sauce, sherry and vinegar.

3. Reheat the oil in the wok. Add the gingerroot and garlic and stir-fry for 30 seconds. Add the ground chuck and stir-fry, breaking up any lumps, until the meat is no longer pink, about 3 minutes. Add the chicken broth mixture to the wok and cook for 1 minute.

4. In a small bowl, stir the cornstarch with 1 tablespoon of water until blended. Pour this mixture into the wok and cook, stirring, until the sauce thickens. Add the beans to the wok and toss to reheat and coat them with the sauce. Serve hot with rice.

Bean Fritters with Parsley Sauce

MAKES ABOUT 20 1½-INCH FRITTERS

Fritters:

1 cup black-eyed peas, soaked overnight and drained
⅓ cup finely chopped onion
¼ cup minced fresh parsley
1 egg
2 teaspoons minced fresh gingerroot
½ teaspoon minced garlic
1 teaspoon whole cumin seeds
1 teaspoon ground coriander
1 teaspoon salt
¼ teaspoon cayenne pepper

Parsley Sauce:

½ cup packed parsley leaves
¼ cup peanut oil
3 tablespoons fresh lemon juice
¼ teaspoon grated lemon zest
¼ teaspoon ground coriander
¼ teaspoon ground cumin
¼ teaspoon salt

Vegetable oil, for deep-frying

1. In a medium bowl, mix all of the ingredients for the fritters. Coarsely puree the mixture in a blender or food processor, in several batches if necessary.

2. Combine all the ingredients for the parsley sauce in a blender or food processor and puree until nearly smooth.

3. Pour 3 inches of oil into a deep-fryer or heavy, deep saucepan. Heat until the oil registers 375°. Drop the fritter batter by rounded tablespoonfuls into the hot oil, 4 or 5 at a time, and cook until crisp and brown, about 2 minutes. Remove with a slotted spoon and drain well on paper towels. Keep warm in a low oven while frying the remaining fritters. Serve hot with the parsley sauce for dipping.

Spiced Baked Beans

This is a cross between old-fashioned Boston baked beans and a bean dish from the Piedmont region of Italy. The preparation is an all-day affair, so plan accordingly. It can be served with cornbread, salad and fruit for dessert to make a complete meal. The dish improves with age, so you can safely make it a couple of days in advance and reheat it in a slow oven. Vegetarians can omit the bacon and add, instead, an additional chopped onion, ¼ cup of vegetable oil and additional salt to taste.

8 SERVINGS

2 cups (1 pound) navy, pea or small white beans, soaked overnight and drained
2 cups chicken or beef stock
1 medium onion, finely chopped (about 1 cup)
4 small garlic cloves, minced
8 slices bacon, preferably nitrite-free, chopped
1 teaspoon salt
½ teaspoon ground cumin
¼ teaspoon mace
¼ teaspoon ground cloves
½ teaspoon pepper
¼ cup blackstrap molasses

1. Preheat the oven to 300°. In a 3- to 5-quart flameproof casserole, combine all the ingredients and stir until mixed. Add 4 cups of water, bring to a simmer on top of the stove, cover and bake for 6 hours.

2. Increase the oven temperature to 350°, uncover the casserole and continue baking until the beans have absorbed all the liquid and formed a slight crust on top, 45 minutes to 1 hour.

Sweet and Sour Beets with Mushrooms

6 SERVINGS

1 pound beets (about 6 medium)
½ cup (1 stick) unsalted butter
3 tablespoons minced shallots
1 pound mushrooms, thinly sliced
2 tablespoons honey
2 tablespoons red wine vinegar
1 cup chicken, turkey or veal stock
1½ tablespoons green peppercorns, drained

1. In a medium saucepan of boiling water, cook the beets until just tender, about 15 minutes. Drain, peel and cut the beets into thin slices.

2. In a medium skillet, melt 6 tablespoons of the butter over moderate heat. Add the shallot and sauté until softened, about 2 minutes. Raise the heat to high and add the beets and mushrooms. Sauté, stirring frequently, for 2 minutes.

3. Add the honey, vinegar and stock. Reduce the heat and simmer, uncovered, until the beets are tender, about 2 minutes. With a slotted spoon, remove the vegetables to a serving bowl.

4. Boil the sauce over high heat until it is reduced to ⅓ cup, about 2 minutes. Swirl in the remaining 2 tablespoons butter, add the peppercorns and pour on the vegetables.

Jade Broccoli with Pecans

Broccoli stalks are often neglected, but this first course makes full use of them; save the florets for another meal

4 SERVINGS

4½ tablespoons unsalted butter
⅓ cup chopped pecans
2½ cups (loosely packed) peeled, shredded broccoli stalks (from about 3 pounds fresh broccoli)
½ teaspoon salt
4 very thin slices Black Forest ham or prosciutto

1. In a small skillet, melt ½ tablespoon of the butter over low heat. Add the pecans and sauté until lightly browned, 2 to 3 minutes.

2. Steam the broccoli shreds until just tender, about 3 minutes. Transfer to a bowl and toss with the remaining four tablespoons butter and the salt.

3. To serve, divide the broccoli among four plates. Sprinkle the pecans on top and arrange a slice of ham on the side.

Broccoli with Pine Nuts and Raisins

6 SERVINGS

1 head of broccoli
¼ cup olive oil
1 dried, hot red pepper
2 garlic cloves, cut into slivers
½ cup (3 ounces) pine nuts (pignoli)
½ cup raisins
2 large tomatoes—peeled, seeded and roughly chopped (about 1 cup)
½ teaspoon salt
⅛ teaspoon pepper

1. Cut the broccoli top into florets. Trim and peel the stalks and cut them on the diagonal into thin slices.

2. In a medium skillet, heat the oil with the red pepper and garlic. Add the pine nuts and raisins and sauté over moderate heat until the nuts just begin to color, about 2 minutes. Add the broccoli and sauté until tender, about 5 minutes.

3. Add the tomatoes and cook just until they are heated through, about 1 minute. Season with the salt and pepper.

Broccoli-Pepper Vinaigrette

6 SERVINGS

1 tablespoon Dijon-style mustard
2 tablespoons red wine vinegar
Zest of 1 large orange
6 tablespoons olive oil
Juice of ½ large orange
½ teaspoon salt
½ teaspoon pepper
¼ teaspoon sugar
2 heads of broccoli, cut into florets
1 red bell pepper, cut into julienne strips (1 by ⅛ inch)

1. Whisk the mustard, vinegar, and orange zest in a small bowl until blended. Slowly whisk in the olive oil; then beat in the orange juice, salt, pepper and sugar.

2. Steam the broccoli until just tender, about 8 minutes. Arrange the warm broccoli in a bowl and immediately pour on the dressing. Toss with the red pepper and serve warm.

Hancock Cabbage in Caraway Cream

This is a delightful, slightly crunchy dish, well-flavored with sour cream and caraway. The recipe is adapted from an old Shaker recipe. Hancock is a Shaker village, located in upstate New York.

4 SERVINGS

2 tablespoons unsalted butter
1 small head of cabbage (about 1¾ pounds)—quartered, cored and coarsely shredded
1 large garlic clove, minced
1¼ teaspoons salt
1 tablespoon cider vinegar
1 tablespoon caraway seed
1 teaspoon sugar
1 teaspoon freshly ground pepper
½ cup sour cream

1. In a large, heavy skillet, melt the butter over moderate heat until sizzling. Add the cabbage, garlic and salt and cook, tossing, until the cabbage is slightly wilted, about 2 minutes. Cover and steam for 7 minutes, or until tender but still slightly crunchy.

2. Season with the vinegar, caraway seed, sugar and pepper. Stir in the sour cream until thoroughly mixed. Serve hot.

Braised Cabbage with Fennel

10 SERVINGS

1 pound bacon, coarsely chopped
2 tablespoons vegetable oil
1 large onion, finely chopped
1 tablespoon fennel seed, slightly crushed
¼ cup golden raisins
1 large head of green cabbage (2½ to 3 pounds), finely shredded
1 teaspoon salt
1 teaspoon freshly ground pepper
2 tablespoons chopped fresh dill

1. In a large skillet, fry the bacon in the oil over moderate heat until it begins to crisp, about 15 minutes.

2. Add the onion and fennel seed and continue to cook, stirring frequently, until the onion is softened and translucent, about 5 minutes. Add the raisins and

cook for 2 minutes longer. Add the cabbage and sauté, tossing frequently, until the cabbage is heated through but still crisp, about 5 minutes.

3. Add the salt, pepper and dill and toss to mix. With two large forks or a slotted spoon, transfer to a heated serving dish, leaving any excess fat in the pan. Serve hot.

Shredded Brussels Sprouts Sautéed in Cream

6 SERVINGS

4 tablespoons unsalted butter
2 teaspoons finely minced garlic
2 cartons (10 ounces each) Brussels sprouts, coarsely shredded
1 teaspoon salt
¼ teaspoon nutmeg
White pepper
⅓ cup heavy cream

In a large skillet, melt the butter over moderate heat. Add the garlic and sauté for 30 seconds. Add the shredded Brussels sprouts and salt and toss well. Cook, stirring frequently, until the Brussels sprouts are wilted and just tender, 3 to 5 minutes. Season with the nutmeg and pepper to taste. Add the cream, stir well and cook for 2 minutes more.

Glazed Carrots with Pearl Onions

6 SERVINGS

4 tablespoons unsalted butter
1 pound (about 18) small white onions (1 inch in diameter), peeled
1 pound carrots, cut into ¼-inch slices
1 can (13¾ ounces) chicken broth
2 teaspoons sugar
Salt and pepper
¼ cup minced fresh parsley

1. In a large heavy skillet, melt the butter over moderate heat. Add the onions and cook for about 10 minutes, shaking the pan occasionally to brown them evenly.

2. Add the carrots and cook, stirring, for 5 minutes. Pour in the chicken stock, bring to a boil, reduce the heat and simmer until the carrots are just tender, about 5 minutes.

3. Remove the vegetables with a slotted spoon. Add the sugar to the liquid in the skillet and bring the mixture to a boil over high heat; reduce the liquid to about ¼ cup. Return the vegetables to the pan. Stir to coat with the glaze. Season with salt and pepper to taste and stir in the parsley.

Herbed Carrots and Green Beans

The subtle lemon and anchovy flavors of this dish marry well with most baked, grilled or broiled fish or chicken dishes.

6 SERVINGS

4 tablespoons unsalted butter
1 medium garlic clove, crushed
¾ pound green beans, cut into 2-inch lengths
6 medium carrots, cut into 2-by-¼-inch julienne strips
¼ teaspoon salt
¼ teaspoon freshly ground pepper
3 tablespoons chopped fresh parsley
2 teaspoons chopped fresh marjoram or ½ teaspoon dried

1 teaspoon finely chopped fresh rosemary or ¼ teaspoon dried, crushed
3 flat anchovy fillets, mashed
Grated zest of 1 lemon
2 teaspoons fresh lemon juice

1. In a large skillet, melt the butter over moderately low heat. Add the garlic and cook until lightly colored, about 2 minutes.

2. Add the beans, carrots, salt, pepper, parsley, marjoram and rosemary. Toss to combine. Cover tightly and cook, tossing occasionally, until just tender, 10 to 12 minutes. If vegetables begin to stick, add 1 or 2 tablespoons of water.

3. Add the anchovies, lemon zest and lemon juice. Cook, tossing, for 2 minutes.

Curried Cauliflower with Peas

6 SERVINGS

1 head of cauliflower (about 2 pounds), cut into 1½-inch florets to yield about 5 cups
1 package (10 ounces) frozen peas or about 1½ pounds unshelled peas (to yield about 1¾ cups)
¼ cup currants
¼ cup vegetable oil
1 tablespoon curry powder
1 cup plain yogurt
1½ teaspoons salt

1. Bring a large saucepan of water to a boil. Add the cauliflower, let the water return to a boil and cook over moderate heat until the cauliflower is just tender, about 5 minutes. Drain into a colander and refresh under cold running water. Drain well and place in a large bowl.

2. In another saucepan of boiling water, cook the peas until just tender, about 2 minutes if using frozen, somewhat longer for fresh peas. Drain, refresh under cold running water and drain well. Add the peas and the currants to the cauliflower.

3. In a small skillet, cook the oil and curry powder over moderate heat, stirring, for 1 minute. In a small bowl, stir together the yogurt and salt. Scrape in the curried oil and stir until smooth.

4. Add the curried yogurt mixture to the vegetables and stir to coat well. Allow to marinate at room temperature for at least 1 and up to 6 hours.

Braised Celery

6 SERVINGS

3 heads of celery
4 tablespoons unsalted butter
¾ cup dry sherry
¾ cup chicken stock or canned broth
1 large garlic clove, sliced
Salt and pepper

Optional Garnish:
2 ounces thinly sliced prosciutto, cut into thin strips
½ ounce dried imported mushrooms—soaked in hot water for 30 minutes, drained and finely chopped
½ cup freshly grated Parmesan cheese

1. Without detaching the ribs, trim away a thin slice from the root end of each celery head. Remove the outer ribs and reserve for another use, such as cream-of-celery soup. Using the celery hearts plus 6 to 8 of the tender ribs attached to each (about 2 pounds total), split each head in half lengthwise.

2. In a large heavy skillet, melt the butter over moderate heat. Working in batches, sauté the celery, cut-sides down, until golden on one side, 5 to 7 minutes. Remove them as they become brown and set aside.

3. Return all the celery, cut-sides up, to the skillet and pour in the sherry. Bring the wine to a boil over moderately high heat and boil, uncovered, until most of the wine has evaporated, about 5 minutes. Add the chicken stock and garlic, and bring the liquid to a boil. Reduce the heat slightly and simmer, covered, until the liquid has reduced to a glaze, about 30 minutes, basting the celery occasionally with the pan broth. Discard the garlic.

4. Place the celery, cut-sides up, on a warm serving platter and spoon the glaze from the pan over them. Season with salt and pepper to taste. Scatter the garnishes over the celery and serve.

Tangy Corn with Lima Beans

6 SERVINGS

6 medium ears of corn
1 package (10 ounces) frozen baby lima beans or 1¾ cups shelled fresh lima beans
1½ cups fresh coriander leaves, loosely packed
¾ teaspoon crushed red pepper
1 teaspoon salt
½ cup corn oil or other vegetable oil
3 tablespoons fresh lime juice

1. Bring a large saucepan of water to a boil and add the corn. Boil for about 8 minutes (less if the corn is very young and fresh), or until tender. Do not overcook. Drain and refresh at once under cold running water for 2 to 3 minutes to stop the cooking. Drain and set aside.

2. In another saucepan of boiling water, cook the lima beans until just tender, 4 to 5 minutes if frozen, slightly longer if fresh. Drain into a colander and refresh under cold running water. Drain well and place in a bowl.

3. Cut the corn kernels from the cobs. Add the kernels to the lima beans.

4. In a blender or food processor, work the fresh coriander, hot pepper, salt, oil and lime juice until the coriander is minced. Pour the dressing over the vegetables and toss to blend well. Let the vegetables marinate at room temperature for at least 1 and up to 6 hours.

Corn-and-Oyster Fritters

Traditional corn fritters are frequently referred to as "oyster" fritters because the flavor of the fried corn is supposed to be similar to that of fried oysters. With that thought in mind, these fritters are cooked with corn *and* oysters. Serve them for breakfast or brunch with eggs and pan-fried tomatoes.

MAKES 15 FOUR-INCH FRITTERS

1 cup milk
½ cup heavy cream
1 whole egg
1 egg yolk
2 tablespoons flat beer
1 cup all-purpose flour

1 cup corn kernels (from 2 to 3 large ears)
1 teaspoon nutmeg
Salt and pepper
5 tablespoons unsalted butter
15 oysters—shucked, drained and chopped

1. Preheat the oven to 300°. In a large bowl, whisk together the milk, cream, whole egg, egg yolk and beer. Sift in the flour and mix well. Stir in the corn, nutmeg and salt and pepper to taste. Chill for 15 minutes.

2. In a large skillet, melt 1 tablespoon of the butter over moderately high heat. Cooking 3 fritters at a time, pour ¼ cup of the batter for each into the skillet. Scatter a tablespoon of the oysters over the tops and cook until bubbles form, 2 to 3 minutes. Turn the fritters over and cook another 2 to 3 minutes, or until golden brown. Transfer to a serving platter and keep warm in the oven. Repeat until all the batter is used. Serve hot.

Martha's Vineyard Corn Pudding

Although a sturdy paring knife works well for removing corn kernels, for especially easy grating you may want to invest in a corn grater. They're available in some kitchen specialty equipment stores, ranging from $1 to $7.

4 SERVINGS

6 large ears of yellow corn
3 tablespoons unsalted butter
2 eggs, lightly beaten
½ cup milk
½ teaspoon salt
¼ teaspoon freshly ground pepper

1. Preheat the oven to 350°. Using a small sharp knife, slit each row of corn kernels lengthwise. Using a corn grater or the blunt edge of a knife, scrape the kernels off each ear. There will be about 2 cups of kernels and juice.

2. Melt 2 tablespoons of the butter. Use ½ tablespoon to lightly grease four ½-cup ramekins. Add the remaining 1½ tablespoons melted butter to the corn. Stir in the eggs, milk, salt and pepper.

3. Divide the corn mixture among the ramekins and bake until a knife inserted in the center comes out clean, 20 to 30

minutes. Cut the remaining 1 tablespoon cold butter into 4 pats and place one atop each pudding.

Millet-and-Eggplant Casserole

This spicy casserole, served with cold yogurt, makes a delicious accompaniment to a roast leg of lamb. To make it a completely vegetarian dish, substitute 1 cup tomato juice and ⅓ cup water for the chicken broth in the ingredient list.

6 SIDE-DISH OR 4 MAIN-COURSE SERVINGS

⅓ cup plus 2 tablespoons olive oil
1 cup millet
1⅓ cups chicken broth
⅔ cup dry vermouth
1 medium eggplant, cut into ½-inch cubes (about 5 cups)
1 large red bell pepper, cut into ½-inch squares (about 2 cups)
1 medium onion, minced (about 1 cup)
2 garlic cloves, minced
¼ teaspoon ground coriander
¾ teaspoon ground cumin
2 teaspoons dried dillweed
1½ teaspoons dry mustard
2 teaspoons dried mint leaves, crumbled
½ teaspoon ground cardamom
¼ teaspoon cayenne
1 teaspoon salt
2 cups plain yogurt

1. Preheat the oven to 400°. In a small skillet, heat 1 tablespoon of the oil over moderately high heat. When the oil is almost smoking, add the millet and stir constantly until toasted and golden, about 4 minutes. Add the chicken broth and vermouth and bring just to a boil. Turn the millet and stock into a shallow

1½-quart casserole, cover tightly, and bake for 20 minutes.

2. While the millet is baking, in a large heavy skillet, heat ⅓ cup of the olive oil over moderately high heat. When the oil is almost smoking, add the eggplant and pepper and stir constantly for 6 minutes. Add the remaining olive oil and the onion and garlic to the pan; continue cooking and stirring over high heat for 3 minutes. Remove from the heat and stir in the remaining spices and herbs all at once. Stir until blended.

3. Add the baked millet and any remaining broth to the skillet. Stir the ingredients together, making sure to incorporate the brown bits that cling to the pan. Turn the entire mixture back into the casserole, cover, and bake for 30 minutes, or until the eggplant is just tender and the peppers still firm. Serve with a side dish of cold yogurt.

Savory Endive Custard

4 SERVINGS

5 tablespoons unsalted butter
4 medium heads of Belgian endive (about 1 pound), cut into julienne strips
⅓ cup crème fraîche
3 whole eggs plus 1 egg yolk
½ teaspoon salt
¼ teaspoon pepper
Pinch of nutmeg

1. Preheat the oven to 300°. Lightly butter four ½-cup ramekins or custard cups with 1 tablespoon of the butter. In a small heavy saucepan, melt the remaining 4 tablespoons butter over moderately high heat. Continue to cook, swirling the pan, until the butter is lightly browned but not burned, 1 to 2 minutes.

2. Pour the browned butter into a large skillet, leaving the residue at the bottom of the pan. Add the endive and cook, stirring occasionally, until wilted, about 6 minutes. In a food processor or blender, puree the endive until smooth. Transfer to a fine sieve and press lightly to remove excess liquid.

3. In a medium bowl, whisk the crème fraîche, whole eggs, egg yolk, salt, pepper and nutmeg until blended. Whisk in the endive puree.

4. Pour the endive mixture into the buttered ramekins, dividing evenly. Place on a rack in a large roasting pan. Add enough warm water to the pan to reach halfway up the sides of the ramekins.

5. Bake until the custard sets and a toothpick inserted in the center emerges clean, 40 to 45 minutes. Let rest for 2 to 3 minutes before unmolding.

Sherried Mushrooms

Buttery and tender, these sautéed mushrooms complement a dry sherry nicely.

3 TO 4 APPETIZER SERVINGS

2 tablespoons unsalted butter
12 medium mushroom caps
2 tablespoons medium-dry sherry
½ teaspoon salt
Freshly ground pepper
3 tablespoons heavy cream

1. In a medium skillet, warm the butter over moderately high heat until sizzling. Add the mushrooms and sauté, turning once, until tender and golden brown, about 12 minutes.

2. Add the sherry and cook, stirring, until reduced to a thick glaze, about 1 minute. Add the salt and pepper to taste. Add the cream and cook, stirring, until reduced to a thick sauce, about 1½ minutes. Spear with toothpicks; serve warm.

Stuffed Mushrooms

MAKES 20

20 medium mushrooms (about 1 pound)
7 tablespoons unsalted butter
2 tablespoons minced shallots
¼ teaspoon salt
¼ teaspoon freshly ground nutmeg
⅛ teaspoon pepper
1 cup fresh bread crumbs, preferably whole-wheat
¼ cup minced parsley
3 tablespoons heavy cream

1. Preheat the oven to 350°. Remove the stems from the mushrooms. Trim the stems and chop them finely. Wipe the mushroom caps and set them aside.

2. Melt 3 tablespoons of the butter and

set aside. In a medium skillet, melt the remaining 4 tablespoons butter over moderate heat. Add the shallots and sauté until softened, about 1 minute. Add the chopped mushroom stems, salt, nutmeg and pepper. Reduce the heat to low and cook, stirring, for 3 minutes. Transfer to a small bowl. Add the bread crumbs, parsley and cream; mix well.

3. Brush the mushroom caps and a baking sheet with the reserved melted butter. Stuff each cap with about 2 rounded teaspoons of filling. Place on the baking sheet and bake for 20 minutes. Serve hot.

Braised Mushrooms with Pancetta and Pine Nuts

Pancetta, a salt-cured meat, can be very salty, so season this dish with discretion. If you cannot find *pancetta*, prosciutto is a good substitute.

6 SERVINGS

1 ounce dried *porcini* or cèpes
¼ pound *pancetta*, cut into ⅛-inch dice
2 to 4 tablespoons olive oil
¼ cup pine nuts (pignoli)
1 large garlic clove, minced
1 small onion, minced
1 pound mushrooms, thinly sliced
¼ cup dry Madeira or tawny port
2 tablespoons heavy cream
¼ cup minced fresh parsley
Salt and pepper

1. In a small bowl, cover the *porcini* with warm water and let soak for 1 hour. Remove the mushrooms. Strain the soaking liquid through several layers of damp cheesecloth; reserve ½ cup.

2. Rinse the mushrooms well to remove any sand; squeeze to remove as much liquid as possible. Chop the mushrooms coarsely and set aside.

3. In a large skillet, cook the *pancetta* in 2 tablespoons of olive oil over low heat until golden brown, 10 to 12 minutes. Remove the *pancetta* with a slotted spoon to a small bowl. Add enough oil, if necessary, to the fat in the skillet to measure 3 tablespoons.

4. Add the pine nuts to the fat and sauté, stirring frequently, over moderate heat until golden, about 3 minutes. Remove with a slotted spoon and add to the *pancetta*.

5. Reduce the heat to low, add the garlic and onion and cook until softened, 2 to 3 minutes.

6. Increase the heat to high, add the reserved *porcini* and fresh mushrooms and cook, tossing, until the mushrooms begin to give up their juices, 5 to 7 minutes.

7. Add the Madeira and the reserved soaking liquid and boil until the liquid is reduced to 2 tablespoons, about 5 minutes. Add the cream, reduce the heat to low and cook until the sauce thickens slightly, about 2 minutes.

8. Stir in the parsley, *pancetta* and pine nuts. Season with salt and pepper to taste.

Crispy Onion Rings

The addition of cornstarch to the batter ensures a delicate, crisp coating.

4 TO 6 SERVINGS

**3 large onions, cut crosswise into
   ½-inch rounds
1 cup all-purpose flour
½ cup cornstarch
1 teaspoon baking soda
½ teaspoon salt
Vegetable oil, for frying**

1. Separate the onions into rings. Soak in a bowl of ice water for about 2 hours.

2. Meanwhile, prepare the batter: Combine the flour, cornstarch, baking soda and salt in a large bowl. Add 1½ cups of ice water all at once and whisk until the batter is smooth. Refrigerate for at least 1 hour before using.

3. Pour 2 inches of oil into a heavy, medium saucepan or deep fryer. Heat until almost smoking (375°). Place all of the onions in the batter and stir to coat.

4. Working in batches to avoid crowding, drop the onion rings, one by one, into the hot oil. Fry, turning once, until crisp and golden brown, 3 to 4 minutes. Drain well on paper towels. Sprinkle with salt and serve hot.

Baked Onions

You'll never know just how sweet and pungent the natural flavor of onions is until you try baking them. The whole onion is simply baked in its skin and served steaming hot with butter.

4 SERVINGS

**4 medium onions (about 1½
   pounds)
Butter
Salt and pepper**

Preheat the oven to 400°. Place the unpeeled onions in a baking dish. Bake for 1 hour, or until tender when pierced with a knife. Serve hot with butter, salt and pepper to taste.

Three-Onion Tart

10 TO 12 SERVINGS

Pastry:
**1½ cups all-purpose flour
½ teaspoon salt
8 tablespoons (1 stick) unsalted
   butter, chilled and cut into thin
   slices
4 to 5 tablespoons ice water
1½ tablespoons Dijon-style mustard**

Filling:
**5 tablespoons unsalted butter
4 medium yellow onions, chopped
   (about 3 cups)
2 medium red onions, cut into ⅛-
   inch slices
¼ pound Gruyère cheese, grated
   (about 1 cup)
12 white onions (about 1 inch in
   diameter)
1 tablespoon sugar
2 whole eggs
1 egg yolk**

**1 cup heavy cream
1 teaspoon coarse (kosher) salt
¼ teaspoon white pepper**

1. Prepare the pastry: Place the flour, salt and butter in a large bowl. Using a pastry blender or two knives, cut the butter into the flour until the mixture resembles coarse meal. Quickly stir in 4 tablespoons of the ice water with a fork. If the dough does not hold together easily when squeezed, blend in as much as 1 tablespoon more of ice water. Do not overmix. Pat the dough into a flat round about 6 inches in diameter; wrap in waxed paper and refrigerate for at least 30 minutes.

2. Preheat the oven to 425°. Roll the chilled pastry into a 12-inch round. Line an 11-inch quiche pan with the pastry. Pierce the dough all over with a fork and fit a piece of aluminum foil into the pastry shell. Fill the foil with dried beans or pie weights and bake for 15 minutes.

3. Remove the foil and weights. Brush the interior of the pastry shell with the mustard and return it to the oven for 5 minutes to crisp the shell. Remove and reduce the oven temperature to 350°.

4. Prepare the filling: In a large skillet, melt 3 tablespoons of the butter over low heat and cook the yellow onions, stirring, until they are soft but not brown, about 5 minutes. Transfer the onions to a plate.

5. Melt 1 more tablespoon of the butter in the skillet. Add a layer of red onion slices and cook over moderate heat until they are slightly colored on the underside. (Do not disturb the slices or they may separate into rings.) Remove with a slotted spoon, set aside, add the remaining slices and cook.

6. Layer the yellow onions over the pastry shell and sprinkle the cheese evenly over them. Arrange the red onion slices on top, cooked sides up, leaving a 1-inch border around the edge.

7. Add the remaining tablespoon of butter to the skillet and cook the white onions for 2 minutes, tossing them so that they can cook on all sides. Sprinkle the sugar over them, and, tossing again, cook them until the sugar caramelizes, about 2 minutes longer. Reserving the glaze in the pan, remove the onions and cut them in half lengthwise. Arrange them, cut-side down, around the edge of the tart. Place the tart on a baking sheet.

8. In a medium bowl, beat together the whole eggs, egg yolk, cream, salt and pepper until blended. Pour the mixture into the tart shell over the onions.

9. Bake the tart for 20 minutes. Reduce the heat to 325° and bake for an additional 10 minutes, or until the filling has set.

10. Meanwhile, add ½ cup of water to the skillet and, stirring to blend in the caramelized sugar, reduce the liquid to about 2 tablespoons. When the tart is done, brush the surface with the glaze reserved in the skillet. Serve warm or at room temperature.

Gratin of Leeks or Scallions

4 TO 6 SERVINGS

8 medium leeks or 18 large scallions
2 cups milk
¾ teaspoon salt
¾ teaspoon thyme
¼ teaspoon freshly grated nutmeg
2 whole cloves
1 bay leaf
6 peppercorns
7½ tablespoons unsalted butter
¼ cup all-purpose flour
Freshly ground white pepper
½ cup grated Gruyère or Swiss cheese
2 tablespoons freshly grated Parmesan cheese
Dash of cayenne pepper

1. Trim the leeks, cutting off the root end but leaving the base intact. Trim off the tough green tops, leaving about 1½ inches of the tender green above the white part. Split each leek lengthwise down to about ½ inch from the base. Rinse well under cold running water to remove all traces of sand. If using scallions, trim off the roots and all but about 3½ inches of the green tops.

2. Bring a large pot of salted water to a boil. Tie the leeks or scallions into 2 or 3 bundles with kitchen string. Lower them into the water and boil until just tender when pierced with a small knife—10 to 15 minutes for the leeks, about 5 minutes for the scallions. Drain and run cold water into the pot until they are cool. Wrap each bundle in paper towels and gently squeeze out excess moisture. Remove the strings and set the vegetables aside on several layers of paper towels while you make the sauce.

3. In a heavy medium saucepan, combine the milk, salt, thyme, nutmeg, cloves, bay leaf and peppercorns. Bring to a simmer over moderate heat. Meanwhile, in another heavy saucepan, melt 6 tablespoons of the butter. Add the flour and cook, stirring, over moderate heat without coloring for about 3 minutes to a make a roux. Whisk the hot milk with the spices into the roux, reduce the heat to moderately low and simmer, stirring frequently, for 25 minutes. Strain the sauce. Season with additional salt and nutmeg and white pepper to taste.

4. Preheat the oven to 375°. Generously butter a shallow baking dish large enough to hold the vegetables in a single layer. Spoon a few tablespoons of the sauce over the bottom of the dish. Give the leeks or scallions a final squeeze in their paper towels and arrange them in the dish. Pour the remaining sauce over the vegetables. Sprinkle on the Gruyère and then the Parmesan cheese. Dot with the remaining 1½ tablespoons butter. Sprinkle lightly with cayenne pepper.

5. Bake for 15 to 20 minutes, or until heated through and bubbly. Increase the temperature to broil and transfer the gratin to the broiler about 4 inches from the heat. Broil for about 3 minutes, checking frequently to prevent burning, until the top is glazed a rich golden brown. Serve hot.

Sautéed Parsnip Sticks

MAKES ABOUT 6 DOZEN

3¾ pounds small parsnips, peeled and cut in half lengthwise
10 tablespoons unsalted butter
½ cup all-purpose flour
½ cup cornmeal
¼ to ⅓ cup vegetable oil
Salt

1. In a large saucepan of boiling salted water, parboil the parsnips until they are slightly spongy, about 2 minutes. Drain them immediately and cut them into matchsticks about 3 inches by ½ inch.

2. In a large skillet, melt 4 tablespoons of the butter over low heat. Roll the parsnips in the butter and transfer them to a platter. Set the skillet aside, along with any remaining butter, and refrigerate the parsnip sticks until the butter coating has hardened, about 20 minutes.

3. Combine the flour and cornmeal in a shallow baking dish or pan and dredge the parsnips in the mixture to coat them.

4. Add 4 tablespoons of the butter along with ¼ cup of the oil to the reserved skillet over moderately high heat. Working in batches, add a single layer of parsnip sticks to the skillet and fry them on all sides until they are crisp and golden, 10 to 15 minutes; drain on paper towels and keep warm. Repeat with the remaining parsnips, adding more oil and butter as necessary. Season with salt to taste and serve.

Peppers with Balsamic Vinegar and Fresh Herbs

Alive with color and flavor, this dish is a natural accompaniment to grilled steak, hamburger or sausage.

8 SERVINGS

¼ cup olive oil
1 large onion, halved and thinly sliced
4 medium red bell peppers, cut into ¼-inch strips
4 medium green bell peppers, cut into ¼-inch strips
⅓ cup minced fresh parsley
⅓ cup shredded fresh basil or 1½ teaspoons dried
1 tablespoon fresh thyme or 1 teaspoon dried
¼ cup balsamic vinegar or good red wine vinegar
Salt and black pepper

1. In a large skillet, warm the oil over moderate heat. Add the onion and cook until softened but not browned, about 3 minutes.

2. Add the red and green peppers and toss to coat with the oil. Cover and cook until the peppers are tender, 10 to 12 minutes.

3. Add the parsley, basil and thyme and cook, uncovered, for another 5 minutes.

4. Stir in the vinegar and continue cooking for 5 minutes. Season with salt and black pepper to taste.

Potato Puree with Scallions

6 SERVINGS

2 pounds baking potatoes
½ cup (1 stick) unsalted butter, at room temperature
About 1 cup half-and-half
¼ cup minced scallions
Salt and pepper

1. Peel the potatoes and cut them into 1½-inch cubes. Place the potatoes in a medium saucepan and add enough water to cover them by 2 inches. Heat to boiling and cook for 15 to 20 minutes, or until soft. Drain and transfer the potatoes to a mixing bowl.

2. Add the butter and ½ cup of the half-and-half to the potatoes. Using an electric mixer, beat until smooth, gradually adding enough additional half-and-half to make a puree with a creamy consistency. Blend in the scallions and season to taste.

Carefree Potatoes

6 SERVINGS

6 baking potatoes
2 tablespoons vegetable oil
Butter

1. Preheat the oven to 400°. Scrub the potatoes well and pat them dry. Cut them in half lengthwise and dry the cut sides with paper towels. Rub the potatoes all over with the oil.

2. Bake the potatoes directly on the rack in the middle of the oven, cut-sides up, for 1 hour and 15 minutes until the tops are crusty and golden brown. Serve with butter.

Steak Fries

We developed this method of frying potatoes in a mere quarter inch of oil. The results are tasty and golden brown without the fuss and expense of deep-frying.

4 SERVINGS

4 large baking potatoes
Vegetable oil, for frying
Salt

1. Peel the potatoes and cut them lengthwise into sticks about 1 inch wide and ½ inch thick. Drop them into a bowl of ice water as they are cut.

2. Pour ¼ inch of vegetable oil into a large, heavy skillet or into 2 large skillets, if you prefer, to save time. Heat over moderately high heat until almost smoking (375°).

3. Meanwhile, drain and pat dry enough potato sticks to fit into a skillet in a single layer without crowding. Place in the hot oil and fry, lowering the heat if they brown too quickly, until crisp and golden brown on the bottom, 5 to 7 minutes. Turn the potato sticks with tongs and fry on the second side for 5 to 7 minutes, or until crisp and golden brown outside

and tender inside. Drain well on paper towels. Keep warm in a low oven while frying the remaining potatoes; add more oil if needed. Sprinkle with salt to taste before serving.

Potato Tart

This warm and buttery tart is delicately seasoned with mint, basil and parsley. It is particularly good served with roasted lamb.

6 TO 8 SERVINGS

1½ pounds (about 3 large) baking potatoes—boiled, peeled and sliced
1 frozen double-crust pie crust (8½ or 9 inches), thawed, or an unbaked homemade flaky pastry crust with top
2 tablespoons unsalted butter, cut into small pieces
2 tablespoons minced fresh mint, or 2 teaspoons dried
1 teaspoon minced fresh basil (optional)
1 teaspoon minced fresh parsley
1 teaspoon salt
¼ teaspoon freshly ground pepper
½ cup heavy cream
1 egg, beaten

1. Preheat the oven to 375°. Layer half of the potatoes in the bottom of the pie crust. Dot with half the butter. Sprinkle with half the mint, basil, parsley, salt and pepper. Layer the remaining potatoes on top and dot with the remaining butter. Sprinkle with the remaining mint, basil, parsley, salt and pepper.

2. Pour the cream over the potatoes. Lightly brush the edge of the pastry with some of the beaten egg. Place the top crust over the potatoes and gently crimp the edges to seal. Brush the top of the tart with the egg. Cut 2 or 3 steam vents into top crust. Bake for 45 minutes, or until the crust is golden brown. Serve warm.

Charley's Potatoes

20 SERVINGS

5 pounds (about 10) baking potatoes, peeled and cut lengthwise into 8 wedges
1 cup (2 sticks) unsalted butter
6 garlic cloves, minced (about 3 tablespoons)
1 tablespoon coarse (kosher) salt
1 teaspoon freshly ground pepper

1. Preheat the oven to 500°. Cook the potatoes in a large pot of boiling water for 5 minutes after the water returns to a boil. Drain thoroughly.

2. In a large skillet melt the butter. Add the garlic and cook over low heat until it is softened but not browned, about 3 minutes. Add the potatoes and stir gently to coat them with the garlic butter.

3. Transfer the potatoes and garlic butter to enough baking dishes or roasting pans to hold the potatoes in a single layer. Sprinkle with the salt and pepper. At this point, the potatoes can be set aside, uncovered, at room temperature until 1 hour before you plan to serve them.

4. Bake the potatoes for 1 hour, stirring gently about every 10 minutes, until they are golden brown and very crisp on the outside. Serve hot.

Oven-Fried Potato Skins

4 SERVINGS

4 medium baking potatoes (about 1½ pounds)
4 tablespoons butter
Salt and pepper

1. Preheat the oven to 450°. Scrub the potatoes thoroughly and pat them dry. Bake directly on the center rack of the oven for about 1 hour, or until tender.

2. Cut the potatoes in half lengthwise and scoop out the insides with a spoon, leaving a shell about ⅛-inch thick; reserve the pulp for another use. Cut each shell lengthwise into ½-inch strips.

3. In a large skillet, melt the butter over low heat. Add the potato skins and toss until well coated. Arrange the strips on a baking sheet, skin side down, and bake for about 15 minutes, or until crisp and golden brown. Sprinkle with salt and pepper to taste. Serve hot or at room temperature.

Spinach, Raisins and Pine Nuts with Romaine Lettuce

This delicate *contorno* complements simple meat dishes, such as sautéed veal, chicken or pork chops. Substitute escarole for romaine lettuce for a slightly bitter and refreshing taste.

6 SERVINGS

2 pounds fresh spinach, stemmed and washed
3 tablespoons unsalted butter
1 tablespoon vegetable oil
⅓ cup raisins
¼ cup pine nuts (pignoli)
1 medium head of romaine lettuce, coarsely chopped
½ teaspoon salt
¼ teaspoon freshly ground pepper
⅛ teaspoon fresh grated nutmeg
¼ cup freshly grated Romano cheese

1. In a large pot, cook the spinach with the water clinging to its leaves over moderately high heat, covered, until the leaves just begin to wilt, about 4 minutes. Rinse under cold running water, drain well and squeeze to remove as much moisture as possible; coarsely chop.

2. In a large skillet, melt the butter in the oil over moderate heat. Add the raisins and pine nuts and sauté, stirring, until the nuts start to color, about 1 minute. Add the lettuce, increase the heat to moderately high and cook, tossing until the lettuce begins to wilt, about 30 seconds. Add the spinach, salt, pepper and nutmeg and cook until the spinach is just heated through, about 1 minute.

3. Remove the pan from heat. Sprinkle on the cheese and toss lightly. Serve hot.

Grilled Spinach and Blue Cheese Sandwiches

2 SERVINGS

1 pound fresh spinach—stemmed, rinsed and coarsely chopped
¼ cup whole-milk ricotta cheese
¼ teaspoon salt
4 thick slices Italian bread
2 tablespoons olive oil, preferably extra-virgin
1 teaspoon coarsely ground pepper
4 ounces double- or triple-crème blue cheese such as Saga, cut into 4 slices
2 scallions (white and light green), cut into thin julienne strips

1. In a medium bowl, combine the spinach, ricotta and salt; mix well.

2. Preheat the broiler. Brush both sides of the bread with the olive oil and sprinkle with the pepper. Place on a cookie sheet and broil about 4 inches from the heat, turning once, until golden brown, about 2 minutes on each side. Remove the bread, but leave the broiler on.

3. Spread the spinach-ricotta mixture over the bread, dividing evenly. Cut each slice of cheese into several strips and distribute them over the sandwiches.

4. Broil about 4 inches from the heat until the cheese melts, about 30 seconds. Sprinkle the scallions over each sandwich and serve hot.

Cheese-Stuffed Swiss Chard

Serve these small, delicately stuffed, steamed leaves as an accompaniment to roast meats, in a chicken broth as a soup, or as a hot hors d'oeuvre.

MAKES ABOUT 18

2 tablespoons olive oil
1 cup chopped onion
1 large garlic clove, crushed and minced
1 pound ricotta cheese
2 teaspoons dried basil
1 cup plus 3 tablespoons freshly grated Parmesan cheese
1 egg, lightly beaten
¼ teaspoon nutmeg

Salt and pepper
1½ pounds young Swiss chard

1. Prepare the filling: In a medium skillet, heat the oil over moderate heat. Add the onion, reduce the heat slightly and cook until the onion is softened and translucent, about 10 minutes. Add the garlic and sauté for 1 minute. Remove from the heat.

2. Place the ricotta in a large bowl and beat it with a spoon until fluffy, about 2 minutes. Stir in the reserved onion mixture along with the basil, 1 cup of the Parmesan cheese, the egg, nutmeg and salt and pepper to taste; set aside.

3. Prepare the chard: Carefully cut off and discard the stems from the leaves, placing 18 of the best leaves, which should range in size from 4 by 4 inches to 6 by 6 inches, aside for stuffing; place the remaining leaves in another stack.

4. Bring a large pot of water to a boil over high heat and add 1 tablespoon salt. Working in batches, drop in the leaves reserved for stuffing and blanch for 1 minute. Carefully remove with a slotted spoon and drain flat on paper towels. Using a paring knife and slicing across the top of each leaf, carefully remove and discard the raised portion of each vein; set the leaves aside. Bring the water back to a boil and add the remaining leaves. Cook for 3 minutes, drain in a sieve, pushing out as much moisture as possible with a wooden spoon, and chop finely (you should have about ½ cup). Mix into the cheese mixture.

5. Stuff the leaves: Place one of the leaves, vein side down, on a work surface. Shape 1 to 2 tablespoons of the filling (depending on the size of the leaf) into a finger shape and place it across the leaf about two-thirds of the way down from the top. Fold the lower third of the leaf over the filling, fold in both side edges and loosely roll the leaf up to enclose the filling. Set it, seam-side down, on a heatproof plate or platter that will fit into your steamer. Continue stuffing and rolling the remaining leaves, adding them to the plate.

6. Cook the leaves: Add water to a steamer to come to 1 inch below the rack placement and bring it to a boil. Add the rack and the plate of chard. Tightly cover and steam for 10 minutes. Serve hot, sprinkled with the remaining 3 tablespoons Parmesan cheese.

Swiss Chard with Chopped Tomatoes

4 SERVINGS

1 pound Swiss chard (about 2 bunches)
1 small onion, diced
¼ cup olive oil
2 tablespoons fresh lemon juice
⅓ cup clarified butter
2 medium, firm tomatoes—peeled, seeded and coarsely chopped
Salt and white pepper

1. Separate the chard stems and leaves. Roughly chop the leaves; peel both sides of the stems.

2. Cook the stems in a medium saucepan of boiling water until tender, about 4 minutes. Drain and coarsely chop.

3. In a small skillet, cook the onion in the oil and lemon juice over moderate heat until translucent and softened, about 2 minutes. Set aside.

4. In a large skillet, heat the butter. Add the chard (stems and leaves) and the tomatoes and sauté over moderate heat, tossing several times, until the chard is just tender, about 4 minutes. Scrape the onion into the skillet and toss to mix. Season to taste with salt and pepper.

Sautéed Tomatoes with Cream

4 SERVINGS

1½ tablespoons unsalted butter
4 slices tomato, each 1-inch thick
Pinch of thyme
Salt
¼ cup light cream

1. In a skillet, melt the butter. Add the tomato slices and sauté until they are slightly soft. Season with the thyme and salt.

2. Pour the cream into the skillet and boil until it has thickened slightly. Serve hot.

Parmesan-Fried Green Tomatoes

6 SERVINGS

About ½ cup all-purpose flour, for dredging
2 eggs
⅓ cup yellow cornmeal
⅓ cup freshly grated Parmesan cheese
2 teaspoons oregano
1 teaspoon salt
¼ teaspoon pepper
4 medium green tomatoes (about 1¼ pounds), cut into ⅛-inch slices
About ½ cup olive oil, for frying

1. Place the flour on a sheet of waxed paper. In a small shallow bowl, lightly beat the eggs. On another sheet of waxed paper, mix the cornmeal, cheese, oregano, salt and pepper until blended.

2. Working with one tomato slice at a time, dip each in the flour, then in the egg and finally in the seasoned cornmeal, being sure to coat both sides completely. As they are coated, place them on a rack or baking sheet in a single layer.

3. In a large heavy skillet, heat 2 to 3 tablespoons of the oil until almost smoking. Add as many tomato slices as fit in a single layer without crowding and fry over moderate heat until crisp and golden brown on the bottom, about 2 minutes. Turn and fry until the other side is golden brown, about 2 minutes. Drain on paper towels. Continue frying the remaining tomato slices in the same manner, adding oil to the skillet as needed. It may be necessary to stop occasionally and wipe particles of burned cornmeal from the pan before frying another batch.

Tomato and Mushroom Pie

The base for this delicious pie is a thick, but light and tasty, pizza-like dough that is flavored with freshly grated Parmesan cheese.

MAKES TWO 12-INCH PIES

Dough:

1½ tablespoons (1½ envelopes) active dry yeast
¼ teaspoon sugar
1 cup warm water (105° to 115°)
About 3 cups all-purpose flour
½ cup (2 ounces) freshly grated Parmesan cheese
4 tablespoons olive oil
1 teaspoon salt

Tomatoes:

2 pounds (about 18) fresh Italian plum tomatoes—peeled, seeded and cut into ½-inch dice
2 teaspoons salt

Topping:

8 medium mushrooms (about 6 ounces), thinly sliced
1 teaspoon oregano
1 teaspoon basil
½ teaspoon freshly ground pepper
8 ounces mozzarella cheese, coarsely shredded
6 tablespoons freshly grated Parmesan cheese
4 tablespoons olive oil

1. Prepare the dough: In a small bowl, combine the yeast and sugar. Add ¼ cup of the warm water and stir briefly to dissolve the yeast; let rest to proof until bubbly, about 5 minutes.

2. In a large bowl, combine 3 cups of flour, the cheese, 3 tablespoons of the oil and the salt. Mix well with a fork, then stir in the remaining ¾ cup warm water and the yeast mixture. Stir until well blended. Turn the dough out onto a lightly floured surface and knead until smooth and elastic, about 10 minutes; add a small amount of additional flour if necessary to prevent sticking. The dough should be soft and moist.

3. Grease a clean large bowl with the remaining 1 tablespoon oil. Place the dough in the bowl, turn it over once to grease the top, cover with a towel and let rise in a warm, draft-free place until doubled in bulk, about 1½ hours.

4. Meanwhile, prepare the tomatoes: Toss the tomatoes with salt and let drain on several thicknesses of paper towel for 15 minutes. Transfer to a sieve placed over a bowl and let drain until you are ready to assemble the pie.

5. Shape the pies: Lightly coat two 12-inch, round pizza pans or small baking sheets with olive oil. Punch the dough and divide it in half. Place each piece on one of the pizza pans and pat out into an 11- or 12-inch circle, pinching the outside edge all around to raise the edge slightly. Cover loosely with kitchen towels or waxed paper and let rise in a warm place until doubled in bulk, about 45 minutes. After about 30 minutes, preheat the oven to 450°.

6. Assemble the pies: If both pies will fit on the floor of your oven at the same time, then assemble both before baking. If only one will fit at a time, assemble one and, while it is baking, assemble the remaining pie. For each pie, arrange half the tomato pieces evenly over one of the dough rounds. Arrange half of the mushroom slices over the tomatoes. Sprinkle evenly with ½ teaspoon of the oregano and basil, and ¼ teaspoon of the pepper. Top with half the mozzarella and half the Parmesan; then drizzle 2 tablespoons of the olive oil over the pie.

7. Bake the pies: Bake in the center of the oven for 12 to 15 minutes, until the crust has puffed, the bottom is lightly browned and the cheese is melted. Transfer the pie, still on the pan, to the floor of the oven if using a gas stove, or to the lowest setting if using an electric stove, and bake for 2 to 3 minutes, until the bottom is golden brown and crisp. Serve hot, cut into wedges.

Broiled Tomatoes

4 SERVINGS

2 large, firm, ripe tomatoes
4 tablespoons unsalted butter, melted
2 tablespoons fresh bread crumbs
2 tablespoons minced parsley
1 teaspoon freshly ground pepper
¾ teaspoon salt

1. Preheat the broiler. Cut each tomato in half crosswise. Brush the cut sides of the tomatoes with a little of the melted butter.

2. In a small bowl, mix the bread crumbs, parsley, pepper and salt with the remaining butter.

3. Place the tomatoes on a small baking sheet and broil about 4 inches from the heat for 3 minutes. Sprinkle the bread-crumb mixture evenly over the tops of the tomatoes and broil until the crumbs are a light, golden brown, about 1 minute.

Orange-Glazed Turnips

4 SERVINGS

4 medium white turnips (1½ pounds)
2 cups orange juice
4 tablespoons unsalted butter
1 seedless orange, separated into segments and coarsely chopped
1 teaspoon salt
¼ teaspoon pepper
¼ cup minced fresh parsley

1. Peel the turnips with a vegetable peeler or a paring knife. Cut the turnips into ¼-inch slices and then into half-rounds.

2. Place the turnip slices and the orange juice in a medium saucepan. Bring the orange juice to a boil over moderate heat. Reduce the heat, and simmer the turnips, covered, until they are tender, 15 to 20 minutes. Remove the turnips with a slotted spoon, setting them aside on a plate.

3. Reduce the orange juice to ¼ cup. Stir in the butter, orange segments, salt, pepper and parsley. Add the turnips and heat gently over low heat until the turnips are hot. Place in a dish and serve immediately.

Zucchini "Spaghetti" with Chive-Cream Sauce

6 SERVINGS

4 medium zucchini
6 tablespoons Fresh Tomato Sauce
  (p. 207) or 1 can (14 ounces)
  peeled Italian tomatoes—seeded,
  drained well and pureed
3 tablespoons clarified butter
¼ cup finely chopped carrot
3 tablespoons finely chopped
  celery
1 tablespoon minced shallots
1 sprig of fresh thyme or ½
  teaspoon dried
1 bay leaf
½ cup dry white wine
2 cups *crème fleurette* (see Note)
⅓ cup finely chopped fresh chives
1 tablespoon fresh lemon juice
½ teaspoon salt
⅛ teaspoon freshly ground pepper
12 large fresh basil leaves,
  shredded

1. If you have a mandoline, cut the zucchini lengthwise into long, thin strips that look like spaghetti. Or with a large knife, cut the zucchini lengthwise into slices ⅛ inch thick. Cut each slice lengthwise again into ⅛-inch strands.

2. If using the tomato sauce, warm it in a double boiler over low heat. If using the pureed tomatoes, cook over moderate heat, stirring occasionally, until reduced by half; keep warm.

3. In a heavy, medium saucepan, heat 1 tablespoon of the clarified butter over moderate heat. Add the carrot, celery, shallots, thyme and bay leaf and cook until the vegetables are softened but not browned, about 3 minutes.

4. Add the white wine and boil until reduced to about 1 tablespoon. Add the *crème fleurette* and boil for 2 minutes.

5. Strain the cream sauce through a fine sieve into another medium saucepan. Add the chives, lemon juice, salt and pepper. Keep hot over very low heat.

6. In a large skillet, heat the remaining 2 tablespoons clarified butter. Add the zucchini and sauté over high heat, stirring, until slightly limp but still *al dente* (resistant to the bite), 2 to 3 minutes. Season with salt and pepper to taste. Drain into a colander.

7. For each serving, place about one-sixth of the zucchini in the center of a large, warm plate and twirl with a fork to form a small nest. Pour about ⅓ cup of the cream sauce around the zucchini, letting it run all over the plate. Spoon about 1 tablespoon of the tomato sauce onto one side of the plate and swirl with the back of a spoon to make a decorative design. Garnish with basil.

NOTE: *Crème fleurette* is a thick French cream that lacks the sour tinge of crème fraîche. To make a good substitute for 2 cups of *crème fleurette*, cook 4 cups (2 pints) heavy cream in a large, heavy saucepan over moderately low heat, so that it does not boil over, whisking frequently, until reduced by half to 2 cups. This will take about 1 hour.

Eggs Verdi

6 SERVINGS

1 package (10 ounces) frozen peas,
  thawed
1 package (10 ounces) frozen
  spinach, thawed and well drained
4 tablespoons unsalted butter,
  melted
¼ cup beef broth
1 tablespoon fresh lemon juice
1 teaspoon salt
½ teaspoon freshly ground pepper
6 thin slices Canadian bacon
6 poached eggs
½ cup sour cream
½ cup (2 ounces) freshly grated
  Parmesan cheese

1. Preheat the oven to 350°. In a medium saucepan, combine the peas and spinach with 2 tablespoons of the butter. Cover and cook over low heat for 10 minutes. Transfer to a blender or food processor.

2. Add the broth, lemon juice, salt and pepper to the spinach and peas and puree until smooth.

3. In a round ovenproof dish, spread a thin layer of the puree. Arrange the bacon in a circle over the puree, spacing evenly. Place a poached egg on top of each slice of bacon. (Since the eggs will be hidden by more sauce, place a toothpick at the edge of the dish next to each egg to indicate position for serving.)

4. Spread the remaining puree in a layer over the eggs. Cover each egg with sour cream, dividing evenly. Top with a sprinkling of Parmesan cheese and drizzle with the remaining 2 tablespoons melted butter.

5. Bake for 10 minutes, until heated through. Serve hot.

Cold Vegetable Platter

4 SERVINGS

1 pound fresh green beans (as thin
  as possible)
French Dressing (recipe follows)
¾ pound whole baby carrots (see
  Note)
½ pound whole small mushrooms,
  or larger mushrooms halved or
  quartered
1 tablespoon toasted sesame seeds

1. Steam the beans until bright green and crisp-tender, 2 to 4 minutes. Transfer to a medium bowl and toss while still warm with half of the French Dressing. Marinate for at least 1 hour.

2. Meanwhile, steam the carrots until bright orange and crisp-tender, 3 to 5 minutes. Transfer to another bowl and toss while still warm with the remaining dressing. Marinate for at least 1 hour.

3. With a slotted spoon, remove the beans and carrots from the vinaigrette and arrange them attractively on a serving platter. Combine the two bowls of vinaigrette; add the mushrooms and toss until well coated. Remove with a slotted spoon and arrange them on the serving platter. Spoon a few tablespoons of the vinaigrette over the vegetables and

sprinkle with the sesame seeds. Serve at room temperature.

NOTE: If you cannot get baby carrots, use large carrots halved crosswise and then halved lengthwise.

French Dressing

MAKES ¾ CUP

¼ cup red or white wine vinegar
2 garlic cloves, crushed through press
Pinch of sugar
½ cup olive oil or other vegetable oil

In a small bowl, combine the vinegar, garlic and sugar. Whisk until the sugar dissolves. Gradually whisk in the oil in a thin stream until blended.

Vegetable Pâté

This pâté should be refrigerated overnight, so plan accordingly.

8 TO 10 SERVINGS

2½ pounds fresh spinach, trimmed and rinsed
2 pounds tomatoes (about 5 large)—peeled, seeded and diced
1 tablespoon coarse (kosher) salt
About 1 tablespoon tomato paste, if necessary
2 tablespoons cornstarch
1 cup crème fraîche
9 eggs
½ teaspoon nutmeg
½ teaspoon pepper
1 tablespoon butter
2 cups (8 ounces) grated Gruyère cheese

1. Place the spinach in a large saucepan and cook, covered, in just the water clinging to the leaves, until wilted, about 5 minutes. Rinse under cold running water; drain well. Squeeze the spinach to remove as much water as possible. Chop the spinach; there should be about 1½ cups.

2. Place the diced tomatoes in a colander and sprinkle them with 1 teaspoon of the salt. Let drain for 30 minutes to draw out moisture. Gently squeeze dry in a kitchen towel or cook for about 10 minutes over moderate heat to evapo-

rate more liquid. There should be about 1 cup fairly solid tomato pulp. If your tomatoes lack flavor and color, add up to 1 tablespoon tomato paste.

3. In a small bowl, stir together the cornstarch and crème fraîche until smooth. In a medium bowl, whisk the eggs, nutmeg, pepper and remaining 2 teaspoons salt until blended. Slowly whisk the crème fraîche mixture into the eggs and beat until smooth.

4. Preheat the oven to 300°. Lightly butter a 6-cup ovenproof glass loaf pan. Line the bottom of the pan with lightly buttered waxed paper.

5. Stir one-third of the egg mixture into the spinach and pour into the pan. Smooth into an even layer. Place the pan in a larger baking pan on the middle rack of the oven. Fill the baking pan with enough boiling water to reach halfway up the sides of the loaf pan. Bake, uncovered, for about 50 minutes, until the spinach layer is just set. Remove the pan from the oven.

6. Stir one-half of the remaining egg mixture into the tomatoes. Layer the tomato mixture evenly over the spinach. Return to the water bath and bake for 40 to 50 minutes, or until the tomato layer is set. Remove the loaf pan from the oven.

7. Stir the cheese into the remaining egg mixture and spoon it on top of the tomato layer. Return to the water bath and bake for 40 to 50 minutes, or until the cheese layer is set around the edges (the center will be slightly soft; it firms after cooling).

8. Let the pâté cool to room temperature; then refrigerate overnight. To serve, invert onto a platter to unmold, remove the waxed paper and cut into ½-inch slices.

Vegetable Stew

8 SERVINGS

2 tablespoons unsalted butter
2 tablespoons vegetable oil
3 medium red onions, thinly sliced
2 garlic cloves, minced
1 pound carrots, cut into 1-inch pieces
1 pound small red potatoes, quartered
1 medium cauliflower (about 1¾ pounds), broken into florets
½ pound medium mushrooms, halved
½ small cabbage (about ½ pound), cored and cut into ½-inch slices
2 teaspoons salt
¼ teaspoon freshly ground pepper
1 teaspoon dried basil or 1 tablespoon minced fresh
3 cups tomato or vegetable juice
3½ cups cooked chick-peas, drained
2 medium green bell peppers, cut into ½-inch strips
2 cups fresh whole-wheat bread crumbs (from about 5 slices)
½ cup (2 ounces) freshly grated Parmesan cheese
½ cup minced fresh parsley

1. Preheat the oven to 350°. In a large flameproof casserole, melt the butter in the oil over moderate heat. Add the onions and garlic and sauté until the onions are soft but not browned, about 5 minutes. Add the carrots, potatoes, cauliflower, mushrooms and cabbage and cook, stirring occasionally, for 20 minutes.

2. Add the salt, pepper, basil and tomato juice. Cover and bring the mixture to a simmer. Stir in the chick-peas and green pepper; cover and bake in the middle of the oven for about 45 minutes, or until the vegetables are tender. Remove from the oven and increase the temperature to 375°.

3. In a small bowl, combine the bread crumbs, cheese and parsley. Sprinkle evenly over the vegetables in the casserole. Return to the oven and bake, uncovered, for 10 minutes, or until the bread crumbs are lightly browned. Serve hot.

PASTA, RICE
& GRAINS

Lasagna with Four Cheeses

This very rich lasagna can be served as a separate pasta course or as a side dish with the meal.

8 TO 10 SERVINGS

8 ounces lasagna noodles
4½ tablespoons unsalted butter
3 tablespoons all-purpose flour
1 quart hot milk
1 cup coarsely grated Swiss Gruyère cheese (4 ounces)
1¼ cups finely grated Parmesan cheese (5 ounces)
¾ cup diced mozzarella cheese (4 ounces)
1 cup grated Pecorino Romano or Italian Fontina cheese (4 ounces)
¾ teaspoon freshly ground white pepper

1. In a large pot of rapidly boiling, salted water, cook the lasagna stirring gently occasionally, until *al dente* (just tender), 10 to 12 minutes. Drain and lay the noodles in a single layer on kitchen towels.

2. Preheat the oven to 350°. Butter a 13-by-9-by-2-inch baking dish.

3. In a large heavy saucepan, melt 3 tablespoons of the butter over moderately low heat. Whisk in the flour and cook, stirring constantly, for 2 to 3 minutes without browning, to make a roux. Gradually whisk in the hot milk in a slow, steady stream, stirring until smooth. Bring to a boil, reduce the heat slightly and cook, stirring frequently, for 5 minutes. Add the Gruyère, 1 cup of the Parmesan, the mozzarella and Pecorino and cook until the cheeses melt, 5 to 7 minutes. Season with the pepper.

4. Line the bottom of the baking dish with one-fourth of the lasagna noodles. Spoon on one-fourth of the cheese filling; spread to cover evenly. Repeat with the remaining ingredients to make 3 more layers of each. Sprinkle the remaining ¼ cup of Parmesan over the top layer of cheese filling and dot with the remaining 1½ tablespoons butter.

5. Bake for 30 to 40 minutes, until bubbly and golden brown. Serve hot.

Vegetable-and-Ricotta-Stuffed Rigatoni

The sauce and the filling for this dish can be made up to several days in advance and stored in the refrigerator.

6 TO 8 SERVINGS

Mushrooms:
1 ounce dried *porcini* mushrooms

Sauce:
6 tablespoons unsalted butter
2 tablespoons olive oil
1 tablespoon finely minced garlic
3 tablespoons finely chopped shallots
½ cup finely chopped green bell pepper
3 tablespoons tomato paste
1 can (35 ounces) whole, peeled tomatoes
1 teaspoon salt

Filling:
6 tablespoons unsalted butter
1½ cups finely chopped carrots
½ cup finely chopped onion
2 teaspoons finely minced garlic
⅔ cup freshly grated Parmesan cheese
3 cups ricotta cheese
1 teaspoon basil
3 tablespoons chopped fresh parsley
1 teaspoon nutmeg
¾ teaspoon salt
½ teaspoon pepper
3 egg yolks
1¼ cups cooked, chopped spinach (1 pound uncooked)

Pasta:
1 pound rigatoni
1 tablespoon salt

Accompaniment: Freshly grated Parmesan cheese

1. Prepare the mushrooms: Soak the *porcini* in 2 cups hot water for 30 to 40 minutes. Drain the mushrooms, reserving 1½ cups of the liquid; squeeze them dry and finely chop. Set aside.

2. Make the sauce: In a deep skillet or medium saucepan, warm the butter in the oil over moderate heat. Add the garlic, shallots and green pepper, reduce the heat to low and cook for 8 to 10 minutes. Stir in the tomato paste, 1 cup of the liquid from the canned tomatoes, the tomatoes, the reserved *porcini* liquid and the salt. Roughly chop the tomatoes with a wooden spoon and then simmer the sauce gently over low heat until thick and rich, about 1½ hours. Cool to room temperature.

3. Meanwhile, make the filling: In a skillet, melt the butter over moderate heat. Add the carrots, onion and garlic, reduce the heat to low and cook for 30 minutes, stirring occasionally. Add the reserved *porcini* and gently cook the mixture until it is a medium caramel color, about 20 minutes longer. Transfer to a bowl with a slotted spoon. Blend in the Parmesan, ricotta, basil, parsley, nutmeg, salt, pepper, egg yolks, and spinach. Refrigerate until ready to use.

4. Prepare the pasta: In a large pot, bring 5 quarts of water to a boil over high heat. Add the pasta and salt, stirring constantly, until the boiling resumes. Then, stirring occasionally, cook the pasta until just *al dente*, 10 to 12 minutes. Drain and return to the pan. Cover the pasta with cold water, and let them rest until you fill them.

5. Preheat the oven to 400°. Butter a large baking dish. Fit a pastry bag with a ½-inch tip, fill it halfway with the vegetable-cheese filling and stuff each rigatoni. Continue until all the pasta and filling have been used.

6. Assemble the dish: Pass the cooled sauce through a food mill to puree it; or puree in a food processor. Then, cover the bottom of the prepared baking dish with ½ cup of the sauce and top with a single layer of stuffed rigatoni. Cover lightly with about ⅔ cup sauce. Continue layering in this way until all the pasta and sauce have been used.

7. Cover the dish with aluminum foil and bake for 20 minutes, or until bubbly. Remove from the oven and let stand, loosely covered, for 10 to 15 minutes before serving. Serve with grated Parmesan.

Top, Tomato Ravioli with Fennel Sausage and Chicken Filling (p. 144). Bottom, Egg Ravioli with Spinach-Ricotta Filling (p. 143) and Creamy Tomato Sauce (p. 207).

Above, East River Shrimp Noodles (p. 140). Left, Summery
Spaghetti with Corn, Coriander and Tomato Sauce (p. 137).

Above left, Valentine Duck Salad
(p. 157). Above right, Oriental-Style
Tomato Salad (p. 152). Right,
Shrimp Salad Hilary (p. 161).
Opposite page, Salad of Duck
Confit with Orange (p. 158).

Left, Salad of Squid, Fennel, Red Peppers and Croutons (p. 161). Below, Celery Root with Celery Dressing (p. 152).

Marinated Tomatoes with Pasta

Fresh tomatoes are marinated in a zesty vinaigrette, then tossed with vermicelli.

4 TO 6 SERVINGS

4 medium-size ripe tomatoes (about 1½ pounds), cut into ½-inch cubes
⅓ cup olive oil
3 tablespoons red wine vinegar
2 teaspoons basil
2 teaspoons coarse (kosher) salt
½ teaspoon freshly ground pepper
1 pound vermicelli or spaghettini
½ cup minced fresh parsley
1 cup (4 ounces) freshly grated Parmesan cheese

1. In a medium bowl, combine the tomatoes, oil, vinegar, basil, salt and pepper; toss gently. Cover and refrigerate until thoroughly chilled, at least 1 hour.

2. Cook the pasta in a large pot of boiling salted water until *al dente* (just tender); drain well. Toss the hot pasta with the cold marinated tomatoes. Serve at room temperature or cover and refrigerate until chilled. Sprinkle with the parsley and pass the cheese on the side.

Tortellini with Pistachio Sauce

4 TO 6 SERVINGS

¾ cup shelled pistachios
5 tablespoons olive oil
1 large garlic clove
1 tablespoon lemon juice
½ cup heavy cream
½ cup freshly grated Parmesan cheese
1 tablespoon salt
1 pound fresh or frozen tortellini
Freshly grated Parmesan cheese and chopped pistachios, for garnish

1. Place the pistachios in a sieve and rinse away the salt under cool running water; pat dry with paper towels. In a small skillet warm 1 tablespoon of the oil over moderate heat. Add the nuts

Smoked Trout (or Salmon) Niçoise (p. 160).

and, stirring constantly, sauté until they are lightly browned, about 2 minutes. Drain on paper towels.

2. Puree the pistachios, the remaining 4 tablespoons oil, the garlic and lemon juice in a blender or food processor. Transfer to a bowl and stir in the heavy cream and Parmesan. Cover and set aside.

3. Bring a large pot of water to a boil over high heat and add the salt and tortellini, stirring constantly when the boiling resumes. Then, stirring occasionally, cook the tortellini until *al dente*, 12 to 15 minutes for frozen, 8 to 12 for air-dried homemade. Drain the tortellini well and return them to the pot in which they were cooked. Toss with the pistachio sauce and serve hot, garnished with the Parmesan and pistachios.

Ziti in Shrimp Sauce

4 TO 6 SERVINGS

4 cups fish stock
1 pound medium shrimp—shelled, deveined and cut into ¼-inch slices
⅓ cup dry white wine
⅛ teaspoon cayenne pepper
8 ounces ziti or mostaccioli macaroni
½ cup heavy cream
¼ cup chopped fresh parsley
2 egg yolks
½ teaspoon salt
¼ teaspoon freshly ground black pepper
¾ cup (3 ounces) freshly grated Parmesan cheese

1. In a medium saucepan, bring the fish stock to a boil over moderate heat. Add the shrimp and cook just until the stock returns to a boil. Turn off the heat and, with a slotted spoon, transfer the shrimp to a bowl.

2. Boil the stock in the saucepan over high heat until it is reduced to 1 cup, about 15 minutes. Add the wine and cayenne pepper and reduce again to 1 cup, about 5 minutes. The sauce will thicken and should coat the back of a spoon.

3. Meanwhile, in a large pot of rapidly boiling salted water, cook the pasta until it is *al dente*, 15 to 18 minutes. Drain and

transfer the pasta to a large bowl set over a saucepan of simmering water. Stir together the cream, parsley, egg yolks, salt and pepper. Add to the pasta and stir to mix well. Cook until the mixture thickens and coats the pasta, 3 to 4 minutes. Add the reserved shrimp and reduced stock and cook until the shrimp is heated through, 1 to 2 minutes. Toss with the Parmesan cheese.

Summery Spaghetti with Corn, Coriander and Tomato Sauce

This is a sprightly, fresh dish, bound with a light, creamy-textured sauce, bright with sweet corn and tomatoes, aromatic with fresh coriander.

🍷 **Beverage Suggestion:**
Pinot Grigio

2 GENEROUS SERVINGS

2 medium tomatoes
1 ear of fresh corn, husked
½ pound spaghettini
1 egg
1 tablespoon red wine vinegar
½ teaspoon sugar
Salt and pepper
1 tablespoon full-flavored olive oil
⅓ cup minced fresh coriander
½ small red onion, chopped (about ½ cup)

1. Bring a large pot of water to a boil. Drop the tomatoes and corn into the boiling water and let the water return to the boil. Remove the tomatoes after 30 seconds. Let the corn boil for 1½ minutes longer. Remove the corn, cover the pot and keep the water at a low boil.

2. Peel and seed the tomatoes; cut into ½-inch dice. Cut the corn kernels from the cob.

3. Drop the spaghettini into the boiling water and cook until barely tender.

4. Meanwhile, in a food processor, whirl the egg until light and fluffy. Add half of the diced tomato, the vinegar, sugar, and salt and pepper to taste. Whirl to blend.

5. Drain the pasta and toss in a hot serving dish with the olive oil. Add the tomato-egg sauce and toss to coat. Add the coriander, onion, the corn and the remaining diced tomato. Toss to mix. Serve hot.

Moroccan Pasta

4 SERVINGS

2 pounds fresh spinach, stemmed
¼ cup olive oil
¼ cup pine nuts (pignoli)
½ cup raisins
1 teaspoon sugar
¼ teaspoon ground cardamom
Zest of 1 lemon, cut into thin
  julienne strips
1 teaspoon fresh lemon juice
¾ teaspoon salt
½ teaspoon freshly ground pepper
3 tablespoons unsalted butter
10 ounces skinless, boneless
  chicken breast, cut crosswise into
  ½-inch pieces
¼ cup dry white wine
½ pound spaghetti or linguine

1. Rinse the spinach well but do not drain. In a large noncorrodible saucepan over high heat, steam the spinach in the water clinging to its leaves until just wilted, about 2 minutes. Drain, rinse under cold running water, then squeeze in a clean linen towel or between several layers of paper towels to remove as much water as possible. Finely chop and set aside.

2. In a medium skillet, warm the oil over moderate heat. Add the pine nuts, raisins, sugar and cardamom. Cook, tossing, until the nuts are golden, about 2 minutes. Add the lemon zest and continue to sauté until the pieces of zest begin to brown around the edges, about 1 minute.

3. Add the spinach and cook, mixing with a fork to evenly distribute the ingredients, for 2 minutes. Season with the lemon juice, ½ teaspoon of the salt and the pepper and set aside.

4. In a medium skillet, melt 1 tablespoon of the butter over moderately high heat. Add the chicken and sauté, tossing, until lightly browned all over, 3 to 4 minutes. Season with the remaining ¼ teaspoon salt and add to the spinach mixture.

5. Pour the wine into the skillet and bring to a boil over high heat, scraping up any browned bits from the bottom to deglaze the pan. Boil until the liquid is reduced to 2 tablespoons, about 2 minutes. Add to the spinach and chicken.

6. Cook the pasta in a large pot of boiling salted water until tender but still firm, 10 to 12 minutes; drain. In a large bowl, toss the hot pasta with the remaining 2 tablespoons butter. Add the spinach and chicken and toss until mixed. Serve warm or at room temperature.

Linguine with Spinach Sauce

The bright green of this spinach sauce contrasts attractively with the pale yellow pasta. The flavor is fresh and mild.

F&W Beverage Suggestion:
Chianti, such as Antinori

4 TO 6 SERVINGS

3 pounds fresh spinach, stemmed
  and rinsed
2 tablespoons unsalted butter
1 garlic clove, minced
2 cups heavy cream
1¼ cups (about 5 ounces) freshly
  grated Parmesan cheese
1 pound linguine
Salt and freshly ground pepper

1. In a large saucepan of boiling water, cook the spinach over high heat, just until wilted, about 10 seconds. Drain and rinse under cold running water until cool; squeeze dry. Coarsely chop the spinach.

2. In a small skillet, melt the butter over low heat. Add the garlic and cook, stirring occasionally, until softened but not browned, about 2 minutes. Scrape into a blender or a food processor. Add the cream. With the machine on, gradually add the spinach and blend until smooth. Add the cheese and blend until mixed. Scrape into a medium saucepan and warm gently over low heat.

3. Meanwhile in a large saucepan of boiling salted water, cook the linguine until tender but still slightly firm—3 to 4 minutes for fresh, 8 to 10 for dried. Drain the pasta and rinse briefly in hot water to remove excess starch. Return the pasta to the saucepan and combine with the spinach sauce, and toss to coat. Season with salt and pepper to taste. Serve hot, with additional Parmesan cheese if desired.

Pasta del Sol

4 TO 6 SERVINGS

4 tablespoons unsalted butter
¼ cup olive oil
¾ cup minced fresh parsley
2 large garlic cloves, minced
1 teaspoon salt
½ teaspoon freshly ground pepper
½ cup heavy cream
1 pound fusilli or linguine
1 cup (4 ounces) freshly grated
  Parmesan cheese

1. In a small saucepan, melt the butter over moderate heat. Add the oil, parsley, garlic, salt and pepper and sauté until the garlic just begins to turn golden, about 2 minutes. Add the cream, reduce the heat and simmer for 3 minutes.

2. Meanwhile, cook the pasta in a large pot of boiling salted water until *al dente*; drain well. Pour the sauce over the pasta and toss. Pass the cheese separately.

Fettuccine Ben Arrivati

F&W Beverage Suggestion:
Galestro, such as Ruffino

6 TO 8 SERVINGS

1½ pounds hot Italian sausage
1½ pounds sweet Italian sausage
2 cups dry white wine
2 tablespoons olive oil
2 medium onions, sliced into rings
2 garlic cloves, chopped
3 medium green bell peppers,
  sliced into rings
2 medium celery ribs, coarsely
  chopped
½ cup chopped fresh parsley
4 tablespoons unsalted butter

3 tablespoons all-purpose flour
1½ cups hot beef stock or canned broth
⅓ cup sweet vermouth
⅓ cup dry vermouth
3 egg yolks
½ cup heavy cream
Salt and freshly ground pepper
1 pound fettuccine
1 cup (4 ounces) freshly grated Parmesan cheese

1. Prick the sausages and place them in a large noncorrodible skillet; add the wine and cook rapidly over moderately high heat until the wine has evaporated and the sausages are glazed, 15 to 20 minutes. Cut the sausages into ½-inch rounds. Remove to a plate and keep warm. Discard the fat in the skillet, but do not wash the pan.

2. In the same skillet, warm the oil over low heat. Add the onions, garlic, peppers and celery and cook until crisp-tender, about 7 minutes. Sprinkle on the parsley, remove to a plate and cover loosely to keep warm.

3. Using the same skillet, melt the butter over low heat. Add the flour and cook, stirring, for 2 to 3 minutes without coloring to make a roux. Off heat, whisk in the hot beef stock. Return to low heat and simmer, stirring occasionally, until thickened and smooth, about 5 minutes.

4. Add the sweet and dry vermouths and simmer for 5 minutes longer.

5. Remove from heat and whisk in the egg yolks, one at a time, beating rapidly until incorporated. Slowly add the cream and return to low heat to warm through; do not allow the sauce to boil. Season with salt and pepper to taste.

6. In a large pot of boiling water, cook the fettuccine until tender but still slightly firm, 2 to 3 minutes for fresh or 8 to 10 minutes for dried. Drain well.

7. Toss the pasta with the sauce to coat. Add the Parmesan cheese and toss again.

8. To serve, place the fettuccine in the middle of a large, warmed platter. Surround with a ring of the reserved pepper and onion mixture and then with a ring of the sausages.

Fettuccine with Smoked Salmon

F&W Beverage Suggestion: California Chardonnay

4 FIRST-COURSE SERVINGS

¼ pound smoked salmon (see Note)
1¼ cups half-and-half
¼ cup chopped fresh dill
2 teaspoons whole pink peppercorns
2 teaspoons tomato paste
¾ teaspoon salt
¼ teaspoon white pepper
2 teaspoons lemon juice
4 to 6 drops hot pepper sauce, to taste
½ pound fettuccine, preferably fresh
4 tablespoons unsalted butter, cut into tablespoons

1. Remove and discard the skin and bones from the salmon and shred it with a fork.

2. In a small saucepan, combine the half-and-half, 2 tablespoons of the dill, the pink peppercorns, tomato paste, salt and white pepper. Bring the mixture to a boil over moderate heat and boil gently until the sauce is slightly reduced and thickened, 3 to 5 minutes. Add the salmon, lemon juice and hot pepper sauce. Remove from the heat and cover to keep warm.

3. In a large pot of rapidly boiling salted water, cook the fettuccine until *al dente*, 45 seconds for fresh, 8 to 10 minutes for dried. Drain well and toss with the butter.

4. Divide the pasta among four plates. Spoon an equal amount of sauce over each portion and sprinkle generously with the remaining dill.

NOTE: Use a relatively less salty variety, such as Nova Scotia, Scottish or Irish salmon.

Maine Scallop and Mussel Fettuccine

F&W Beverage Suggestion: California white table wine, such as Trefethen Eschol White

6 SERVINGS

1½ cups dry white wine
3 large shallots, finely chopped
1½ cups heavy cream
2 bunches of fresh basil (1½ cups packed leaves), thick stems reserved
½ teaspoon salt
¼ teaspoon freshly ground pepper
1 large garlic clove
2 teaspoons grated orange zest
1 red bell pepper
1 small onion, coarsely chopped
8 parsley stems
½ cup bottled clam juice
2 small dried hot red peppers
2 dozen mussels, scrubbed and debearded
4 tablespoons unsalted butter
12 ounces sea scallops, sliced crosswise in half
1 pound fresh spinach fettuccine
½ cup freshly grated Parmesan cheese
3 cooked artichoke bottoms, cut into small wedges
Sprigs of fresh basil, for garnish

1. Combine 1 cup of the wine and the shallots in a small, noncorrodible saucepan. Boil over moderately high heat until reduced to ¼ cup, about 7 minutes. Strain, pressing with the back of a spoon to extract as much liquid as possible; discard the shallots.

2. In a large, heavy saucepan, combine the heavy cream and the stems from the basil and cook over moderately high heat until reduced to ¾ cup, about 10 minutes. Strain, discard the stems and combine the basil cream with the reduced wine. Season with the salt and pepper.

3. Grind the basil leaves, garlic and grated orange zest to a coarse paste using a mortar and pestle or a food processor. Add to the reserved cream-wine mixture.

4. Roast the red pepper on top of a gas burner or under the broiler, turning, until evenly charred. Place in a paper bag and let steam for 5 minutes. Scrape off the blackened skin. Remove the seeds and ribs and cut the pepper into thin strips. Add to the sauce.

5. In a heavy, medium saucepan, combine the onion, parsley stems, clam juice, hot peppers and remaining ½ cup wine. Bring to a boil over moderately high heat, add the mussels, cover and steam until the mussels open, 3 to 4 minutes. Remove the mussels from their shells and add to the sauce; discard any that do not open. Strain the cooking liquid and reserve for another use if desired. (The recipe can be prepared 2 to 3 hours ahead to this point.)

6. Bring a large pot of salted water to a boil.

7. Meanwhile, melt the butter in a large skillet. Add the scallops and cook over low heat until they just lose their translucency, 3 to 4 minutes. Remove from the heat and set aside.

8. Cook the fettuccine in the boiling water until *al dente*, 2 to 4 minutes. Drain well and toss with the scallops and their butter, the cheese and artichokes. Reheat the sauce, pour over the pasta, and toss until coated. Serve hot, garnished with sprigs of basil.

East River Shrimp Noodles

This is an irresistible tumble of egg noodles, shrimp, slivered ham and scallion, bound in an engagingly sweet sauce. All the preparations may be done a day in advance. Passing the shrimp through hot oil to cook the outside before stir-frying, gives the shrimp a texture reminiscent of lobster.

2 SERVINGS

1 large egg white (2 tablespoons)
2 tablespoons Chinese rice wine or dry sherry
1½ tablespoons cornstarch
1¾ teaspoons coarse (kosher) salt
½ pound medium shrimp, shelled and deveined
½ pound thin (1/16 inch) Chinese egg noodles, fresh or defrosted frozen (see Note)
1½ teaspoons Oriental sesame oil
½ cup plus 1 tablespoon rich, unsalted chicken stock or canned broth
1 teaspoon soy sauce
4 teaspoons cream sherry
3½ teaspoons sugar
3 cups corn or peanut oil
4 medium scallions, cut into 1-inch lengths, white part split lengthwise
½ cup slivered Black Forest ham
Freshly ground pepper

1. In a food processor or blender, beat the egg white, 1 tablespoon of the wine, 1 tablespoon of the cornstarch and ½ teaspoon of the salt until smooth and milkshake thick, about 1 minute.

2. Place the shrimp in a shallow bowl, scrape the egg-white mixture over them and toss well with your fingers to coat. Place in an airtight container and refrigerate for 8 to 24 hours. (The longer the shrimp marinate, the plumper and more tasty they will be.)

3. In a large saucepan, bring 4 quarts of water to a boil over high heat. Fluff the noodles to separate the strands, add them to the boiling water and cook until just tender, about 2 minutes. Drain and rinse under cold running water. Shake to remove excess water and gently toss in a large bowl with the sesame oil and 1 teaspoon of the salt; set aside. (The noo-

dles may be cooked and then refrigerated, covered, for up to 2 days.)

4. In a small bowl, combine ½ cup of the stock, the soy sauce, cream sherry and sugar to make the sauce. Set aside.

5. About 20 minutes before serving, heat the oil in a wok or large heavy skillet to 275°; turn off the heat. Stir the shrimp to separate the pieces, then slide them into the hot oil. Stir gently to separate the shrimp and "cook" until barely white, 15 to 20 seconds; immediately remove with a slotted spoon. Reserve the frying oil.

6. Heat a clean wok or skillet over high heat until hot enough to evaporate a bead of water on contact. Add 2 tablespoons of the frying oil and reduce heat to moderately high. When the oil is sizzling hot, add the scallions. Cook, tossing briskly, to glaze, 1 to 2 minutes. Sprinkle with the remaining ¼ teaspoon salt and 1 tablespoon wine, and toss to combine. Add the ham, toss again to mix; then remove the mixture to a plate.

7. Return the pan to moderately high heat; add 3 tablespoons of the frying oil. When the oil is sizzling hot, shower the noodles into the pan. Using two spoons, toss until evenly glazed, 15 to 30 seconds, adjusting the heat to avoid scorching and adding 1 or 2 tablespoons additional frying oil if necessary, to prevent sticking. Once glazed, alternately toss the noodles and press them against the side of the pan until they brown and crisp in spots and are heated through, about 3 minutes.

8. Return the shrimp to the pan and toss to combine. Stir the sauce mixture, add to the pan and toss again. Bring to a low simmer; cover the pan and cook for 30 seconds; reduce the heat to low.

9. Dissolve the remaining ½ tablespoon cornstarch in the remaining 1 tablespoon stock and pour evenly over the noodles. Toss gently until the sauce turns glossy and thickens slightly, about 10 seconds.

10. Return the scallions and ham to the pan and toss gently to mix. Season with pepper to taste. Transfer to a heated serving platter and serve at once.

NOTE: Chinese egg noodles are available fresh and frozen in 1-pound bags in Chinese groceries. Thin fresh or dried Italian egg noodles can be substituted; dried Chinese egg noodles are lacking in flavor.

Capelli d'Oro

This extravagant pasta was a favorite at *Food & Wine*. The sparkling golden caviar creates an effect that is as beautiful as it is delicious. The recipe can serve four as a first course.

2 GENEROUS SERVINGS

6 large shallots, finely chopped
2 cups heavy cream
2 tablespoons Cognac or brandy
2 tablespoons olive oil
8 ounces capelli d'angelo (angel hair) or capellini pasta
2 tablespoons unsalted butter, melted
1 teaspoon salt
½ teaspoon white pepper
1 jar (7½ ounces) domestic golden caviar (about ¾ cup)*
*Available at specialty food shops

1. In a medium saucepan set over low heat, cook the shallots and cream until the cream is reduced by half, about 25 minutes. Add the Cognac and cook 5 minutes more.

2. Strain the mixture through a fine sieve, pushing the solids with the back of a spoon. Return to the saucepan set over very low heat and keep warm, stirring occasionally.

3. Meanwhile, bring 6 quarts of salted water to a boil. Add the oil, then the pasta and cook until just *al dente*, 4 to 5 minutes. Drain well.

4. Pour the butter into a well-heated, deep bowl. Add the pasta, cream sauce, salt, pepper and all but 2 tablespoons of the caviar. Toss gently until coated.

5. Divide the pasta onto two heated plates or arrange in nests on a large platter. Divide the remaining 2 tablespoons of caviar between the portions and serve at once.

Rarebit Noodles

4 TO 6 SERVINGS

1 pound good-quality Cheddar cheese, grated (4 cups)
3 tablespoons unsalted butter
½ cup beer
2 tablespoons Dijon-style mustard
⅛ teaspoon freshly ground pepper
6 ounces egg noodles
½ pound sliced boiled ham, cut into ¼-inch-wide strips
1 cup (4 ounces) freshly grated Parmesan cheese
½ cup coarse dried bread crumbs
2 tablespoons minced fresh parsley

1. Preheat the oven to 400°. Combine the Cheddar, 2 tablespoons of the butter, the beer, mustard and pepper in a double boiler. Cook over simmering water, stirring occasionally, until all the cheese has melted and the mixture is smooth, about 10 minutes.

2. Meanwhile, in a large pot of salted boiling water, cook the noodles until they are tender but still firm, 5 to 7 minutes. Drain thoroughly.

3. In a large bowl, combine the noodles with the melted cheese mixture, the ham and the Parmesan, stirring gently to mix well.

4. Turn the noodle mixture into a medium baking dish. Sprinkle evenly with the bread crumbs and dot with the remaining 1 tablespoon butter.

5. Bake for 30 minutes, or until the bread crumbs are lightly browned. Sprinkle the parsley around the edges and serve hot.

Pasta with Parsley Pesto

If fresh basil is not available, this parsley pesto makes a nice alternative. It freezes well and will keep for about a week in the refrigerator.

8 TO 10 SERVINGS

2 garlic cloves
4 cups lightly packed, fresh parsley leaves
2 tablespoons dried basil
¼ cup (1 ounce) pine nuts (pignoli) or walnut pieces
1 teaspoon salt
½ cup olive oil
1½ pounds fresh pasta
Freshly grated Parmesan cheese

1. Using a food processor or blender, grind the garlic, parsley, basil, nuts and salt to a coarse paste, scraping the sides of the container as necessary. With the machine on, gradually add the oil and continue to blend until it is incorporated and the sauce has a fine texture.

2. Cook the pasta in a large pot of rapidly boiling, salted water until *al dente*, about 1 minute after the water returns to a rapid boil; drain well.

3. Pour the sauce over the pasta and toss. Serve with freshly grated Parmesan cheese.

Uncooked Tomato Sauce with Olives

Lively as a marinara sauce, this version of a very popular dressing has a distinctive southern Italian accent. Fully ripe plum tomatoes and fresh basil are essential. Thin spaghetti goes best with this sauce.

FOR 1 POUND OF PASTA

1½ pounds very ripe plum tomatoes (about 9 medium)— peeled, seeded and cut into 1½-inch strips
¼ pound Gaeta olives (about 40) or any small black oil-cured olives, halved and pitted
1 large garlic clove, minced
2 tablespoons chopped fresh basil
½ teaspoon salt
¼ teaspoon freshly ground pepper
½ cup olive oil

1. In a large serving bowl, combine the

tomatoes, olives, garlic, basil, salt, pepper and oil.

2. Let stand at room temperature for 1 to 3 hours before tossing with 1 pound of cooked and drained pasta. Serve at room temperature.

Ham Sauce

This quick, hearty sauce from Apulia gets a lot of mileage out of a quarter-pound of boiled ham. We like it best on rigatoni or similar broad, tubular macaroni shapes. For those who like spicy food, add a small *peperoncino* (hot red pepper) with the garlic and remove it before serving.

FOR 1 POUND OF PASTA

¼ cup plus 2 tablespoons olive oil
2 large garlic cloves, minced
¼ pound lean boiled ham, sliced ¼ inch thick and cut into ¼-inch dice
1 can (35 ounces) Italian peeled tomatoes, with their juice
½ teaspoon freshly ground pepper
1 cup (about 4 ounces) freshly grated Pecorino Romano cheese
¼ cup minced fresh basil
Salt

1. In a large skillet, heat the oil. Add the garlic and ham and sauté over moderate heat until the garlic is lightly browned, 3 to 5 minutes.

2. Add the tomatoes with their juice and the pepper. Bring to a boil, reduce the heat to moderately low and simmer, uncovered, for 15 minutes. Add the cheese, basil and salt to taste when tossing the sauce with pasta.

Cauliflower Sauce

The combination of anchovies, raisins and pine nuts in this sauce is typical of Moorish-inspired dishes of Sicily. The use of only 2 tablespoons of tomato paste is the characteristically light way in which that ingredient is treated in southern Italy. We recommend serving this sauce with pasta shells (conchiglie) or similar-shaped macaroni because they act as tiny catch basins for the flavorful sauce.

FOR 1 POUND OF PASTA

⅓ cup golden raisins
1 small cauliflower, divided into florets
6 tablespoons olive oil
1 large onion, coarsely chopped
2 tablespoons tomato paste dissolved in 1 cup water
12 flat anchovy fillets packed in olive oil, drained, with oil reserved
⅓ cup pine nuts (pignoli)
1 cup (about 4 ounces) freshly grated Pecorino Romano cheese
¼ cup chopped fresh basil and/or parsley

1. Soak the raisins in lukewarm water for 15 minutes, or until softened, then drain.

2. Meanwhile, in a large pot of boiling salted water, blanch the cauliflower for 2 minutes. Drain and rinse under cold running water to stop the cooking.

3. In a large skillet, heat 3 tablespoons of the olive oil, add the onion and sauté over moderately low heat until softened and translucent but not browned, about 3 minutes. Add the dissolved tomato paste. Cover and simmer for 15 minutes.

4. In a small skillet, stir the anchovy fillets in the remaining 3 tablespoons oil over low heat until the anchovies dissolve.

5. Add the cauliflower to the onion-to-mato sauce and simmer, covered, for 5 minutes. Add the reserved anchovy oil, the pine nuts and raisins and cook until the cauliflower is tender but still holds its shape, about 10 minutes longer. Serve over pasta, sprinkled with the cheese and basil.

Basic Ravioli

This is the basic technique for forming and cooking ravioli. Use the following recipes for flavored pasta doughs and ravioli fillings to create various combinations. The ravioli can be sauced with any number of sauces, including Creamy Tomato Sauce (p. 207) and Béchamel Sauce with Cheese (p. 208).

MAKES ABOUT 6 DOZEN 2-INCH RAVIOLI

1 recipe Egg, Spinach or Tomato Pasta (recipes follow)
1 recipe Spinach-Ricotta Filling; Fennel Sausage and Chicken Filling; or Potato, Onion and Cheese Filling (recipes follow)

1. Divide the dough into sixths. Working with one piece at a time, pat the dough into a rectangle roughly 6 by 4 inches. Knead the dough by passing it through a pasta machine at the widest setting 2 or 3 times, until it is silky smooth and no longer sticky.

2. Continue to pass the dough through the pasta machine, reducing the space between the rollers by one number each time, until the pasta has passed through the thinnest setting.

3. Cut the band of dough into two even lengths. Place one strip of dough on a flat work surface. Spoon or pipe mounds (about 1½ teaspoons) of filling onto the strip of dough, about ½ inch in from the edges and spaced about ½ inch apart.

4. Paint the exposed areas of dough lightly with water. Drape the second sheet of dough on top and shape the ravioli with your fingers, pressing out the air and sealing the edges. Cut the ravioli apart with a sharp knife, a jagged pastry wheel or a ravioli stamp.

5. Cook the ravioli, 12 at a time, in a large pot of boiling salted water until the pasta is *al dente*, 6 to 7 minutes; the filling will be hot and cooked. Do not overcrowd or the ravioli may stick.

NOTE: An easy way to form ravioli is to use a ravioli mold. Although it is a specialized piece of equipment, it is inexpensive and much simplifies the ravioli-making task.

Egg Pasta

MAKES 1¼ TO 1½ POUNDS, ENOUGH FOR
ABOUT 6 DOZEN 2-INCH RAVIOLI

**About 2½ cups all-purpose or
bread flour
3 whole eggs
1 egg yolk
2 teaspoons olive oil
Pinch of salt**

1. Place 2½ cups flour in a medium bowl. Make a well in the center and add the whole eggs, egg yolk, oil and salt. Using your fingers or a fork, mix together the ingredients in the well.

2. Gradually work in the flour until the mixture is blended and the dough begins to mass and pull away from the side of the bowl. It should be soft, pliable and slightly sticky. If the dough is too dry and stiff or will not absorb all the flour, add up to 2 tablespoons water, 1 teaspoon at a time. If it is too wet and sticky, add additional flour, 1 tablespoon at a time.

3. Turn the dough out onto a lightly floured surface and knead for 8 to 10 minutes, until smooth and elastic.

4. Shape into a ball, dust lightly with flour and cover with plastic wrap. Let rest for at least 1 hour before rolling out.

Tomato Pasta

MAKES 1¼ TO 1½ POUNDS, ENOUGH FOR
ABOUT 6 DOZEN 2-INCH RAVIOLI

**About 2½ cups all-purpose or
bread flour
5 tablespoons tomato paste
2 whole eggs
1 egg yolk
2 teaspoons olive oil
Pinch of salt**

1. Place 2½ cups flour in a medium bowl. Make a well in the center and add the tomato paste, whole eggs, egg yolk, oil and salt. Using your fingers or a fork, mix together the ingredients in the well.

2. Complete the recipe by following Steps 2 and 3 in the Egg Pasta recipe. This dough does not need a resting period and is best rolled out immediately, though it can be made the night before.

Spinach Pasta

MAKES 1¼ TO 1½ POUNDS, ENOUGH FOR
ABOUT 6 DOZEN 2-INCH RAVIOLI

**1 pound fresh spinach, washed and
stemmed, or 1 package (10
ounces) frozen spinach
About 2½ cups all-purpose or
bread flour
2 whole eggs
1 egg yolk
2 teaspoons olive oil
Pinch of salt**

1. If using fresh spinach, steam for 2 to 3 minutes, or until wilted and tender but still bright green. If using frozen, cook as directed on the package. Drain and rinse under cold running water until cooled, to refresh and preserve the color; drain well. Squeeze the spinach by handfuls to remove as much water as possible. Puree in a food processor or food mill; scrape out onto a clean kitchen towel. Bundle the spinach puree in the towel and wring tightly to remove as much moisture as you can; there will be about ⅓ cup spinach puree.

2. Place 2½ cups flour in a medium bowl. Make a well in the center and add the spinach, whole eggs, egg yolk, oil and salt. Using your fingers or a fork, mix together the ingredients in the well.

3. Complete the recipe by following Steps 2 and 3 in the Egg Pasta recipe. This dough does not need a resting period and is best rolled out immediately, though it can be made the night before.

Potato, Onion and Cheese Filling

MAKES ABOUT 2½ CUPS, ENOUGH FOR
6 DOZEN 2-INCH RAVIOLI

**2 medium baking potatoes (about 8
ounces each), peeled and
quartered
1 tablespoon olive oil
2 medium onions, chopped
½ cup freshly grated Parmesan
cheese
8 ounces farmer's cheese
1 egg
1¼ teaspoons salt**

**¼ teaspoon white pepper
¼ teaspoon freshly grated nutmeg**

1. In a medium saucepan of boiling salted water, cook the potatoes until tender, 15 to 20 minutes. Drain; then put through a ricer or the medium disk of a food mill.

2. Meanwhile, in a medium skillet, heat the oil. Add the onions and sauté over moderate heat until softened and translucent, about 5 minutes. Puree the onions in a food processor or pass through the medium disk of a food mill.

3. In a large bowl, combine the potatoes, onions, Parmesan cheese, farmer's cheese, egg, salt, pepper and nutmeg. Mix until well blended.

Spinach-Ricotta Filling

MAKES ABOUT 2¼ CUPS, ENOUGH FOR
6 DOZEN 2-INCH RAVIOLI

**1½ pounds fresh spinach, washed
and stemmed, or 1½ packages
(15 ounces) frozen spinach
1 container (10 ounces) whole-
milk ricotta cheese
1 cup (4 ounces) freshly grated
Parmesan cheese
2 eggs
1 teaspoon salt
⅛ teaspoon pepper
¼ teaspoon freshly grated nutmeg**

1. If using fresh spinach, steam for 2 to 3 minutes, until wilted and tender but still bright green. If using frozen, cook as directed on the package. Drain and rinse under cold running water until cooled. Squeeze the spinach by handfuls to remove as much water as possible.

2. Place the spinach in a food processor. Add the ricotta cheese, Parmesan cheese, eggs, salt, pepper and nutmeg. Puree for about 1 minute, until the spinach is finely chopped and thoroughly mixed with the other ingredients.

Fennel Sausage and Chicken Filling with Garlic

MAKES ABOUT 2¼ CUPS, ENOUGH FOR 6 DOZEN 2-INCH RAVIOLI

2 tablespoons olive oil
1 whole skinless, boneless chicken breast, about 10 ounces
6 links (about 1¼ pounds) sweet Italian sausages with fennel, casings removed
2 garlic cloves, crushed through a press
¼ cup heavy cream
Salt and freshly ground pepper

1. In a heavy, medium skillet, heat the oil. Add the chicken breast and sauté over moderate heat, turning once, until lightly browned and resistant to the touch, about 10 minutes. Remove from the skillet and let cool.

2. Add the sausage to the same skillet. Sauté over moderate heat, stirring to break up the meat, for 4 minutes. Add the garlic and continue to cook until the meat begins to brown and there is no trace of pink, about 2 to 3 minutes longer. With a slotted spoon, remove the sausage from the skillet. Let cool to room temperature.

3. Cut the chicken into pieces; place in a food processor. Add the sausage, garlic and cream and chop for about 1 minute, until well blended. Season with salt and pepper to taste.

Shrimp-Garlic Risotto

F&W Beverage Suggestion:
Vernaccia di San Gimignano

4 TO 6 SERVINGS

5 tablespoons unsalted butter
2 garlic cloves, finely chopped
1 pound medium shrimp—shelled, deveined and sliced lengthwise
2 tablespoons minced fresh parsley
About 5 cups fish stock or 2½ cups bottled clam juice diluted with 2½ cups water
1 large leek (white and tender green), thinly sliced
1½ cups Arborio rice
½ cup dry white wine
¼ teaspoon freshly ground pepper
Salt

1. In a large skillet, melt 2 tablespoons of the butter. Add the garlic and cook over low heat until softened, about 2 minutes.

2. Increase the heat to moderate, add the shrimp and cook, stirring occasionally, until just opaque, 1 to 2 minutes. Add the parsley and set aside.

3. In a medium saucepan, bring the stock to a simmer; maintain at a simmer over moderately low heat.

4. In a large noncorrodible saucepan or flameproof casserole, melt the remaining 3 tablespoons butter over moderate heat. Add the leek and cook until softened, 3 to 4 minutes.

5. Add the rice and stir for 1 to 2 minutes, until well coated with butter and slightly translucent. Add the wine and cook until it evaporates.

6. Add ½ cup of the simmering stock and cook, stirring constantly, until the rice has absorbed most of the liquid. Adjust the heat, if necessary, to maintain a simmer. Gradually adding stock, ½ cup at a time, cook, stirring constantly, until the rice is almost tender but still crunchy in the center, 20 to 25 minutes.

7. Add the pepper and salt to taste and continue to cook, stirring and adding stock as necessary, ¼ cup at a time, until the rice is tender but still firm and is bound with a creamy sauce, 3 to 6 minutes longer.

8. Stir in the shrimp mixture, including any accumulated juices, and serve immediately.

Cheese Risotto

4 TO 6 SERVINGS

About 5 cups chicken stock or 2½ cups canned broth diluted with 2½ cups water
3 tablespoons olive oil
⅓ cup minced onion
1½ cups Arborio rice
½ cup freshly grated Parmesan and/ or a melting cheese, such as mozzarella, Fontina or Gorgonzola
½ teaspoon freshly ground pepper
Salt
2 tablespoons unsalted butter

1. In a medium saucepan, bring the stock to a simmer; maintain at a simmer over moderately low heat.

2. In a large noncorrodible saucepan or flameproof casserole, heat the oil over moderate heat. Add the onion and cook until it is softened and translucent, about 2 minutes.

3. Add the rice and stir for 1 to 2 minutes, until well coated with oil and slightly translucent.

4. Add ½ cup of the simmering stock and cook, stirring constantly, until the rice has absorbed most of the liquid. Adjust the heat if necessary to maintain a simmer. Gradually adding stock, ½ cup at a time, cook, stirring constantly, until the rice is almost tender but still slightly crunchy in the center, 20 to 25 minutes.

5. Add the cheese and season with the pepper and salt to taste. Continue to cook, stirring and adding stock as necessary, ¼ cup at a time, until the rice is tender but still firm and is bound with a creamy sauce, 3 to 6 minutes longer.

6. Stir in butter and serve immediately.

Vegetable Risotto: Reduce the cheese to ¼ cup. Add 1 to 1½ cups sautéed vegetables (such as artichoke hearts, peas, mushrooms or green beans) in Step 5.

Seafood Risotto: Omit the cheese. Add ¼ cup dry white wine after Step 3 and cook, stirring, until it almost evaporates. In Step 4, substitute fish stock or bottled clam juice diluted by half with water for the chicken stock. Add 1 pound of cooked seafood (such as bass, squid, tilefish, scallops or salmon) in Step 5.

Tomato-Basil Risotto

4 TO 6 SERVINGS

About 5 cups chicken stock or 2½ cups canned broth diluted with 2½ cups water
5 tablespoons unsalted butter
1 medium onion, finely chopped
3 ounces prosciutto, finely chopped (⅓ cup)
2 tablespoons tomato puree
1½ cups Arborio rice
¼ cup freshly grated Parmesan cheese
½ teaspoon freshly ground pepper
Salt
1½ pounds plum tomatoes— peeled, seeded and coarsely chopped
¼ cup shredded basil leaves

1. In a medium saucepan, bring the stock to a simmer; maintain at a simmer over moderately low heat.

2. In a large noncorrodible saucepan or flameproof casserole, melt 3 tablespoons of the butter. Add the onion and prosciutto and sauté over moderate heat until the onion is softened and translucent, about 3 minutes.

3. Stir in the tomato puree and cook for 1 minute.

4. Add the rice and stir for 1 to 2 minutes, until well coated with butter and tomato puree and slightly translucent.

5. Add ½ cup of the simmering stock and cook, stirring constantly, until the rice has absorbed most of the liquid. Adjust the heat if necessary to maintain a simmer. Gradually adding stock, ½ cup at a time, cook, stirring constantly, until the rice is almost tender but still slightly crunchy in the center, 20 to 25 minutes.

6. Add the cheese and season with the pepper and salt to taste. Continue to cook, stirring and adding stock as necessary, ¼ cup at a time, until the rice is tender but still firm and is bound with a creamy sauce, 3 to 6 minutes longer.

7. Stir in tomatoes, basil and remaining 2 tablespoons butter; serve immediately.

Balkan Braised Rice

4 TO 6 SERVINGS

3 tablespoons olive oil
2 cups thinly sliced onions (about 2 medium)
1 small, dried red hot pepper, seeded and minced
1 garlic clove, minced
1 teaspoon oregano
1 teaspoon imported sweet paprika
1 can (1 pound 12 ounces) Italian plum tomatoes—drained, seeded and chopped
1 red and 1 green bell pepper (or 2 green peppers), thinly sliced
2 medium zucchini, cut into ¼-inch dice
1 teaspoon salt
¼ teaspoon black pepper
½ teaspoon loosely packed thread saffron
2 cups chicken stock or canned broth
¾ cup short-grain rice, preferably Italian Arborio
2 tablespoons minced fresh parsley and rings of roasted red peppers, for garnish

1. In a deep heavy 10-inch skillet, heat the olive oil. Add the onions and hot pepper and cook over moderate heat, stirring occasionally, until the onion is lightly browned, about 10 minutes. Reduce the heat to low, cover and cook, stirring several times, until the onion is soft and golden brown, about 30 minutes.

2. Add the garlic, oregano, paprika, tomatoes, bell peppers and zucchini. Simmer uncovered, for 20 minutes. Season with the salt and black pepper.

3. Crumble the saffron into the chicken stock and let stand until softened. When the vegetables are cooked, add the rice and saffron-flavored chicken stock to the skillet. Stir well to mix. Bring to a boil, lower the heat and cook, covered, over very low heat until the rice is tender and the liquid is absorbed, about 30 minutes. Do not uncover or stir the rice during cooking.

4. Taste the rice and season with additional salt and pepper if necessary. Garnish with the parsley and roasted peppers.

Baked Rice with Peppers

Goat's-milk mozzarella cheese is recommended for this recipe. Whole-milk mozzarella is an acceptable substitute. The dish can be prepared ahead of time (up to Step 2) and refrigerated until 1 hour before serving.

8 SERVINGS

1 small onion, chopped
3 tablespoons lard or unsalted butter
1 cup long-grain rice, washed and drained
2 cups chicken stock or canned broth
1 cup dry white wine
1 or 2 small hot green peppers, such as jalapeños, seeded and finely chopped
¾ teaspoon salt
2 small bell peppers, preferably 1 green and 1 red, cut into ¼-inch dice (about 1 cup)
1 celery rib, cut into ¼-inch dice (about ½ cup)
1½ cups (12 ounces) sour cream
2½ ounces Gruyère cheese, cut into ¼-inch dice (about ½ cup)
2½ ounces sharp Cheddar cheese, cut into ¼-inch dice (about ½ cup)
2½ ounces mozzarella cheese, cut into ¼-inch dice (about ½ cup)

1. Preheat the oven to 350°. In a medium ovenproof skillet, sauté the onion in the lard over moderately high heat until soft but not brown, about 3 minutes. Add the rice and stir until coated with butter. Stir in the stock, wine, hot peppers and salt. Bring to a boil, cover and place in the oven. Bake for 15 to 20 minutes, or

until all the liquid has been absorbed. Remove from the oven.

2. Transfer the rice to a large bowl. Stir in the bell peppers, celery, sour cream, Gruyère, Cheddar and mozzarella cheeses and transfer the mixture to a lightly buttered, 2-quart baking dish. If preparing the rice ahead, cover the dish tightly and refrigerate until about 50 minutes before serving.

3. Increase the oven temperature to 400°. Bake the rice, uncovered, for 20 minutes, or until lightly browned on top. If the rice has been prepared through Step 2 and refrigerated, bake it at 300° for 30 minutes and then at 400° for 10 minutes.

Savory Pistachio Strudel with Sour Cream-Dill Sauce

This special strudel makes a perfect appetizer or meatless main course. For even nuttier flavor, use a specialty long-grain white rice, such as Indian *basmati* or wild pecan rice from Louisiana.

6 TO 8 SERVINGS

Mushroom Duxelles:
½ pound mushrooms
2 tablespoons unsalted butter
3 tablespoons minced shallots
1 garlic clove, minced
¼ teaspoon salt
⅛ teaspoon pepper

White Rice Layer:
2 teaspoons unsalted butter
1 teaspoon olive oil
¼ cup long-grain white rice
1½ teaspoons minced fresh dill
Salt and pepper

Brown Rice Layer:
½ cup chopped pistachio nuts
2 teaspoons unsalted butter
1 teaspoon olive oil
¼ cup short-grain brown rice, rinsed and drained
Salt and pepper

Assembly:
12 sheets phyllo dough (about 16½ by 12 inches)
½ cup (1 stick) unsalted butter, melted

Sauce:
1 cup sour cream
1 cup plain yogurt
1 tablespoon Dijon-style mustard
2 teaspoons minced fresh dill

1. Make the duxelles: Chop the mushrooms finely. A handful at a time, squeeze them in a cotton or linen kitchen towel to remove moisture. In a medium skillet, melt the butter over moderate heat. Add the shallots and garlic and sauté for 2 minutes. Add the mushrooms, salt and pepper. Increase the heat to high and sauté stirring frequently, until the pieces of mushroom have separated and all the liquid has evaporated, 5 to 7 minutes.

2. Prepare the white rice: In a small saucepan, heat the butter and oil over moderate heat. Add the white rice and sauté, stirring frequently, until the rice turns pale gold and smells toasted, 3 to 4 minutes. Add ⅔ cup of water and bring to a boil. Reduce the heat to very low, cover and cook for about 30 minutes, or until all the water is absorbed. Let the rice stand, covered, for 10 minutes; then season with the dill and salt and pepper to taste. Set aside, uncovered, and let cool to room temperature.

3. Prepare the brown rice: In a small ungreased skillet, cook the pistachio nuts over moderate heat, stirring frequently, until lightly toasted, 1 to 2 minutes.

4. In a small saucepan, heat the butter and oil over moderate heat. Add the brown rice and sauté, stirring frequently, until the rice begins to brown and smells toasted, about 5 minutes. Add ⅔ cup of water and bring to a boil. Reduce the heat to very low, cover and cook for about 1 hour, or until all the water is absorbed. Remove from the heat and let stand, covered, for 10 minutes. Stir in the toasted pistachio nuts and salt and pepper to taste. Set aside, uncovered, and let cool to room temperature.

5. Assemble the strudel: Preheat the oven to 400°. Generously butter a large baking sheet.

6. On a damp kitchen towel, place 1 sheet of the phyllo dough. Keep the remaining sheets covered with a damp towel while you work. Lightly brush the first sheet with melted butter. Place a second sheet over the first and brush

lightly with more melted butter. Repeat this layering and buttering with the remaining 10 sheets of phyllo dough.

7. After buttering the top sheet, spread the white rice evenly over the dough, leaving a 1½-inch border all around the edges. Layer the mushroom duxelles over the white rice. Spread the brown rice evenly over the mushrooms. Make sure all the edges are even.

8. Fold in the long borders. Starting at one of the short sides, and using the towel as a guide to help you lift the dough, roll up the strudel like a jelly roll. Carefully transfer the roll to a baking sheet. Brush the strudel all over with melted butter.

9. Bake in the oven for 30 minutes, until the strudel is golden brown and crisp.

10. Meanwhile, make the sauce: In a small bowl, whisk the sour cream, yogurt, mustard and dill until blended. Let the sauce stand for about 30 minutes to come to room temperature and to allow the flavors to mellow.

11. Remove the strudel from the oven and let rest for 15 minutes before slicing. Serve with the sour cream-dill sauce.

Oriental Poultry Stuffing

Glutinous rice must be soaked overnight, but the stuffing does not take long to prepare.

MAKES ABOUT 8 CUPS

3 cups glutinous rice*
2 tablespoons peanut oil
1 cup minced shallots (about ½ pound)
½ cup minced scallions
½ cup Chinese rice wine or pale dry sherry
½ pound Chinese pork sausage*, cut into ¼-inch dice
½ pound Chinese duck liver sausage* (see Note), cut into ¼-inch dice
3 cups chicken stock
1 teaspoon salt
¼ teaspoon pepper
1½ pounds fresh water chestnuts*, or ½ pound jicama, peeled and coarsely chopped (about 2 cups)
1 small red bell pepper, diced
1½ teaspoons tarragon

1 teaspoon thyme
¼ cup chopped fresh Chinese chives*, chives or scallion greens
*Available at Oriental groceries

1. Place the rice in a large bowl. Add 6 cups of water and let soak overnight. Drain well.

2. In a large skillet or wok, heat the peanut oil over moderately high heat. Stir-fry the shallots and scallions until softened, about 30 seconds. Add the wine and cook until almost no liquid remains in the skillet, about 4 minutes. Add the pork and liver sausages and cook, stirring once or twice, for 1 minute. Add the rice, the stock and the salt and pepper. Cook, uncovered, stirring occasionally to prevent sticking, until all the stock is absorbed, about 8 minutes.

3. Add the water chestnuts, red pepper, tarragon, thyme and chives and cook, stirring frequently, for 3 minutes. Remove from the heat and let the stuffing cool to room temperature.

4. Use as much stuffing as needed to stuff the bird. Spoon the remainder into a greased baking dish and bake at 350° for 45 minutes.

NOTE: Use another ½ pound of Chinese pork sausage if duck liver sausage is unavailable.

Almond and Currant Pilaf

8 TO 10 SERVINGS

2 tablespoons unsalted butter
1 small onion, chopped
2 cups long-grain rice
½ cup currants
3 cups chicken stock or canned broth
¼ cup (1 ounce) toasted, slivered almonds

1. In a medium flameproof casserole, melt the butter over moderate heat. Add the onion and sauté until softened, about 2 minutes. Add the rice and stir until the grains are well coated; stir in the currants.

2. Add the stock and bring to a boil. Cover the casserole, reduce the heat to low and simmer until all the liquid is absorbed, about 15 minutes. Remove from the heat and stir in the almonds. Serve hot.

NOTE: To serve as a cold rice salad, toss the hot pilaf with about 5 tablespoons of mint sauce or mint vinegar and about 2 tablespoons of olive or vegetable oil. Chill before serving.

Spinach Rice

Serve this colorful combination with roast lamb, beef or game.

4 SERVINGS

1 tablespoon unsalted butter
1 small green bell pepper, finely chopped
1 small onion, finely chopped
2 eggs, beaten
2 cups milk
3 cups cooked rice (made from about 1 cup raw rice)
2 cups loosely packed spinach, washed and roughly chopped (about 1 pound)
1½ teaspoons salt
½ teaspoon freshly ground pepper

1. Preheat the oven to 350°. In a small skillet, melt the butter over moderate heat. Add the green pepper and onion and sauté over moderate heat until softened but not browned, 3 to 4 minutes.

2. In a medium bowl, whisk together the eggs and the milk until blended.

3. In a medium bowl, combine the cooked rice with the pepper-onion mixture, the milk-egg mixture, the spinach and the salt and pepper. Stir gently to mix all the ingredients. Turn into a lightly buttered medium casserole.

4. Bake for 45 minutes, or until the top is lightly browned and the custard is set.

Wild Rice with Bacon and Mushrooms

This wild rice dish is colorful and flavorful. It goes well with all game birds and with venison. The recipe is easily increased, if you are serving more people, or halved for two.

4 SERVINGS

½ cup wild rice, well washed
2½ teaspoons salt
1 tablespoon unsalted butter
2 ounces slab bacon, cut into 1½-by-¼-inch strips
⅓ cup chopped onion
⅓ cup chopped mushrooms (about 2 ounces)
½ teaspoon freshly ground pepper
⅓ cup cooked white rice (optional, see Note)

1. Place the wild rice in a medium saucepan. Add 4 cups of water with 2 teaspoons of the salt. Bring to a boil over moderately high heat, reduce the heat and simmer, uncovered, stirring frequently, until tender, about 1 hour. Drain the rice, rinse under cold running water and drain well.

2. In a heavy medium skillet, melt the butter over moderately high heat. Add the bacon and cook, tossing frequently, for 4 minutes. Add the onion and mushrooms and cook for 3 to 4 minutes, or until they begin to brown.

3. Add the wild rice, stir until mixed and season with the remaining ½ teaspoon of salt and the pepper. Stir in the white rice and serve hot.

NOTE: The addition of this small amount of white rice lightens the texture and adds visual interest. Simply add 2 tablespoons of rice to a small saucepan of boiling salted water and boil, uncovered, for about 10 minutes, or until tender. Drain well before adding to the wild rice.

Polenta with Cheese and Raisins

6 SERVINGS

2 tablespoons unsalted butter
2 large onions, finely chopped
1 cup polenta (yellow cornmeal)
1 cup boiling water
1 teaspoon salt
½ pound Monterey Jack cheese, thinly sliced and cut into 1½-inch squares
½ cup pine nuts (about 3 ounces), toasted (see Note)
¼ cup golden raisins
¼ cup freshly grated Parmesan cheese

1. Preheat the oven to 350°. In a large skillet, melt the butter over very low heat. Add the onions and sauté, stirring occasionally, until softened but not browned, about 10 minutes.

2. In a medium bowl, mix the polenta with 2 cups of cold water until smooth. Stir in the boiling water and salt until blended. Immediately pour into the skillet with the onions and bring to a boil over moderately low heat, stirring constantly. Continue to cook, stirring frequently, until the mixture is thick and pulls away from the bottom and sides of the pan, about 7 minutes.

3. Spread half the polenta into a buttered 8-inch-square baking dish. Layer half the Monterey Jack evenly over the polenta and sprinkle with half the toasted pine nuts and all the raisins. Spread out the remaining polenta to create a second layer and top with the rest of the Monterey Jack and nuts. Sprinkle evenly with the Parmesan and bake for 45 minutes, or until the top is golden. Cover with foil and continue to bake for another 15 minutes. Remove from the oven and let rest for 15 minutes before cutting into small squares or slices.

NOTE: To toast pine nuts, place them on an ungreased baking sheet and bake in a 375° oven, shaking the pan once or twice until lightly browned, about 5 minutes.

Bulgur Wheat, Peppers and Bean Curd

Although completely vegetarian, this colorful dish has enough complementary protein to be as nutritious as meat.

4 MAIN-COURSE SERVINGS

1 cup coarse or medium bulgur wheat
4 tablespoons unsalted butter
3 garlic cloves, minced
1 teaspoon ground cumin
2 red bell peppers, seeded and cut into julienne strips
3 tablespoons cider vinegar
10 ounces fresh spinach—washed, stemmed and coarsely chopped
4 small, firm-style bean curd cakes (about 12 ounces), cut into cubes
1 teaspoon salt
½ teaspoon freshly ground pepper

1. Place the bulgur in a small bowl and rinse several times to remove any impurities. Add cold water to cover by 1½ inches and let soak for 45 minutes, or until tender. Drain in a fine sieve, pressing to remove as much moisture as possible.

2. In a large skillet, melt the butter over moderately low heat. Add the garlic and sauté until fragrant but not browned, about 30 seconds. Stir in the cumin and add the peppers, cover and cook for 5 minutes. Add the vinegar and bulgur and cook uncovered for 5 minutes, stirring frequently to prevent scorching. Add the spinach and bean curd, cover and simmer until the spinach wilts, about 5 minutes. Season with the salt and pepper.

Kasha and Red Peppers

6 SERVINGS

3 to 4 medium-size red bell peppers (or a combination of red and green)
1 medium-large onion, cut into ½-inch dice
2 tablespoons olive oil
1 egg
1½ cups whole-grain kasha
1½ teaspoons salt
1 teaspoon dried summer savory leaves, crumbled
2¼ cups boiling water
Pepper

1. Drop the peppers into a large pot of boiling water; let them boil for 5 minutes, turning to cook all sides. Run under cold water to cool. Gently and carefully pull off the skins. Remove stems, ribs and seeds. Cut into ½-inch dice.

2. In a heavy saucepan, cook the onion in the oil until slightly softened. Add the peppers and cook a minute over high heat. Scrape into a dish and set aside. Keep the saucepan handy.

3. In a small bowl, beat the egg. Add the kasha and stir until all the grains are coated. Scrape the mixture into the pan in which the vegetables were cooked and stir over moderate heat for a few minutes, or until all the grains are dried and separated. Add salt, savory, boiling water, pepper to taste and the cooked vegetables. Return to a boil.

4. Turn the heat to its lowest point, cover the pan and cook 15 minutes. Remove from the heat and let stand 15 minutes or so. Turn into a fairly wide, ovenproof serving dish, fluffing the grains. Let rest at room temperature until you serve dinner; or cool, cover and refrigerate overnight.

5. To reheat and serve, set the foil-covered dish in a 375° oven and leave until heated through, about 30 minutes if chilled, slightly less if room temperature.

SALADS:
SIDE-DISH

Portsmouth Salad

A light, tart sweet salad, appropriate for a simple lunch or as part of a multicourse dinner.

6 SERVINGS

2 medium cucumbers, well washed
1 small ripe pineapple, cut into ⅜-inch dice
2 tart red-skinned apples, such as McIntosh, cut into ⅜-inch dice
¼ cup olive oil
½ teaspoon brown sugar
¼ teaspoon salt
¼ teaspoon freshly ground pepper
1 head of Bibb or Boston lettuce

1. Using a fork with sharp tines, score the skin of the cucumbers. Cut in half lengthwise; scoop out the seeds with a spoon. Cut the cucumber into ⅜-inch dice; place in a large bowl.

2. Using your hands, gently squeeze handfuls of the pineapple over a small bowl to collect 2 tablespoons of fresh juice; reserve the juice. Add the pineapple and the apples to the cucumber.

3. In a small bowl, combine the oil, brown sugar, salt and pepper with the reserved pineapple juice. Beat until blended; pour over the salad and toss lightly to mix.

4. Arrange several lettuce leaves on 6 small plates or in 6 shallow champagne glasses. Divide the salad evenly over the lettuce and serve at room temperature.

Salad Walker Percy

Though this recipe calls for finely chopped chives, parsley and basil, it is delicious made with a number of combinations of fresh herbs.

4 SERVINGS

Salad:
1 medium head of Bibb or Boston lettuce, torn into bite-size pieces
6 cups spinach leaves (or a combination of spinach and red-leaf lettuce), torn into bite-size pieces
1 large carrot, cut into 1½-by-⅛-inch julienne strips
1 small leek, cut into 1½-by-⅛-inch julienne strips

Finely grated zest of 1 lemon
¼ teaspoon salt
¼ teaspoon pepper
¾ cup pecan halves
Dressing:
6 tablespoons peanut oil
2 tablespoons distilled white or white wine vinegar
1 tablespoon sherry vinegar
2 tablespoons finely chopped chives
2 tablespoons finely chopped parsley
2 tablespoons finely chopped basil
½ teaspoon salt
2 tablespoons liquid from water-packed green peppercorns (optional)
Pepper to taste

1. Preheat the oven to 450°. In a large noncorrodible ovenproof bowl, combine the salad ingredients.

2. In a separate bowl, combine the dressing ingredients, then pour over the salad and toss.

3. Heat the salad in the oven for about 15 seconds, or just until the chill has been taken off the greens. Serve the salad on room-temperature plates.

Cabbage, Mushroom and Green Pea Salad

6 TO 8 SERVINGS

½ medium head of red cabbage, coarsely chopped (about 6 cups)
5 tablespoons vegetable oil
½ pound fresh peas, shelled (about ½ cup)
6 medium mushrooms, sliced
1 tablespoon white wine vinegar
1 teaspoon Dijon-style mustard
Salt and freshly ground pepper

1. In a large serving bowl, toss the cabbage with 2 tablespoons of the oil; let stand for about 1 hour. Add the peas and toss to mix. Arrange the mushrooms on top of the salad around the edge of the bowl.

2. In a small bowl, whisk the vinegar, remaining 3 tablespoons of oil, the mustard and salt and pepper to taste. Before serving, pour the dressing over the salad and toss.

Calico Corn Salad

8 SERVINGS

1 cup medium cracked wheat (bulgur)
2 cups boiling water
⅔ cup olive oil
2½ to 3 cups corn kernels (from 5 to 7 large ears, husks reserved)
1 cup minced scallions (about 6 medium)
1 cup minced fresh parsley
1 cup minced fresh mint
1 tablespoon finely minced lemon zest
1 cup finely chopped red bell pepper (about 2 medium)
⅓ cup lemon juice
1½ to 2 teaspoons salt
Pepper

1. Place the cracked wheat in a bowl with the boiling water and let rest for 1 hour. Drain in a fine sieve, rinse under cold water and, with the back of a large spoon, press out all excess moisture; transfer to a large bowl and set aside.

2. In a medium skillet, warm 3 tablespoons of the oil over moderately high heat. Add the corn and stir-fry for 2 minutes. Remove from the heat and let cool to room temperature.

3. Add the corn, scallions, parsley, mint, lemon zest and red pepper to the cracked wheat and gently combine. Mix in the remaining oil. Add the lemon juice, salt and pepper to taste and mix again. Chill, covered, for several hours or overnight.

4. To serve select 8 of the most attractive of the reserved corn husks; rinse well and pat dry. Place each on a salad plate and mound generously with the salad.

Salad of Spinach Crowns

Spinach crowns are the root ends of the plant with about 2 inches of the stem attached. The Chinese call them "parrot beaks," because of their colorful red tips. Save the spinach leaves for another recipe. The crowns tend to toughen as they sit, so prepare this salad no more than an hour before you plan to serve.

2 SERVINGS

16 to 20 spinach crowns (roots and 2 inches of the stem from about 2 pounds of fresh spinach)
¼ cup soy sauce
1 teaspoon Oriental sesame oil
1 teaspoon rice vinegar

1. Trim off any woody parts from the roots and remove any stems that look bruised or spoiled. Rinse well in at least two changes of clean, cold water (sand tends to collect between the stems).

2. In a medium saucepan of boiling salted water, blanch the crowns until tender but still bright green, about 4 minutes. Drain and rinse under cold running water until cool.

3. In a medium bowl, combine the soy sauce, oil and vinegar with 2 tablespoons of water. Add the crowns and toss to coat with the dressing. Divide between two plates and pour any dressing that remains in the bowl over the salads.

Spinach Salad with Warm Anchovy Dressing

A classic spinach, mushroom and bacon salad takes on a whole new dimension with this warm, anchovy-flavored dressing.

4 TO 6 SERVINGS

1 can (2 ounces) flat anchovy fillets, with 1 teaspoon of the oil
3 tablespoons olive oil
1 teaspoon Oriental sesame oil
2½ tablespoons red wine vinegar
2 teaspoons capers
1½ tablespoons Dijon-style mustard
1 pound fresh spinach, rinsed, dried and trimmed
3 hard-cooked eggs, thinly sliced
½ pound mushrooms, thinly sliced
8 slices cooked bacon, crumbled

1. In a small saucepan, heat the anchovies, anchovy oil, olive oil and sesame oil over moderate heat, stirring until the anchovies dissolve, 2 to 3 minutes. Turn off the heat and stir in the vinegar, capers and mustard.

2. Place the spinach in a large bowl. Scatter the egg and mushroom slices along the sides of the bowl and the bacon in the middle. Bring the dressing to a boil over moderately high heat for about 5 seconds; drizzle over the salad and toss.

Spinach and Avocado Salad

4 SERVINGS

Salad:
¾ pound fresh spinach, washed and thoroughly dried
1 large or 2 small avocados
Fresh lemon juice
4 scallions (white and some of the green), sliced

Dressing:
2 tablespoons fresh lemon juice
6 tablespoons salad oil
3 to 4 dashes hot pepper sauce
Salt to taste

1. Prepare the salad: Remove the stems from the spinach and tear the leaves into bite-size pieces. Arrange the spinach on a serving plate or in a salad bowl.

2. Peel and slice the avocados. To preserve their fresh color, place the slices in a bowl, squeeze a little lemon juice over them, and toss until they are well coated. Arrange the avocado slices on top of the spinach. Sprinkle the scallions on top.

3. Prepare the dressing: Combine all the dressing ingredients while beating well with a fork. Pour into a serving dish and place on the table with the salad; dress the salad at the table.

Honeydew and Green Grape Salad with Lime Vinaigrette

This light salad of sweet, ripe fruit can be served with the entrée or afterward as a separate course. To test a honeydew melon, keep in mind that the outer skin of a ripe melon will have a velvety rather than a slick texture and a sweet fragrance.

4 SERVINGS

½ medium honeydew melon, seeded
½ pound (1¼ cups) seedless green grapes, halved
2 tablespoons olive oil
1 tablespoon fresh lime juice
¼ teaspoon sugar
⅛ teaspoon salt
Freshly ground black pepper

1. Cut the melon lengthwise into long, thin slices; trim off the rind. Divide the melon slices into four equal portions and arrange attractively on four plates. Sprinkle the grapes over the melon, dividing evenly.

2. Whisk the oil, lime juice, sugar, salt, and pepper to taste until blended. Drizzle about 2 teaspoons of dressing over each salad. Serve at room temperature.

Three-Green Salad with Pears

6 TO 8 SERVINGS

3 large, firm ripe pears
1½ tablespoons fresh lemon juice
2 heads of Boston lettuce
2 bunches of watercress, large stems removed
3 heads of Belgian endive
1 egg yolk
6 tablespoons olive oil
2 tablespoons walnut oil
2 tablespoons sherry vinegar or red wine vinegar
2 tablespoons dried mint
½ teaspoon anchovy paste
1 teaspoon salt
1 teaspoon pepper

1. Peel and core the pears; cut them into fine julienne strips, about 2½ inches long. Place them in a bowl of ice water with ½ tablespoon of the lemon juice; set aside.

2. Arrange the lettuce leaves around the sides and bottom of a salad bowl and mound the watercress in the center.

3. Trim the stem end off each endive and cut the leaves crosswise into ½-inch pieces. Sprinkle over the watercress.

4. Place the egg yolk in a bowl and gradually whisk in the olive and walnut oils. One at a time, add the remaining 1 tablespoon lemon juice, the vinegar, mint, anchovy paste, salt and pepper, whisking to blend thoroughly.

5. Drain the pears and dry with paper towels. Arrange them in a fan shape over the greens.

6. At the table, pour the dressing over the salad and toss before serving.

Oriental-Style Tomato Salad

8 SERVINGS

1 ounce (about 14 medium) dried shiitake mushrooms
2 cups boiling water
3 tablespoons Oriental sesame oil
¼ cup soy sauce
¼ cup rice vinegar
1 cup sliced scallions (about 10)
2 cans (8 ounces each) water chestnuts, drained and cut into 2-by-⅛-inch julienne strips
1 tablespoon shredded, peeled fresh gingerroot
3 pounds (about 6 large) firm ripe tomatoes, seeded and cut into ½-inch cubes.

1. Place the mushrooms in a medium bowl. Pour on the boiling water and let the mushrooms soak until softened, about 30 minutes. Drain and squeeze out the excess water. Trim off any woody stems and cut the caps into ⅛-inch slivers.

2. In a medium bowl, combine the mushroom slivers, sesame oil, soy sauce and vinegar; mix well. Stir in the scallions, water chestnuts and gingerroot. Add the tomatoes and toss gently. Cover and refrigerate until chilled, at least 1 hour, before serving.

Grated Carrots with Pernod

4 SERVINGS

½ pound carrots, peeled
3 tablespoons olive oil
1 teaspoon balsamic vinegar or 2 teaspoons red wine vinegar
1 teaspoon Pernod, or to taste
Salt and pepper

Coarsely shred the carrots by hand or through the shredding disk of a food processor. In a medium serving bowl, whisk the oil, vinegar and Pernod until blended. Add the carrots and season with salt and pepper to taste. Cover and refrigerate until chilled. Serve within 24 hours.

Beet and Chicory Salad

6 TO 8 SERVINGS

Red Wine Vinaigrette:
2 tablespoons red wine vinegar
1½ tablespoons fresh lemon juice
1½ teaspoons Dijon-style mustard
½ garlic clove or small shallot, minced
¼ teaspoon salt
¼ teaspoon freshly ground pepper
¼ cup olive oil
¼ cup vegetable oil

Salad:
3 pounds fresh beets (weighed without tops)
1 teaspoon lemon zest
¼ cup fresh lemon juice
3 tablespoons olive oil
1 teaspoon salt
½ teaspoon freshly ground pepper

1 head of chicory, torn into bite-size pieces
¼ cup chopped fresh parsley
½ cup toasted (see Note) coarsely chopped walnuts, for garnish

1. Make the vinaigrette: In a small bowl, whisk the vinegar, lemon juice, mustard, garlic, salt and pepper until blended. Gradually whisk in the oils in a slow, thin stream.

2. Prepare the salad: Preheat the oven to 450°. Wrap the beets tightly in aluminum foil. Place on a baking sheet and bake about 45 minutes, or until the beets are tender when pierced with a small knife. Let cool slightly.

3. Rub the skins off the beets under cold running water. Cut in half crosswise; cut each half into ¼-inch slices. In a medium bowl, toss the beets with the lemon zest, lemon juice, olive oil, salt and pepper. Let marinate at room temperature for at least 20 minutes, or up to several hours.

4. In a large bowl, toss the chicory and parsley with enough of the vinaigrette to coat lightly; place in a serving bowl or on a platter. Remove the beets from the marinade and arrange them over the greens. Scatter the walnuts over the top, if desired. Drizzle any remaining beet marinade over the salad. Pass any remaining vinaigrette separately.

NOTE: To toast the walnuts, preheat the oven to 350°. Scatter the nuts in a baking pan and bake, turning the nuts frequently, until lightly toasted, about 10 minutes.

Celery Root with Celery Dressing

8 SERVINGS

2 cups chopped celery (4 to 6 ribs), including some of the leaves
1 large garlic clove, sliced
1 small onion, chopped
1 teaspoon salt
½ cup plus 1 tablespoon olive oil
2 egg yolks, at room temperature
3 tablespoons fresh lemon juice
⅓ cup sour cream
1½ tablespoons Dijon-style mustard
1 teaspoon sugar
½ teaspoon ground cumin
¼ teaspoon celery seed
¼ teaspoon freshly ground pepper

2 pounds celery root, peeled and cut into 2-by-¼-inch julienne strips

1. In a medium saucepan, combine the celery, garlic, onion, ½ teaspoon of the salt, 1 tablespoon of the oil and 2 cups of water. Bring to a boil over moderately high heat. Boil, uncovered, until the water has evaporated and the vegetables begin to sauté in the oil, 15 to 20 minutes. Continue to cook, stirring constantly, until the celery is dry, about 2 minutes.

2. Puree the celery mixture through the medium disk of a food mill. Transfer the puree to a fine sieve set over a bowl and let any excess moisture drain off.

3. In a medium bowl, using a whisk or an electric mixer on low speed, beat the egg yolks and 1 tablespoon of the lemon juice until blended. Gradually beat in the remaining ½ cup oil in a thin stream to make a mayonnaise; the dressing should be smooth and thick. Stir in the celery puree, sour cream, mustard, sugar, cumin, celery seed, the remaining ½ teaspoon salt, the pepper and the remaining 2 tablespoons lemon juice. Cover and refrigerate.

4. Bring a large pot of lightly salted water to a boil. Add the celery root, return to a boil and cook for 1 minute. Drain and rinse under cold running water; drain well. Dry with paper towels.

5. Toss the celery root with the celery dressing. If desired, stir in additional lemon juice or mustard to taste. Cover and refrigerate until chilled before serving.

Panzanella

This rustic Italian salad is usually served as a first course. It is traditionally made of Tuscan bread, a salt-free, chewy Italian loaf, which dries rock hard. Buy the bread at least three days before you make the salad, so it will be completely stale.

<u>8 SERVINGS</u>

1 loaf (1 pound) crusty Italian bread, preferably Tuscan
4 ripe, medium tomatoes, cut roughly into ½-inch cubes (about 4 cups)

1 large cucumber, peeled and thinly sliced
5 scallions, chopped (about 1 cup)
¼ cup chopped fresh basil
6 tablespoons olive oil, preferably extra-virgin Tuscan
3 tablespoons red wine vinegar
1 teaspoon salt
1 teaspoon freshly ground pepper, or to taste

1. Three days before assembling the salad, cut the bread roughly into 1-inch cubes and leave out, uncovered, turning several times, so that the bread becomes stale and hard throughout.

2. The day you make the salad, spread the stale bread cubes, crust-side down, in a large, shallow baking dish; the bread should be no more than 2 cubes deep. Drizzle 4 cups of cold water over the bread; be sure to moisten all the cubes. Let soak for 10 minutes, no longer.

3. One handful at a time, pick up the bread and squeeze out as much water as possible. Place the bread on one half of a large kitchen towel and pat out to about ¼ inch. Repeat until you have squeezed all the bread and spread it out in a thin layer over half the towel. Fold over the other half of the towel to cover the bread, slide onto a baking sheet and refrigerate until chilled, about 2 hours.

4. Meanwhile, place the tomatoes, cucumber, scallions and basil in a large salad bowl. Cover and refrigerate until chilled.

5. Transfer the cold bread to a dry towel. Form the bread into a long, narrow cylinder; roll it up in the towel and twist it to squeeze out as much additional water as possible.

6. Remove the vegetables from the refrigerator. Using your fingers, tear off small pieces of the bread and crumble it into the salad bowl; the bread will be sticky.

7. In a small bowl, whisk the oil, vinegar, salt and pepper until blended. Pour the dressing over the salad. With a fork, rake through the salad to mix the bread with the vegetables. Serve chilled.

Tomato-Potato Salad

A refreshing version of potato salad, this one is loaded with cherry tomatoes and flavored with fragrant fresh coriander.

<u>12 SERVINGS</u>

3 pounds (about 24) small red potatoes
3 teaspoons salt
2 large green bell peppers, cut into ¼-inch dice
4 celery ribs, cut into ¼-inch dice
¼ cup (packed) minced fresh coriander (cilantro)
¼ cup grated onion (optional)
2 pints cherry tomatoes—halved crosswise, squeezed to remove seeds and excess juice, then halved again
1½ cups mayonnaise, preferably homemade
2 tablespoons Dijon-style mustard
½ teaspoon freshly ground pepper

1. Place the potatoes in a large saucepan; fill with cold water and add 1 teaspoon of the salt. Partially cover and bring to a boil over high heat. Reduce the heat to moderate and cook until just tender when pierced with a fork, 20 to 30 minutes. Drain the potatoes, let cool to room temperature and refrigerate until chilled.

2. Peel the potatoes and cut them into ¾-inch cubes. Place them in a large bowl and add the green peppers, celery, coriander, onion and tomatoes; toss gently to avoid breaking the potatoes.

3. In a small bowl, mix the mayonnaise, mustard, the remaining 2 teaspoons salt and the pepper until blended. Add the dressing to the potato mixture and toss gently until the vegetables are coated. Season with more salt, if desired. Serve chilled.

Arugula, Potato and Red Pepper Salad with Caper Mayonnaise

6 SERVINGS

1½ pounds small red potatoes, halved and cut into ⅜-inch slices
1½ teaspoons salt
2 large red bell peppers
1 garlic clove
1 tablespoon capers
1 egg yolk
2 teaspoons fresh lemon juice
¼ teaspoon freshly ground black pepper
¾ cup olive oil
1½ cups lightly packed arugula (1 large bunch), coarsely chopped
Bibb lettuce, for garnish

1. Place the potatoes and 1 teaspoon of the salt in a medium saucepan; add enough cold water to cover by 1 inch. Bring to a boil, reduce the heat to a simmer and cook, uncovered, until the potatoes are just tender, about 10 minutes. Drain and rinse under cold running water; drain well.

2. Roast the red peppers over an open flame or broil about 4 inches from the heat, turning, until the skins are completely blackened. Put the charred peppers in a paper bag and let steam for about 5 minutes to loosen the skins. Scrape off the blackened skin and remove the seeds and stems. Cut the peppers lengthwise into ⅜-inch strips.

3. Mash the garlic and capers to a paste with a mortar and pestle. (If you don't have a mortar and pestle, chop the capers and garlic very fine, sprinkle with ¼ teaspoon of the salt, then slide the flat side of the knife over the top several times to mash to a paste.) Transfer to a small bowl.

4. Add the egg yolk, lemon juice, black pepper and remaining salt to the bowl. Whisk until well blended.

5. Begin slowly whisking in the olive oil drop by drop to make a mayonnaise. When the emulsion thickens after about half of the oil has been incorporated, whisk in the remaining oil in a thin stream.

6. Toss the potatoes and arugula with the mayonnaise until coated. Line a plat-ter with lettuce leaves if desired. Mound the potato salad on the platter and surround with bundles of the red pepper strips.

Northwest Roquefort Apple Slaw

8 TO 10 SERVINGS

½ small head of green cabbage (about 1 pound), finely shredded
¼ head of red cabbage (about ½ pound), finely shredded
1 cup finely shredded savoy cabbage (about ¼ pound)
2 large unpeeled Delicious apples, cored and cut into ¼-inch dice
1 small, sweet red onion, chopped (½ cup)
1 celery rib, cut into ¼-inch dice
1 tablespoon plus 2 teaspoons sugar
½ cup dry white wine
⅓ cup fresh lemon juice
¼ cup salad or walnut oil
4 hard-cooked egg yolks, mashed
1 tablespoon German-style mustard, preferably Dusseldorf
1 teaspoon salt
Freshly ground pepper
½ cup heavy cream, lightly whipped to hold soft peaks
4 ounces Roquefort cheese, crumbled (about 1 cup)
Walnut halves, for garnish

1. In a large bowl, combine the green, red and savoy cabbages, the apples, onion, celery and 2 teaspoons of the sugar.

2. In a separate bowl, whisk together the wine, lemon juice, oil, egg yolks, mustard, remaining 1 tablespoon sugar, the salt and pepper to taste until well blended. Fold in the cream.

3. Pour the dressing over the vegetables and toss. Add the cheese and toss again. Garnish with the walnuts, if desired.

Creole Rice Salad

Distinctly Southern, this tasty rice and bean salad can be made as spicy-hot as you like. Add cooked meat to transform it from a side dish into a main course.

F&W Beverage Suggestion: Chilled imported lager beer

6 TO 8 SERVINGS

2 teaspoons salt
1¼ cups long-grain white rice
⅓ cup olive oil
¼ cup red wine vinegar
1½ teaspoons Worcestershire sauce
3 medium garlic cloves, minced
½ teaspoon oregano
½ teaspoon thyme
½ teaspoon paprika
¼ teaspoon freshly ground black pepper
¼ to ½ teaspoon cayenne pepper, to taste
1 can (15¼ ounces) red kidney beans, drained
⅓ cup (2 ounces) unsalted roasted peanuts
1 large tomato—peeled, seeded and coarsely chopped
1 large red or green bell pepper, coarsely chopped
1 medium onion, coarsely chopped
1 pound diced cooked chicken, smoked sausage, ham or shrimp or a mixture of these meats (optional)

1. In a medium saucepan, bring 2½ cups of cold water and 1 teaspoon of the salt to a boil. Sprinkle in the rice, return to a boil and cover. Reduce the heat to moderately low and cook until the rice is tender but still firm, about 18 minutes.

2. Meanwhile, in another medium saucepan, combine the oil, vinegar, Worcestershire, garlic, oregano, thyme, paprika, black pepper and cayenne to make a dressing. Heat just to a simmer, stirring to blend well. Remove from the heat.

3. Put the cooked rice in a large bowl. Add the kidney beans, peanuts, tomato, bell pepper and onion; toss briefly to mix. Pour the dressing over the salad, add the cooked meat, if desired, and toss to coat thoroughly. Serve at room temperature or cover and refrigerate to chill and allow the flavors to mellow.

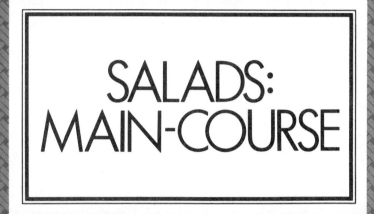

SALADS:
MAIN-COURSE

Summer Vegetable Salad

4 SERVINGS

Vegetables:

2 medium carrots cut into 1-by-¼-inch julienne strips (about 1 cup)
10 tablespoons dry white wine
¼ pound snow peas, cut into thirds lengthwise (about 1 cup)
6 thin scallions, including all the green portions, cut into 1¼-inch pieces on the diagonal (about ⅔ cup)
1 pound Jerusalem artichokes, peeled and cut into ⅛-inch-thick slices (about 1¾ cups)
4 medium beets, peeled and cut into ¼-inch dice (about 1½ cups)

Dressing:

1 teaspoon anchovy paste
2 tablespoons sherry vinegar
2 tablespoons walnut oil
¼ cup olive oil
Salt

1. Prepare the vegetables: Steam the carrots, covered, for 2 minutes over high heat. Transfer the carrots to a small bowl, pour 2 tablespoons of the wine over them and set aside to cool. Repeat this procedure with each vegetable separately, steaming the snow peas and scallions for 2 minutes, the Jerusalem artichokes for 5 minutes, and the beets for 6 to 7 minutes. Keep the vegetables in separate bowls.

2. Make the dressing: Place the anchovy paste and vinegar in a small bowl and beat with a fork until well combined. Slowly add the walnut and olive oils, beating constantly until thoroughly incorporated. Add salt to taste. Toss each vegetable separately with about 1½ tablespoons of the dressing.

3. Assemble the salad: On individual plates or a large serving plate, make separate mounds of beets, carrots, snow peas and Jerusalem artichokes. Arrange the scallions decoratively on top of each and serve at room temperature.

Shredded Chicken Salad with Ginger and Sesame

F&W Beverage Suggestion:
A hearty California red, such as Petite Sirah

4 TO 6 SERVINGS

2 slices (quarter-sized), plus 1 tablespoon finely shredded fresh gingerroot
3 tablespoons sherry wine vinegar
Green tops from 1 bunch of scallions
3 peppercorns
1 teaspoon salt
1 pound skinless, boneless chicken breasts
¾ pound carrots, cut into 2-by-¼-inch sticks
½ pound green beans, cut into 2-inch lengths
1 tablespoon Dijon-style mustard
2 tablespoons soy sauce
½ teaspoon freshly ground pepper
2 tablespoons Oriental sesame oil
2 tablespoons vegetable oil

1. In a large, deep, noncorrodible skillet or flameproof casserole, put the ginger slices, 1 tablespoon of the vinegar, the scallion tops, peppercorns, salt and 6 cups of water. Bring to a boil, reduce the heat and simmer for 15 minutes.

2. Add the chicken, reduce the heat to low and simmer until the chicken is almost cooked through but still slightly pink in the center (it will finish cooking as it cools), about 10 minutes. Remove the chicken to a rack and let cool.

3. Meanwhile, in a medium saucepan of boiling salted water, cook the carrots until crisp-tender, about 2 minutes. Drain and rinse under cold running water; drain well.

4. In another medium saucepan of boiling salted water, cook the green beans until crisp-tender, about 2 minutes. Drain and rinse under cold running water; drain well.

5. In a small bowl, whisk the mustard, soy sauce, ground pepper and remaining 2 tablespoons vinegar until blended. Slowly whisk in the sesame and vegetable oils in a thin stream to make a dressing.

6. With your fingers, tear the chicken into shreds about the same size as the carrots. In a large bowl, combine the chicken with the carrots, green beans and shredded ginger. Pour on the dressing, toss well to coat and serve at room temperature.

Minted Chicken Salad with Tropical Fruits

This is a delicate salad that is cooled by the mint and fresh fruits. It is a pleasant and refreshing lunch or supper dish when served in crisp lettuce cups with a marinated green bean and shallot salad, and a chilled Gewürztraminer alongside.

6 SERVINGS

3½ tablespoons vegetable oil
2 teaspoons minced fresh gingerroot
1 teaspoon minced garlic
¼ teaspoon crushed hot red pepper flakes
1 pound skinless, boneless chicken breasts, cut into 1-inch pieces
½ teaspoon salt
Freshly ground black pepper
⅓ cup chicken stock or water
¼ cup chopped fresh mint
¼ cup mayonnaise, preferably homemade
¼ cup plain yogurt
1 tablespoon fresh lemon juice
1¼ teaspoons grated lemon zest
½ mango, peeled and diced
½ papaya, peeled and diced
1 medium banana, sliced
⅓ cup diagonally sliced scallions
Fresh mint sprigs, for garnish

1. In a large skillet or wok, heat the oil. Add 1 teaspoon of the ginger, ½ teaspoon of the garlic and the red pepper flakes and cook over moderately high heat for 10 seconds. Add the chicken and stir fry until just cooked through, about 2 minutes; transfer to a sieve placed over a bowl to catch any juices. Season the chicken with the salt and pepper to taste.

2. Add the chicken stock, 1 tablespoon of the mint and any juices from the chicken to the skillet. Boil over high heat until reduced to about 1 tablespoon, scraping the bottom of the pan to loosen any brown bits.

3. Strain the reduced liquid into a medium bowl and let cool slightly. Stir in the mayonnaise, yogurt, lemon juice, lemon zest, the remaining 1 teaspoon ginger, ½ teaspoon garlic and the remaining chopped mint. Season with additional salt and pepper to taste.

4. Toss the cooled chicken with the dressing. Add the mango, papaya, banana and scallions and toss gently. Place in a serving dish, cover and refrigerate for at least 2 hours to chill and to allow the flavors to meld. Serve at room temperature, garnished with fresh mint sprigs.

Valentine Duck Salad

2 SERVINGS

Duck:
4½- to 5-pound duck
Coarse (kosher) salt and pepper
1 tablespoon honey
1 tablespoon frozen orange juice
    concentrate
½ teaspoon ground cloves
1 tangerine

Dressing:
6 tablespoons olive oil
2 tablespoons red wine vinegar
1 tablespoon medium-dry sherry
¼ teaspoon anchovy paste
2 tablespoons finely chopped
    scallions

Garnish:
4 tangerines peeled (white pith
    removed), and sliced into very
    thin rounds

1. Prepare the duck: Preheat the oven to 350°. Rinse and dry the duck thoroughly. Rub it, inside and out, with salt and pepper.

2. Combine the honey, orange juice concentrate and cloves in a small bowl to make a glaze for the duck.

3. Prick the tangerine all over with the tines of a fork and place it in the cavity of the duck. Close the cavity with skewers

or thread. Transfer the duck to a rack set in a roasting pan and roast, breast-side down, for 30 minutes. Turn the bird on one side and roast for 15 minutes; turn the duck on the other side and roast for 15 minutes more. Turn the bird breast-side up and roast for an additional 1½ hours, brushing with the glaze every 15 minutes during the last hour of cooking.

4. Allow the duck to rest until it is cool enough to handle. Preheat the oven to 350°. Gently remove as much of the skin as possible, preferably in large sheets. Arrange the skin on a baking sheet, outer side up, and bake for 30 minutes, or until crisp.

5. Meanwhile, carefully remove the two breast halves from the duck, keeping each in 1 solid piece. Cut the meat diagonally into thin slices. Cut off the legs (with thighs attached) and reserve. Cut off the wings and save for another purpose. Trim any remaining meat from the carcass; reserve the carcass for stock.

6. Prepare the dressing: In a medium bowl, whisk the oil, vinegar, sherry and anchovy paste until blended; stir in the scallions.

7. Assemble the salad: Mound the untidy-looking meat on the center of a platter. Arrange the breast meat neatly over it. Place a leg at either end of the platter. Pass the dressing through a sieve onto the meat, pressing on the solids with the back of a spoon.

8. Coarsely chop the duck-skin cracklings and sprinkle them over the salad. Arrange the tangerine slices around the edges. Cover loosely and set aside at room temperature until serving time.

Artichoke Salad with Chicken and Dried Monterey Jack

4 SERVINGS

2 tablespoons fresh lemon juice
4 large uncooked artichoke
    bottoms, with 20 leaves reserved
2 cups chicken stock or canned
    broth
2 skinless, boneless chicken breast
    halves
3 tablespoons olive oil, preferably
    Californian
¼ teaspoon salt
¼ teaspoon freshly ground pepper
¼ cup coarsely grated dried
    Monterey Jack cheese or mild
    Parmesan
2 tablespoons finely chopped
    parsley

1. Place 1 tablespoon of the lemon juice in a small bowl. One at a time, cut each artichoke bottom into ⅛-inch julienne strips and add to the bowl, tossing until coated with the lemon juice to prevent discoloration.

2. In a medium, noncorrodible saucepan, bring 1 quart of water to a boil. Add the julienned artichokes with lemon juice and the 20 reserved leaves. Blanch until barely tender, about 1 minute. Drain and rinse under cold running water; drain well. Transfer to a medium bowl.

3. In a medium saucepan, bring the stock and 2 cups of water to a boil over moderately high heat; reduce to a simmer. Add the chicken and poach 10 minutes, or until firm to the touch. Let cool, then cut into ¼-inch julienne strips. Add to the artichokes.

4. In a small bowl, whisk together the olive oil, remaining 1 tablespoon lemon juice, the salt and pepper. Pour over the artichokes and chicken and toss to coat. Arrange 5 artichoke leaves around the edge of each of 4 plates. Pile one-quarter of the artichoke-chicken mixture on each plate. Sprinkle each serving with 1 tablespoon Monterey Jack, a grind of black pepper and ½ teaspoon chopped parsley.

Curried Turkey Salad with Grapes and Almonds

8 SERVINGS

Turkey Breast:

1 turkey breast, about 5 pounds
2 medium carrots, cut up
1 medium onion, cut up
2 celery ribs with leaves, cut up
Bouquet garni: 2 bay leaves, 6
 peppercorns, 4 sprigs of parsley,
 2 teaspoons thyme tied in a
 double thickness of cheesecloth

Curry Mayonnaise:

2 cups mayonnaise
1½ tablespoons curry powder
2 tablespoons mango chutney,
 finely chopped
¼ teaspoon ground cumin
2 to 3 tablespoons chopped fresh
 basil or 1 teaspoon dried
⅛ teaspoon cayenne
2 tablespoons dry white wine
2 tablespoons lemon juice
Salt and pepper

Assembly:

1½ tablespoons unsalted butter
8 ounces slivered, blanched
 almonds (about 2 cups)
2 pounds seedless grapes
1 to 2 bunches of watercress, for
 garnish

1. Poach the turkey breast: Place the turkey breast in a stockpot with 5 quarts of water, the carrots, onion, celery, and bouquet garni. Simmer over moderate heat until the juices run clear when the meat is pierced with a fork, or when a meat thermometer registers an internal temperature of 165°, 1½ to 2 hours. Let the meat cool to room temperature in the stock to help keep the meat moist.

2. Meanwhile, make the curry mayonnaise: In a medium bowl, mix the mayonnaise with the curry powder, chutney, cumin, basil and cayenne. Add the white wine and lemon juice and mix well. Season with salt and pepper to taste; cover and refrigerate until needed.

3. Assemble the salad: In a small skillet, melt the butter, add the almonds and sauté over moderate heat until golden brown.

4. Remove the turkey breast from the stock. (Strain the stock and reserve for another use.) Separate the turkey meat from the bone and tear or cut into strips about ¼ inch wide and 2 to 3 inches long. Mix the strips with 1½ cups of the curry mayonnaise, adding more if the mixture seems dry. Add the almonds and grapes and gently incorporate them. Cover and refrigerate for at least 30 minutes.

5. To serve: Place the salad in a mound in the center of a large, chilled serving dish and surround with the watercress.

Salad of Duck Confit with Orange

The breasts of either duck or goose *confit* can be attractively sliced for this salad.

4 APPETIZER OR 2 MAIN-COURSE SERVINGS

2 pieces of duck *confit*, preferably
 breast
3 tablespoons sherry vinegar or red
 wine vinegar
1 teaspoon Dijon-style mustard
¼ teaspoon salt
⅛ teaspoon freshly ground pepper
½ cup walnut oil
½ cup broken walnut pieces
1 tablespoon chopped fresh parsley
2 teaspoons minced fresh chives
1 head of lettuce, preferably
 Boston, Bibb or lamb's lettuce
 (*mâche*)
2 oranges, peeled and sectioned

1. Preheat the broiler. Scrape off any excess fat from the pieces of *confit*. Place the duck, skin-side up, on a rack in a broiling pan about 4 inches from the heat and broil until the skin is crisp and brown, 3 to 5 minutes. Let rest until cool enough to handle. Cut the breasts into very thin diagonal slices; discard the bones. Set the meat aside.

2. In a small bowl, whisk the vinegar, mustard, salt and pepper until blended. Gradually whisk in the oil.

3. Place the duck and walnuts in a shallow dish. Spoon half the vinaigrette over them and sprinkle with the parsley and chives. Let marinate at room temperature for 30 minutes, tossing once.

4. Toss the lettuce with the remaining dressing. Divide the lettuce among the individual plates. Lift the duck out of the marinade and arrange it and the orange sections in a flowerlike pattern on top of the lettuce. Sprinkle with the marinated walnuts and serve at room temperature.

Orzo Salad with Vegetables

32 SERVINGS

1 cup currants
1 cup cream sherry
¼ cup loosely packed, chopped
 fresh mint or 2 tablespoons dried
3 cups plus 3 tablespoons olive oil
3 pounds orzo
¼ cup fresh lemon juice
1 cup red wine vinegar
3 tablespoons salt
2 tablespoons freshly ground
 pepper
2 cups thinly sliced scallions
 (about 2 bunches)

**Vegetable Accompaniments
(recipes follow):**

Honey Carrots Vinaigrette
Tangy Cauliflower with Poppy
 Seeds
Dilled Green Beans with Walnuts
Limey Cherry Tomatoes

1. In a medium saucepan, combine the currants, sherry and mint. Bring to a boil, remove from the heat and set aside for 30 minutes.

2. Meanwhile, in a large pot, bring 8 to 10 quarts of salted water to a boil. Add 3 tablespoons of the oil and pour the orzo into the water, stirring to prevent sticking. Cook for 8 minutes, or until tender. Drain; then spread the orzo in a single layer on a clean surface or onto 2 or 3 baking sheets and allow to dry for up to 30 minutes.

3. Add the remaining 3 cups oil, the lemon juice, vinegar, salt and pepper to the currant-sherry mixture, blend well.

4. Transfer the orzo to a large bowl. Pour on the dressing, add the scallions and mix well. Set aside for 1 hour at room temperature to blend the flavors. If not using immediately, cover and refrigerate; allow the salad to return to room temperature before serving.

5. To serve, mound the orzo in the center of a large platter and arrange the vegetable accompaniments around the edge, using some vegetables to decorate the center.

Honey Carrots Vinaigrette

2 pounds carrots, cut into 2½-by-⅛-inch julienne strips
1 cup olive oil
⅓ cup red wine vinegar
⅓ cup honey
2 tablespoons fresh lemon juice
3 tablespoons finely chopped fresh parsley
Salt and pepper

1. Steam the carrots for about 5 minutes, until crisp-tender. Drain well.

2. In a medium bowl, whisk the oil, vinegar, honey, lemon juice, parsley and salt and pepper to taste until blended. Add the warm carrots and toss to coat well.

Tangy Cauliflower with Poppy Seeds

2 pounds cauliflower (1 large or 2 medium heads), cut into florets
1 cup olive oil
⅓ cup red wine vinegar
2 teaspoons anchovy paste
2 teaspoons fresh lime juice
Salt and pepper
3 tablespoons poppy seeds

1. Steam the cauliflower for 6 to 8 minutes, until just tender; do not overcook. Drain well.

2. In a medium bowl, whisk the oil, vinegar, anchovy paste, lime juice and salt and pepper to taste until blended. Stir in the poppy seeds. Add the warm cauliflower and toss to coat well.

Limey Cherry Tomatoes

½ cup olive oil
¼ cup fresh lime juice
3 tablespoons chopped chives
Salt and pepper
4 pints cherry tomatoes

In a medium bowl, whisk the oil, lime juice, chives and salt and pepper to taste. Add the tomatoes and toss to coat well.

Dilled Green Beans with Walnuts

2 pounds green beans, trimmed
1 cup olive oil
⅓ cup red wine vinegar
2 tablespoons fresh lemon juice
Salt and pepper
3 hard-cooked eggs, coarsely chopped
2 tablespoons finely chopped walnuts
3 tablespoons minced fresh dill

1. Steam the beans for about 6 minutes, until crisp-tender. Drain and rinse briefly under cold water to refresh; drain well.

2. In a medium bowl, whisk the oil, vinegar, lemon juice and salt and pepper to taste until blended. Stir in the eggs, walnuts and dill. Add the warm green beans and toss to coat well.

Cold Rice Salad

12 SERVINGS

Rice:
2 cups long-grain brown rice
2 tablespoons lemon juice

Marinated Zucchini:
3 small zucchini (about 1 pound), cut into ½-inch cubes
1 tablespoon olive oil
2 teaspoons red wine vinegar
¼ teaspoon salt
¼ teaspoon pepper
1 teaspoon chopped dill

Marinated Eggplant:
1 medium eggplant (about 1½ pounds)
2 teaspoons salt
4 tablespoons olive oil

1 tablespoon minced garlic
2 tablespoons red wine vinegar
1 tablespoon finely minced flat-leaf parsley
¼ teaspoon pepper

Dressing:
1 large garlic clove, crushed
1 cup olive oil
⅓ cup red wine vinegar
2 tablespoons lemon juice
½ teaspoon pepper
1½ teaspoons salt
4 tablespoons chopped dill
5 fresh basil leaves or ½ teaspoon dried
3 sprigs of flat-leaf parsley, stems removed

Assembly:
1½ cups cooked peas
½ cup chopped red onion
1 cup chopped red bell pepper
Salt and pepper
Cherry tomato halves, sprig of dill and 1 to 2 bunches arugula or watercress, for garnish

1. Prepare the rice: In a large saucepan, bring 5 cups of salted water to a boil over high heat. Stir in the rice, and reduce the heat to low. Simmer the rice, covered, until barely tender, 40 to 45 minutes. Remove from the heat and let rest, covered, for 15 minutes. Rinse under cold running water, drain and transfer to a large bowl. Toss with the lemon juice and reserve.

2. Meanwhile, prepare the zucchini: Cook the zucchini in boiling salted water for 3 minutes. Drain and rinse under cold running water. Place the zucchini in a medium bowl and coat with the olive oil. Add the vinegar, salt, pepper and dill, and toss well. Cover and chill.

3. Prepare the eggplant: Peel the eggplant and cut into ½-inch cubes. Place the cubes in a colander and sprinkle with the salt. Toss and set over a bowl to drain for about 30 minutes. Rinse, drain and pat dry with paper towels.

4. In a large skillet, heat the olive oil over high heat until almost smoking. Add the eggplant and garlic and sauté, stirring frequently, until the eggplant is brown and tender, 7 to 8 minutes. Transfer the mixture to a medium bowl and add the vinegar, parsley and pepper; toss well. Cool to room temperature.

5. Make the dressing: Place all the dressing ingredients in a blender or food processor and blend for 1 minute, or until the garlic is completely incorporated into the mixture.

6. Assemble the salad: Reserving one-third of the dressing in a small serving bowl or cruet, add the remainder to the rice along with the peas, red onion and red pepper. Mix well and season with salt and pepper to taste. Chill for at least 1 hour.

7. Mound the rice mixture in the center of a large platter and edge it with a row of cherry tomato halves, cut-sides down. Along the rim of the platter, place small, alternating mounds of the eggplant and zucchini mixtures. Place two cherry tomato halves and a sprig of dill on top of the salad and garnish the platter with the arugula or watercress. Serve cold with the remaining dressing.

Salmon-Pasta Salad

16 TO 18 SERVINGS

Salad:
1½ pounds small pasta shells
3 tablespoons olive oil
4½ cups coarsely chopped scallions (about 5 bunches)
¾ cup finely chopped parsley
1¼ cups coarsely chopped black olives
¼ cup capers, drained
1½ pounds smoked salmon, cut into thin julienne strips

Dressing:
¾ cup olive oil
¼ cup red wine vinegar
3 tablespoons fresh lemon juice
½ teaspoon anchovy paste
¾ teaspoon salt
¾ teaspoon freshly ground pepper

1. Boil the shells in a large pot of salted water until *al dente*, 10 to 12 minutes.

Drain thoroughly and immediately transfer to a large bowl. Toss the hot shells with the olive oil. Add the scallions, parsley, olives, capers and salmon and toss to mix.

2. In a small bowl, whisk all the dressing ingredients until thoroughly blended. Pour over the salad and toss to coat. Serve at room temperature.

Smoked Trout (or Salmon) Niçoise

6 TO 8 SERVINGS

1½ pounds small red potatoes
½ pound snow peas
1 pound green beans
1 pint cherry tomatoes
1 red onion, thinly sliced
1 cup Niçoise olives
10 ounces skinned and boned smoked trout or salmon, cut into chunks (about 2½ cups)
4 hard-cooked eggs, halved lengthwise
⅓ cup white wine vinegar
⅔ cup olive oil
1 tablespoon minced shallot
1 tablespoon minced fresh dill
½ teaspoon salt
Black pepper
Sprigs of fresh dill, for garnish

1. Cook the potatoes in a large pot of boiling water until tender, 15 to 20 minutes. Drain and rinse under cold running water until they are cool enough to handle. Slip the skins off the potatoes and cut them into quarters.

2. Meanwhile, in another pot of boiling water, cook the snow peas until they swell slightly and turn bright emerald green, 2 to 3 minutes. Remove them with a slotted spoon and rinse until cool. Cook the green beans in the same boiling water until tender but still firm, 7 to 10 minutes. Drain the beans and rinse them under cold running water until cool.

3. Arrange the potatoes, snow peas, green beans, cherry tomatoes and onion decoratively on a large platter. Scatter the olives over the vegetables. Mound the smoked trout in the center. Place the eggs decoratively around the salad. If not serving immediately, cover and refrigerate.

4. In a small bowl, whisk the vinegar and oil until blended. Whisk in the shallot, minced dill, salt and pepper, to taste.

5. Just before serving, whisk the dressing and drizzle it over the salad. Garnish with the dill sprigs.

Sesame Noodle Salad

6 TO 8 SERVINGS

1 pound fresh linguine or 12 ounces dried
¼ cup Oriental sesame oil
3 tablespoons soy sauce or tamari
¼ teaspoon freshly ground black pepper
¼ cup chopped watercress leaves
¼ cup finely diced red bell pepper
1 small garlic clove, minced

1. In a large pot of boiling salted water, cook the linguine until tender but still slightly firm, 2 to 3 minutes for fresh pasta, 8 to 9 minutes for dried. Drain in a colander, then immediately submerge in a bowl of cold water to stop the cooking. Drain well.

2. In a large bowl, combine the sesame oil, soy sauce and black pepper. Add the linguine and toss well to coat. Add the watercress, red pepper and garlic; toss until mixed. Serve at room temperature.

Shrimp Salad Hilary

In this delicately colored, creamy salad, the characteristic tartness of sour cream and plain yogurt is shaded with mustard and smoothed with a touch of Cognac. There is a lot of sauce, which doubles as a dressing for the bed of romaine lettuce.

8 FIRST-COURSE SERVINGS

2½ tablespoons coarse (kosher) salt
2 pounds medium shrimp in their shells
1 pound thinly sliced Canadian bacon
4 medium tomatoes—peeled, seeded and chopped
½ cup finely chopped scallions
2 cups sour cream
2 cups plain yogurt
¼ cup Cognac
¼ cup prepared Dijon-style mustard
1 teaspoon freshly ground pepper
2 small heads of romaine lettuce—separated into leaves, rinsed and dried

1. **Prepare the shrimp:** In a large pot, bring 6 quarts of water to a boil with 2 tablespoons of the salt. When the water has reached a rolling boil, add all the shrimp at once. Cook, uncovered, until the shrimp are pink and tender, about 3 minutes. Drain the shrimp into a colander and rinse immediately under cold running water to prevent further cooking; drain well. Shell the shrimp and devein, if desired. Split them in half lengthwise and place in a large bowl.

2. Cut the bacon into ½-inch pieces. Add to the shrimp. Add the tomatoes and scallions.

3. In a medium bowl, combine the sour cream, yogurt, Cognac, mustard, remaining ½ tablespoon salt and the pepper; stir until blended. Pour the dressing over the shrimp salad and toss gently until mixed. Refrigerate, covered, until chilled.

4. Before serving, arrange the lettuce in an attractive pattern on each salad plate. Divide the shrimp salad among the plates, adding as much sauce as desired. Let stand at room temperature for 15 minutes before serving.

Scallop and Orange Salad

4 SERVINGS

Salad:
1 navel orange
About 1⅓ cups orange juice
1 pound bay or sea scallops
2 tablespoons thinly slivered fresh gingerroot
1 garlic clove, minced
1 tablespoon honey

Dressing:
¼ cup sherry or white wine vinegar
½ cup olive oil
½ teaspoon salt
Pepper
1 tablespoon minced fresh coriander
⅓ cup thinly sliced scallions
1 medium red bell pepper, cut into ¾-by-⅛-inch julienne strips

1. **Prepare the oranges:** Using a swivel-bladed peeler, remove the zest in pieces as large as possible from the orange and cut into thin strips; place in a bowl, cover with cold water and set aside. Working over a large bowl to collect the juices, section the orange, removing as much of the pith and membrane as possible. Reserve the orange sections; measure any juice and add as much as needed to measure 1⅓ cups.

2. **Poach the scallops:** (If using sea scallops, halve them horizontally, then cut into wedge-shaped quarters.) Rinse the scallops and pat them dry. In a noncorrodible saucepan, bring the orange juice and the scallops to a boil over moderate heat. Reduce the heat to low and poach for 30 to 60 seconds, or until the scallops are just cooked through (do not overcook or they will toughen). Remove them from the pan with a slotted spoon and set aside.

3. Add the ginger, garlic and honey to the orange juice in the pan. Bring the mixture to a boil over high heat; lower the heat to moderate and, stirring frequently, reduce the mixture to ½ cup. Cool to room temperature.

4. **Prepare the dressing:** In a medium bowl, whisk together the vinegar, oil, salt, pepper and coriander. Chop half the reserved orange zest and add it to the dressing, along with half the scallions and all the red pepper.

5. **Marinate the scallops:** Add the reserved scallops to the dressing and toss well. Cover and chill for at least 1 hour.

6. **Assemble the salad:** Mound the scallop salad in the center of a chilled platter. Dip the reserved orange sections into the reduced orange juice mixture. Then, garnish the platter with "butterflies", using 2 glazed orange sections for the wings and 2 strips of orange zest for the antennae of each butterfly. Sprinkle the remaining scallions over the salad and top with remaining strips of orange zest.

Salad of Squid, Fennel, Red Peppers and Croutons

This meaty, satisfying salad is subtly seasoned with fennel and crisped with croutons. If you cannot spare the time to prepare them, you can substitute 1½ to 2 cups commercially produced croutons for the homemade. If fresh fennel is elusive, use the tender, inner stalks of celery instead.

4 SERVINGS

2 bay leaves
½ teaspoon fennel seed
3 garlic cloves
¼ cup dry vermouth
¼ cup olive oil
1½ pounds small, cleaned squid (about 2 pounds if not cleaned)
4 tablespoons lemon juice
3 thin slices of firm-textured white bread
Salt
1 medium fennel bulb
3 medium red peppers, cut into thin julienne strips about 1½ inches long

Green part of 3 or 4 scallions, thinly sliced
Large head of Boston lettuce— cleaned, dried and torn into pieces
Pepper

1. Make a stock: Combine the bay leaves, fennel seed, 2 of the garlic cloves, the vermouth, 2 tablespoons of the olive oil and 1½ cups of water in a medium saucepan. Boil gently, covered, for 10 minutes.

2. Meanwhile, slice the squid into rings about ¼ inch wide. Halve or quarter the tentacles lengthwise.

3. Strain the solids from the stock and return the liquid to the saucepan. Add the squid and simmer, stirring, until opaque and curled at the edges, 1 or 2 minutes. With a slotted spoon transfer the squid to a small bowl and let cool.

4. Boil the stock gently, stirring occasionally, until reduced to ½ cup, about 15 minutes. Pour over the squid, add 2 tablespoons of the lemon juice, then season to taste with salt, if desired. Cover and refrigerate.

5. Meanwhile, preheat the oven to 325°. Place the bread slices in a baking pan and bake until somewhat firm, but not yet crisped through, about 10 minutes. Peel and halve the remaining garlic clove. Rub both sides of the bread with garlic, cutting the clove again as you go to expose a fresh surface for each side of bread. Cut the bread into ¼- to ½-inch squares. Return to the oven and toast until crisp and browned, tossing occasionally, 10 to 15 minutes longer. Reserve the croutons until serving time.

6. Trim the feathery tops from the fennel and set aside. Separate the bulb from the stalks and reserve the stalks for another use. Discard any stringy, pithy outer sections of the bulb and coarsely chop the remainder. There should be about 1½ cups. In a large bowl, toss the fennel with the red peppers, scallions, remaining 2 tablespoons lemon juice and remaining 2 tablespoons oil. Cover and refrigerate until serving time.

7. Arrange the lettuce in a wide serving dish or bowl. Toss the squid with the vegetables and croutons. Season with salt, pepper and additional lemon juice and oil, if desired. Spread over the let-

tuce. Mince a few tablespoons of the reserved fennel tops and sprinkle over the top. Serve at once.

Shrimp and Endive Salad

4 SERVINGS

½ pound large shrimp, shelled and deveined
4 small heads of Belgian endive
1 can (8 ounces) water chestnuts, drained and sliced
1 tablespoon soy sauce
2 teaspoons cornstarch
1 teaspoon sugar
1½ teaspoons salt
1 jar (3 ounces) pimientos, drained and cut into 2-inch strips
1 large grapefruit—halved, sectioned and juice reserved
1 teaspoon grated fresh gingerroot

1. Cut each shrimp into three pieces and set them aside. Separate the leaves from the heads of endive; cut the largest leaves in half crosswise. Wash them and pat them dry with paper towels. Toss the water chestnuts with the soy sauce and allow them to rest for 3 minutes; discard any soy sauce that has not been absorbed.

2. In a small bowl, mix the cornstarch with 1 teaspoon water, the sugar, and the salt; set aside.

3. In a large noncorrodible bowl, combine the shrimp, endive, water chestnuts, pimientos, and the grapefruit along with any reserved juice; toss gently.

4. In a large noncorrodible skillet, gently stir-fry the shrimp mixture over moderately high heat, until the shrimp have turned pink and the other ingredients are hot, 3 to 4 minutes.

5. Using a slotted spoon, quickly transfer the salad to a bowl. Add the cornstarch mixture to the pan, and, stirring constantly, cook until the liquid thickens, about 1 minute. Toss the salad with the dressing and ginger; arrange on a platter and serve.

Crab-Pecan Salad

Beverage Suggestion:
California Chardonnay, such as St. Clement

4 SERVINGS

1 cup mayonnaise, preferably homemade
1 tablespoon fresh lemon juice
1 teaspoon Dijon-style mustard
½ cup minced fresh parsley
½ cup minced fresh dill
2 tablespoons minced fresh chives
1½ pounds lump crabmeat, preferably Dungeness, broken up
⅓ cup thinly sliced celery (1 small rib)
Tender leaves from 1 large head of Boston lettuce, washed and well dried
½ cup (about 2 ounces) pecan halves, slivered and lightly toasted (see Note)
Lemon wedges, for garnish

1. In a small bowl, stir the mayonnaise with the lemon juice and mustard until blended.

2. Set aside 1 tablespoon each of the parsley and dill and 1 teaspoon of the chives for garnish. Fold the remaining parsley, dill and chives into the mayonnaise.

3. In a medium bowl, toss the crabmeat with the celery; gently fold about ⅔ cup of the mayonnaise into the crab mixture (enough to moisten and flavor the salad).

4. Arrange the lettuce leaves on chilled dinner plates or a large platter; loosely mound the crabmeat on the leaves. Sprinkle the reserved parsley, dill and chives and the pecan slivers attractively on top. Garnish with the lemon wedges. Serve with the remaining mayonnaise.

NOTE: Using a small sharp knife, cut the pecans lengthwise into ⅛-inch slivers. Toast them in a preheated 350° oven for about 10 minutes, tossing once or twice until lightly colored.

Filet Mignon Salad

2 SERVINGS

Boston or Bibb lettuce
2 tablespoons olive oil
2 tablespoons fresh lemon juice
Salt and freshly ground pepper
5 ounces filet mignon, sliced paper thin
Chinese black mushrooms, softened if dried
Black truffles (optional)

1. Line 2 small plates with lettuce leaves. Mix 1 tablespoon of the oil, 1 tablespoon of the lemon juice and salt and pepper to taste and drizzle over the lettuce.

2. In a small bowl, combine the remaining 1 tablespoon oil and lemon juice and salt and pepper to taste. Dip the slices of filet mignon in the mixture for 2 seconds on each side. Arrange on top of the lettuce. Garnish each plate with Chinese mushrooms and/or truffles.

Madrigal Salad

Have all the ingredients ready before you begin to cook the salad, as it is finished in only a few minutes.

4 SERVINGS

½ pound flank steak
2 tablespoons olive oil
1 garlic clove, minced
1⅓ cups (one 35-ounce can) Italian plum tomatoes—drained, seeded and cut into ½-inch dice
1 cup thinly sliced scallions, including some of the green portions
½ cup mayonnaise
½ teaspoon salt
½ teaspoon freshly ground pepper
¼ cup chopped fresh parsley leaves, for garnish

1. Trim away and discard any fat from the steak. Thinly slice the steak across the grain and then cut the slices into 3-inch-long strips.

2. Combine the oil and the garlic. In a large heavy skillet or wok, heat the oil and garlic over moderate heat. When the oil is hot, add the meat and stir-fry over high heat for 1 minute; remove the meat with a slotted spoon and set it aside. Add the tomatoes and scallions to the pan and cook over high heat, stirring gently or until the tomatoes are hot, about 30 seconds.

3. Remove the pan from the heat and return the meat to it. Add the mayonnaise, salt and pepper; toss until the meat and vegetables are well coated with the mayonnaise.

4. Arrange the salad on a serving plate and sprinkle the chopped parsley over the top; serve immediately.

Avocado and Veal Salad with Walnuts

F&W Beverage Suggestion: California Petite Sirah

4 TO 6 SERVINGS

3 pounds boneless veal shank or shoulder
3 medium carrots, cut into 2-inch lengths
2 celery ribs, cut into 2-inch lengths
3 medium onions, unpeeled, quartered
12 parsley stems (from about ½ bunch)
4 medium garlic cloves, unpeeled
10 black peppercorns
1 teaspoon thyme
1¼ teaspoons salt
½ cup walnut oil
⅓ cup walnut pieces
2 tablespoons sherry wine vinegar
1 teaspoon green peppercorns, finely chopped
2 ripe avocados

1. Put the veal, carrots, celery, onions, parsley stems, garlic, black peppercorns, thyme and ½ teaspoon of the salt into a stockpot. Add water to cover and simmer, skimming, until the meat is very tender, about 2½ hours. Remove the meat (see Note) and when cool enough to handle, shred into pieces about ½ by 2 inches (there will be about 3½ packed cups).

2. Toss the veal with ½ teaspoon of the salt and 2 tablespoons of the walnut oil; set aside.

3. In a small skillet, heat 1 tablespoon of the walnut oil. Add the walnut pieces and cook, tossing, over moderate heat until toasted, about 3 minutes.

4. In a medium bowl, whisk together the remaining 5 tablespoons walnut oil, the vinegar, green peppercorns and remaining ¼ teaspoon salt to make a dressing.

5. Pit and peel the avocados and cut each half lengthwise into 6 slices. Add to the dressing, tossing gently to coat.

6. To assemble, mound the veal in the center of a large platter. Remove the avocado slices from the dressing and reserve the dressing. Arrange the avocado around the veal. Sprinkle the walnuts over the avocado. Drizzle the reserved dressing over the salad.

NOTE: Strain the cooking liquid, which is delicious, and use as a stock or soup base.

Sweetbread Salad with Spring Vegetables

This unusual salad is a perfect dish for a spring or summer luncheon. If you prepare the sweetbreads the night before, the final dish will only take about 30 minutes to put together.

3 SERVINGS

1 pound veal sweetbreads
Salt
3 tablespoons fresh lemon juice
8 ounces green beans, trimmed to 2½-inch lengths
3 medium carrots, cut into 2½-by-¼-inch julienne strips
1 head of chicory, separated into leaves
¾ cup peanut oil, preferably French
¼ cup sherry vinegar
1 tablespoon Dijon-style mustard
1½ tablespoons ketchup (optional)
Pepper
½ cup flour
4 tablespoons unsalted butter
1 small lime
1 bunch of fresh chervil or parsley

1. Prepare the sweetbreads: Place the sweetbreads in a large bowl. Add 2 teaspoons of salt and cold water to cover. Let soak for at least 1½ hours, changing the salted water every 30 minutes. In a large, noncorrodible saucepan or Dutch oven, place 3 quarts of cold water, the lemon juice and 1 tablespoon salt. Add the sweetbreads to the cold water, bring to a boil over moderately high heat and cook for 5 minutes. Drain and plunge into a bowl of cold water.

2. As soon as the sweetbreads are cool enough to handle, peel off the outer membrane and cut out any connective tubes with a small, sharp knife. Line a jelly-roll pan with a clean towel, place the sweetbreads on top and cover with another towel. Place another pan or cookie sheet on top and weigh down with a couple of large cans or a bag of flour. Refrigerate and press the sweetbreads for at least 3 hours or overnight.

3. Prepare the vegetables: Place the green beans in a medium saucepan of boiling salted water and cook until the beans are crisp-tender, 6 to 7 minutes.

Rinse under cold running water and drain well.

4. Place the carrots in a medium saucepan of boiling salted water; as soon as the water returns to a simmer, about 1 minute, remove, rinse under cold running water and drain. Cut the chicory into bite-size pieces and set aside.

5. Make the vinaigrette: In a medium bowl, whisk the oil, vinegar, mustard, ketchup (if desired), and salt and pepper. Taste for seasoning and set aside.

6. Sauté the sweetbreads: Cut the sweetbreads on the diagonal into slices about a half inch thick. Season the flour with 1 teaspoon salt and ½ teaspoon pepper and place on a large plate. Lightly dredge the sweetbreads and shake off any excess. In a large skillet, melt the butter over moderate heat. When the foam subsides, add the sweetbreads and sauté for about 2 minutes on each side, until golden. Set aside and keep warm.

7. Arrange the salad: Toss the carrots and green beans with enough of the vinaigrette to moisten. Place the chicory on a serving platter and moisten with a little vinaigrette. Arrange the vegetables on top of the chicory and place the warm sweetbreads over the top. Squeeze the lime over the sweetbreads. Garnish with fresh chervil or parsley. Serve the remaining vinaigrette on the side.

Ham Salad with Raspberries and Pearl Onions

2 SERVINGS

4 ounces tiny white pearl onions
2 cups dry red wine
⅔ cup fresh orange juice
¼ cup sugar
1 navel orange
12 ounces hickory smoked ham, or other fine smoked ham, sliced ¼ inch thick
16 small spinach leaves, well rinsed and dried
1 cup fresh raspberries
¼ teaspoon coarsely ground pepper

1. Cut the root ends off the pearl onions. In a large pot of boiling water, blanch the onions for 2 minutes. Drain and rinse under cold running water until cool enough to handle; slip off the skins.

2. In a large skillet, combine the wine, orange juice and sugar. Bring to a boil over high heat. Stir to dissolve the sugar; continue to boil for 6 minutes. Add the onions and cook for 6 minutes longer, until the onions are tender and the liquid is reduced to about ½ cup of syrup.

3. Meanwhile, remove 1 large piece of zest from the orange with a swivel-bladed vegetable peeler and cut into very fine slivers. Blanch for 30 seconds in boiling water, run cold water over to cool; reserve.

4. Using a sharp knife, cut away the remaining peel and all of the inner white membrane from the orange. Cut down on either side of the dividing membranes to section the orange. Halve each section crosswise and set aside in a strainer to drain off any juice.

5. Trim the ham of any fat and then cut into 2-by-½-by-¼-inch strips. Arrange the spinach leaves around the edges of each of two plates.

6. Add the ham to the hot wine sauce and heat through for about 1 minute, stirring to coat with the sauce. Add the orange sections, berries and pepper and toss again just to coat. Using a slotted spoon, divide the salad between the two spinach-lined plates. Pour the remaining sauce over the top. Garnish with the orange zest. Serve warm.

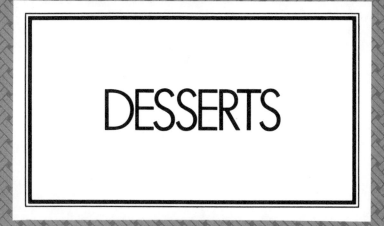

DESSERTS

Pear Brandy Tart

8 SERVINGS

Tart Shell:

1 cup all-purpose flour
1½ tablespoons sugar
¼ teaspoon salt
⅓ cup (5 tablespoons plus 1
    teaspoon) cold unsalted butter
1 egg yolk, lightly beaten with 2
    teaspoons brandy

Filling:

¾ cup sugar
1¼ pounds Anjou pears (about 4
    medium)—peeled, cored and cut
    into ½-inch slices
3 eggs
1 cup heavy cream
1 teaspoon grated lemon zest
2 tablespoons fresh lemon juice
3 tablespoons melted unsalted
    butter, cooled to room
    temperature
¼ cup brandy

Garnish:

2 tablespoons unsalted butter
1 medium Anjou pear—peeled,
    cored, and cut into ½-inch slices
1 teaspoon sugar
2 tablespoons brandy

1. Prepare the pastry: In a medium bowl, combine the flour, sugar and salt. Cut in the cold butter until the mixture resembles coarse meal. Gradually add the egg-yolk mixture to the flour mixture, stirring with a fork, until the dough begins to mass together. If necessary, add a few drops of cold water. Gently pat into a ball and flatten into a disk about 6 inches in diameter. Wrap in waxed paper and chill for at least 1 hour.

2. Make the filling: In a medium skillet, dissolve the sugar in ¼ cup of water over low heat. Add the pear slices and bring to a boil. Reduce the heat, cover and simmer the pears until they are soft, about 35 minutes; drain. Transfer the pears to a medium bowl. Using a wooden spoon, mash them into a puree.

3. Preheat the oven to 400°. Oil or butter a 9½-inch tart pan with a removable bottom. Roll out the pastry between two sheets of generously floured waxed paper to an 11-inch round, about ⅛ inch thick. Carefully peel off the top sheet of waxed paper. Invert the pastry into the tart pan and without stretching, gently ease the pastry into the pan, fitting it against the sides of the pan. Peel off the waxed paper and remove the excess pastry by pressing the rolling pin over the rim of the pan. With a fork, lightly prick the dough all over. Refrigerate for 15 minutes.

4. Line the pastry shell with aluminum foil and fill with dried beans or pie weights. Bake for 12 minutes; remove the liner and weights. Reduce the oven temperature to 350° and continue to bake the shell another 2 minutes, or until the bottom of the pastry is dry. Let the shell cool in its pan on a rack while you finish the filling.

5. In a large bowl, beat the eggs until frothy. Stir in the cream, lemon zest, lemon juice, melted butter, brandy and pear puree. Set the tart pan on a baking sheet; pour the pear custard into the tart pan and bake for 30 minutes or until the custard is set. Let cool for 2 hours at room temperature.

6. Prepare the garnish: In a small skillet, melt the butter. Add the pear slices, sprinkle with the sugar and sauté until lightly browned and tender. Pour in the brandy and ignite, shaking the pan until the flames subside. With a slotted spoon, transfer the pears to a shallow dish and let cool to room temperature.

7. Before serving, remove the sides of the tart pan. Arrange a circle of pear slices on top of the tart, about 2 inches in from the edge. Serve at room temperature, or chilled if desired.

Strawberry Tart

MAKES ONE 9-INCH TART

**Vanilla Pastry Cream (recipe
    follows)**
Prebaked Tart Shell (p. 202)
1 pint strawberries
⅓ cup red currant jelly

1. About 2 hours before serving, spread the pastry cream into the cooled tart shell.

2. Reserving one attractive berry for the center, cut the strawberries lengthwise into ⅛-inch slices, placing the solid-colored end pieces in a separate pile. Arrange the center-cut berries in two overlapping circles around the outer edge of the crust. Arrange the solid-colored end sections in two inner circles and place the whole berry in the center.

3. In a small heavy saucepan, melt the jelly over low heat. Brush the berries very lightly with the warmed jelly. Refrigerate for 30 minutes or up to 2 hours before serving.

Vanilla Pastry Cream

MAKES ABOUT 1¼ CUPS

1 cup milk
½ vanilla bean, split
3 egg yolks, at room temperature
⅓ cup sugar
2 tablespoons all-purpose flour
1 tablespoon stiffly whipped cream
    (optional)

1. In a small saucepan, scald the milk with the vanilla bean over moderately low heat. Remove from the heat and set aside.

2. In a medium bowl, whisk together the egg yolks and sugar until pale and thickened, about 3 minutes. Whisk in the flour, 1 tablespoon at a time.

3. Strain the hot milk and then whisk it into the egg mixture.

4. Pour the mixture into a clean, small, heavy saucepan and cook over moderately low heat, whisking constantly, until it boils. Reduce the heat to low and cook, stirring constantly, until the pastry cream loses its raw flour taste, about 2 minutes.

5. Scrape the pastry cream into a small bowl and lay a piece of buttered waxed paper over the surface to prevent a skin from forming. Let cool to room temperature; this can be accomplished quickly by stirring the cream over a bowl of ice and water. Fold in the whipped cream, if desired, for a lighter pastry cream.

Golden Delicious Apple Tart

MAKES ONE 9½-INCH TART

Pastry:

1 cup all-purpose flour
1 tablespoon sugar
Pinch of salt
½ cup (1 stick) unsalted butter, chilled and cut into small bits
About 3 tablespoons ice water

Filling and Glaze:

4 Golden Delicious apples, as small as possible
¼ cup sugar
4 tablespoons unsalted butter, thinly sliced
¼ cup apricot preserves
1 tablespoon rum

1. Make the pastry: Mix the flour, sugar and salt in a bowl. Cut in the butter until the mixture resembles flakes of oatmeal. Dribble in the ice water while tossing the flour mixture with a fork, adding just enough water to form the dough into a rough ball. On a lightly floured surface, press away a few tablespoons of the dough at a time with the heel of your hand, pushing quickly to form a smear about 5 inches long. Scrape together into a ball.

2. Continuing on a lightly floured surface, shape the dough into a rough rectangle about 4 inches wide and 6 inches long. Fold up the bottom third, then fold the top third over that. Rotate the dough a quarter-turn counterclockwise, so that it looks like a book you are about to open. Roll out to form an even rectangle about ¼ inch thick. Fold into thirds again, wrap in plastic and refrigerate for about 1 hour.

3. Bang the chilled dough with a rolling pin to flatten slightly and let soften briefly so that it can be rolled. On a lightly floured surface, roll out to form a circle 12 to 13 inches in diameter. Fit the pastry loosely into a 9½-inch tart pan with a removable bottom. Roll the pin across the top to cut off excess pastry. Press the pastry firmly into the pan. Prick the bottom at 1-inch intervals with a fork. Chill for about 1 hour.

4. Preheat the oven to 450°. Using a corer, neatly cut the cores from the apples. Peel, then halve each apple. Place one apple half, flat-side down, on your work surface and cut crosswise into very thin slices, retaining the shape of the apple by keeping the slices together. (Do *not* slice lengthwise, from stem to blossom.) Repeat with the remaining apple halves. Set one half in the pastry with the wider, stem end against the edge. Fan the slices very slightly apart, tipping toward the center of the pie. Do the same with five more halves, leaving the center of the pastry uncovered. Arrange the remaining 2 apple halves in a rough flower shape in the center, fanning out the overlapping slices. Sprinkle with the sugar and evenly distribute the butter over the top.

5. Set the tart on the lowest rack of the oven and bake until the apples are lightly browned and somewhat caramelized and the crust is a rich brown, about 40 minutes.

6. Remove the sides of the tart pan and, using the largest spatula available, gently slide the tart from the base onto a rack.

7. In a small pan, heat the preserves and rum, stirring until smooth. If the mixture is too thick to pour, add 1 tablespoon of water. Strain into a cup. Brush the warm glaze evenly over the warm tart. Serve immediately or within a few hours. Re-warm the tart if it has become completely cool.

Apricot Almond Crêpes

Make the filling a day ahead of time. The crêpes and sauce may be prepared early on the day you plan to entertain and reheated just prior to serving. When frying the crêpes, don't be dismayed if the first couple are not perfect. The pan often takes several minutes to adjust to the proper heat. This recipe makes enough for seconds or dessert the next day.

4 SERVINGS

Almond Filling:

4 ounces cream cheese, at room temperature
¼ cup confectioners' sugar
¾ cup heavy cream
1 teaspoon almond extract
1 tablespoon amaretto liqueur
1 tablespoon ground almonds

Apricot Crêpes:

½ cup all-purpose flour
1 egg, lightly beaten
¾ cup milk
1 tablespoon unsalted butter, melted
3 tablespoons apricot brandy

Apricot Sauce:

1 cup apricot nectar
½ cup apricot brandy
½ cup apricot preserves
2 tablespoons fresh lemon juice

Vegetable oil, for crêpe pan

1. Make the almond filling: Beat the cream cheese with an electric mixer or in a food processor until smooth and fluffy. Gradually blend in the sugar, scraping down the sides of the bowl as necessary.

2. In a chilled bowl with chilled beaters, whip the heavy cream until stiff. Fold half of the whipped cream into the cream cheese; gently fold in the almond extract, amaretto and almonds. Fold in the remaining whipped cream.

3. Line four ½-cup *coeur à la crème* molds (or a 2-cup woven basket) with a double layer of moistened cheesecloth. Mound the cream-cheese mixture into the molds; tap on a surface to settle the contents and fold the cheesecloth over the top. Place the molds in a shallow dish (the basket on a rack in a shallow pan) to catch any moisture, and refrigerate overnight.

4. Prepare the crêpe batter: Place the flour in a medium bowl and make a well in the center. Add the egg and mix with the flour until partially incorporated. Slowly whisk in the milk. Add the butter and brandy and whisk until smooth. Refrigerate, covered, for at least 2 hours.

5. Meanwhile, make the apricot sauce: Combine the apricot nectar, brandy and preserves in a small saucepan. Cook over moderate heat until reduced by half, about 20 minutes. Strain through a fine sieve and stir in the lemon juice.

6. Cook the crêpes: Lightly oil a 6½- to 7½-inch crêpe pan or a small nonstick skillet and set it over moderate heat. When the pan just begins to smoke, remove it from the heat and pour 2 tablespoons of the batter into the center of the pan. Immediately tilt the pan in all directions so the batter spreads uniformly into a thin film. Return the pan to the heat and cook until the edges begin to turn a golden brown, 10 to 20 seconds. Flip the crêpes by holding one edge with the fingers and turning it over. Cook for another 5 to 7 seconds to brown the bottom slightly, and slide the crêpe onto a plate. Lightly wipe the inside of the pan

with a paper towel moistened with oil. Continue making crêpes and seasoning the pan until all the batter is used; only about 8 of the crêpes will be pretty enough to use. Stack the cooked crêpes one on top of the other; cover with a sheet of waxed paper and set aside.

7. To serve: Preheat the oven to 300°. Place the crêpes on a heatproof plate and warm them in the oven for 10 minutes. Place the sauce over moderately low heat and warm gently; transfer it to a serving bowl or pitcher. Unmold the cream-cheese hearts onto a serving platter and gently remove the cheesecloth. At table, wrap 2 tablespoonfuls of the cream-cheese filling in each crêpe and pass the warmed sauce separately. Store any leftover filling in the refrigerator, lightly wrapped with plastic. Wrap leftover crêpes in waxed paper and reheat as above.

Brioche Bread Pudding

6 SERVINGS

¼ **cup currants**
¼ **cup orange liqueur, such as Grand Marnier**
8 ounces leftover brioche (see Note), cut into ¼-inch slices
3 tablespoons unsalted butter, softened
2½ cups milk
1 vanilla bean
2 whole eggs
3 egg yolks
1 cup sugar
Heavy cream (optional)

1. In a small bowl, combine the currants and orange liqueur. Set aside for 30 minutes.

2. Preheat the oven to 350°. Lightly butter both sides of each slice of brioche. Place in the preheated oven and bake, turning once, until lightly toasted, about 5 minutes; set aside. Leave the oven on.

3. Butter a shallow, 8-inch square baking dish. Overlap the slices of brioche in the dish. Drain the currants, reserving the orange liqueur, and sprinkle them over the brioche.

4. In a medium saucepan, bring the milk with the vanilla bean to a simmer over moderate heat. Remove from heat and add the reserved orange liqueur.

5. In a large bowl, beat the whole eggs and egg yolks with the sugar until thickened and light colored.

6. Remove the vanilla bean and gradually pour the milk into the egg-sugar mixture, stirring constantly. Pour over the brioche.

7. Place the baking dish in a larger dish or roasting pan on the middle rack of the oven. Add enough warm water to reach halfway up the dish's sides. Bake for 30 to 35 minutes, or until the custard is set. Remove from the oven and let cool to room temperature before serving. (The pudding can be covered and refrigerated overnight; the flavors will improve. Let return to room temperature before serving.) Serve with a pitcher of heavy cream, if desired.

NOTE: Any shape stale brioche is ideal for this recipe, though fresh can be used.

Baked Marmalade Pancake

This is a lovely idea for a Sunday brunch or a last-minute dessert.

4 SERVINGS

2 eggs
½ cup all-purpose flour
½ cup milk
¼ teaspoon almond or vanilla extract
½ cup (1 stick) unsalted butter
6 tablespoons orange marmalade or any other citrus marmalade
2 tablespoons confectioners' sugar

1. Preheat the oven to 400°. In a medium bowl, whisk the eggs, flour, milk and almond extract until blended.

2. In a large ovenproof skillet, melt the butter over moderate heat. Remove the skillet from the heat and pour in the batter, tilting to cover the bottom of the pan evenly. Immediately place in the oven and bake for 15 minutes, or until puffed and golden brown.

3. Transfer to a serving plate, spread with the marmalade and dust with the sugar; serve immediately.

Top, Creamy Four-Fruit Sherbet (p. 190); bottom, Glazed Apple Cake (p. 178).

Strawberry Soufflé (p. 187) and individual Orange Truffle Soufflés (p. 188).

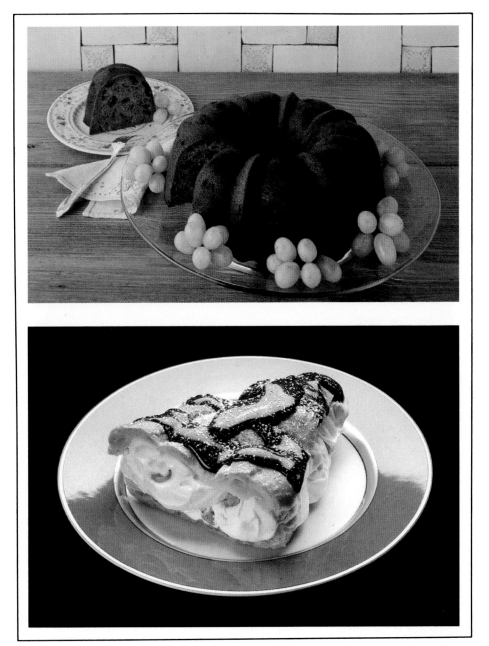

Top, Hunt Fruitcake (p. 183). Bottom, Chocolate-Orange Cream Puff Strip (p. 179).

171

*Above, Pear Brandy Tart (p. 166). Opposite page, top,
Moravian Sugar Bread (p. 201); bottom, Chocolate Soufflé
with Chocolate Sauce (p. 181).*

Stuffed Pain Perdu (p. 194).

Top, English Muffins (p. 195); bottom, Potato Scones (p. 194).

Peach Parfait Cake

24 TO 30 SERVINGS

Cake:

6 eggs
⅔ cup sugar
1 teaspoon vanilla extract
1⅓ cups sifted flour
3 tablespoons unsalted butter,
  melted and cooled slightly

Filling and Decoration:

10 medium peaches, preferably
  freestone (about 3½ pounds)
¼ cup lemon juice
4 or 5 cups heavy cream
1½ teaspoons almond extract
1 cup sifted confectioners' sugar

Glaze:

1 jar (12 ounces) peach preserves
3 tablespoons brandy

1. Preheat the oven to 350°. Lightly butter a 4-quart stainless-steel bowl and dust it with a little flour, shaking out the excess; set aside. Chill a bowl and beaters for whipping the cream later.

2. Prepare the cake: In a mixing bowl set over simmering water, beat the eggs with a whisk until frothy, about 1 minute. Whisk in the sugar, beating until it has dissolved and the eggs are just warm to the touch. Remove from the heat and beat until it has tripled in volume, 3 to 5 minutes. The mixture should be cool, light in color and run off in a ribbon when the whisk is lifted. Beat in the vanilla.

3. Sift the flour over the egg mixture a third at a time, quickly folding it in with a rubber spatula. Fold in the melted butter and pour the batter into the prepared bowl. Bake the cake in the center of the oven for 45 to 50 minutes, or until the center springs back when lightly touched. Cool for about 5 minutes. Then place a rack over the bowl and invert both, unmolding the cake onto the rack; cool completely.

4. Prepare the filling: Peel the peaches, halve them lengthwise, pit and cut them into slices about ½ inch thick. Place them in a bowl and toss with the lemon juice.

Sprouted Wheat Berry Bread (p. 197).

5. If you are going to pipe designs on the cake, you will need to whip 5 cups of the cream; otherwise 4 cups will be enough. Using the chilled bowl and beaters and working in two batches, whip the cream until soft peaks form. Add the almond extract and confectioners' sugar and beat until the cream is very stiff. Cover and refrigerate.

6. Prepare the glaze: Place the preserves in a small saucepan and bring to a boil over moderate heat. Using a wooden spoon, force the preserves through a strainer into a bowl. Stir in the brandy.

7. Assemble the cake: Using a long, serrated knife, split the cake horizontally into four equal layers, using toothpicks to mark out the layers before cutting if necessary. Place the bottom layer on a cake plate and brush the top of it with one-third of the glaze. Spread ¼ inch of the whipped cream over the glaze and arrange 1½ cups of the peach slices over the cream. Top the peaches with another ¼ inch of the whipped cream and add the next layer of cake. Brush the second layer with half the remaining glaze and top it with ¼ inch of whipped cream, 1 cup of peach slices and another ¼ inch of whipped cream. Add the third layer of cake, brush with the remaining glaze, spread with ¼ inch of whipped cream, add 1 cup of the peach slices and ¼ inch more of the whipped cream. Top with the remaining cake layer.

8. Decorate the cake: Reserving about 2 cups of the whipped cream if you wish to pipe designs on the cake, frost the cake evenly with whipped cream, using a spatula. To decorate, fit a pastry bag with a ¼-inch star tip and fill it with the reserved whipped cream. Arrange 8 of the remaining peach slices on the top of the cake in a spoke design; evenly space 10 or 11 peach slices around the base. Decoratively pipe whipped cream on the tops and sides of the cake. Chill the cake, uncovered, until serving time or up to 12 hours. Serve cold.

Lemon-Lime Meringue Pie

MAKES ONE 9-INCH PIE

1 Sweet Pastry Crust (p. 202),
  prebaked

Filling:

1 cup sugar
6 tablespoons cornstarch
¼ teaspoon salt
5 tablespoons unsalted butter
4 egg yolks, at room temperature
¼ cup fresh lemon juice
¼ cup fresh lime juice
1 teaspoon grated lemon zest
1 teaspoon grated lime zest

Meringue:

4 egg whites, at room temperature
¼ teaspoon salt
¼ teaspoon cream of tartar
½ cup sugar

1. Prepare and bake the Sweet Pastry Crust.

2. Prepare the filling: In a medium saucepan, bring the sugar, cornstarch, salt, butter and 2 cups of water to a boil over moderate heat. Cook for 1 minute, stirring constantly with a wooden spoon, until thickened and smooth; remove from the heat.

3. In a small bowl, lightly whisk the egg yolks. Whisk in the lemon and lime juices. Gradually whisk the yolk mixture into the sugar mixture in the saucepan. Over low heat, bring the mixture to a boil, stirring constantly. Remove from the heat and stir in the lemon and lime zests. Let the mixture cool for 10 minutes covered, and then pour it into the pie shell. Lay a sheet of waxed paper on the filling and chill for at least 5 hours or overnight.

4. Prepare the meringue: Preheat the oven to 350°. In a medium bowl, beat the egg whites with the salt and cream of tartar until soft peaks form. Gradually add the sugar and continue beating until the whites stand in stiff peaks and are very glossy; do not overbeat or the meringue will be dry.

5. Assemble and bake the pie: Pile the meringue on the filling, mounding it in the center and spreading it out to the very edge of the crust all around. If desired, make small peaks all over the meringue with the back of a spoon. Bake the pie in the center of the oven for 15 minutes, or until the meringue turns golden. Chill for at least 3 hours before serving. To slice evenly, dip a knife into hot water before making each cut.

Ricotta-Orange Pie

The inside of this prebaked pie shell is coated with melted chocolate before it is filled. This prevents it from becoming soggy during baking and adds a delicious flavor to the pie.

MAKES ONE 9-INCH PIE

1 Cookie Crumb Crust (p. 202)
3 ounces semisweet chocolate
1½ cups ricotta cheese
⅔ cup sugar
½ cup sour cream
3 eggs, separated
1½ tablespoons finely minced orange zest
½ teaspoon almond extract
¼ teaspoon salt

1. Prepare and bake the Cookie Crumb Crust.

2. Heat the chocolate in the top of a double boiler set over simmering water until it is melted. Quickly spread it in an even layer over the bottom of the pie shell. Chill for 15 to 20 minutes.

3. Meanwhile, preheat the oven to 350°. In a large bowl, blend the ricotta with ½ cup of the sugar, the sour cream, egg yolks, orange zest, almond extract and salt. Beat until smooth and set aside.

4. In another large bowl, beat or whisk the egg whites until soft peaks form. Gradually beat in the remaining sugar and continue beating until stiff peaks form. Do not overbeat. Gently but thoroughly fold the egg whites into the ricotta mixture. Pour the mixture into the pie shell and bake in the center of the oven for 30 minutes, or until the filling is puffy and golden. Cool to room temperature (the pie will settle during cooling) and then chill thoroughly before serving.

Cherry-Apricot Upside-Down Cake

8 SERVINGS

6 tablespoons unsalted butter
½ cup plus 2 tablespoons packed dark brown sugar
About 12 large Bing cherries, halved and pitted
⅓ cup coarsely chopped walnuts
2 large fresh apricots, pitted and cut lengthwise into ⅜-inch slices
3 eggs, separated
½ cup granulated sugar
⅓ cup milk
½ teaspoon vanilla extract
1 cup all-purpose flour
1 teaspoon baking powder

1. Preheat the oven to 325°. Melt the butter in a 9-inch round cake pan over low heat. Add the brown sugar and cook, stirring frequently, until the mixture caramelizes and foams and bubbles; immediately remove from the heat.

2. Arrange a ring of cherry halves, cut-side up, in the caramel around the outer edge of the cake pan. Make a ring of the chopped nuts inside the cherries. Overlap the apricot slices in a ring inside the nuts. Fill the center with any remaining cherries.

3. Beat the egg whites until stiff; set aside. In a mixer bowl, beat the egg yolks with the granulated sugar until light and lemon colored. Add the milk and vanilla and beat well. Stir in the flour and baking powder, then beat to form a smooth batter. Gently fold in the reserved beaten egg whites. Pour the batter evenly over the fruit in the cake pan.

4. Bake for 45 to 55 minutes, or until a toothpick inserted in the center comes out clean.

5. Remove the cake from the oven. Run a knife around the edge of the pan and invert the cake onto a platter while still hot. Let cool slightly before serving.

Glazed Apple Cake

The lightness of this cake comes from beating the whole eggs over warm water, then off the heat until cooled and tripled in volume and then from carefully folding in the flour and melted butter, as in a génoise. For this recipe, you will need a total of two 6-ounce cans of frozen apple juice concentrate.

F&W Beverage Suggestion:
Joseph Phelps Johannisberg Riesling, Late Harvest

8 SERVINGS

Cake:

3 eggs, at room temperature
Pinch of salt
½ cup thawed, unsweetened frozen apple juice concentrate, at room temperature
1 teaspoon vanilla extract
⅔ cup sifted all-purpose flour
1 teaspoon ground cardamom
2 teaspoons unsalted butter, melted and cooled to room temperature

Apple Topping:

3 tablespoons unsalted butter
2 tart green cooking apples (1 pound)—peeled, cored and cut into ½-inch slices
1 cup thawed, unsweetened frozen apple juice concentrate

Whipped Cream (optional):

½ cup heavy cream, chilled
1 tablespoon apple juice glaze (reserved from above)
¼ teaspoon vanilla extract

1. **Prepare the cake:** Preheat the oven to 350°. Butter a 9-inch round cake pan; line the bottom with waxed paper and butter the paper. Dust the pan with flour; tap out the excess.

2. In a medium, stainless-steel bowl, beat the eggs and salt with an electric hand-mixer until frothy, about 30 seconds. Place the bowl over a pan filled with 1 inch of simmering water; be sure the bowl does not touch the water. Over low heat, gradually beat in the apple juice concentrate in a slow, steady stream. Beat at high speed until the mixture is warm to the touch, 3 to 4 minutes. Remove the bowl from the heat and con-

tinue to beat at high speed until the batter has tripled its original volume and cooled to room temperature, about 2 minutes.

3. Stir in the vanilla. Sift one-third of the flour and cardamom over the batter and fold in quickly and thoroughly with a rubber spatula; repeat with another third of the flour and cardamom. Sift the remaining flour and cardamom over the batter, drizzle on the melted butter and fold quickly just until blended. Pour mixture into the pan and tap gently but firmly to settle the batter.

4. Place immediately in the oven and bake for 22 to 25 minutes, until the edges of the cake begin to pull away from the pan and the top springs back when touched gently in the center. The cake will be about 1 inch high. Cool in the pan for 5 minutes; then turn out onto a rack, peel off the waxed paper and let cool completely.

5. Prepare the topping: In a large heavy skillet, melt the butter over moderately high heat. Add the apples in a single layer and sauté for about 3 minutes on each side, or until lightly browned. Add the apple juice concentrate, bring to a boil, reduce the heat and simmer for 2 minutes, turning the apples once. Remove from the heat.

6. Using a slotted spoon, remove the apple slices and arrange them decoratively on top of the cake. Remove 1 tablespoon of the apple juice glaze from the skillet and reserve. Boil the remaining glaze, if necessary, until reduced to about 3 tablespoons. Drizzle the glaze over the cake and apples.

7. Prepare the cream: Beat the cream until stiff. Blend in the reserved 1 tablespoon apple juice glaze and the vanilla. Serve with the cake.

Chocolate-Orange Cream Puff Strip

This dessert is best assembled shortly before serving, to prevent the cream puff pastry from becoming soggy. The pastry itself can be baked ahead and then crisped in a 325° oven for about 3 minutes. The cream filling can be refrigerated, covered, for up to 2 hours.

6 SERVINGS

Cream Puff Strip:
4 tablespoons unsalted butter
½ teaspoon sugar
⅛ teaspoon salt
½ cup sifted all-purpose flour
2 eggs

Cream Filling:
¼ cup golden raisins
¼ cup Cointreau or other orange liqueur
1 cup heavy cream, chilled
2 tablespoons sugar
¾ teaspoon vanilla extract
2 tablespoons grated orange zest

Assembly:
2 ounces semisweet chocolate, melted
2 tablespoons confectioners' sugar

1. Make the cream puff strip: Preheat the oven to 400°. Butter a 15-by-11-inch jelly roll pan. In a medium saucepan, combine the butter, sugar and salt with ½ cup of water. Bring to a boil over moderately high heat.

2. Add the flour all at once and beat with a wooden spoon over low heat until the mixture masses and pulls away from the sides of the pan, about 1 minute.

3. Remove from the heat and continue beating for 2 minutes longer to cool the mixture slightly. Add the eggs, beating them in 1 at a time, until the mixture is smooth and has a satinlike sheen.

4. Spoon onto the prepared jelly roll pan in an even strip about 2 inches wide and 15 inches long.

5. Bake in the preheated oven until puffed and golden brown, about 35 minutes. Remove from the oven and let cool on a wire rack.

6. Meanwhile, make the filling: In a small saucepan, combine the raisins and

Cointreau. Cook over low heat until warmed through. Remove from the heat and let stand for 1 hour to plump the raisins. Drain the raisins, reserving the liqueur.

7. Beat the cream until soft peaks form. Add the sugar, vanilla and the reserved liqueur and beat until stiff peaks form. Fold in the orange zest and raisins.

8. To assemble: With a serrated knife, split the pastry strip horizontally in half. Spread the cream filling over the bottom. Cover with the top half of the pastry. Spread or drizzle the melted chocolate over the top. Sift the confectioners' sugar over the chocolate.

Narsai's Original Chocolate Decadence

Chocolate lovers turn rapturous just thinking about this dense, dark, fudgy cake with its whipped cream icing and raspberry sauce. The last is a touch of genius; the tart raspberries seem to cut through the unctuousness of the devastatingly rich cake.

12 SERVINGS

1 pound dark sweet chocolate
10 tablespoons unsalted butter
4 whole eggs
1 tablespoon sugar
1 tablespoon all-purpose flour
1 cup heavy cream, whipped
Shaved bittersweet chocolate
1 package (10 to 12 ounces) frozen raspberries

1. Flour and butter an 8-inch round cake pan. Cut waxed paper to fit the bottom, butter it and lay it on the bottom of the pan. Preheat the oven to 425°.

2. In a small saucepan over very low heat (or set into a larger saucepan of hot water), melt the chocolate with the butter. Set it aside. In the deep top of a double boiler, combine the eggs with the sugar. Beat the eggs and sugar over the hot water until the sugar dissolves and the mixture is just lukewarm. Remove the top of the double boiler from the heat and beat the eggs until they quadruple in volume and become quite thick.

3. Fold the flour into the eggs. Stir one-fourth of the egg mixture into the chocolate. Then, fold the chocolate back into the rest of the egg mixture. Pour and scrape the batter into the cake pan. Bake it for 15 minutes. The cake will still be liquid in the center. Freeze the cake overnight in the pan.

4. To unmold the cake, carefully dip the bottom of the pan in hot water. Invert it onto a cake plate. Remove the pan and gently remove the waxed paper. Decorate the cake with the whipped cream and shaved chocolate. Refrigerate until serving.

5. Puree the raspberries and their juice in a blender or food processor. Strain out the seeds and serve a tablespoon of this puree as a sauce with each portion.

Viennese Chocolate Torte

8 TO 10 SERVINGS

Torte:

11 tablespoons unsalted butter, softened
6 tablespoons all-purpose flour
3 ounces semisweet chocolate
½ cup sugar
3 eggs, separated, at room temperature
6 tablespoons finely ground walnuts
1 cup canned, pitted tart red cherries, drained

Glaze:

6 ounces semisweet chocolate
¼ cup strongly brewed coffee

1. Preheat the oven to 350°. Using 1 tablespoon of the butter and 2 tablespoons of the flour, lightly grease and flour a 9-inch springform pan; tap out excess flour and set the pan aside.

2. In a double boiler, melt the chocolate over boiling water; cool to room temperature.

3. Meanwhile, in a large bowl, beat the remaining 10 tablespoons butter until creamy. Gradually beat in the sugar until the mixture is light and fluffy. Beat in the melted chocolate and then the egg yolks one at a time.

4. In a small bowl, combine the walnuts and the remaining flour. In a separate bowl, beat the egg whites until stiff but not dry. Working in three additions, gently fold the egg whites into the chocolate mixture alternately with the walnut mixture.

5. Spoon the mixture into the prepared pan and shake it until evenly distributed. Pat the cherries dry with paper towels and scatter them evenly over the top of the batter. Bake for 50 to 55 minutes, or until a cake tester inserted in the center comes out clean. Cool the torte thoroughly on a rack and then remove the springform ring.

6. Prepare the glaze: Place the chocolate and the coffee in the top portion of a double boiler set over boiling water. Stir occasionally until the chocolate is melted. Spread the glaze over the top and sides of the torte. Chill until the glaze has set. Cut into thin slices to serve.

Chocolate-Chocolate-Chocolate-Chocolate-Chocolate-Chip Fudge Cake

10 TO 12 SERVINGS

Cake Layers:

⅔ cup unsalted butter, at room temperature
2 cups granulated sugar
3 eggs
2 cups sifted all-purpose flour
¾ cup unsweetened cocoa powder, preferably Dutch processed
1¼ teaspoons baking soda
¼ teaspoon baking powder
½ teaspoon salt
1½ cups milk
1 teaspoon vanilla extract
¼ cup chocolate-mint liqueur, such as Vandermint

Chocolate Fudge Filling:

⅔ cup granulated sugar
½ cup heavy cream
2½ ounces (2½ squares) unsweetened baking chocolate
1 tablespoon light corn syrup
2 tablespoons unsalted butter

Chocolate Cream:

2½ cups heavy cream
3½ tablespoons unsweetened cocoa powder, preferably Dutch processed
7 tablespoons confectioners' sugar

Assembly and Chocolate Syrup:

3 tablespoons chocolate chips
2 tablespoons unsweetened cocoa powder, preferably Dutch processed
2 tablespoons light corn syrup
1 tablespoon granulated sugar

1. Prepare the cake layers: Preheat the oven to 350°. Line two 9-inch round cake pans with waxed paper; butter and flour the pans; tap out any excess flour.

2. In a mixer bowl, beat the butter until light and fluffy. Gradually add the sugar and continue beating until smooth. Beat in the eggs, 1 at a time, until well-blended.

3. Sift together the flour, cocoa, baking soda, baking powder and salt. Add to the egg mixture in thirds, alternating with the milk, mixing only until blended. Blend in the vanilla and liqueur.

4. Divide the batter evenly between the two prepared pans. Bake until the tops of the cakes are springy to the touch, 40 to 45 minutes. Remove from the oven and set on racks to cool for 30 minutes. Loosen the edges with a knife and unmold. Peel off the waxed paper. Set the cakes on a rack and let cool completely.

5. Prepare the filling: Combine the sugar, cream, chocolate and corn syrup in a small heavy saucepan. Bring to a simmer over moderate heat, stirring frequently. Reduce the heat to low and cook for 10 minutes, or until the mixture thickens. Remove from the heat, dot the top with the butter and let cool to room temperature, about 15 minutes. When cool, stir in the butter until the fudge filling is smooth and creamy.

6. Meanwhile, make the chocolate cream: Beat the cream and cocoa until soft peaks form. Gradually add the confectioners' sugar and continue beating until stiff.

7. Assemble the cake: Cover one cake layer with all of the fudge filling. Sprinkle evenly with the chocolate chips. Spread ½ cup of the chocolate cream on top of the chips. Cover with the second cake layer and cover the top and sides of the cake with half of the remaining chocolate cream. Use the remainder in a pastry bag to decorate the cake as desired. Refrigerate for up to 3 hours before serving time.

8. Prepare the syrup: Combine the cocoa, corn syrup, sugar and 2 tablespoons of water in a small heavy saucepan. Bring to a simmer over low heat and cook, stirring constantly, for 2 minutes. Transfer the syrup to a small bowl and let cool to room temperature, stirring once or twice, to prevent a skin from forming.

9. Just before serving, drizzle the syrup over the top of the cake in a lacy design.

Chocolate Soufflé with Chocolate Sauce

The combination of semisweet chocolate and sour cream gives this soufflé so much body that it needs no flour. Part of the soufflé base is used to make a rich chocolate sauce.

Beverage Suggestion:
Champagne or mature Muscat from Australia, such as Brown Brothers Reserve

8 SERVINGS

11 ounces semisweet chocolate, coarsely chopped
1¼ cups sour cream
10 eggs, separated
1 tablespoon confectioners' sugar
1 tablespoon orange liqueur, such as Grand Marnier
3 to 4 tablespoons milk
2 teaspoons grated orange zest
1 quart vanilla ice cream
Confectioners' sugar, for garnish
1 large navel orange—peeled, sliced and cut into small triangles, for garnish

1. Preheat the oven to 425°. Butter and flour the bottom of a large gratin dish or ovenproof skillet.

2. In a heavy medium saucepan, melt 8 ounces of the chocolate over very low heat. Whisk in 1 cup of the sour cream, then whisk in the egg yolks, 1 at a time. Cook, stirring, over low heat until the mixture thickens slightly, 4 to 5 minutes; do not allow to boil. Remove from the heat.

3. Beat the egg whites until they begin to mound. Sprinkle on the confectioners' sugar and beat until soft peaks form.

4. Gently fold three-quarters (about 2 cups) of the chocolate mixture into the beaten egg whites until incorporated; reserve the remainder for the sauce. Pour into the prepared skillet and bake for 10 to 15 minutes, until the soufflé is puffed but still slightly wobbly in the center.

5. Meanwhile, in a small heavy saucepan, melt the remaining 3 ounces of chocolate over very low heat. Whisk in the remaining ¼ cup sour cream. Scrape this chocolate-sour cream mixture into the chocolate mixture reserved from the soufflé. Stir in the liqueur and 3 tablespoons of the milk. The sauce should be thin enough to pour; if necessary, add the additional tablespoon milk to reach the desired consistency. Stir in the orange zest.

6. To serve, spoon about 3 tablespoons of the sauce onto each serving plate. Place a scoop of vanilla ice cream in the center of each plate and top with a portion of the hot soufflé. Sprinkle with confectioners' sugar and garnish with the orange triangles.

Ginger Génoise with Whipped Cream and Candied Orange Peel

This cake can be made a day ahead and stored, tightly wrapped, at room temperature. To avoid sogginess, fill it with the whipped cream and garnish as close to serving as possible.

8 SERVINGS

Ginger Génoise
⅔ cup all-purpose flour
2 teaspoons ground ginger
3 eggs
¼ cup dark molasses, heated and cooled to room temperature
2 tablespoons dark brown sugar
½ teaspoon vanilla extract
1½ tablespoons unsalted butter, melted and cooled to room temperature

Orange-Ginger Whipped Cream:
1 cup heavy cream, chilled
1 tablespoon orange liqueur, such as Grand Marnier
3 tablespoons confectioners' sugar
2 teaspoons minced orange zest
1 tablespoon minced preserved stem ginger*

Garnish:
Strips of candied orange peel, preferably homemade (see Note)
Slices of preserved stem ginger*
*Available at specialty food shops

1. Prepare the ginger génoise: Preheat the oven to 350°. Generously butter a 9-inch round cake pan. Dust the pan with flour; tap out any excess.

2. Sift together the flour and ginger.

3. Place the eggs in a metal mixing bowl and whisk until frothy, about 1 minute. Add the molasses and brown sugar and set the bowl over a saucepan of barely simmering water. With a whisk or portable electric mixer, beat until the sugar is dissolved, about 1 minute. Continue to beat until the eggs are just warm to the touch, 2 to 3 minutes.

4. Remove the bowl from the pan and beat with an electric mixer until the mixture has cooled and is almost triple in volume, 5 to 7 minutes. Add the vanilla and beat 30 seconds.

5. Sift ⅓ of the gingered flour into the batter and fold quickly but gently until incorporated. Be sure to scrape the bottom of the bowl. Repeat 2 more times with the remaining gingered flour. Just before the last addition is completed, quickly fold in the butter. Immediately pour the batter into the prepared pan. Tap gently to settle.

6. Bake for about 25 minutes in the center of the oven or until the cake has pulled away slightly from the sides of the pan and springs back when pressed in the center. Remove from the oven and cool in the pan on a rack for 3 minutes. Invert the cake onto a rack and let it cool completely.

7. Prepare the whipped cream: Using a chilled bowl and beaters, begin whipping the cream and orange liqueur on medium speed until the mixture starts to thicken, about 1 minute. Increase the speed to high and gradually add the confectioners' sugar, 1 tablespoon at a time. Continue beating until the cream is just stiff, 2 to 3 minutes (do not overbeat). Fold in the orange zest and minced stem ginger. Chill, covered, until ready to use.

8. Assemble and garnish the cake: Using a long, sharp knife, split the cake horizontally into 2 layers. Shortly before serving, spread the bottom layer with half of the whipped cream. Cover with the second layer and spread the remaining whipped cream over the top; do not frost the sides. Decorate the cake with the slivers of candied orange peel and slices of preserved ginger.

NOTE: To prepare enough candied orange peel to garnish the cake, remove the zest from 1 large navel orange in thin strips with a zester. Combine ¾ cup sugar and ¼ cup water in a small, heavy saucepan. Heat over moderate heat, stirring, until the sugar dissolves and the syrup comes to a boil, about 5 minutes. Reduce the heat to low, add the orange peel and simmer uncovered for 10 minutes. Remove from the heat and, with a fork, transfer the orange peel, 1 strip at a time, to a rack. Let dry for at least 1 hour.

Pecan-Bourbon Torte with Bourbon Buttercream Frosting

12 TO 14 SERVINGS

Torte:

4 eggs, separated
1 cup sugar
3 tablespoons bourbon
1⅔ cups (6 ounces) ground pecans

Frosting:

3 egg yolks
1 tablespoon bourbon
¼ teaspoon vanilla extract
Pinch of salt
⅓ cup sugar
6 tablespoons butter, cut into ½-inch pieces, at room temperature

Decoration:

1½ ounces bittersweet or semisweet chocolate
Candied violets (optional)

1. Make the torte: Preheat the oven to 325°. Lightly butter the bottom of a 9-inch springform pan.

2. In a large bowl, beat the egg yolks, sugar and bourbon until the mixture is light and frothy. In another bowl, beat the egg whites until stiff but not dry. Spoon the beaten whites onto the yolk mixture, sprinkle the nuts on top of the whites and fold gently just until no streaks of white remain.

3. Pour the batter into the springform pan; gently smooth the top with a rubber spatula. Bake in the middle of the oven

for about 30 minutes, or until the edges of the cake pull away from the pan and the center springs back when lightly touched. Cool the torte completely before removing it from the pan; the layer will be about 1½ inches high.

4. Prepare the frosting: In a medium bowl, beat the egg yolks, bourbon, vanilla and salt with an electric mixer on medium speed until the mixture begins to thicken, 2 to 3 minutes.

5. In a small saucepan, combine the sugar with 2 tablespoons of water. Bring to a boil over moderate heat, using a wet pastry brush to wash down any crystals of sugar that cling to the sides of the pan. Reduce the heat to low and simmer until the syrup reaches 250° on a candy thermometer, or until a drop of syrup forms a firm ball when dropped into a glass of cold water, 5 to 7 minutes.

6. Gradually beat the hot syrup into the egg yolk mixture, in a slow, steady stream; continue to beat on medium speed until cooled to room temperature, 2 to 3 minutes. Add the butter, 2 or 3 pieces at a time, and beat on low speed until the butter is thoroughly incorporated and the mixture is completely smooth, about 5 minutes. Chill until the frosting is of spreading consistency, 30 to 45 minutes.

7. Frost and decorate the torte: Spread the buttercream evenly over the sides and top of the torte. Refrigerate until the frosting has set (about 30 minutes) before decorating.

8. Melt the chocolate in the top of a double boiler over simmering water. Remove the pan from the heat. Let the chocolate cool for 5 minutes.

9. Make a paper cone: Tear off a 12-inch length of waxed paper; fold diagonally in half to make a triangle. Roll up tightly to form a cone that is almost sealed at the tip. Tape the outside so the cone doesn't unfold.

10. Fill the cone with the melted chocolate and fold down the top to seal. Trim the tip on a diagonal to create a ⅛-inch opening and pipe the chocolate onto the frosted torte in concentric circles. Decorate with candied violets, if you wish. Refrigerate if not served immediately. Then let stand at room temperature for 15 to 20 minutes before serving.

Filbert Torte

14 TO 16 SERVINGS

12 eggs, separated
2 cups sugar
¼ cup all-purpose flour
1 teaspoon grated lemon zest
2 tablespoons fresh lemon juice
1½ teaspoons vanilla extract
½ teaspoon salt
¼ teaspoon cinnamon
1 pound filberts (hazelnuts), finely
   ground
Confectioners' sugar

1. Preheat the oven to 325°. Lightly butter the sides and bottom of a 10-inch tube pan, preferably with a removable bottom. Cut a piece of waxed paper to fit the bottom; place the paper in the pan and butter the paper.

2. In a large bowl, beat the egg yolks with an electric mixer. Gradually beat in the sugar; continue beating until light and lemon-colored. Beat in the flour, lemon zest, lemon juice, vanilla, salt, cinnamon and ground nuts. The mixture will be very stiff.

3. In another large bowl, beat the egg whites until stiff but not dry. Fold about 2 cups of the beaten whites into the nut mixture to lighten the batter. Gently fold the remaining egg whites into the nut mixture until no streaks of white remain.

4. Pour the batter into the tube pan; gently smooth the top with a rubber spatula. Bake in the middle of the oven for about 1¼ hours, or until the edges of the cake pull away from the pan and the center springs back when lightly touched.

5. Cool the torte in the pan on a wire rack for 10 minutes. Run a narrow spatula or knife around the tube and outside edge of the pan to loosen the torte. Invert the torte onto a wire rack, peel off the waxed paper and let cool completely. Just before serving, dust the top of the torte with confectioners' sugar.

Pistachio Lace Cookies

MAKES ABOUT 3 DOZEN

1 cup shelled pistachios
9 tablespoons unsalted butter
⅔ cup packed brown sugar
⅓ cup light corn syrup
2 tablespoons orange liqueur
1 teaspoon grated orange or lemon
   zest
1 cup flour

1. Place the nuts in a sieve and rinse away the salt under cool running water; pat dry with paper towels and chop coarsely. In a small skillet, melt 1 tablespoon of the butter over moderate heat. Add the nuts and stir-fry until lightly browned, about 2 minutes. Drain on paper towels.

2. Preheat the oven to 375°. Lightly butter one or two baking sheets. In a medium-size saucepan, bring the remaining 8 tablespoons butter, the brown sugar, corn syrup, liqueur and zest to a boil over moderate heat, stirring constantly. Remove from the heat and gradually beat in the flour. Stir in the nuts.

3. Drop the cookie dough onto the baking sheet(s) by mounded teaspoonfuls, leaving about 3 inches between each. Bake for about 5 minutes, or until the cookies have spread to 3 or 4 inches and become bubbly and golden brown. Cool the cookies on the sheet for 3 to 5 minutes and then transfer them to a cooling rack with a spatula. Cool the baking sheet(s) and repeat the procedure with the remaining cookie dough.

Hunt Fruitcake

18 SERVINGS

¾ pound (3 sticks) unsalted butter,
   cut into ¼-inch slices
4 cups all-purpose flour
1¾ cups packed light brown sugar
2 teaspoons grated lemon zest
1 cup (4 ounces) dark raisins
1 cup (4 ounces) golden raisins
1 cup (4 ounces) chopped walnuts
⅔ cup (4 ounces) mixed candied
   fruit
2 teaspoons allspice
1 teaspoon cinnamon
¼ teaspoon nutmeg
4 bottles (6⅓ ounces each) stout or
   dark ale
1 teaspoon baking soda
4 eggs, well beaten

1. Preheat the oven to 325°. Generously butter a 12-cup Bundt or tube pan. In a large bowl, rub the butter into the flour with your fingertips until the mixture resembles bread crumbs. Add the brown sugar and lightly toss with your hands to mix. Add the lemon zest, dark raisins, golden raisins, walnuts, candied fruit, allspice, cinnamon and nutmeg; stir until blended.

2. Empty 3 bottles of the stout into a medium saucepan and heat until lukewarm (not hot). Remove from the heat and stir in the baking soda and eggs. Gradually add the liquids to the flour mixture, stirring constantly; be sure the batter is well blended. Pour the batter into the pan.

3. Bake the cake in the middle of the oven for 1 hour. Reduce the heat to 300° and continue to bake for 1 hour longer, or until a toothpick inserted into the center of the cake comes out clean. Cool in the pan on a rack for 30 minutes. Unmold and let cool completely.

4. Wrap the cooled cake in a kitchen towel that has been soaked in the remaining bottle of stout. Store the wrapped cake in a cool, dry place overnight or in the refrigerator for up to 5 days before serving.

Golden Syrup and Ginger Pudding

This traditional English pudding is made with an imported product called Golden Syrup. You may use this or substitute our homemade facsimile.

6 SERVINGS

⅓ cup Golden Syrup (p. 217)
½ cup (1 stick) unsalted butter, at room temperature
½ cup sugar
2 eggs, lightly beaten
1 cup plus 2 tablespoons all-purpose flour
1 teaspoon baking powder
1 teaspoon powdered ginger
2 tablespoons milk
2 tablespoons diced (¼-inch) preserved stem ginger* (optional)
Custard Sauce (p. 212)
*Available at specialty food stores

1. Pour the Golden Syrup into the bottom of a buttered 4-cup pudding basin.

2. In a medium bowl, beat together the butter and sugar until they are pale and creamy. Beat in half of the eggs. Sift together the flour, baking powder and powdered ginger and stir half of these dry ingredients into the egg mixture. Stir in the remaining eggs and then the rest of the dry ingredients. Stir in the milk and the optional preserved ginger.

3. Spoon the batter into the basin. Cover the basin with a sheet of buttered waxed paper and a sheet of aluminum foil, pleated together in the center, to allow for expansion. Twist and crimp the ends tightly around the rim of the basin or tie securely with string. Lower the pudding basin onto a rack or folded towel in a steamer or large, deep pot filled with enough boiling water to reach halfway up the sides of basin.

4. Cover and steam the pudding over moderate heat for 1½ hours. Replenish with boiling water at regular intervals. To test for doneness at the end of the cooking time, remove from the heat, uncover and carefully raise an edge of the papers. Insert a skewer or sharp knife into the center; it should come out almost clean. If there is wet batter clinging to it, re-cover and steam the pudding a bit longer.

5. To serve, unmold the pudding with its syrup onto a serving platter. Cut into wedges and serve hot with Custard Sauce.

Jam Roly-Poly

6 SERVINGS

1½ cups all-purpose flour
1½ teaspoons baking powder
½ teaspoon salt
1 cup grated suet, loosely packed (2½ ounces), chilled
¾ cup plum jam, at room temperature
Custard Sauce (p. 212)

1. Sift the flour, baking powder and salt into a medium bowl. Add the suet, toss with a fork and stir in enough cold water (about ⅔ cup) to make a soft, but not sticky, dough; do not overmix.

2. Turn the dough out onto a lightly floured surface and roll out into an 8-by-10-inch rectangle. Spread the dough to within 1 inch of the edges with the jam.

3. Dampen the edges of the dough with water and roll up from one of the long sides like a jelly roll. Press along the seam and at both ends to seal in the jam. Tear off a sheet of aluminum foil 16 inches long. Lay a sheet of waxed paper the same size on top of the foil and butter the waxed paper. Place the jam roll lengthwise in the center of the paper. Fold and crimp the edges of both sheets to seal, leaving room around the roll to allow for expansion.

4. Place a rack in a large steamer or turkey roaster. Add enough boiling water to come just below the rack. Lower the jam roll onto the rack, cover and steam over moderate heat for 1½ hours longer, replenishing the water at regular intervals.

5. Remove the foil and waxed paper and place the pudding on a platter. Cut into slices and serve with Custard Sauce.

Pumpkin Cheesecake

14 TO 16 SERVINGS

2 tablespoons unsalted butter, softened
⅓ cup gingersnap crumbs
4 packages (8 ounces each) cream cheese, at room temperature
1½ cups firmly packed dark brown sugar
5 eggs
¼ cup all-purpose flour
1 teaspoon cinnamon
1 teaspoon allspice
¼ teaspoon ground ginger
¼ teaspoon salt
2 cups (one 16-ounce can) pumpkin puree
Maple syrup and walnut halves, for garnish
Unsweetened whipped cream (optional)

1. Generously butter a 9-inch springform pan with the softened butter. Sprinkle the gingersnap crumbs into the pan and shake to coat the bottom and sides evenly.

2. Preheat the oven to 325°. In a large bowl, beat the cream cheese with a wooden spoon until fluffy. Gradually beat in the brown sugar. Add the eggs, 1 at a time, mixing thoroughly after each addition. Sift in the flour, cinnamon, allspice, ginger and salt. Blend well. Beat in the pumpkin puree. Pour the batter into the prepared pan.

3. Bake in the center of the oven for 1½ to 1¾ hours, until the cake pulls away from the sides of the pan and a toothpick inserted in the center comes out clean. Remove from the oven and cool in the pan on a rack for 1 hour. Carefully remove the ring from the springform and let the cake finish cooling to room temperature. Refrigerate, covered, until chilled.

4. Brush the top of the cake with maple syrup and garnish with walnuts. Serve with whipped cream, if desired.

Double-Cream Cheesecake with Chocolate Crust

Though the directions given for the filling call for a food processor, this recipe can just as easily be prepared with a hand mixer or fork. The cake must be made a day ahead of time, so plan accordingly.

<u>10 TO 12 SERVINGS</u>

Crust:

1 box (8½ ounces) chocolate wafer cookies
¼ cup sugar
1 teaspoon cinnamon
Pinch of salt
6 tablespoons unsalted butter, melted

Filling:

3 packages (8 ounces each) cream cheese, softened
⅔ cup sugar
½ teaspoon salt
3 eggs
3 cups sour cream
1 tablespoon lemon juice
1½ tablespoons bourbon or dark rum
1 teaspoon vanilla extract
2 tablespoons unsalted butter, melted

1. Make the crust: In a food processor or blender, grind the cookies into moderately fine-textured crumbs. Add the sugar, cinnamon and salt and process briefly to blend. Transfer to a bowl, pour the butter over the crumbs and toss with a fork to moisten evenly. Gently press the crumbs evenly over the bottom and sides of a 9-inch springform pan.

2. Prepare the cheesecake filling: Preheat the oven to 350°. In a food processor, combine the cream cheese, sugar, salt and eggs; blend until smooth, scraping down the sides of the container as necessary. Add the sour cream (see Note), lemon juice, bourbon, vanilla and butter and blend.

3. Pour the filling into the cookie-crumb shell and bake in the middle of the oven for 45 minutes. Turn off the oven, prop the oven door open slightly and allow the cake to rest in the oven for another 60 minutes. Cool on a rack and refrigerate for at least 8 hours.

NOTE: If the container of the food processor is not large enough, add only 1 cup of sour cream in Step 2. Pour about half the mixture into a mixing bowl; add the remaining 2 cups of sour cream to the processor and blend. Combine both batches in the mixing bowl and stir to blend.

Blueberry Flan

<u>12 SERVINGS</u>

Pastry:

2 cups all-purpose flour
⅔ cup superfine sugar
⅛ teaspoon salt
⅔ cup unsalted butter, chilled and cut into bits
1 egg yolk
2 tablespoons ice water

Blueberry Filling:

1 pound fresh or frozen blueberries (about 4 cups)
2 tablespoons lemon juice
1 teaspoon grated lemon zest
½ cup sugar
1 tablespoon arrowroot

Chestnut Cream Filling:

1 cup canned chestnut puree
1 cup plus 2 tablespoons heavy cream
¼ cup Irish whiskey
2 tablespoons sugar

1. Prepare the pastry: In a medium bowl, combine the flour, sugar and salt. Cut in the butter until the mixture resembles coarse meal. Make a well in the center, add the egg yolk and blend with a fork. Sprinkle on the ice water and blend until the mixture begins to hold together. With floured hands, form the pastry into a flat, 5-inch circle, wrap in plastic wrap and refrigerate for at least 30 minutes.

2. Roll out the pastry between floured sheets of waxed paper into a 14-inch circle. Gently fit the pastry into an 11-inch tart pan with a removable bottom. Trim the pastry even with the top of the pan. Refrigerate for 30 minutes.

3. Preheat the oven to 350°. Bake the pastry shell for 25 minutes, until golden brown. Cool thoroughly before assembling the flan.

4. Meanwhile, prepare the blueberry filling: In a medium saucepan, combine the blueberries, lemon juice and lemon zest. If using fresh blueberries, add 2 tablespoons of water. Bring to a boil over moderate heat. Mix the sugar and arrowroot and stir into the blueberries. Cook, stirring constantly, until the mixture thickens, 2 to 3 minutes. Set aside to cool completely.

5. Prepare the chestnut cream filling: In a bowl, beat together the chestnut puree, 2 tablespoons of the cream, the whiskey and the sugar. In a chilled bowl with chilled beaters, beat the remaining 1 cup cream until stiff. Add half the whipped cream to the chestnut puree and blend thoroughly. Gently fold in the remaining whipped cream.

6. Assemble the flan: Spoon the chestnut cream into the cooled pastry shell; smooth the top. Spread the cooled blueberry filling evenly over the chestnut cream. If desired, sprinkle with confectioners' sugar and serve with crème fraîche, whipped cream or Devonshire cream.

Vanilla Cream Ring with Raspberries

This is a Scandinavian-American dessert, similar to the puddinglike creams of Sweden. The cream needs to chill and set overnight, so plan accordingly.

<u>10 SERVINGS</u>

2 cups heavy cream
¾ cup superfine sugar
1 envelope (¼ ounce) unflavored gelatin
2 cups sour cream
1 teaspoon vanilla extract

1 pint (2 cups) fresh raspberries (or substitute other fresh berries)
¼ cup orange liqueur, such as Grand Marnier

1. In a small saucepan, cook the cream over low heat until warm but not hot. Gradually add the sugar and stir until dissolved, 3 to 5 minutes; remove from the heat.

2. In another small saucepan, soften the gelatin in ½ cup of cold water. Bring to a boil, stirring to dissolve the gelatin; remove from the heat. Blend into the cream mixture.

3. Place the sour cream in a large bowl. Slowly pour in the cream-gelatin mixture, whisking until smooth. Stir in the vanilla. Pour the cream into an ungreased 4-cup ring mold. Cover and refrigerate overnight, until firm.

4. Shortly before serving, toss the berries with the liqueur and let macerate for 15 to 30 minutes.

5. Unmold the ring onto a plate. Fill the center with half of the berries; scatter the remaining berries around the outside. Serve slightly chilled.

Tea-Flavored Bavarian Cream

Tea is steeped in milk and sweetened with honey to make this deliciously different Bavarian cream. Although you can make it in any 4-cup mold, a simple one is easier to unmold than a very decorative one.

6 TO 8 SERVINGS

1½ envelopes unflavored gelatin
⅓ cup dark, heavy rum
2 cups milk
5 tea bags
5 egg yolks
½ cup honey
1 teaspoon vanilla extract
1 cup heavy cream

1. Lightly oil a 4-cup mold, turn it upside down on a layer of paper towels and let the excess oil drain out.

2. In a small mixing bowl, sprinkle the gelatin over the rum.

3. In a small saucepan, scald the milk over low heat. Remove the pan from the heat, add the tea bags and let them steep for 5 minutes. Remove the tea bags, squeezing as much liquid as possible back into the pan, and set the mixture aside.

4. In a medium mixing bowl, beat the egg yolks until lemon-colored. Slowly beat in the honey and then the hot tea-milk mixture, beating until smooth.

5. Transfer the mixture to a heavy saucepan and cook over low heat, stirring constantly, until it has a custardlike consistency, about 8 minutes. (Do not allow the mixture to come to a boil or it may curdle.) Off heat, stir in the gelatin, rum and vanilla. Pour the mixture into a shallow bowl and cover it with a piece of waxed paper. Cool to room temperature, stirring the custard occasionally as it cools (do not refrigerate).

6. In a mixing bowl, beat the cream until firm peaks form. Fold two large spoonfuls of the whipped cream, one at a time, into the custard to lighten it. Fold in the remaining whipped cream until the mixture is thoroughly blended and the color is even. Pour into the prepared mold, cover with waxed paper, and refrigerate at least 5 hours or overnight.

7. Unmold the Bavarian onto a serving platter. Refrigerate until ready to serve.

Grand Marnier Crème Caramel

8 TO 10 SERVINGS

2¼ cups granulated sugar
5 whole eggs
1 egg yolk
3¼ cups milk
¼ cup plus 2 tablespoons Grand Marnier
1 cup heavy cream
2 tablespoons confectioners' sugar

1. In a heavy medium saucepan, combine 1½ cups of the granulated sugar with ½ cup of water. Cook over moderate heat, stirring once or twice to dissolve the sugar, until the mixture turns a rich golden brown and begins to caramelize, about 12 minutes. Immediately remove from the heat and pour the caramel into a 6- to 7-cup metal ring mold. Using pot holders to protect your hands (the caramel makes the mold extremely hot), quickly swirl the caramel up and around to coat the mold.

2. Preheat the oven to 325°. In a large bowl, whisk the whole eggs and the additional egg yolk with the remaining ¾ cup granulated sugar until well blended but not frothy. Stir in the milk and ¼ cup of the Grand Marnier. Pour this mixture into the caramel-lined mold.

3. Place the mold in a roasting pan on the middle shelf of the oven and add enough simmering water to the pan to reach about halfway up the sides of the mold. Bake until a knife inserted in the middle of the custard comes out clean, about 1 hour 30 minutes.

4. Remove the mold from the roasting pan and set on a rack to cool to room temperature, about 2 hours. Cover and refrigerate for at least 2 hours, or until well chilled.

5. Run a knife around the edges of the mold to loosen the custard. Invert to unmold onto a platter; refrigerate, covered, if not serving immediately. Most of the solid caramel will remain in the mold. If you have used a lightweight aluminum mold, you can crack and release the caramel by slightly twisting the mold the way you remove ice cubes from a plastic tray. With a heavier mold, it's best to rap the mold several times sharply on a flat surface and then dig out the pieces with a heavy spoon; do not use a knife. Place the chunks of caramel in a sturdy plastic bag and crush into small bits with a rolling pin.

6. Beat the cream until soft peaks form. Add the confectioners' sugar and beat until stiff. Stir in the remaining 2 tablespoons Grand Marnier.

7. Just before serving, mound the whipped cream in the center of the custard ring and garnish the top with the bits of cracked caramel.

Fruit Loaf with Raspberry Sauce

Since this spectacular light fruit loaf must set for at least 8 hours, it is best to prepare this easy dessert a day ahead.

F&W Beverage Suggestion: Sauternes or Barsac, such as Château Rayne-Vigneau or Coutet

8 TO 10 SERVINGS

Raspberry Sauce:

1 pint fresh raspberries (see Note)
About ¼ cup sugar, or to taste, depending on the sweetness of the berries
About 1 tablespoon fresh lemon juice

Fruit Loaf:

5 teaspoons unflavored gelatin
1½ cups milk
1 large or 2 small vanilla beans, split
1 cup plus 2 tablespoons sugar
4 egg yolks
1 cup heavy cream, chilled
2 cups cubed, peeled ripe peaches
½ pint fresh raspberries
¾ cup strawberries, preferably small
¾ cup blackberries

1. Make the sauce: Sprinkle the fresh raspberries with the sugar, cover and refrigerate overnight. Puree the raspberries in a food processor or blender; strain to remove the seeds. Adjust the flavor with the lemon juice and more sugar if necessary. Cover and refrigerate until serving time.

2. Make the loaf: Line a 7-cup loaf pan (9 by 5 by 3 inches) with plastic wrap; oil the wrap lightly. Gently work out as many air bubbles as possible. Set aside.

3. In a small saucepan, sprinkle the gelatin over ½ cup of the milk and allow to soften.

4. Meanwhile, in a heavy, medium, non-corrodible saucepan, combine the remaining 1 cup milk with the vanilla bean and ⅓ cup of the sugar. Bring to a simmer over moderate heat, stirring to dissolve the sugar. Remove from the heat.

5. In a medium bowl, whisk the egg yolks and the remaining sugar until thick and lemon colored.

6. Gradually whisk ¼ cup of the hot milk into the egg yolk mixture. Slowly add the mixture to the saucepan containing the remaining milk. Cook over moderately low heat, stirring constantly with a wooden spoon, until the mixture becomes thick enough to coat the back of the spoon, 5 to 8 minutes; do not allow the mixture to boil or it will curdle. Remove from the heat and continue to stir for about 1 minute, to cool the custard slightly and help stop the cooking.

7. Place the saucepan of softened gelatin over low heat and warm gently, stirring frequently, until completely dissolved, 3 to 4 minutes. Stir the dissolved gelatin into the custard, mixing well. Strain into a stainless-steel bowl and let cool to room temperature; then cover and refrigerate, stirring every 5 or 10 minutes, until the mixture is thick enough to mound but not set.

8. Beat the cream, preferably in a chilled bowl with chilled beaters, over ice and water, until stiff and doubled in volume. (The whipped cream and custard should be at the same temperature when you combine them.) Using a large spatula, gently fold the whipped cream into the thickened custard.

9. Immediately fold in the fruits, taking care not to crush them. Spoon the mixture into the prepared loaf pan. Tap gently to settle, cover and chill for at least 8 hours or overnight, until completely set.

10. Before serving, invert the loaf onto a chilled platter and peel off the plastic wrap. Using a thin, sharp knife dipped in hot water and wiped dry, cut into even slices, about ¾ inch thick. Place on individual serving dishes. Encircle each slice with several spoonfuls of the raspberry sauce.

NOTE: For the sauce, 2 packages (10 ounces each) of frozen raspberries may be substituted for the pint of fresh berries, but the ¼ cup of sugar should be omitted. However, to create the lovely mosaic of the fruit loaf, firm fresh berries are necessary. If fresh raspberries are unavailable or prohibitively expensive, substitute more strawberries. Out of season, drained canned peaches and blackberries or fresh blueberries may be used.

Strawberry Soufflé

F&W Beverage Suggestion: Muscat Beaume de Venise

8 SERVINGS

1 quart strawberries
2 envelopes (¼ ounce each) unflavored gelatin
6 eggs, separated, at room temperature
⅔ cup superfine sugar
1 tablespoon framboise or kirsch
1 cup heavy cream, chilled
Strawberries and whipped cream, for garnish
Strawberry Sauce (recipe follows)

1. Fasten a paper collar around a 5½-cup soufflé dish.

2. Puree the strawberries in a blender or food processor. Pass through a strainer to remove the seeds. Place the puree in a small bowl, sprinkle on the gelatin and set aside until softened. Place the bowl in a pan of hot water and stir occasionally until the gelatin dissolves, about 3 minutes. Set aside in the hot water.

3. In a double boiler, beat the egg yolks and sugar over barely simmering water until the mixture is light-colored, creamy and warm to the touch, about 5 minutes. Remove from the heat and continue to beat until the mixture cools, thickens and forms a ribbon when the beater is lifted, about 3 minutes. Stir in the framboise, scrape the mixture into a large bowl and set aside.

4. Beat the cream until it is doubled in volume and forms soft peaks.

5. Beat the egg whites until they form soft peaks.

6. Stir the gelatin mixture into the beaten egg yolks. Place the bowl into a larger bowl half-filled with ice and water and stir with a rubber spatula until the mixture begins to thicken and mound, 2 to 4 minutes depending on the type of bowl used (metal chills faster than glass or ceramic).

7. Immediately remove from the ice water and fold in the whipped cream: With a broad rubber spatula, cut straight down the center to the bottom of the bowl; turn the spatula as you lift. Repeat, rotating the bowl slightly until the cream is incorporated. Fold in the egg whites, about one-third at a time, using the same technique, until no streaks of white remain; do not overmix. Turn into the prepared soufflé dish, cover loosely with waxed paper and refrigerate until thoroughly chilled, at least 4 hours.

8. Before serving, remove the paper collar. Garnish the top with strawberries and whipped cream, if desired. Serve chilled, with Strawberry Sauce.

Strawberry Sauce

MAKES ABOUT ¾ CUP

1 pint strawberries
1 tablespoon superfine sugar
1 tablespoon framboise or kirsch

Puree the strawberries in a blender or food processor. Pass through a strainer to remove the seeds. Transfer the puree to a small bowl. Stir in the sugar and framboise. Refrigerate, covered, until chilled.

Orange Truffle Soufflés

These individual orange soufflés have a surprise chocolate truffle buried in the center.

6 SERVINGS

1 envelope (¼ ounce) unflavored gelatin
½ cup fresh orange juice
5 eggs, separated, at room temperature
½ cup superfine sugar
1 teaspoon grated orange zest
3 tablespoons orange liqueur, such as Grand Marnier or Curaçao
1 cup heavy cream, chilled
6 chocolate truffles
Strips of orange zest and whipped cream, for garnish

1. Fasten paper collars around six ⅔-cup soufflé dishes.

2. In a small bowl, sprinkle the gelatin over the orange juice and set aside until softened. Place the bowl in a pan of hot water and stir occasionally until the gelatin dissolves, about 3 minutes. Set aside in the hot water.

3. In a double boiler, beat the egg yolks and sugar over barely simmering water until the mixture is light-colored, creamy and warm to the touch, about 5 minutes. Remove from the heat and continue to beat until the mixture cools, thickens and forms a ribbon when the beater is lifted, about 3 minutes. Stir in the orange zest and liqueur. Scrape into a large bowl and set aside.

4. Beat the cream until it is doubled in volume and forms soft peaks.

5. Beat the egg whites until they form soft peaks.

6. Stir the gelatin mixture into the beaten egg yolks. Place the bowl in a larger bowl half-filled with ice and water and stir with a rubber spatula until the mixture begins to thicken and mound, 2 to 4 minutes, depending on the type of bowl used (metal chills faster than glass or ceramic).

7. Immediately remove from the ice water and fold in the whipped cream: With a broad rubber spatula, cut straight down through the center to the bottom of the bowl, turn the spatula as you lift. Repeat, rotating the bowl slightly each

time, until the cream is incorporated. Fold in the egg whites about one-third at a time, using the same technique, until no streaks of white remain; do not overmix.

8. Spoon ½ cup of the mousse mixture into each soufflé dish and place a truffle in the center. Divide the remaining mousse among the dishes to bury the truffles. Smooth the tops, cover loosely with waxed paper and place on a tray in the refrigerator until set and chilled, about 2½ hours.

9. Before serving, remove the paper collars. Decorate the tops with whipped cream and strips of orange zest, if desired. Serve chilled.

Sweet Chestnut Croquettes

🍷 F&W Beverage Suggestion:
Asti Spumante, such as Bonardi

8 SERVINGS

Croquette Mixture:
1 cup milk
1 vanilla bean, split, or 1 teaspoon vanilla extract
3 egg yolks
¼ cup sugar
2½ tablespoons all-purpose flour
1 teaspoon unsalted butter, at room temperature
1 cup ground roasted chestnuts* (about 5 ounces)
½ cup coarsely chopped glazed chestnut pieces*

Coating Mixture:
1 cup all-purpose flour
2 eggs, beaten
2 cups fresh bread crumbs (made from 5 or 6 slices of firm-textured white bread, crusts removed)
1½ to 2 quarts peanut oil, for deep-frying
Confectioners' sugar, for garnish
*Available at specialty food shops

1. Prepare the croquette mixture: In a heavy medium saucepan, bring the milk with the vanilla bean to a boil over moderately high heat; immediately reduce the heat to low and simmer for 5 minutes.

2. Meanwhile, in a medium bowl, whisk the egg yolks and sugar together until thickened and lemon colored. Beat in the flour until blended.

3. Remove the vanilla bean from the milk (see Note) and, whisking constantly, gradually pour the hot milk into the egg yolk mixture. Return to the saucepan and bring to a boil over moderately high heat, stirring constantly. Cook, stirring constantly, until the pastry cream is thick and smooth and begins to pull away from the sides of the pan, about 3 minutes. Scrape into a small bowl; dot the surface with the butter to prevent a skin from forming and let cool to room temperature.

4. Fold the ground and chopped chestnuts into the pastry cream. Cover tightly and refrigerate until well chilled, about 3 hours or overnight.

5. Form and coat the croquettes: Place the flour in a shallow dish, the eggs in a second dish and the bread crumbs in a third shallow dish. To make each croquette, scoop out 1 tablespoon of the pastry cream and quickly roll it into a small ball between your palms. Roll each ball in flour to coat all over; shake lightly on your fingers to remove any excess. Dip into the beaten eggs, letting the excess drip back into the dish. Roll in the bread crumbs until completely coated. Roll lightly between your palms to remove excess crumbs.

6. Fry the croquettes: Heat 2½ inches of oil in a deep-fat fryer or deep heavy saucepan to 375°. Fry the croquettes in batches without crowding for about 3 minutes, or until golden brown. Remove and drain on paper towels. Serve hot, sprinkled with confectioners' sugar, if desired.

NOTE: The vanilla bean can be rinsed off, dried and used again.

Jigsaw Pears

6 SERVINGS

2 cups dry white wine
1 cup sugar
2 tablespoons almond extract
6 large pears
3 tablespoons finely chopped pecans
1 tablespoon finely chopped mint leaves
6 mint sprigs and 6 mint leaves, for garnish

1. In a large noncorrodible saucepan, bring the wine, sugar, almond extract and 5 cups of water to a boil. Reduce the heat to low and simmer for 10 minutes.

2. Meanwhile, peel the pears, leaving the stems intact. Place a pear upright on a work surface and insert a paring knife at an angle into its "equator"; cutting almost to the core in a zigzag fashion, work around the circumference. Repeat with the remaining pears. Secure the halves of each pear together by pushing toothpicks up through the base.

3. Using a slotted spoon, transfer the pears to the simmering liquid, cover and poach for 10 to 15 minutes, or until tender when pierced with a knife point. Transfer to a plate and set aside until cool enough to handle.

4. Meanwhile, reduce the poaching liquid over high heat for about 20 minutes, or until 1½ cups are left. Remove the pan from the heat and let cool to room temperature.

5. Remove the toothpicks and gently separate the pear halves. Scoop out the cores in each base, but do not cut through to the blossom end.

6. Toss the pecans and mint together in a small bowl. Fill each pear cavity with 2 teaspoons of the mixture and replace the pear tops. Set the pears in shallow dessert bowls and spoon about ¼ cup of the syrup around each. For garnish, place a mint leaf near each stem and float a mint sprig in each bowl.

Pickled Strawberries

6 SERVINGS

2 pints strawberries, hulled and sliced
2 tablespoons sugar
Pinch of cinnamon
2 teaspoons balsamic vinegar
1 bottle (about 3 cups) dry or semisweet sparkling white wine

1. Place the strawberries in a bowl. Sprinkle them with the sugar and cinnamon and toss gently. Let the strawberries stand at room temperature for 30 minutes, tossing 2 or 3 times.

2. Sprinkle on the vinegar, toss and refrigerate, covered, until serving time.

3. Divide the strawberries into 6 large goblets or dessert bowls. Pour about ½ cup of wine into each goblet and serve.

Pineapple Brûlé

8 SERVINGS

4 tablespoons unsalted butter
1¼ cups loosely packed dark brown sugar
½ cup dark rum
½ teaspoon lemon juice
¼ teaspoon almond extract
2 ripe pineapples, quartered lengthwise, with leafy tops attached

1. In a small saucepan, melt the butter over low heat. Add 1 cup of the brown sugar, the rum, lemon juice and almond extract. Cook, stirring frequently, for 10 minutes; set aside.

2. Using a sharp knife, cut the flesh of the pineapple away from the skin, leaving a ½-inch shell. Cut away and discard the core. Cut the pineapple into wedges about 1 inch thick. Return the wedges to the shell and push every other wedge from the center toward the opposite side of the shell to create a pattern.

3. Preheat the broiler. Wrap the leafy tops in foil to prevent them from burning. Place as many pineapple quarters as will fit in a large, shallow heatproof pan. Spoon about 2 tablespoons of the rum sauce over each quarter and sprinkle with the remaining ¼ cup brown sugar.

4. Broil 6 inches from the heat for 4 to 5 minutes, or until the sugar begins to bubble. Broil the remaining batches in the same manner. Remove the foil and serve hot.

Apricot Compote

This compote must sit for at least 12 hours before serving, so plan accordingly.

6 SERVINGS

½ **pound dried apricots**
¼ **cup sugar**
¼ **cup currants**
¼ **cup golden raisins**
2 **cups Sauternes**
3 **whole cloves**
⅓ **cup crystallized ginger, chopped**
2 **tablespoons pine nuts**

1. In a medium saucepan, combine the apricots and sugar with 2 cups of water. Cover, bring to a simmer and cook over low heat for about 30 minutes, or until the apricots are soft. Drain the cooking liquid into another saucepan and set the apricots aside. Boil the liquid over moderately low heat until it is reduced to 1 cup, about 15 minutes.

2. In a large bowl, combine the reserved apricots, the reduced syrup, the currants, raisins, Sauternes and cloves. Cover and refrigerate for 12 to 24 hours.

3. Just before serving, add the ginger and pine nuts to the compote. Serve cold.

Pears Baked with Wine

4 SERVINGS

1¼ **cups dry red or white wine**
About 2 **tablespoons brown sugar**
Zest of ¼ **lemon**
4 **whole cloves**
4 **medium pears, preferably Bosc**

1. Preheat the oven to 450°. In a small saucepan, combine the wine, 2 tablespoons brown sugar, the lemon zest and cloves and bring to a boil. Reduce the heat and simmer, covered, for 5 minutes.

2. Peel, halve and core the pears. Arrange them with cut-sides down in a baking/serving dish to fit tightly in one layer. Pour the flavored wine over the pears. Cover the dish with foil, then cut a few slits in the foil.

3. Set the dish in the oven and bake until the pears are somewhat tender, 20 to 25 minutes. Gently turn over the pears, recover with the foil and bake for about 20 minutes longer, or until the fruit is tender. Uncover, baste and bake for 10 to 15 minutes longer, until the syrup has reduced somewhat.

4. Remove from the oven and taste for sweetness, adding a bit more brown sugar if necessary. Spoon some syrup over the pears to moisten them, then set aside to cool until dessert time. Or if you are making the dish the night before, let cool, cover and refrigerate.

Creamy Four-Fruit Sherbet

This is really a cross between an ice cream and a sherbet. Usually both contain mounds of refined sugar, so weight watchers will be pleased with the delectable results of this fruit-sweetened dish.

MAKES ABOUT 5½ CUPS

2 **pints ripe strawberries**
1 **can (6 ounces) frozen unsweetened pineapple, tangerine or orange juice concentrate**
3 **ripe bananas**
½ **cup unsweetened white grape juice**
1 **cup sour cream**
2 **teaspoons vanilla extract**

Place all the ingredients in a blender or food processor and puree until smooth. Transfer to an ice cream maker and freeze according to the manufacturer's instructions. Place in the freezer for at least 2 hours and then let stand at room temperature for about 15 minutes before serving.

Pineapple-Buttermilk Sherbet

MAKES ABOUT 1½ QUARTS

1 **quart buttermilk**
1 **can (20 ounces) crushed pineapple in heavy syrup**
1 **cup sugar**

1. Combine the buttermilk, the pineapple with its syrup and the sugar in a large bowl; stir to dissolve the sugar.

2. Pour the mixture into two standard ice cube trays (without ice cube dividers), filling them to within ¼-inch of the top. Place the trays in the freezer until partially frozen, about 45 minutes, then stir to break up the ice crystals. Return the trays to the freezer, stirring every 30 minutes, until completely frozen. If you are not serving the sherbet the same day, transfer it to a freezer container with a tight-fitting lid.

Papaya Sherbet

MAKES ABOUT 1 QUART

3 **ripe papayas, about 3 pounds**
½ **cup fresh lime juice (from about 4 limes)**
1 **cup sugar**
2 **egg whites**

1. Cut the papayas in half lengthwise and remove the black seeds with a small spoon. Scoop out the flesh. Puree the papaya with the lime juice in a blender or food processor until smooth, 1 to 2 minutes.

2. In a medium noncorrodible saucepan, combine the sugar with 1 cup of water. Bring to a boil over moderate heat, stirring to dissolve the sugar. Reduce the heat and simmer for 5 minutes. Add the papaya puree, reduce the heat and simmer, stirring constantly, for 5 minutes. Remove from the heat and let cool to room temperature.

3. Pour the mixture into the chilled canister of an ice cream maker and freeze according to the manufacturer's directions, until partially frozen.

4. Beat the egg whites until stiff. Once the ice cream is partially frozen, add the beaten whites. Complete the freezing process. Place the sherbet in the freezer for 1 to 2 hours for extra firmness, if desired.

Rhubarb Sherbet

6 TO 8 SERVINGS

1 cup sugar
2 cups diced fresh rhubarb (about 3 stalks)
2 teaspoons fresh lemon juice
½ cup drained, canned crushed pineapple
1 egg white
⅛ teaspoon salt
2 tablespoons confectioners' sugar
1 cup heavy cream
1 teaspoon vanilla extract

1. In a medium saucepan, combine the sugar, rhubarb and 1 cup of water. Simmer over moderate heat until the rhubarb is tender, about 10 minutes. Transfer the mixture to a bowl and refrigerate until cold.

2. Stir the lemon juice and pineapple into the rhubarb. Pour into a 6-cup shallow baking dish or freezer trays. Freeze for 1 hour, or until firm.

3. In a medium bowl, beat the egg white with the salt until foamy. Gradually add the sugar and continue beating until the egg white is stiff but not dry.

4. In a separate bowl, beat the cream and vanilla until stiff. Transfer the rhubarb mixture to a medium bowl. Fold in the beaten egg white and then the whipped cream. Return the sherbet to the baking dish or freezer trays and freeze until firm, about 30 minutes. Stir thoroughly to break up the ice crystals and freeze for another 30 minutes before serving.

Frozen Coffee Cream

Semi-freddo al Caffè, as this smooth, rich dessert is called in Italian, is a snap to prepare, and the distinctive flavor combination of coffee and chocolate makes it especially suitable for entertaining.

8 SERVINGS

4 egg yolks
½ cup sugar
2 cups heavy cream, chilled
2 tablespoons instant espresso, such as Medaglia d'Oro
Whipped cream and grated sweet chocolate, for garnish

1. In a medium mixer bowl, beat the egg yolks on high speed until smooth. Slowly add the sugar and beat until thick and pale, 2 to 3 minutes.

2. In a large mixer bowl, beat the cream until soft peaks form.

3. Sprinkle the coffee over the cream and fold in gently just until mixed.

4. Stir one-quarter of the cream mixture into the egg mixture to lighten it. Fold in the remaining cream until incorporated. Spoon the coffee cream into individual ½-cup ramekins. Cover lightly with plastic wrap and place in the freezer until firm but not hard, 1 to 1½ hours. Serve garnished with whipped cream and grated chocolate.

Hazelnut Ice Cream

The color of this ice cream is a pretty, pale tan, and the texture is either nubbly or silken depending on whether you leave the ground hazelnuts in or strain them out of the mixture before freezing.

MAKES ABOUT 2½ CUPS

¾ cup (3 ounces) hazelnuts
2 cups half-and-half
½ cup sugar
1 teaspoon Frangelico (hazelnut liqueur)
About ¼ teaspoon fresh lemon juice

1. Preheat the oven to 350°. Spread the nuts on a jelly roll pan and toast in the middle of the oven until the nuts are pale brown beneath the skin, about 12 minutes; shake the pan midway to ensure even browning. Rub the hot nuts in a dry kitchen towel to remove as much of the brown skin as possible. (Don't worry about getting off every bit. Those bits lend a good color and flavor in the end.)

2. In a food processor, grind the nuts to a smooth, oily paste, about 60 seconds, scraping down the bowl midway.

3. Add the half-and-half and the sugar; process for 30 seconds to blend the mixture and dissolve the sugar. If you want a smooth-textured ice cream, strain through a fine sieve to remove the nuts.

4. Add the liqueur and stir to blend; then add the lemon juice, several drops at a time, stirring and tasting frequently until the flavor peaks on your tongue. Freeze in an ice cream maker according to the manufacturer's instructions.

Pomegranate Ice Cream

Here is an unusual ice cream, with a delicious twang of sourness underscoring the sweetness. The color is soft pink, and the texture is exceedingly smooth. Serve it on a ring of thin blood orange slices garnished with fresh pomegranate seeds. Unsweetened pomegranate juice can be found in health food stores. It has a rather odd smell, which happily disappears in the freezing process.

MAKES ABOUT 5 CUPS

1 cup unsweetened bottled pomegranate juice
2 cups half-and-half
½ cup plus 1 tablespoon sugar
1 tablespoon grenadine or crème de cassis
3 to 4 teaspoons fresh lemon juice

1. Blend the pomegranate juice and half-and-half in a food processor. Add the sugar and grenadine and mix for 15 seconds to dissolve the sugar.

2. Stir in 3 teaspoons of the lemon juice, taste, then add additional lemon juice ¼ teaspoon at a time, stirring and tasting, until the flavor peaks on your tongue. Freeze in an ice cream maker according to the manufacturer's instructions.

Ice-Cream Fritters with Raspberry Sauce

Don't be hesitant about the idea of frying ice cream. If you follow our procedure, the results will be extremely exciting. Each fritter has a hot, crispy nut coating within which is a frozen ice-cream center. These can be prepared ahead of time and frozen, but they must be served immediately after frying.

5 SERVINGS

Ice-Cream Balls:
1 pint high-quality vanilla ice cream
1 egg white, lightly beaten
1 cup chopped toasted almonds

Raspberry Sauce:
½ cup seedless raspberry jam
2 tablespoons framboise or raspberry liqueur

Vegetable oil, for deep-frying

1. Prepare the ice-cream balls: Using an ice-cream scoop, shape the ice cream into ten 1½-inch balls and freeze them for 1 hour.

2. Quickly roll the ice-cream balls in the beaten egg white, the almonds, again in the egg white, and again in the almonds; replace the balls in the freezer until ready to deep-fry, either immediately or for as long as a week stored in airtight containers.

3. Prepare the raspberry sauce: In a small saucepan, heat the jam over moderate heat, stirring constantly until it has melted. Stir in the framboise.

4. In a deep-fryer with a deep-frying basket inserted, heat about 3 inches of oil to 375°. Using a slotted spoon, lower up to four fritters into the basket in the oil; fry for 15 seconds. Remove with the basket and drain briefly. Immediately place two fritters each in small, stemmed serving dishes. Repeat with the remaining ice-cream balls. Spoon raspberry sauce over the fritters and serve immediately.

Frozen Ginger Soufflé

8 TO 10 SERVINGS

2 envelopes (¼ ounce each) unflavored gelatin
1 cup sake
8 eggs, separated, at room temperature
⅔ cup superfine sugar
½ teaspoon powdered mace
½ teaspoon powdered ginger
1 cup heavy cream, chilled
¼ cup finely diced crystallized ginger
Slivered almonds, crystallized ginger and whipped cream, for garnish

1. Fasten a paper collar around a 5½-cup soufflé dish.

2. In a small bowl, sprinkle the gelatin over the sake and set aside until softened. Place the bowl in a pan of hot water without allowing any water into the bowl and stir occasionally until the gelatin dissolves, about 3 minutes. Set aside in the hot water.

3. In a double boiler, beat the egg yolks, sugar, mace and powdered ginger over barely simmering water until the mixture is light-colored, creamy and warm to the touch, about 5 minutes. Remove from the heat and continue to beat until the mixture cools, thickens and forms a ribbon when the beater is lifted, about 3 minutes. Scrape into a large bowl and set aside.

4. Beat the cream until it is doubled in volume and forms soft peaks.

5. Beat the egg whites until they form soft peaks.

6. Stir the dissolved gelatin mixture and the crystallized ginger into the beaten egg yolks. Place the bowl in a larger bowl half-filled with ice and water and stir with a rubber spatula until the mixture begins to thicken and mound, 2 to 4 minutes, depending on the type of bowl used (metal chills faster than glass or ceramic).

7. Immediately remove from the ice water and fold in the whipped cream: With a broad rubber spatula cut straight down through the center to the bottom of the bowl; turn the spatula as you lift. Repeat, rotating the bowl slightly each time, until the cream is incorporated. Fold in the egg whites, about one-third at a time, using the same technique, until no streaks of white remain; do not overmix. Turn into the prepared soufflé dish, cover loosely with waxed paper and freeze until firm, at least 6 hours.

8. Before serving, remove the paper collar. Decorate the sides with slivered almonds and the top with crystallized ginger and whipped cream, if desired. Serve frozen.

Iced Lemon Soufflé

8 GENEROUS SERVINGS

6 eggs, separated
1 cup sugar
⅓ cup plus 1 tablespoon fresh lemon juice (from 2 to 3 lemons)
Pinch of salt
1½ cups heavy cream

1. Make a 2-inch foil collar and securely attach it around the top of a 6-cup soufflé dish. Lightly oil the dish and the collar.

2. Beat the egg yolks with the sugar until well blended. Beat in the lemon juice.

3. Beat the egg whites with the salt until stiff but not dry. Add the egg whites to the egg-yolk mixture and fold until blended.

4. Whip the cream just until soft peaks form. Gently fold the whipped cream into the egg mixture until blended. Turn into the soufflé dish. Freeze for at least 4 hours, or overnight.

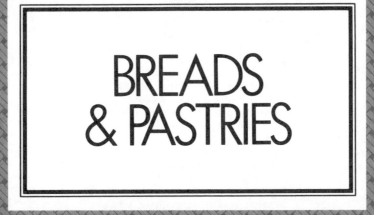

BREADS
& PASTRIES

Vanilla French Toast

4 TO 6 SERVINGS

8 eggs
½ cup heavy cream
1 teaspoon vanilla extract
1 loaf Italian bread (8 ounces,
about 16 by 4 inches)
3 to 4 cups corn oil or other
flavorless vegetable oil
2 tablespoons confectioners' sugar
Maple syrup (optional)

1. In a large bowl, whisk the eggs, cream and vanilla until well blended. Pour half of the egg mixture into another bowl.

2. Cut the bread crosswise in half. Then cut each piece lengthwise in half to give you 4 long wedges. Slice each wedge into 1½-inch pieces. There will be about 20 pieces of bread.

3. Place half of the bread pieces in one bowl of egg mixture. Let them soak, turning several times with a spoon, until they have absorbed the egg mixture, about 5 minutes.

4. Meanwhile, pour enough oil into a deep skillet or large saucepan to measure 1 inch. Heat until the oil registers 370°.

5. With a slotted spoon, place the soaked bread, 1 piece at a time, in the hot oil. Fry the bread over moderate heat, turning occasionally, until each piece is evenly browned all over, 4 to 5 minutes. While the bread is cooking, soak the remaining bread in the second bowl of egg mixture.

6. Remove the toast with a slotted spoon and drain well on crumpled paper towels. Keep warm in a very low oven while you fry the remaining bread.

7. To serve, arrange half of the French toast on a large plate and sift half of the sugar over it. Make a second layer of French toast and sift on the remaining sugar. Serve hot, with maple syrup if desired.

Stuffed Pain Perdu

One of our favorite brunch dishes, this savory French toast has a cream cheese-sausage filling sandwiched into the bread. It is dipped in a light beer batter and fried.

8 SERVINGS

1 cup all-purpose flour
1 teaspoon baking powder
1¼ teaspoons salt
2 eggs, lightly beaten
1½ cups beer
2 tablespoons unsalted butter
½ cup finely chopped onion
½ pound breakfast sausage links,
finely chopped (about 1 heaping
cup)
¼ pound bacon
4 ounces cream cheese, softened
½ teaspoon pepper
1 unsliced loaf firm-textured white
bread (about 12 ounces, 10 by
4½ by 4½ inches)
1½ cups vegetable oil
1½ tablepoons paprika

1. In a medium bowl, sift together the flour, baking powder and 1 teaspoon of the salt. Make a well in the center and add the eggs. Slowly pour in the beer while stirring with a fork; mix thoroughly. Let the batter stand, covered, at room temperature for at least 2 hours.

2. In a small skillet, melt the butter over moderate heat. Add the onion and sausage and sauté until the onion is softened, about 7 minutes; drain off and discard the fat. Meanwhile, in another skillet, cook the bacon until golden brown and crisp; drain on paper towels.

3. In a medium bowl, combine the onion and sausage, cream cheese, the remaining ¼ teaspoon salt and the pepper. Crumble in the bacon and blend well. This mixture can be set aside at room temperature or refrigerated, covered, until you are ready to fill and fry the bread.

4. Cut the loaf of bread into ½-inch slices but do not cut all the way through on the first cut and every alternating cut; leave about ½ inch attached at the bottom. There will be 8 or 9 pairs of slices attached at one end. Stuff each pair of slices with 2½ tablespoons of the sausage mixture.

5. In a large skillet, heat the oil to 370°. Two at a time, dip the stuffed bread into the batter, turning to cover all surfaces. Let any excess batter drip back into the bowl. Fry the *pain perdu*, turning once, until golden brown on both sides, about 1 to 2 minutes per side. Drain on paper towels and keep warm in a very low oven while dipping and frying the remaining bread. Sprinkle with paprika just before serving.

Potato Scones

MAKES 8 SCONES

1¼ pounds baking potatoes (about
3), peeled and quartered
2 tablespoons unsalted butter
1 medium onion, finely chopped
1 cup all-purpose flour
2 teaspoons baking powder
1 teaspoon salt
½ teaspoon pepper
¼ cup milk
Vegetable oil and butter, for
griddle

1. Cook the potatoes in a medium saucepan of boiling salted water for 20 to 25 minutes, or until tender. Drain well, mash with a fork and measure 2 cups of the mashed potato into a medium bowl. Save any leftovers for another use.

2. Meanwhile, in a small skillet, melt the butter over low heat. Add the onion and cook until softened but not brown, about 5 minutes. Preheat the griddle.

3. Scrape the onion into the potatoes and stir to mix. Sift on the flour, baking powder, salt and pepper. Stir lightly to combine; do not beat. Stir in the milk. Divide the mixture in half. Place one half on a lightly floured work surface and pat or roll into a flat disk about 6 inches in diameter and ½ inch thick. Cut into 4 equal wedges. Repeat with the other half of the dough.

4. When the griddle is very hot, brush it lightly with oil and about 1 teaspoon of butter. Using a spatula, transfer the scones to the griddle. Reduce the heat to moderately low and cook the scones for 8 minutes, checking after about 5 minutes, until the undersides are nicely browned. Turn and cook for 4 minutes, or until the second side is browned.

English Muffins

MAKES ABOUT 16 MUFFINS

1 envelope (¼ ounce) active dry
    yeast
1 teaspoon sugar
1 cup warm water (105° to 115°)
2 cups buttermilk
4 cups all-purpose flour
1 teaspoon salt
1 teaspoon baking soda
Vegetable oil, for griddle
Unsalted butter, for muffin rings

1. In a small bowl, stir the yeast and sugar into ¼ cup of the warm water. Set aside in a warm, draft-free place until frothy, about 10 minutes.

2. Place the buttermilk in a small saucepan over low heat until it is just warm to the touch. Measure the flour and salt into a large bowl. Stir in the yeast mixture and the warm buttermilk. Beat with a wooden spoon until smooth and elastic, about 3 minutes. Cover and set in a warm, draft-free place until doubled in bulk, about 1 hour.

3. Dissolve the baking soda in the remaining ¾ cup warm water and beat it vigorously into the dough for 1 minute. Cover and let rise in a warm place for 30 minutes.

4. Meanwhile, preheat the griddle. When it is hot, reduce the heat to moderately low and brush with oil. Place buttered 3-inch muffin rings (or clean tuna cans open at both ends) on the griddle and, using a buttered spoon and your finger, scoop 3 rounded teaspoons of dough into each ring. If necessary, spread the mixture evenly. Cook over moderate heat until the muffins rise about ¾ inch, are almost dry on top and golden brown underneath, 6 to 7 minutes. Remove the rings with tongs and turn the muffins over with a spatula. Cook until the second side is browned, about 2 minutes longer. Butter the rings again and repeat with the remaining dough. Cool for 15 minutes on a wire rack.

5. Split with a fork, toast and serve buttered while still hot.

Raspberry-Corn Muffins

MAKES 12 MUFFINS

2 eggs
1 cup milk
1 teaspoon vanilla extract
1½ cups all-purpose flour
¾ cup sugar
¾ cup yellow cornmeal
1 tablespoon plus 1 teaspoon
    baking powder
½ teaspoon salt
¾ cup fresh raspberries
4 tablespoons unsalted butter,
    melted

1. Preheat the oven to 400°. Lightly grease 12 muffin cups, 2½ inches in diameter.

2. In a medium bowl, beat the eggs, milk and vanilla until frothy.

3. In a large bowl, stir together the flour, sugar, cornmeal, baking powder and salt.

4. In a small bowl, gently toss the raspberries with 2 tablespoons of the flour mixture until lightly coated.

5. Pour the egg-milk mixture and the melted butter into the remaining flour mixture. Stir quickly until just blended; the batter will be slightly lumpy.

6. Spoon about 2 tablespoons of batter into each muffin cup. Working quickly, scatter 3 or 4 floured raspberries in each cup; spoon the remaining batter over the top, dividing equally among the cups.

7. Bake for about 15 minutes, or until the muffins are golden and the tops spring back when touched.

Fresh Apple Fritters

MAKES 40 TO 50 SMALL FRITTERS

1 egg, beaten
1 cup milk
4 tablespoons unsalted butter,
    melted
1 teaspoon vanilla extract
1 large navel orange
1 large tart apple, peeled and
    chopped
About 2 quarts peanut oil, for deep
    frying
3 cups sifted all-purpose flour
½ cup granulated sugar
1 tablespoon baking powder
½ teaspoon salt
Confectioners' sugar

1. In a medium bowl, whisk together the egg, milk, butter and vanilla.

2. Finely grate the zest from the orange; squeeze the juice. Add the zest and juice to the egg mixture. Stir in the apple.

3. In a deep-fryer or heavy deep saucepan, heat 1¾ inches of oil to 350°.

4. Into a large bowl, sift the flour, granulated sugar, baking powder and salt. Make a well in the center. Gradually pour the egg-apple mixture into the well while stirring in the flour from around the edge to make a thick batter.

5. Fry level tablespoons of the batter in batches without crowding until the fritters are brown and crisp, about 5 minutes. Drain on paper towels. Dust with confectioners' sugar and serve hot.

Crêpes Pernod

MAKES ABOUT 20 CRÊPES

½ cup cold club soda
½ cup cold milk
2 eggs
1 cup all-purpose flour
2 tablespoons Pernod
½ teaspoon salt
½ teaspoon white pepper
5 tablespoons unsalted butter,
    melted

1. Combine the club soda, milk, eggs, flour, Pernod, salt, pepper and 3 tablespoons of the melted butter in the jar of a blender. Mix for 30 seconds; scrape down the sides of the container and blend for 3 to 4 seconds more. Cover and refrigerate for at least 2 hours.

2. Lightly coat a 7-inch skillet (preferably nonstick) with some of the remaining melted butter. Set over moderately high heat until the pan begins to smoke slightly.

3. Ladle 1½ to 3 tablespoons of the batter into the pan. Tilt and quickly swirl the pan around to thinly coat the bottom with batter. Pour any excess batter back into the bowl.

4. Cook the crêpe until the edges are very lightly browned and the slightly bubbly surface has lost its gloss, about 30 seconds; the underside should be golden brown. Using a spatula or your fingers, flip the crêpe and cook the second side for about 30 seconds, or until it is scattered with browned spots. Transfer the crêpe to a plate, grease the pan if necessary and make crêpes with the remaining batter, stacking them as they finish cooking.

Cream Cheese Tea Biscuits

MAKES ABOUT 2 DOZEN

1 cup all-purpose flour
2 teaspoons baking powder
½ teaspoon salt
¼ pound (1 stick) unsalted butter, at room temperature
1 small package (3 ounces) cream cheese, at room temperature
About 2 tablespoons cherry preserves

1. Preheat the oven to 400°. In a small bowl, sift together the flour, baking powder and salt.

2. In a medium bowl, blend the butter and cream cheese together. Stir in the flour mixture until well blended.

3. On a heavily floured surface, roll out the dough into a circle ½ inch thick. With a floured, 1¼-inch round cutter, cut out as many biscuits as possible. The dough is very soft and will stick to the cutter. Using your finger or the handle of a table knife, push the biscuits out of the cutter onto a lightly floured baking sheet. Form a small indentation in the center of each biscuit. Spoon ¼ teaspoon of the preserves into each indentation.

4. Bake on a lightly greased baking sheet for 10 to 12 minutes in the middle of the oven, or until the biscuits are pale gold.

Tomato-Basil Biscuits

MAKES ABOUT 3 DOZEN

1½ cups all-purpose flour
4 teaspoons baking powder
½ teaspoon salt
6 tablespoons unsalted butter, cut into thin slices
1½ cups grated mozzarella cheese (6 ounces), chilled
3 tablespoons finely chopped onion
1½ teaspoons oregano
1½ teaspoons basil
3 tablespoons tomato paste dissolved in ⅓ cup milk
2 tablespoons milk
3 tablespoons freshly grated Parmesan cheese

1. Preheat the oven to 425°. Into a large mixing bowl, sift together the flour, baking powder and salt. Using a pastry blender or two knives, cut the butter into the flour until the mixture resembles coarse meal.

2. Stir in the cheese, onion, oregano and basil. Pour in the tomato paste mixture and stir lightly with a fork until the dough can be formed into a ball; do not overmix.

3. Turn the dough out onto a lightly floured work surface and quickly roll or pat it to a ½-inch thickness. Using a lightly floured 1½-inch biscuit cutter or small glass, cut out the biscuits. Gather the scraps and quickly pat them to a ½-inch thickness; cut as many additional biscuits as possible. Lightly grease a baking sheet with oil, place the biscuits on it and brush the tops with the 2 tablespoons of milk. Sprinkle each biscuit with a pinch of Parmesan cheese. Place the pan on the middle rack of the oven and bake for 10 to 12 minutes, or until the cheese is golden brown. Serve while still warm.

Lemon-Parsley Biscuits

MAKES ABOUT 3 DOZEN

1½ cups all-purpose flour
4 teaspoons baking powder
1 teaspoon salt
6 tablespoons unsalted butter, cut into thin slices
2 teaspoons grated lemon zest (from 1 lemon)
¾ cup finely chopped fresh parsley
2 tablespoons lemon juice
½ cup plain yogurt
1 egg, beaten

1. Preheat the oven to 425°. Sift the flour, baking powder and salt into a large mixing bowl. Using a pastry blender or two knives, cut in the butter until the mixture resembles coarse meal. Blend in the lemon zest.

2. Sprinkle the parsley with the lemon juice and add it to the flour mixture along with the yogurt. Using a fork, quickly mix the dough.

3. Turn the dough out onto a lightly floured work surface and quickly roll or pat it to a ½-inch thickness. Using a lightly floured 1½-inch biscuit cutter or small glass, cut out the biscuits. Gather the scraps and quickly pat them to a ½-inch thickness; cut as many additional biscuits as possible. Lightly grease a baking sheet with oil, place the biscuits on it and brush the tops with the beaten egg. Place the pan on the middle rack of the oven and bake for 10 to 12 minutes, or until the biscuits are golden. Serve while still warm.

Orange Popovers

MAKES 8 POPOVERS

1 cup sifted all-purpose flour
1 tablespoon finely grated orange
  zest
¼ teaspoon salt
1 tablespoon sugar
1 tablespoon vegetable oil
½ cup orange juice
½ cup milk
2 eggs

1. Preheat the oven to 450°. Thoroughly butter eight 2½-inch muffin cups.

2. In a large mixing bowl, combine the flour, orange zest, salt and sugar.

3. In a medium bowl, beat the oil, orange juice, milk and eggs together until well combined. Pour the mixture into the dry ingredients, beating with a wire whisk until the batter is very smooth, 2 to 3 minutes.

4. Pour the batter into the prepared cups, filling each about halfway. Bake for 30 minutes, or until the popovers are deep golden brown. Serve at once.

Virginia Spoon Bread

4 TO 6 SERVINGS

4 ears of fresh corn
2 cups milk, at room temperature
3 eggs
3 tablespoons unsalted butter,
  melted
¾ cup water-ground white
  cornmeal
2 teaspoons sugar
½ teaspoon salt
3½ teaspoons single-acting baking
  powder (see Note)

1. Preheat the oven to 375°. Husk the corn. Using a sharp knife, score each row of kernels lengthwise down the cob. Over a bowl, scrape the knife downward along the cob to remove the milky insides of the kernels.

2. In a blender, combine the scraped corn with the milk and liquefy at high speed for about 15 seconds. Add the eggs and melted butter and blend for 15 seconds. Add the cornmeal, sugar, salt and baking powder and blend for 3 seconds.

3. Pour the mixture into a buttered 1½-quart soufflé dish or deep casserole. Bake for 45 to 50 minutes, until slightly puffed and golden. Let stand for about 5 minutes before serving.

NOTE: To make single-acting baking powder, sift together 2 teaspoons cream of tartar, 1 teaspoon baking soda and 1½ teaspoons cornstarch. Store in a tightly closed jar.

Cornbread

MAKES ONE 13-BY-9-INCH SHEET

1½ cups yellow cornmeal
½ cup all-purpose flour
1 tablespoon baking powder
1 teaspoon salt
3 eggs
1¼ cups milk
1 tablespoon honey or sugar
4 tablespoons butter, melted

1. Preheat the oven to 400°. Lightly grease a 13-by-9-inch baking pan.

2. In a large bowl, sift together the cornmeal, flour, baking powder and salt. In another bowl, beat the eggs with the milk and honey. Add the egg mixture to the dry ingredients and mix thoroughly. Stir in the melted butter and pour the batter evenly into the prepared pan. Bake for 15 to 18 minutes, or until a toothpick inserted in the center comes out clean.

Sprouted Wheat Berry Bread

The wheat berries take 2 days to sprout, so plan accordingly.

MAKES 2 LOAVES

¾ cup whole wheat berries*
1 envelope (¼ ounce) active dry
  yeast
3 cups warm water (105° to 115°)
2 tablespoons honey
2 tablespoons molasses
2 cups unbleached white flour
7 to 8 cups whole wheat flour
¼ cup safflower or other vegetable
  oil
1 scant tablespoon salt
1 cup soy flour*
1 egg beaten with ¼ cup water, for
  egg wash
1 tablespoon sesame seeds
*Available at health-food stores

1. Soak the wheat berries in 4 cups of water for 10 to 12 hours. Drain and divide evenly among two or three 1-quart jars. Cover the tops with sprouting lids or cheesecloth and secure with rubber bands. Turn the jars sideways and shake them to distribute the berries up the sides (so they aren't all piled on the bottom). Place the jars on their sides in a cool, dry, dark place. Rinse and drain the berries thoroughly 2 or 3 times a day for 2 days. The sprouts are ready to be used when the shoots are as long as the grains. Rinse, drain and dry them on paper towels; coarsely chop the sprouts with a cleaver or in a food processor and refrigerate, stored in plastic bags.

2. In a large bowl, dissolve the yeast in the warm water. Add the honey and molasses, and stir to mix. Using a wooden spoon and adding the flour 1 cup at a time, stir in the white flour and 2 cups of the whole wheat flour, blending well after each addition. The mixture will be thick; stir it 100 times, until smooth. Cover the bowl with a damp cloth and set aside in a warm, draft-free place until bubbly, about 1 hour.

3. Fold in the oil and salt until the oil is incorporated. Add the chopped wheat sprouts and blend well. Fold in the soy flour. Stir in 2 cups of the remaining whole wheat flour, 1 cup at a time, blending well after each addition. The dough should begin to pull away from the sides of the bowl and will be quite sticky.

4. Mound 1 cup of whole wheat flour on a work surface and scrape the dough out of the bowl onto the flour. Add 1 cup of the remaining whole wheat flour and knead for 10 to 15 minutes, working in the flour and adding enough of the remaining flour, as necessary, until the dough is stiff and smooth.

5. Shape the dough into a ball. Oil a large bowl and place the dough in it, seam-side up. Turn the dough over, cover with a clean towel, and set aside to rise in a warm place for 1 hour.

6. Punch down the dough and allow it to rise, covered, until doubled in bulk, 45 to 50 minutes.

7. Punch down the dough a second time and turn it onto a lightly floured work surface. Knead into a ball and, using a sharp knife, halve it. Shape each half into a ball.

8. Generously oil two 9-by-5-by-3-inch bread pans. Shape each ball of dough into a loaf and place it, seam-side up, into each pan. Turn the loaves over and make 2 or 3 diagonal slashes in the top of each loaf. Cover and let rise until the dough has risen slightly over the tops of the pans, about 30 minutes. Preheat the oven to 350°.

9. Brush the dough with some of the egg wash and sprinkle 1½ teaspoons of the sesame seeds over each loaf. Brush again with the egg wash to "paste" the seeds onto the dough. Bake the loaves for 35 minutes; brush again with the egg wash and bake for 10 to 15 minutes, until the bread is golden brown and sounds hollow when tapped.

10. Turn the loaves out onto a rack and cool completely. To store, wrap each loaf in plastic wrap and seal in plastic bags or wrap in foil. This bread freezes well.

Airi's Oat Bread

<u>MAKES 2 LOAVES</u>

2 envelopes (¼ ounce each) active dry yeast
1½ cups warm water (105° to 115°)
3½ cups old-fashioned rolled oats
⅔ cup white vegetable shortening
½ cup sugar
2 tablespoons salt
2½ cups milk
7 cups sifted all-purpose flour
2 eggs, lightly beaten

1. In a small bowl, dissolve the yeast in ½ cup of the warm water. In a large bowl, combine 3 cups of the oats, the shortening, sugar and salt. Scald 2 cups of the milk and pour over the oat mixture; let stand for 5 minutes, stirring once or twice.

2. Add the remaining 1 cup warm water to the hot oat mixture and let cool to lukewarm. Beat in 1 cup of the flour, the eggs and the dissolved yeast. Gradually add enough of the remaining flour, about 1 cup at a time, to make a moderately stiff dough. Knead on a lightly floured surface until very smooth, about 10 minutes. Shape into a ball, place in a large greased bowl and turn once to grease the top. Cover and let rise in a warm, draft-free place until doubled in bulk, about 1¼ hours.

3. Punch the dough down and divide in half. Let rest, covered, for 10 minutes. Meanwhile, soak the remaining ½ cup oats in the remaining ½ cup milk until softened.

4. Grease two 9-by-5-by-3-inch metal loaf pans (see Note). Roll out each half of the dough to form a 17-by-9-inch rectangle about ½ inch thick. Starting with

one short side, roll up like a jelly roll, pinching and pressing the ends to seal. Place the loaves, seam-side down, in the pans.

5. Drain the softened oats in a sieve over a small bowl, reserving the milk. Brush the tops of the loaves with the milk and sprinkle with the oats. Loosely cover the loaves and let rise in a warm place until doubled, about 45 minutes. About 15 minutes before baking, preheat the oven to 375°.

6. Bake for 60 minutes, or until the loaves are golden brown and sound hollow when the bottoms are tapped. Remove from the pans and cool on a rack.

NOTE: If using glass pans, bake at 350°.

Finnish Cardamom Bread

<u>MAKES 5 BRAIDS</u>

Dough:
1 can (13 ounces) evaporated milk
1 cup (2 sticks) unsalted butter
2 cups plus 1 tablespoon sugar
2 envelopes (¼ ounce each) active dry yeast
12 to 13 cups all-purpose flour
3 eggs, at room temperature, lightly beaten
1 tablespoon salt
Seeds from 24 cardamom pods, ground, or 1¾ teaspoons ground cardamom

Glaze and Topping:
2 egg yolks
1 teaspoon milk
2 tablespoons sugar, preferably coarsely granulated

1. Prepare the dough: In a medium saucepan, heat the milk, butter and 2½ cups of water until the butter melts. Transfer to a large bowl and stir in 1 tablespoon of the sugar. Let cool to lukewarm (about 110°).

2. Add the yeast and stir until dissolved. Whisk in 4 cups of the flour to make a thin paste. Cover and let rest in a warm, draft-free place until spongy and doubled in bulk, about 30 minutes.

3. In another large bowl, beat together the eggs, salt, the remaining 2 cups sugar and the cardamom until the eggs are pale, 3 to 5 minutes. Stir the yeast sponge and pour it over the egg mixture; stir until blended. Add enough of the remaining flour—1 cup at a time, beating until blended between additions—to make a soft, sticky dough.

4. Turn out onto a floured surface and knead in just enough of the remaining flour to prevent sticking. Knead until smooth and elastic, about 15 minutes. Place the dough in a large lightly oiled bowl and turn once to oil the top. Cover and let rest in a warm, draft-free place until doubled in bulk, about 1½ hours.

5. Shape the braids: Generously grease 5 bread pans (8 by 4 by 2½ inches) or 2 baking sheets (12 by 17 inches). Punch down the dough and let it rest for 10 minutes. Divide the dough into 5 equal parts.

6. Working with one piece at a time, divide each piece of dough into three equal sections; roll out each section on a lightly floured surface to form a 12-inch rope. Pinch the three ropes together at one end and braid loosely; pinch the other ends to seal. Place each braid in a bread pan, tucking the pinched ends under; or arrange the braids three-across on one sheet and two on the second sheet.

7. Cover loosely and let rise in a warm, draft-free place until doubled in bulk. About 15 minutes before baking, preheat the oven to 325° and adjust the oven racks so that you can bake on two levels at one time.

8. Glaze the braids: In a small bowl, lightly beat the egg yolks and milk until blended. Brush the tops of the loaves liberally with the egg glaze, letting it run down into the crevices of the braids. Sprinkle with the sugar.

9. Bake, reversing the pans or baking sheets after 20 minutes, for about 45 minutes, until the loaves are golden brown and sound hollow when the bottoms are tapped. Let cool for 10 minutes; then remove from the pans and cool on wire racks.

Portuguese Beer Bread

This rough, moist bread owes its malty flavor to the stale beer used as the liquid ingredient, and its tweedy texture to a mixture of whole wheat and unbleached flours.

MAKES 2 (7- TO 8-INCH) ROUND LOAVES

2 envelopes (¼ ounce each) active dry yeast
2 tablespoons sugar
About 4½ cups sifted unbleached all-purpose flour
1½ cups lukewarm flat beer (105° to 115°)
1½ cups unsifted whole wheat flour
2 teaspoons salt
½ cup milk, scalded and cooled to lukewarm (105° to 115°)
¼ cup vegetable oil

1. In a large, warm bowl, combine the yeast, sugar and 1 cup of the all-purpose flour. Add ¾ cup of the beer and beat with a wooden spoon until smooth. Cover the bowl with a kitchen towel, set in a warm, draft-free place and let rise until spongy and doubled in bulk, about 20 minutes.

2. Stir the yeast mixture down. Blend in the remaining ¾ cup beer, the whole wheat flour, salt, milk and oil. Add enough of the remaining flour, 1 cup at a time, to make a stiff but workable dough (about 3½ cups). Turn the dough out onto a lightly floured work surface and knead for 5 minutes, until smooth and elastic.

3. Shape the dough into a ball and place smooth-side down in a warm, lightly greased bowl; turn the dough over to coat with oil. Cover the bowl with a towel, set in a warm, draft-free place and let rise until doubled in bulk, 1 to 1¼ hours.

4. Punch the dough down. Turn out onto a lightly floured work surface and knead vigorously for 5 minutes. Again, shape the dough into a ball and place smooth-side down in a warm, lightly greased bowl; turn the dough over. Cover the bowl with a kitchen towel, set in a warm draft-free place and let rise until doubled in bulk, about 50 minutes.

5. Punch the dough down, turn onto a lightly floured work surface. Using only enough flour to keep the dough from sticking, knead vigorously for 5 minutes. Divide the dough in half and vigorously knead each piece of dough for 3 minutes. Shape each piece into a ball and place each ball into a lightly greased 8- or 9-inch round cake pan. Lightly dust the tops of each ball with some whole wheat flour. Cover each pan with a kitchen towel, set in a warm draft-free place and let rise until doubled in bulk, about 45 minutes.

6. Meanwhile, improvise a brick-and-steam oven (which will produce the thick, brown crust and moist, chewy interiors typical of Portuguese country breads). Place 3 or 4 unglazed bricks close together in a large, shallow baking pan and set the pan on the oven floor. Place an oven rack in the exact center of the oven. Preheat the oven and pan of bricks a full 20 minutes at 500°.

7. When the breads are doubled in bulk, quickly drizzle about 1 cup of ice water over the hot bricks. Immediately place the loaves on the center rack of the oven, arranging the pans so they are not touching the oven walls or each other. Quickly shut the oven door and bake the loaves for 15 minutes, quickly drizzling the bricks with ice water every 5 minutes.

8. Lower the temperature to 400° and bake for 15 minutes longer, drizzling the bricks with ice water every 5 minutes.

9. Remove the breads and test for doneness. They should be a deep brown and sound hollow when thumped on the bottom. Transfer to wire racks to cool.

Smoked Pork Bread

MAKES 2 LOAVES

¾ cup milk
1½ tablespoons unsalted butter
2 teaspoons salt
1 teaspoon sugar
2 envelopes (¼ ounce each) active dry yeast
1¾ cups warm water (105° to 115°)
1¼ teaspoons pepper
6 to 7 cups unbleached all-purpose flour
½ cup grated Parmesan cheese
1½ cups diced (⅜-inch) smoked pork (about ¾ pound)
1 cup diced (⅜-inch) provolone cheese
1 egg yolk
½ teaspoon paprika

1. In a small saucepan, heat the milk, butter, salt and sugar over moderate heat until the butter melts. Set aside and let cool to room temperature

2. In a small bowl, dissolve the yeast in the warm water and let it stand for 10 minutes.

3. Combine the cooled milk mixture and the yeast in a large bowl. Add the pepper and stir in 3 cups of the flour, one cup at a time, until the batter is thick and smooth. Stir in the Parmesan. Gradually add 2 more cups of the flour, stirring until the dough pulls away from the sides of the bowl. Turn the dough out onto a floured surface and knead, adding more flour as needed, until the dough is smooth, satiny and elastic, 8 to 10 minutes. Form the dough into a ball.

4. Place the dough smooth-side down in an oiled bowl and turn to coat it well. Cover with a kitchen towel and let rise in a warm, draft-free place until doubled in bulk, about 1 hour.

5. Punch down the dough and flatten it out to a 14-inch round on a floured surface. Spread the pork and diced cheese over the dough. Knead the dough, folding and rotating it in quarter turns, until the pork and cheese are evenly incorporated.

6. Divide the dough in half. Divide each half into thirds and let rest for 10 minutes. With your hands, roll each piece of dough into a rope about 20 inches long. Braid three of the ropes together; form

the braid into a ring and pinch all the loose ends together to seal. Transfer the ring to a greased cookie sheet. Repeat with the remaining three ropes, placing the ring on another cookie sheet. Cover and let rise in a warm place until nearly doubled in bulk, about 45 minutes.

7. Preheat the oven to 350°. Beat the egg yolk with 1 teaspoon of water and the paprika to make a glaze. Brush the loaves all over with the glaze. Adjust two racks in the oven, one in the top third and the other in the bottom third.

8. Bake the loaves 12 minutes, then exchange shelves and bake for 20 minutes more. The bread is done if it sounds hollow when tapped and the crust is golden brown and shiny. Cool the loaves on a rack before slicing.

Baltimore Cheese Bread

12 SERVINGS

¼ cup plus 1 teaspoon sugar
3 tablespoons warm water (105° to 115°)
1 envelope (¼ ounce) active dry yeast
2 eggs
1 cup milk
½ cup (1 stick) unsalted butter, melted and cooled to room temperature
1 teaspoon salt
About 5 cups unbleached flour
1 pound Svenbo, Jarlsberg or Swiss cheese, grated (about 4 cups)

Glaze: 1 egg, lightly beaten

1. In a small bowl, stir 1 teaspoon of the sugar into the warm water; stir in the yeast and set aside until dissolved.

2. In a large bowl, lightly beat the eggs. Mix in the remaining sugar, the milk,

butter and salt. Blend in the yeast mixture and then stir in 2 cups of the flour to make a dough. Stir in another 1½ cups flour, turn the dough onto a work surface and knead in enough of the remaining flour to make a soft, smooth dough. Knead the dough until it is smooth and satiny, about 15 minutes.

3. Place the dough in a lightly oiled bowl, turn it to lightly grease the surface, cover with a tea towel and allow it to rise in a warm place until doubled in bulk, about 1½ hours.

4. Thoroughly grease a 9-inch pie pan. Punch down the dough and roll it into a 16-inch round. Center the dough in the pie pan, pressing it snugly against the edges of the pan and allowing the excess to hang over. Mound the cheese in the center and fold and pleat the dough into a turban shape by gathering it into 6 or 7 equally spaced folds, stretching the dough slightly as you draw each pleat over the filling. Holding the ends of the dough in your hand, twist them together tightly on top. Glaze the surface by brushing it with the lightly beaten egg. Set it aside in a warm place and let it rise until doubled in bulk, about 45 minutes.

5. Preheat the oven to 325°. Bake the bread in the center of the oven for about 50 minutes, or until the top is golden brown and the bread sounds hollow when lightly tapped on the side. Cool for 15 minutes, remove it from the pan and let rest another 30 minutes before slicing into wedges and serving.

Quick Loaf Bread

This bread takes just 2 hours from start to finish. It also looks nice as a braid; braid it after the first rising and let it rise again before baking.

MAKES 2 LOAVES

2⅔ cups lukewarm water (105° to 115°)
2 envelopes (¼ ounce each) active dry yeast
2 teaspoons honey or sugar
6½ to 7½ cups unbleached bread or all-purpose flour
2 teaspoons salt

1. In a large bowl, combine the water, yeast and honey. Stir briefly and let stand until the yeast dissolves and begins to foam, 5 to 10 minutes.

2. Stir 3 cups of the flour and the salt into the yeast mixture and beat well until smooth and bubbly. Gradually add enough of the remaining flour, 1 cup at a time, to make a fairly soft dough; do not add more flour than the dough can absorb.

3. Turn out onto a lightly floured surface and knead lightly until the dough is just barely nonsticky, about 2 minutes. Place in an oiled bowl and turn to coat with a light film of oil. Cover and let rise in a warm, draft-free place until doubled in bulk, about 30 minutes.

4. Punch down the dough and divide in half; place each half in a well-greased 9-by-5-by-3-inch loaf pan. Cover and let rise in a warm, draft-free place until doubled in bulk, about 30 minutes. Meanwhile, preheat the oven to 400°.

5. Bake the loaves for 30 minutes, or until the tops are browned and the bottoms sound hollow when tapped. Turn out onto racks and let cool before storing.

Holiday Fig-and-Nut Bread

This bread may be made a day or two ahead, but the glaze and decorations should not be applied until about 1 hour before serving.

MAKES 2 LOAVES

Dough:
7 to 8 cups all-purpose flour
2 envelopes (¼ ounce each) active dry yeast
2 cups milk
½ cup honey
½ cup (1 stick) unsalted butter
2 teaspoons salt
2 eggs

Filling:
¼ cup honey
4 tablespoons unsalted butter
1½ teaspoons cinnamon
1 teaspoon ground cloves

1 cup chopped dried figs
1 cup (4 ounces) finely chopped walnuts

Glaze and Decoration:
½ cup red currant jelly
Candied pineapple—red, green and yellow*
Candied angelica*
Glacéed apricots*
***Available at specialty food shops**

1. Make the dough: In a large bowl, combine 3 cups of the flour with the dry yeast. In a small saucepan, heat the milk, honey, butter and salt over low heat until the butter is melted. Cool to lukewarm (about 110°); then add to the flour and yeast. Stir briefly to mix and add the eggs. With an electric mixer, beat the batter on high speed for 3 minutes.

2. Stir in 3 to 4 cups of the remaining flour, 1 cup at a time, to form a stiff dough. Turn the dough out onto a well-floured surface. Gradually work in as much of the remaining flour as necessary to prevent sticking. Knead until the dough is smooth and elastic, 8 to 10 minutes. Place the dough in a greased bowl and turn it over to coat. Cover the bowl with a kitchen towel, place in a warm, draft-free place and let the dough rise until doubled in bulk, about 1 hour.

3. Punch down the dough, turn it out onto a lightly floured surface and knead briefly. Divide the dough in half and let rest for 10 minutes.

4. Prepare the filling: In a small saucepan, warm the honey and butter over low heat until the butter melts. Remove from the heat and stir in the cinnamon and cloves; set aside. In a small bowl, combine the figs and walnuts; set aside.

5. Preheat the oven to 350°. Grease two 9-by-5-by-3-inch loaf pans. Roll out one piece of the dough on a lightly floured surface into a rectangle about 15 by 8 inches. Spread the rectangle with half the honey-butter mixture, leaving a 1-inch border all around the edge. Cover the honey-butter with 1 cup of the fig and walnut mixture. Starting at one of the short ends, roll up the dough tightly like a jelly roll. Moisten the edges with a little water and pinch the ends of the loaf and along the seam to seal. Place the loaf, seam-side down, in one of the pre-

pared pans. Repeat with the remaining dough and filling. Cover, place in a warm draft-free place and let rise until doubled in bulk, about 45 minutes.

6. Bake the loaves for 50 minutes to 1 hour, until they sound hollow when tapped. Remove from the pans and cool completely on a rack before glazing.

7. Make the glaze and decorate the bread: In a small saucepan, melt the jelly over low heat. Cut the pineapple, angelica and apricots into decorative shapes. Brush the loaves with the jelly and decorate as desired. Lightly brush the decorations with jelly after applying them. Allow the glaze to set before serving.

Moravian Sugar Bread

24 SERVINGS

1 cup lukewarm water (105° to 115°)
1 envelope (¼ ounce) active dry yeast
⅓ cup plus 1 teaspoon granulated sugar
1 cup mashed potatoes (about 2 medium all-purpose potatoes)
3½ cups all-purpose flour
2 eggs, lightly beaten
1 cup (2 sticks) unsalted butter, at room temperature
¾ teaspoon salt
1 tablespoon milk
1 cup (packed) light brown sugar
1 teaspoon cinnamon

1. Place the water in a mixer bowl. Add the yeast and 1 teaspoon granulated sugar; stir until the yeast dissolves. Stir in the mashed potatoes, 2 cups of the flour, the remaining ⅓ cup granulated sugar, the eggs, ½ cup of the butter and the salt. Beat on medium speed for 5 minutes. Using a dough hook, gradually add the remaining flour and continue beating another 5 minutes; alternatively, if you do not have a dough hook, stir in the flour, turn out onto a floured surface and knead until the dough is soft and very elastic, 10 to 15 minutes. Cover and let rise in a warm place until doubled in bulk, about 2 hours.

2. Butter a 15½-by-10½-by-1-inch jelly roll pan. With lightly oiled hands, spread the dough evenly into the prepared pan.

Cover and let rise for 1 hour, or until the dough appears light and bubbly.

3. Preheat the oven to 350°. Brush the dough with the milk. Combine the brown sugar and cinnamon and sprinkle over the top. With two floured fingers together, make 30 indentations evenly spaced in the dough. Melt the remaining ½ cup of butter and spoon over the surface of the dough and into each indentation. Bake for 35 minutes, or until golden brown and firm to the touch. Serve warm.

Prebaked Tart Shell

MAKES ONE 9-INCH SHELL

1½ cups all-purpose flour
1 tablespoon sugar
¼ teaspoon salt
½ cup (1 stick) unsalted butter,
    chilled and cut into small bits
1 egg, lightly beaten

1. In a medium bowl, combine the flour, sugar and salt. Cut in the butter until the mixture resembles coarse meal. Add the egg and stir quickly to moisten the dry ingredients. Squeeze the dough together. If it seems very dry, add a few drops of cold water.

2. Gather the dough into a ball and place on a lightly floured work surface. With the heel of one hand, rapidly press small pieces of the pastry away from you until it has all been worked. (This quick, final blending, or kneading, is known as *fraisage*.) Form the dough into a flat, 6-inch disk, wrap in waxed paper or plastic wrap and refrigerate for at least 1 hour and up to 3 days.

3. Before rolling out the dough, place a 9-inch tart pan with removable bottom in the refrigerator to chill. Remove the dough from the refrigerator; if it has been chilled for more than an hour, you may need to let it sit at room temperature for 15 minutes to soften slightly. On a lightly floured surface, roll out the dough, working with quick short strokes from the center to the farthest edge; do not roll the pin over the edges if you can avoid it. Turn the dough about a quarter of a turn in one direction and roll again; repeat until the dough forms a 12-inch circle about ⅛ inch thick. If the dough sticks, dust with a little more flour.

4. Place the chilled tart pan close to the pastry circle. Drape the pastry over the rolling pin and lower into the pan. Fit the pastry into the bottom of the pan and press against the sides without stretching the dough. Trim the edges with scissors, leaving a ½-inch overhang. Fold down this extra dough and press against the pan to reinforce the sides. Prick the bottom all over with a fork. Place the tart pan on a cookie sheet and refrigerate for 1 hour, until thoroughly chilled.

5. Preheat the oven to 400°. Line the pastry with aluminum foil and fill with pie weights or dried beans. Bake on the cookie sheet for 20 minutes. Remove from the oven and reduce the oven temperature to 375°. Lift out the foil and the weights and bake for 15 minutes, or until the tart shell is golden. Unmold while still warm and slide onto a rack. Let cool completely before filling.

Cookie Crumb Crust

MAKES ONE 9-INCH SHELL

1 cup crushed vanilla wafers
⅓ cup finely chopped almonds
2 tablespoons sugar
5 tablespoons unsalted butter,
    melted

Preheat the oven to 350°. In a medium bowl, combine the vanilla wafer crumbs, almonds and sugar. Pour the butter over and blend with a fork until the crumbs are moistened. Butter the bottom of a 9-inch pie plate (not the sides or the shell may fall during baking) and distribute the crumbs evenly over it. Gently press the crumbs evenly over the bottom and then up at the sides of the pan. Bake in the center of the oven for 8 minutes. Cool to room temperature before filling.

Sweet Pastry Crust

This recipe can be doubled easily.

MAKES ONE 9-INCH SHELL

1 cup all-purpose flour
1½ tablespoons sugar
¼ teaspoon salt
⅓ cup (5 tablespoons plus 1
    teaspoon) unsalted butter
½ large egg, lightly beaten (see
    Note)

1. In a medium bowl, combine the flour, sugar and salt. Cut in the butter until the mixture resembles coarse meal. Gradually add the egg to the mixture, stirring with a fork, until the dough begins to mass together. If necessary add a few drops of cold water. Gently pat into a ball and flatten it into a round about 6 inches in diameter. Wrap in waxed paper and chill for at least 1 hour. (Tightly wrapped in plastic wrap, the pastry will keep for up to 3 days in the refrigerator or for up to 3 months in the freezer.)

2. Oil or butter a 9-inch pie plate. To roll out the pastry, place the round between two sheets of generously floured waxed paper. With a rolling pin, roll the pastry from the center out to the edges, turning the pastry a few degrees clockwise after each stroke. Roll and turn the pastry until it forms an 11- to 12-inch round. Carefully peel off the top sheet of waxed paper. Invert the pastry into the pie plate and peel off the remaining waxed paper. Without stretching it, gently fit the pastry into the pie plate and trim off the overhang evenly to ½ inch. Fold the edge under and crimp decoratively. With a fork, lightly prick the dough all over. Refrigerate for 15 minutes.

3. To prebake the shell, preheat the oven to 400°. Line the pastry shell with aluminum foil and fill with dried beans, rice or pie weights. Bake for 12 minutes and remove the liner and weights. Reduce the heat to 350° and bake for another 8 minutes. Cool the shell completely on a rack before filling.

NOTE: For ½ egg, beat 1 egg lightly with a fork and measure out 1½ tablespoons.

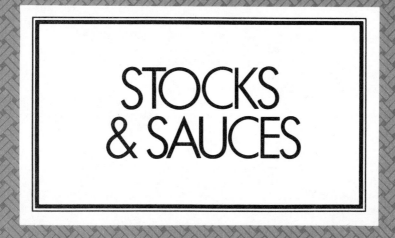

STOCKS
& SAUCES

Chicken Stock

Although this deliciously rich stock calls for two whole chickens in addition to chicken parts, the whole birds are removed as soon as they are cooked, so you can eat them as is or use the meat for other dishes, salads or sandwiches. You may substitute additional chicken parts for the whole chickens. Use this stock as a base for soups or sauces.

MAKES ABOUT 3 QUARTS

4 pounds chicken backs, necks and/or wings
2 whole chickens (about 3 pounds each), including neck and gizzards
3 large carrots, sliced
2 large onions, sliced
4 medium leeks—split lengthwise, rinsed and sliced crosswise (or, substitute 1 extra onion)
2 celery ribs with leaves, sliced
Bouquet garni: 8 sprigs of parsley, 1 teaspoon thyme, 1 bay leaf, ½ teaspoon peppercorns and 3 whole cloves tied in a double thickness of cheesecloth

1. Place the chicken parts in a large, heavy stockpot; place the whole chickens on top. Add 6 quarts of cold water and place over low heat. Heat to simmering without stirring; for a clear stock, this should take about an hour. While the water is heating, skim off any scum that rises to the surface.

2. Add the carrots, onions, leeks, celery and bouquet garni. Simmer, partially covered, without stirring, for about 45 minutes. Remove both chickens. Continue simmering the stock, without stirring, for about 4 hours, skimming occasionally. (The meat can be removed from the two chickens as soon as they are cool enough to handle and the bones returned to the pot.)

3. Ladle the stock carefully through a colander lined with several layers of dampened cheesecloth. Strain a second time, if desired, for an even clearer stock. Let cool to room temperature; then cover and refrigerate. Remove the congealed fat from the top. If using the hot stock immediately, remove the fat by first skimming and then blotting the surface with paper towels, or use a degreasing utensil designed for that purpose.

Brown Chicken Stock

Use this rich, dark stock as the base for sauces to accompany poultry and game birds.

MAKES ABOUT 1 QUART

3 to 4 pounds of chicken backs, wings and/or necks
1 medium onion, unpeeled and quartered
1 celery rib, coarsely sliced
1½ cups dry white wine
2 medium tomatoes, quartered
1 sprig of fresh thyme or ¼ teaspoon dried
½ bay leaf
½ teaspoon peppercorns

1. Preheat the oven to 500°. Place the chicken, onion and celery in a roasting pan and roast, turning the bones once or twice, until they are a dark, golden brown, about 30 minutes.

2. Transfer the chicken and vegetables to a stockpot. Deglaze the roasting pan with the wine and pour into the stockpot. Add the tomatoes, thyme, bay leaf, peppercorns, and enough water to cover by 1 inch. Bring to a boil over high heat, reduce the heat and simmer for 3 hours, skimming off the foam and fat occasionally as they rise to the top.

3. Strain the stock into a large saucepan; there should be about 2 quarts. Skim off any fat. Boil until reduced by half.

Brown Stock

Deep, amber, flavorful brown stock forms the basis for many sauces.

MAKES 4 TO 5 QUARTS

6 pounds beef shin with bones
6 pounds veal bones
6 carrots, cut into 2-inch lengths
3 onions—unpeeled, halved and each half stuck with 1 whole clove
3 leeks (white part only), split lengthwise, plus 1 leek (including green top), quartered
2 celery ribs with leaves, cut into 2-inch lengths
1 small white turnip

2 cups coarsely chopped tomatoes, canned or fresh
Bouquet garni: 6 sprigs of parsley, 1 teaspoon thyme, 1 large bay leaf, 7 peppercorns and 2 unpeeled garlic cloves tied in a double thickness of cheesecloth

1. Preheat the oven to 450°. Place the meat and bones in a large roasting pan in 1 or 2 layers, or in 2 roasting pans if necessary. Bake, uncovered, for 30 minutes. Add the carrots and onions and bake, turning occasionally, until the bones are deep brown but not charred, 30 to 60 minutes longer.

2. Transfer the bones and vegetables to a large stockpot. Pour off and discard any fat from the roasting pan. Add 2 to 3 cups of cold water to the pan and deglaze over medium heat, scraping up any browned particles that cling to the bottom. Pour the liquid into the stockpot, add enough additional cold water to cover the bones—about 4 quarts—and bring the water slowly to a simmer over low heat; to insure a clear stock, this slow heating should take about 1 hour. Skim off all the scum that rises to the surface.

3. Add the leeks, celery, turnip, tomatoes, bouquet garni and enough additional water to cover. Simmer, partially covered, over low heat for 5 to 8 hours, skimming the surface occasionally. Add additional water to cover as necessary.

4. Carefully ladle the stock into a large bowl through a colander lined with several thicknesses of dampened cheesecloth. Do not press on the bones and vegetables, or the resulting stock will be cloudy. Refrigerate, uncovered, overnight; then remove any fat from the surface. The stock may be refrigerated for 3 to 4 days, then reboiled, or frozen for several months.

White Veal Stock

Use this clear, delicate stock to create sauces for veal, chicken or fish dishes.

MAKES 2 TO 3 QUARTS

4½ pounds veal bones
3 pounds veal stew meat, such as shank, breast, neck
2 leeks (white part only), cut into 2-inch lengths
2 medium onions, quartered
2 celery ribs with leaves, cut into 2-inch lengths
2 carrots, cut into 2-inch lengths
Bouquet garni: 6 sprigs of parsley, ½ teaspoon thyme, 1 bay leaf, 2 unpeeled garlic cloves, 3 whole cloves and 4 peppercorns tied in a double thickness of cheesecloth

1. Place the veal bones and meat in a large stockpot. Add enough cold water to cover, about 3 quarts. Cover the pot and bring to a boil over high heat. Lower the heat to moderate and boil gently for 5 minutes. Drain, discarding the water, and rinse the bones under cold running water. Rinse out the pot. Return the bones and meat to the stockpot and add enough cold water to cover. Bring to a simmer over low heat and skim off any scum that rises to the surface. Add 1 cup cold water and when the liquid has returned to a simmer, skim again. Repeat the cold water-skimming process until the liquid is clear.

2. Add the leeks, onions, celery, carrots and bouquet garni. Simmer, partially covered, for 4 to 5 hours, adding water to cover as necessary.

3. When the stock is ready, carefully ladle it through a colander lined with several thicknesses of dampened cheesecloth into a large bowl. Allow to cool. Cover and refrigerate. After the stock has jelled, remove any fat that has accumulated on the surface.

Vegetable Stock

MAKES ABOUT 1½ QUARTS

3 celery ribs, cut into 2-inch lengths
2 large carrots, cut into 2-inch lengths
2 small onions, unpeeled and quartered
1 large boiling potato, cut into 1-inch slices
½ pound mushrooms, roughly chopped
4 small leeks (white part only), split lengthwise
2 small white turnips, peeled and quartered
6 garlic cloves, unpeeled
1½ teaspoons salt
1½ teaspoons Hungarian sweet paprika
Bouquet garni: 10 sprigs of parsley, 1½ teaspoons marjoram, 2 bay leaves and 8 peppercorns tied in a double thickness of cheesecloth

1. Place all the vegetables in a stockpot. Add the garlic, salt, paprika, bouquet garni and 3 quarts of water and bring to a boil over moderate heat.

2. Reduce the heat to low and simmer the stock, partially covered, until reduced by half, about 1½ hours.

3. Strain through a double thickness of dampened cheesecloth, pressing lightly on the vegetables with the back of a spoon.

Fish Stock

When cleaning whole fish, save the heads and frames for stock; or, inquire at your local fish market. Use this stock for a variety of sauces.

MAKES ABOUT 2 QUARTS

4 pounds fish bones and trimmings (heads, tails, skin)
3 tablespoons vegetable oil
1 medium onion, cut into eighths
1 large celery rib, cut into 1-inch lengths
1 large carrot, cut into 1-inch lengths
Bouquet garni: 3 sprigs of parsley, ½ teaspoon thyme, 1 bay leaf and 8 to 10 peppercorns tied in a double thickness of cheesecloth

1. Rinse the fish bones and trimmings under cold running water to remove any blood; drain.

2. Heat the oil in a large, heavy stockpot. Add the fish bones and trimmings and sauté over moderate heat for 5 minutes, breaking them up occasionally with a wooden spoon. Cook, partially covered, for 5 minutes longer.

3. Add the onion, celery, carrot and bouquet garni. Pour in 3 quarts of cold water. Bring the mixture to a boil over high heat, skimming off any foam from the surface. Reduce the heat to low and simmer, uncovered, for 30 minutes. Strain through a fine sieve lined with several layers of dampened cheesecloth.

Espagnole Sauce

MAKES ABOUT 2 CUPS

5 tablespoons unsalted butter
⅔ cup chopped onion
⅔ cup chopped carrot
⅓ cup all-purpose flour
3½ cups hot brown stock
1⅓ cups dry white wine
1½ tablespoons tomato paste
Bouquet garni: 3 sprigs of parsley, ½ teaspoon thyme and 1 bay leaf tied in a double thickness of cheesecloth
1 teaspoon salt
¼ teaspoon pepper

1. In a medium saucepan, melt the butter over moderately low heat. Add the onion and carrot and sauté, stirring occasionally, until soft but not brown, 10 to 12 minutes. Remove from the heat and blend in the flour. Return to low heat and cook, stirring frequently, until the roux turns golden brown, 8 to 10 minutes. Whisk in the stock, wine and tomato paste; add the bouquet garni.

2. Bring to a boil over high heat. Reduce the heat and simmer, stirring occasionally, until the sauce is reduced by half to about 2½ cups, 35 to 45 minutes. Season with the salt and pepper. Strain the sauce through a fine sieve.

Bordelaise Sauce

A rich, unctuous sauce, perfect over steaks and often served with kidneys.

MAKES ABOUT 1 CUP

1½ ounces beef marrow, cut into
 ¼-inch slices (about ⅓ cup)
1 tablespoon unsalted butter
1 tablespoon minced shallot
½ cup dry red wine
1 cup Espagnole Sauce (p. 205)
1 tablespoon minced fresh parsley
Salt and pepper

1. Gently rinse the marrow under cold running water to remove any blood. Drop into a small saucepan of boiling water. Immediately remove from the heat and let stand until the marrow softens, 2 to 3 minutes. Drain and set aside.

2. In a small saucepan, melt the butter over low heat. Add the shallot and cook, stirring frequently, until softened, about 2 minutes. Add the wine, increase the heat to high and boil until the liquid is reduced to ¼ cup, 2 to 3 minutes. Reduce the heat to low, add the Espagnole Sauce, parsley and salt and pepper to taste. Cook over low heat, stirring frequently, for 2 minutes.

3. Just before serving, heat through. Strain the sauce through a fine sieve. Gently fold in the marrow.

Fish Sauce Aurore

If not served immediately, this sauce can be kept warm in a double boiler or water bath for up to 1 hour.

MAKES ABOUT 2 CUPS

4 cups fish stock
3 tablespoons tomato paste
¾ teaspoon salt
¼ teaspoon white pepper
½ cup (1 stick) cold unsalted
 butter, cut into tablespoons

1. In a large heavy saucepan, boil the stock over high heat until reduced to 1½ cups, about 15 minutes.

2. Reduce the heat to low and stir in the tomato paste, salt and pepper. Remove from the heat and gradually whisk in the butter, 2 tablespoons at a time.

Velouté Sauce

A properly made velouté sauce is light and velvety. Serve over the appropriate meat, fish or vegetable—depending upon which stock you used as a base—or enrich and season to make one of the more complex sauces that follow.

MAKES ABOUT 2 CUPS

4 tablespoons unsalted butter
4 tablespoons all-purpose flour
2 cups hot stock—chicken, white
 veal or fish stock
Salt and white pepper

1. In a small saucepan, melt the butter over moderate heat. Whisk in the flour until smooth and cook, stirring, for 2 minutes, without browning, to make a roux.

2. Off the heat, whisk in the hot stock. Return to moderate heat and cook, stirring constantly, until the sauce boils. Continue to cook for 1 minute, whisking until smooth. Season with salt and pepper to taste.

Sauce Fines Herbes

Serve this delicately flavored sauce over baked, broiled or poached fish or scallops.

MAKES ABOUT 2 CUPS

1 tablespoon unsalted butter
1½ tablespoons chopped shallot
2 cups Velouté Sauce (above)
 made with fish stock
½ cup heavy cream
1 tablespoon minced fresh parsley
1 tablespoon minced fresh chives
½ teaspoon dried dillweed
¼ teaspoon chervil
Salt and white pepper

In a medium saucepan, melt the butter over low heat. Add the shallot and cook until softened but not browned, about 3 minutes. Add the Velouté Sauce, cream, parsley, chives, dill and chervil. Simmer over low heat until the sauce is reduced to 2 cups, about 8 minutes. Season with salt and pepper to taste.

Tarragon Cream Sauce

Light and fragrant, this sauce is lovely over poached chicken breasts or eggs.

MAKES ABOUT 1½ CUPS

1 tablespoon chopped fresh
 tarragon or 1 teaspoon dried
¼ cup dry white wine
1½ cups Velouté Sauce (at left)
 made with chicken stock
3 tablespoons heavy cream

1. Place the tarragon and wine in a small saucepan and boil over moderately low heat until reduced by half, about 2 minutes.

2. Strain through a fine sieve into the Velouté Sauce. Stir in the heavy cream, place in a clean small saucepan and heat until hot.

Tomato Sauce

Serve this hearty, all-vegetable sauce over pasta, sautéed or broiled eggplant, zucchini or mushrooms.

MAKES ABOUT 3 CUPS

1 small onion, finely chopped
1 small garlic clove, chopped
3 tablespoons olive oil
3 tablespoons all-purpose flour
2 large cans (35 ounces each)
 Italian peeled tomatoes—drained,
 seeded and roughly chopped
3 cups Vegetable Stock (p. 205)
½ teaspoon oregano
½ teaspoon sugar
⅛ teaspoon pepper
Salt

1. In a large saucepan, sauté the onion and garlic in the olive oil over moderately low heat until softened, about 2 minutes. Blend in the flour and cook, stirring, for about 2 minutes, without browning, to make a roux.

2. Stir in the tomatoes, stock, oregano, sugar and pepper and bring to a boil. Reduce the heat and simmer for 1 hour, stirring occasionally. Season with salt to taste.

3. Pass the sauce through the medium disk of a food mill or coarsely puree in a blender or food processor.

Creamy Tomato Sauce

MAKES ABOUT 1½ CUPS

1 can (2 pounds 3 ounces) Italian
peeled tomatoes, drained
Bouquet garni: 5 sprigs of parsley,
½ teaspoon thyme and 5
peppercorns tied in a double
thickness of cheesecloth
¾ cup heavy cream
½ teaspoon salt
Freshly ground pepper

1. Place the tomatoes in a blender or
food processor and puree until smooth.
Strain through a coarse mesh sieve to
remove the seeds.

2. In a large skillet, bring the tomato
puree with the bouquet garni to a boil
over moderate heat. Boil, uncovered, for
5 minutes to reduce slightly. Stir in the
cream and add the salt. Discard the bouquet garni. Season with additional salt
and pepper to taste.

Saucè Américaine

MAKES 1½ CUPS

8 tablespoons (1 stick) unsalted
butter
1 medium carrot, coarsely chopped
1 medium onion, coarsely chopped
Shells from 1 pound medium
shrimp (about 2½ cups)
½ cup Cognac or brandy
¼ cup tomato paste
½ cup dry white wine
2 bottles (8 ounces each) clam
juice
1 sprig of parsley
½ bay leaf
¼ teaspoon freshly ground pepper
½ cup heavy cream

1. In a large heavy saucepan, melt 4 tablespoons of the butter. Add the carrot,
onion and shrimp shells; sauté over
moderate heat until the vegetables are
softened but not browned, about 5 minutes. Reduce the heat to low, cover and
cook for 5 minutes.

2. In a small saucepan, warm the Cognac over low heat. Remove the cover
from the large saucepan, ignite the Cognac and pour it into the pan, being
careful to avoid the flames.

3. When the flames subside, stir in the
tomato paste, wine, clam juice, parsley,
bay leaf, pepper and 1 cup of water.
Bring to a boil and cook over moderate
heat until reduced by half, about 30 minutes. Strain into a bowl, pressing on the
solids with the back of a wooden spoon
to extract as much liquid as possible.
Discard the solids.

4. Pour the liquid into a medium saucepan and boil over high heat until reduced to about 1¼ cups. Add the cream
and boil until the sauce is reduced to 1¼
cups. (The sauce can be done ahead to
this point, covered and refrigerated for
up to 2 days or frozen.)

5. Shortly before serving, heat the sauce
to boiling and remove from the heat.
Gradually whisk in the remaining 4 tablespoons butter, 1 tablespoon at a time.

Fresh Tomato Sauce

MAKES ABOUT 3½ CUPS

1 tablespoon olive oil
3 shallots, finely chopped
2 pounds firm, ripe tomatoes—
peeled, seeded and quartered
1 garlic clove, crushed
Bouquet garni: 6 sprigs parsley, ½
teaspoon thyme and 1 bay leaf
tied in a double thickness of
cheesecloth
Salt and pepper

1. In a medium saucepan, heat the oil.
Add the shallots and cook over moderately low heat until softened but not
brown, about 1 minute. Add the tomatoes, garlic, bouquet garni and ½ cup
water. Simmer, uncovered, over moderate heat for 20 minutes.

2. Remove the bouquet garni. In a food
processor or blender, puree the tomato
sauce. Season with salt and pepper to
taste.

Green Herb Sauce
with Champagne

MAKES ABOUT 1 CUP

½ cup fish stock or bottled clam
juice
1 large shallot, thinly sliced
1 cup champagne
½ cup heavy cream
1 cup of two or more of the
following: tarragon, marjoram,
parsley, watercress, torn spinach
leaves or chopped dill
1 cup fresh sorrel leaves or 2
tablespoons sorrel paste
½ cup mayonnaise
Salt and pepper
Lemon juice

1. In a small saucepan, cook the fish
stock, shallot and champagne over moderately high heat until reduced to ½ cup,
15 to 20 minutes. Add the heavy cream
and cook again until reduced to ½ cup, 8
to 10 minutes. Let cool.

2. In a medium saucepan, bring 1 cup of
water to a boil. Add the herbs and
greens, except the sorrel, and blanch for
2 minutes; drain and run under cold
water for about 1 minute to set the color
and stop the cooking. Drain well and
squeeze out any excess moisture.

3. Combine the sorrel with the mayonnaise in a blender or food processor.
Add the blanched greens and herbs and
blend again. Slowly add the cream-stock
reduction and blend until smooth and
creamy. Season with the salt, pepper and
lemon juice to taste. Transfer to a small
bowl, cover and chill until ready to use.

Green Caper Sauce

MAKES ABOUT 1 CUP

½ cup olive oil
3 tablespoons fresh lemon juice
½ cup drained capers, chopped (1½
jars, 3¼ ounces each)
¼ cup chopped green bell pepper
1 tablespoon chopped fresh chives
1 tablespoon chopped fresh parsley
Salt and pepper to taste

In a small bowl, whisk the olive oil and
lemon juice until well blended. Stir in
the remaining ingredients.

Anchovy and Red Pepper Sauce

This pungent sauce is delicious served over poached fish or chicken.

2 SERVINGS

1 small red bell pepper
5 anchovy fillets (about 1 ounce), rinsed and chopped
5 tablespoons unsalted butter, chilled
½ teaspoon coarsely ground black pepper

1. Roast the red pepper by placing it directly on a gas burner, or broil as closely to the heat as possible, turning frequently, until completely charred. Place in a brown paper bag; seal and let steam for about 10 minutes. Peel under cold running water; seed and finely dice.

2. In a small saucepan, combine the anchovies with 3 tablespoons of water. Cover and simmer for about 5 minutes, or until the anchovies dissolve. Swirl in the butter, 1 tablespoon at a time; strain the sauce through a fine sieve. Stir in the red pepper and the black pepper and serve warm.

Béchamel Sauce with Cheese

MAKES ABOUT 1½ CUPS

2 cups milk
Bouquet garni: 5 sprigs of parsley, ¼ teaspoon thyme and ½ bay leaf tied in a double thickness of cheesecloth
2 tablespoons unsalted butter
3 tablespoons all-purpose flour
½ teaspoon salt
Pinch of freshly ground white pepper
Pinch of nutmeg
½ cup freshly grated Parmesan cheese

1. In a heavy, medium saucepan, bring the milk with the bouquet garni to a boil.

2. Meanwhile, in another heavy, medium saucepan, melt the butter over moderate heat. Add the flour and cook, stirring, for 1 to 2 minutes without browning to make a roux.

3. Whisking constantly, strain the boiling milk into the roux. Return to the boil and cook, whisking, until the sauce is thickened and smooth, 3 to 4 minutes. Season with the salt, pepper and nutmeg and stir in the cheese.

Basic Mayonnaise

Mayonnaise works best if all the ingredients are at room temperature before you begin. The emulsion (the suspension of the particles of oil within the yolk) will not form if the oil or the yolks are too cold. On a chilly day, warm the bowl and the whisk in hot water, then dry well before starting.

MAKES ABOUT 1½ CUPS

3 egg yolks, at room temperature
1 teaspoon Dijon-style mustard
½ teaspoon salt
Pinch of white pepper
1 tablespoon fresh lemon juice
½ cup olive oil mixed with ½ cup light vegetable oil (see Note)
1 tablespoon white wine vinegar
1 tablespoon boiling water

1. In a medium bowl, whisk the egg yolks until they lighten in color and begin to thicken. Beat in the mustard, salt, pepper and lemon juice and continue whisking until the mixture thickens enough to leave a trail when the whisk is drawn across the bottom of the bowl.

2. Very gradually, begin whisking in the oil by droplets. The emulsion will not form if the oil at this stage is added too quickly.

3. Once the emulsion forms and the mayonnaise begins to thicken, you can add the oil more rapidly, but never faster than in a thin stream.

4. After all the oil has been incorporated, whisk in the vinegar and the boiling water. (The vinegar will lighten and flavor the sauce, the boiling water will help stabilize it.) Taste the mayonnaise and adjust the seasonings according to your taste and the planned use. Cover and refrigerate for up to 5 days.

NOTE: We find this combination of oils produces the perfect balance of flavor and lightness for an all-purpose mayonnaise. You can adjust the proportions according to your taste and particular use.

Sauce Rémoulade

Serve with cold fish, pork or meat.

MAKES ABOUT 1¾ CUPS

Make the Basic Mayonnaise (at left), using 4 egg yolks instead of 3. Stir in 1 teaspoon Dijon-style mustard, ½ teaspoon anchovy paste, 1 tablespoon finely chopped capers, 1 tablespoon finely chopped cornichons, 1 tablespoon chopped fresh parsley and 1 tablespoon chopped fresh chives.

Sauce Andalouse (Tomato Mayonnaise with Pimiento)

Serve with cold poultry or beef.

MAKES ABOUT 1¾ CUPS

Make the Basic Mayonnaise (at left), using 4 egg yolks instead of 3. Whisk in ¼ cup tomato paste until blended and stir in 2 tablespoons of pimiento cut into fine julienne strips.

Watercress-Mustard Mayonnaise with Cucumber

Serve with cold poached fish, lamb or beef.

MAKES ABOUT 1 CUP

1 bunch of watercress
2 tablespoons grainy mustard
¼ cup mayonnaise
¼ teaspoon salt
¼ teaspoon freshly ground pepper
1 large cucumber—peeled, seeded and finely diced

1. Holding the stems, dip the bunch of watercress in and out of a saucepan of boiling water. Rinse under cold running water; squeeze dry, cut off the stems and finely chop the leaves.

2. In a medium bowl, stir the mustard, mayonnaise, salt and pepper until blended. Fold in the watercress and cucumber.

Blender Hollandaise

1 cup (2 sticks) unsalted butter
3 egg yolks
Pinch of salt
Pinch of white pepper
1 tablespoon fresh lemon juice

1. Melt the butter over low heat and keep warm.

2. Place the egg yolks, salt, pepper and the lemon juice in the bowl of a blender. Mix at high speed until blended thoroughly.

3. While blending at high speed, add the hot butter in a thin stream; do not add the milky residue at the bottom of the pan. Taste and adjust the seasonings.

Sauce Maltaise

MAKES ABOUT 1 CUP

Make the Blender Hollandaise (above). Stir in 2 tablespoons grated orange zest and 2 tablespoons fresh orange juice.

Béarnaise

Béarnaise sauce is hollandaise's bolder cousin. Instead of the delicate lemon of hollandaise, béarnaise is made lively with a tarragon-flavored vinegar reduction, sharpened with shallots and black peppercorns. Its stronger flavor stands up well to grilled meats, to which it is a classic accompaniment.

MAKES ABOUT 1 CUP

1 cup (2 sticks) unsalted butter
3 tablespoons dry white wine
3 tablespoons tarragon vinegar or white wine vinegar
2 tablespoons finely chopped shallots
3 tablespoons chopped fresh tarragon or 1 tablespoon dried
10 black peppercorns, crushed
3 egg yolks
¼ teaspoon salt
Pinch of white pepper
1 tablespoon chopped fresh parsley or chervil

1. Melt the butter in a small saucepan over low heat. Set aside and let cool until tepid.

2. In a heavy, medium, noncorrodible saucepan, boil the wine, vinegar, shallots, 1 tablespoon of the tarragon and the peppercorns over high heat until reduced by two-thirds to about 2 tablespoons, 2 to 3 minutes. Set aside and let cool until tepid.

3. Whisk the egg yolks and the salt into the cooled vinegar reduction. Cook over low heat, whisking constantly, until the sauce thickens just enough to leave a trail when the whisk is drawn across the bottom of the pan.

4. Immediately remove from the heat and begin whisking in the butter in droplets. When the sauce begins to thicken, whisk in the remaining butter in a thin stream; do not add the milky residue at the bottom of the pan.

5. Strain the sauce through a fine sieve. Add the white pepper, remaining 2 tablespoons chopped tarragon and the parsley. Taste and adjust the seasonings if necessary.

Beurre Blanc

If not served immediately, this sauce can be kept warm in a pan of hot—not simmering—water for up to 30 minutes.

MAKES ABOUT 1½ CUPS

2 tablespoons minced shallots
¼ cup dry white wine
¼ cup white wine vinegar
1½ cups (3 sticks) cold unsalted butter, cut into tablespoons
½ teaspoon salt
⅛ teaspoon white pepper

1. In a heavy noncorrodible saucepan, combine the shallots, wine and vinegar. Bring to a boil over high heat and continue to boil until the liquid is reduced to 1 tablespoon, 4 to 5 minutes.

2. Remove from the heat and whisk in 4 tablespoons of the butter, 2 tablespoons at a time, until incorporated. Return the pan to very low heat and gradually whisk in the remaining butter, 2 tablespoons at a time. Season with the salt and pepper.

Cucumber Beurre Blanc

Serve with steamed or poached fish.

MAKES ABOUT 1½ CUPS

Make the Beurre Blanc (above) with the following adjustments. In Step 1, reduce the minced shallots to 1 tablespoon and add 2 tablespoons peeled, seeded, finely diced cucumber to the pan; reduce to 2 tablespoons. After incorporating all the butter in Step 2, strain the mixture through a fine sieve and then season with the salt and pepper.

Fennel Mustard Sauce

A tasty sauce for poached fish, grilled chicken, steamed vegetables or leeks.

MAKES ABOUT 1 CUP

2 cups heavy cream
2 tablespoons fennel seed, bruised
8 large garlic cloves, peeled
2 tablespoons grainy mustard
2 teaspoons white wine vinegar
¼ teaspoon salt

1. In a medium saucepan, combine the cream, fennel seed and garlic. Bring to a boil over moderate heat. Reduce the heat to low and simmer, stirring occasionally, until the cream is reduced to 1 cup and the garlic is soft, about 30 minutes.

2. Pour the sauce through a fine strainer set over a small pan. Press the garlic through the strainer into the sauce; discard the fennel seed. Whisk in the mustard, vinegar and salt. Reheat.

Sherry-Mustard Sauce

Spoon this buttery sauce over grilled steak, veal or lamb chops.

MAKES ABOUT 1 CUP

¼ cup sherry or red wine vinegar
1⅓ cups dry sherry
½ cup grainy mustard
½ cup (1 stick) unsalted butter, chilled and cut into 8 pieces

1. In a small saucepan, boil the vinegar over high heat until reduced to 1 tablespoon, about 2 minutes.

2. Add the sherry and boil until reduced

to ¼ cup of syrupy liquid, about 6 minutes. Stir in the mustard and reduce the heat to low.

3. Swirl in the butter one piece at a time, waiting until each piece has been fully incorporated before adding the next. Serve immediately.

Dilled Sour-Cream Sauce

MAKES ABOUT ¾ CUP

½ cup mayonnaise
6 tablespoons sour cream
¼ cup chopped dill
¼ teaspoon salt
1½ teaspoons minced garlic
½ teaspoon lemon juice
1½ teaspoons Dijon-style mustard
White pepper to taste

Blend all the ingredients in a blender or food processor until smooth and creamy. Transfer to a small bowl, cover and chill until ready to use.

Yogurt Sauce

MAKES ABOUT 2½ CUPS

1 cup plain yogurt
1 cup sour cream
2 tablespoons fresh lime juice
3 tablespoons finely minced
  scallions (white and light green)
¼ teaspoon white pepper
1 teaspoon coarse (kosher) salt

Combine all the ingredients in a bowl and refrigerate, covered, for several hours or overnight.

Crème Fraîche

2 cups heavy cream
⅓ cup active-culture buttermilk

1. In a small saucepan, gently heat the cream and buttermilk to just under 100° (higher will kill the culture).

2. Pour into a clean glass jar, cover and place in a saucepan filled with warm (100°) water; or put in a thermos bottle. Allow to stand for 8 to 36 hours, or until thickened, replenishing the warm water from time to time. The longer you culture the cream, the tangier it will become.

3. Refrigerate until chilled. Crème fraîche will keep in the refrigerator for a week to 10 days.

Creamy Green Peppercorn Dressing

This dressing is at its best over slices of cold ham decorated with hard-cooked egg slices and asparagus spears.

MAKES ABOUT 1½ CUPS

2 egg yolks
2 tablespoons white wine vinegar
1 teaspoon salt
½ cup olive oil
½ cup vegetable oil
¼ teaspoon sugar
1 tablespoon green peppercorns,
  roughly chopped
¼ cup sour cream

1. Have all ingredients at room temperature before you begin. In a mixing bowl, place the egg yolks, vinegar and salt. If you have an electric mixer, beat at moderately high speed for a minute. If you are whisking the emulsion by hand, beat 2 minutes.

2. Combine the olive oil and the vegetable oil in a measuring cup with a spout and add, a drop at a time, 1 tablespoon of it to the egg-yolk mixture, beating constantly until each drop has been completely absorbed before adding another. Add about ⅓ cup more of the oil a few drops at a time. (As the emulsion forms, the mixture will thicken and become homogenous.) Add the remaining oil in a thin, continuous stream, making sure that all the oil is being completely absorbed as you pour. The emulsion will become progressively thicker.

3. Stir in the sugar, green peppercorns and sour cream. Taste for flavor; for a more piquant flavor, add more vinegar.

Creamy Tarragon Vinaigrette

MAKES ABOUT 1⅓ CUPS

½ cup dry white wine
½ cup white wine vinegar
10 whole black peppercorns
2 large shallots, finely chopped
  (about 3 tablespoons)
2 tablespoons dried tarragon,
  crushed
1 egg yolk, at room temperature
1 teaspoon Dijon-style mustard
¼ teaspoon salt
⅛ teaspoon white pepper
1 cup safflower oil

1. In a small, noncorrodible saucepan, combine the wine, vinegar, peppercorns, shallots and tarragon. Boil until the liquid is reduced to ⅓ cup, about 10 minutes. Strain through several layers of dampened cheesecloth and set aside to cool to lukewarm.

2. In a large bowl, whisk together the egg yolk, mustard, salt and white pepper and 2 tablespoons of the wine reduction. Start whisking in the oil in a very thin stream. After about one-third of the oil has been added and the mixture starts to thicken, add 2 more tablespoons of the reduction. Whisk in another third of the oil, then add the remaining reduction. Whisk in the remaining oil.

Horseradish Sauce

This sauce is the perfect accompaniment to any beef dish. It also lends a sharp, creamy flavor to baked or boiled potatoes.

MAKES ABOUT 2 CUPS

1 cup heavy cream
¼ cup prepared white horseradish,
  drained
2 teaspoons lemon juice
¾ teaspoon Worcestershire sauce
½ teaspoon Angostura bitters
½ teaspoon salt

1. In a chilled mixing bowl with chilled beaters, whip the cream until almost stiff.

2. In a small bowl, stir the horseradish, lemon juice, Worcestershire, bitters and salt until blended; fold into the whipped cream.

All-American Barbecue Sauce

MAKES ABOUT 1¾ CUPS

1 can (6 ounces) tomato paste
1 cup dry vermouth
⅓ cup fresh lemon juice
⅓ cup tarragon vinegar
⅓ cup honey
¼ cup Worcestershire sauce
3 tablespoons Dijon-style mustard
2 tablespoons soy sauce
1 tablespoon hot pepper sauce
1 teaspoon ground cumin
2 tablespoons unsalted butter
1½ tablespoons olive oil
1 medium onion, minced
4 garlic cloves, minced
1 bay leaf

1. In a medium bowl, mix the tomato paste, vermouth, lemon juice, vinegar, honey, Worcestershire sauce, mustard, soy sauce, hot sauce and cumin until blended.

2. In a medium noncorrodible saucepan, warm the butter and oil over moderate heat. Add the onion and garlic and sauté, stirring, until softened and translucent, about 4 minutes.

3. Add the sauce mixture and the bay leaf and simmer, uncovered, over moderately low heat, stirring occasionally until thick, about 20 minutes.

Hakka Chili Sauce

1 tablespoon Chinese chili sauce (see Note)
1 teaspoon unseasoned Japanese rice vinegar
½ teaspoon sugar

In a small dish, combine the chili sauce, vinegar and sugar with 1 tablespoon of hot water; stir to dissolve the sugar. Let stand at least 15 minutes and stir before serving.

NOTE: Chinese chili sauce is a fruity-hot blend of chili and spices. Use Szechwan brand, available in a black-labeled can in Chinese groceries and through mail order. Do not confuse chili sauce with hot bean paste or a product labeled "chili paste with garlic."

California Barbecue Sauce

MAKES ABOUT 3½ CUPS

1½ cups pineapple juice or apricot nectar
1 cup (packed) light brown sugar
1 cup ketchup
1 cup cider vinegar
2 tablespoons cornstarch

In a medium noncorrodible saucepan, combine 1 cup of the fruit juice, the brown sugar, ketchup and vinegar. Bring to a boil over moderate heat, stirring occasionally. In a small bowl, dissolve the cornstarch in the remaining ½ cup juice. Whisk into the hot sauce, and simmer, stirring constantly, until the sauce is thickened and slightly translucent, about 3 minutes.

Apple and Plum Sauce

6 SERVINGS

2 pounds Golden Delicious apples (about 4 large)
1 teaspoon fresh lemon juice
1 tablespoon sugar
½ cup (4 ounces) Chinese plum sauce*

*Available at Oriental groceries

1. Peel and core the apples and cut them into 1-inch chunks. Place them in a medium saucepan and toss with the lemon juice.

2. Add the sugar and enough water to barely cover the apples. Bring the water to a boil over moderate heat. Reduce the heat and simmer the apples, uncovered, until soft, about 10 minutes. Drain the apples and allow to cool to room temperature.

3. Puree the apples with the plum sauce in a blender or food processor.

Parsley-Lime Hot Sauce

This piquant sauce is excellent for perking up a simple broiled chicken, roast pork or plain fish.

MAKES ABOUT 1 CUP

1 tablespoon unsalted butter
½ tablespoon minced lime zest
½ tablespoon all-purpose flour
1 cup heavy cream
½ cup packed parsley leaves
2 jalapeño peppers—roasted, peeled and deveined, and cut into strips
½ small onion, coarsely chopped
2 tablespoons fresh lime juice
¼ teaspoon salt

1. In a small saucepan, melt the butter over low heat. Add the lime zest and cook for about 30 seconds. Whisk in the flour and cook, stirring, for 3 to 4 minutes to make a roux. Gradually stir in the cream and bring the sauce to a boil. Cook, stirring, until smooth and slightly thickened, 1 to 2 minutes. Remove from the heat.

2. Coarsely puree the parsley, jalapeños, onion and lime juice in a food processor or blender. Gradually stir into the cream sauce, 1 tablespoon at a time. Add the salt and heat over low heat until the sauce is warm.

Sweet-and-Sour Grape and Raisin Sauce

Serve hot or warm over slices of ham.

MAKES ABOUT 2½ CUPS

½ cup seedless golden raisins
½ cup dry sherry
3 cups seedless green grapes
2 teaspoons Dijon-style mustard
3 tablespoons brown sugar
2 tablespoons sherry wine vinegar
½ cup unsweetened applesauce
1 teaspoon arrowroot
½ cup chicken broth

1. In a small saucepan, combine the raisins and sherry and bring to a boil over medium heat. Reduce the heat and simmer until the liquid has almost evaporated. Remove from the heat and set aside.

2. Place 2 cups of the grapes into the container of a food processor or blender and puree (the consistency will be rather watery).

3. Place the grape puree in a medium saucepan along with the mustard, brown sugar, vinegar and applesauce. Bring the mixture to a boil over moderate heat, stirring occasionally. Stir in the raisins.

4. Dissolve the arrowroot in the chicken broth; stir the mixture into the sauce. Cook over moderate heat, stirring constantly, until the sauce thickens, 2 to 3 minutes.

5. Peel the remaining grapes or simply cut them in half and add them to the sauce.

Sharp-and-Fragrant Ginger Sauce

This tangy sauce goes nicely with smoked ham or chicken.

MAKES ABOUT 1½ CUPS

¼ cup sliced scallions, including some of the green
¼ cup plus 2 tablespoons shredded fresh gingerroot
½ cup dry white wine
¾ cup rice vinegar
½ teaspoon salt
½ teaspoon sugar
White pepper
½ pound (2 sticks) unsalted butter, cut into small bits

1. In a medium saucepan, combine the scallions, ¼ cup of the ginger, the white wine, rice vinegar, salt and sugar. Bring the mixture to a boil over high heat.

Reduce the heat slightly and boil, stirring occasionally, until it is reduced to a thick pulp. Stir in white pepper to taste and the remaining 2 tablespoons ginger.

2. Place a sieve over the top of a double boiler. Using a wooden spoon, force the ginger mixture through the sieve into the pan; discard the solids. Scrape any puree on the outside of the sieve into the pan.

3. Place the mixture over simmering water (if more than an occasional bubble should rise from the bottom of the mixture, the temperature is too high). Using a wire whisk, beat in two or three pieces of the butter; when they have been thoroughly incorporated, beat in two or three additional pieces. (As the emulsion forms, the mixture will thicken and become homogenous.) Continue with this procedure until all the butter has been added. Serve warm. (This sauce can be kept warm in a double boiler over hot water, but it cannot be reheated.)

Mango Sauce

Delicious over ice cream, warm bread pudding or pancakes, this is an excellent way to use an overripe mango.

MAKES ABOUT 1 CUP

⅓ cup plus 1 tablespoon sugar
1 large ripe mango, peeled and pitted
1½ tablespoons fresh lemon juice

1. Place the sugar and ⅓ cup plus 1 tablespoon water in a small saucepan over medium high heat. Bring to a boil, stirring until the sugar is dissolved; boil for about 1 minute. Remove from the heat and let cool completely.

2. Place the mango in a food processor and puree until very smooth (see Note).

3. Add the cooled sugar syrup and lemon juice and process just to mix. Store in a covered jar in the refrigerator for up to 3 or 4 days.

NOTE: Overripe mangoes occasionally become fibrous. If this seems to be true of yours, press through a fine mesh sieve after pureeing it in the food processor.

Sour Lemon Sauce

MAKES ABOUT 1½ CUPS

6 tablespoons fresh lemon juice
1½ teaspoons grated lemon zest
1 cup sugar
½ cup (1 stick) unsalted butter, cut into tablespoons
2 eggs

1. In the top of a double boiler, combine the lemon juice, lemon zest, sugar and butter. Cook over barely simmering water, stirring occasionally, until the butter is melted and the sugar is dissolved, about 10 minutes.

2. In a small bowl, whisk the eggs together until blended. Stir in about 2 tablespoonfuls of the warm lemon mixture. Strain the eggs into the remaining lemon mixture and stir over simmering water until smooth and slightly thickened, about 10 minutes. Serve warm.

Custard Sauce

MAKES ABOUT 1 CUP

1 whole egg
2 egg yolks
2 tablespoons sugar
1 cup milk
½ teaspoon vanilla extract

1. In a small bowl, beat together the whole egg, egg yolks and 1 tablespoon of the sugar until well blended.

2. In the top of a double boiler, bring the milk to a boil with the remaining 1 tablespoon sugar. Remove from the heat and stir about 2 tablespoons of the hot milk into the egg mixture. Gradually stir the egg mixture into the remaining milk and cook over boiling water, stirring constantly with a wooden spoon, until the custard thickens enough to lightly coat the back of the spoon. Immediately transfer the saucepan to a bowl of ice water to stop the cooking. Stir in the vanilla. Serve warm.

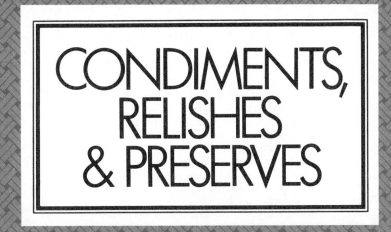

CONDIMENTS,
RELISHES
& PRESERVES

Celery Salt

To make this fresh-tasting homemade seasoning, whole celery seeds are crushed to release their flavor and then combined with salt. Sprinkle it on meats or poultry before roasting, or use it to flavor soups, casseroles or breads.

MAKES ABOUT 2 TABLESPOONS

1 teaspoon celery seeds
2 tablespoons coarse (kosher) salt

1. Place the celery seeds in a mortar or spice grinder and pulverize. Transfer to a bowl and work in the salt with a pestle or the back of a wooden spoon.

2. Place the celery salt in a small, covered jar and store with your spices and herbs.

Onion Jam

This is a lovely tart accompaniment to pâtés or simply roasted poultry and meats.

MAKES 1½ TO 2 CUPS

3 medium onions (about 1 pound)
2 cups dry red wine
⅓ cup red wine vinegar
1 teaspoon sugar
1 tablespoon grenadine syrup

Cut the onions in half lengthwise and then cut them into thin half-rounds. In a small saucepan, combine them with the red wine, vinegar, sugar and grenadine. Bring the mixture to a boil over moderate heat. Reduce the heat to low and simmer, stirring occasionally, until the liquid has almost evaporated, about 1 hour.

Pickled Onions

MAKES 2 TO 2½ CUPS

1 pound pearl onions, peeled and
**   trimmed (about 4 cups)**
4 tablespoons coarse (kosher) salt
1 cup dry vermouth
½ cup distilled white vinegar

1. Bring a large pot of water to boil, add the onions and 1 tablespoon of the salt. When the boiling resumes, cook for 3

minutes. Drain and transfer to a large bowl; add 1 cup cold water and the remaining salt, stirring until the salt is dissolved. Let rest, covered, overnight.

2. Drain and rinse under cold water. Add the vermouth and vinegar and let rest, covered, overnight.

Pickled Brussels Sprouts

MAKES ABOUT 3 CUPS

1 carton (10 ounces) Brussels
**   sprouts, trimmed and halved**
**   (about 2½ cups)**
3 tablespoons plus 1 teaspoon salt
½ cup olive oil
⅓ cup lemon juice
2 large garlic cloves, sliced
1 tablespoon chopped fresh thyme
**   or 1 teaspoon dried**
2 large bay leaves
½ teaspoon instant coffee dissolved
**   in 1 tablespoon water**

1. In a large bowl, combine the Brussels sprouts with 3 tablespoons of the salt and 1 tablespoon of water. Cover and let rest overnight.

2. Drain and rinse the Brussels sprouts. Blanch them in a pan of rapidly boiling water for 2 minutes. Drain and transfer to a bowl or jar.

3. In a small noncorrodible saucepan, bring the remaining ingredients to a boil over high heat. Remove from the heat, pour the hot liquid over the Brussels sprouts and let cool, uncovered, to room temperature.

4. Strain the liquid into a small noncorrodible saucepan and bring to a boil over high heat. Pour the liquid over the Brussels sprouts, cool to room temperature, cover and let rest overnight.

Marinated Mushrooms

MAKES ABOUT 1 QUART

2 pounds mushrooms, quartered
¼ cup lemon juice
2 cups distilled white vinegar
1 cup olive oil
1 tablespoon salt
½ teaspoon pepper
3 garlic cloves, lightly crushed
2 teaspoons dried oregano or 2
**   tablespoons chopped fresh**
2 teaspoons dried basil or 2
**   tablespoons chopped fresh**

1. Place the mushrooms in a bowl and cover with water; add the lemon juice.

2. In a medium noncorrodible saucepan, bring the remaining ingredients to a boil; remove from heat.

3. Drain the mushrooms, discarding the liquid, return them to the bowl and pour the hot marinade over. Cool to room temperature, cover and let rest 8 hours or overnight, tossing occasionally.

Kim Chee

MAKES ABOUT 1 QUART

½ small head of cabbage (about ½
**   pound)**
2 large ribs of celery, sliced ¼ inch
**   thick on the bias (about 1 cup)**
1 large carrot, peeled and cut into
**   paper-thin rounds (about 1 cup)**
1 tablespoon coarse (kosher) salt
5 tablespoons soy sauce
3 tablespoons sugar
4 garlic cloves, thinly sliced
3 to 4 small, dried, hot chiles, split
1 tablespoon distilled white vinegar

1. Cut the cabbage in half through the core and then into 1-inch cubes, core included. In a large bowl, toss the cabbage, celery and carrot with the salt, 1 tablespoon of the soy sauce and ½ cup of water. Cover and let stand overnight, tossing occasionally.

2. Drain the vegetables (do not rinse) and return to the bowl. Combine the remaining soy sauce with the sugar, stirring to partially dissolve the sugar. Add to the vegetables along with the garlic, chiles, vinegar and 1 cup water. Toss and transfer to a quart jar or similar container, submerge by weighting with a heavy glass jar or saucer and let stand for 48 hours.

Three-Pepper Relish

MAKES 3 PINTS

3 cups finely chopped red bell peppers (about 3 pounds)
2 cups finely chopped green bell peppers (about 2 pounds)
1 cup finely chopped Italian frying peppers (about 1 pound)
1½ cups finely chopped onions (about 2 large)
1½ cups finely chopped celery (about 3 ribs)
1 cup granulated sugar
⅓ cup firmly packed light brown sugar
1 cup cider vinegar
1½ tablespoons mustard seed
2 teaspoons coarse (kosher) salt

1. In a large mixing bowl, combine the red and green bell peppers, the Italian frying peppers, the onions and the celery. Pour enough boiling water over the vegetables to barely cover them; let stand for 5 minutes.

2. Drain the vegetables and transfer to a large saucepan. Stir in the granulated sugar, brown sugar, vinegar, mustard seed and salt, stirring to mix well. Bring to a boil over high heat. Reduce the heat to moderately high and cook, uncovered, until the vegetables are tender but still slightly crunchy, about 5 minutes.

3. Using a slotted spoon, divide the relish among 3 hot pint canning jars. Fill each jar with enough of the cooking liquid (about ½ cup) to come to within ¼ inch of the rim. Cover with lids, and tighten the screw bands to seal.

4. Lower the jars onto a rack in a large pot of boiling water or into a water-bath canner; the tops should be covered by 1 to 2 inches of water. Return to the boil and process for 15 minutes. Store on a cool, dark shelf for 2 weeks before using.

Pickled Red Cabbage

This pickled cabbage is best when eaten within two months after preserving.

MAKES 6 PINTS

1 quart distilled white vinegar
1½ cups sugar
1 tablespoon salt
2 bay leaves
½ teaspoon whole black peppercorns
½ teaspoon whole cloves
2 large heads of red cabbage (about 3½ pounds each), finely shredded

1. Place the vinegar, sugar and salt into a large, noncorrodible saucepan with 1 quart of water. Tie the bay leaves, peppercorns and cloves in a double thickness of cheesecloth and add to the pot. Bring to a boil over high heat, reduce the heat and simmer for 15 minutes.

2. Add half the cabbage and cook until just tender, about 2 minutes. Remove from the heat. Using a slotted spoon or tongs, remove the cabbage from the cooking liquid and tightly pack it into three hot pint canning jars. Fill each jar with about ½ cup of the cooking liquid to reach ¼ inch from the rim. Cover with lids and tighten the screw bands to seal.

3. Return the remaining liquid to a boil and repeat the cooking and filling with the remaining cabbage.

4. Lower the jars onto a rack in a large pot of boiling water or into a water-bath canner; the tops should be covered by 1 to 2 inches of water. Return to a boil and process the jars for 15 minutes. Store on a cool, dark shelf for 1 week before serving.

Mixed Pickled Vegetables

MAKES 4 PINTS

1 quart distilled white vinegar
1½ cups sugar
1 tablespoon salt
1 blade of mace
1 bay leaf
½ pound carrots—quartered lengthwise and cut into 4-inch lengths
1 small head of cauliflower, cut into 1-inch florets
½ pound green beans
1 medium red onion, cut into ¼-inch rings
4 small, dried hot red peppers (optional)
1 teaspoon oregano

1. In a noncorrodible saucepan, heat the vinegar, sugar, salt, mace, bay leaf and ½ cup of water to boiling. Reduce the heat and simmer for 15 minutes.

2. Meanwhile, cook the carrots in a medium saucepan of boiling water until crisp-tender, about 5 minutes; remove with a slotted spoon and drain. Add the cauliflower to the water and boil until crisp-tender, about 4 minutes, remove and drain. Boil the green beans until crisp-tender, about 4 minutes and drain. All the vegetables should remain crunchy.

3. Dividing the vegetables evenly, pack them into 4 hot pint canning jars, interspersing the cooked vegetables with onion rings. Add a dried hot pepper to each jar, if desired, and ¼ teaspoon of oregano.

4. Strain the hot vinegar to remove the herbs and return it to a boil. Pour the boiling vinegar over the vegetables in the jars to ¼ inch of the rim. Cover with lids and tighten the screw bands to seal. Lower the jars onto a rack in a large pot of boiling water or into a water-bath canner; the tops should be covered by 1 to 2 inches of water. Return to a boil and process the jars for 15 minutes. Store on a cool, dark shelf.

Curried Corn Relish

MAKES 4 PINTS

2 cups finely chopped cabbage (8 ounces)

2 green bell peppers, seeded and finely chopped (1½ cups)

2 red bell peppers, seeded and finely chopped (1½ cups)

1 medium onion, finely chopped (1 cup)

2 celery ribs, finely chopped (1 cup)

⅓ cup sugar

2 tablespoons curry powder

2 teaspoons dry mustard

1 tablespoon salt

½ teaspoon white pepper

1½ cups cider vinegar

6 cups tender young corn kernels, fresh or frozen

1. Place all of the ingredients, except the corn, into a large saucepan. Add ½ cup of water. Bring to a boil, cover and cook over moderate heat for 10 minutes. Stir in the corn kernels. Return to a boil, cover and cook for 5 minutes longer.

2. Pack the relish tightly into 4 hot pint jars to within ¼ inch of the rim. Cover with lids and tighten the screw bands to seal. Lower the jars onto a rack in a large pot of boiling water or into a water-bath canner; the tops should be covered by 1 to 2 inches of water. Return to a boil and process the jars for 15 minutes. Store on a cool, dark shelf.

Pear-and-Walnut Relish

MAKES ABOUT 1 QUART

¾ cup chopped walnuts (about 3 ounces)

3 pounds Bartlett pears (about 6 large)—peeled, cored and cut into 1-inch cubes

2 celery ribs, halved lengthwise and cut crosswise into thin slices

Zest of ½ medium orange, cut into 1-by-⅛-inch julienne strips (about 1½ tablespoons)

⅓ cup sugar

2 tablespoons cider vinegar

½ teaspoon cinnamon

¼ teaspoon mace

¼ teaspoon allspice

1. Toast the walnuts in a small, ungreased skillet over moderate heat, stirring several times, until they are golden brown and crispy, about 5 minutes.

2. In a large saucepan, combine the pears, celery, orange zest, sugar, vinegar, cinnamon, mace and allspice. Add ½ cup of water and bring to a boil over moderately high heat. Boil, stirring gently several times, until the relish thickens, about 15 minutes.

3. Remove from the heat and stir in the nuts. Let cool to room temperature, cover and refrigerate until chilled.

Mango Chutney

MAKES 5 PINTS

6 large, firm ripe mangoes, peeled and sliced into 2½-by-½-inch strips

1 large yellow onion, thinly sliced

1 large red onion, thinly sliced

2 green and 2 red bell peppers, thinly sliced

3 small or 2 large, fresh, hot green chiles, sliced into thin rounds

¼ cup pickled hot cherry peppers, caps and stems removed, sliced into thin rounds

1 cup brown sugar

¾ cup honey

2 teaspoons grated orange zest

¾ cup fresh grapefruit juice

¾ cup cider vinegar

½ cup currants

½ cup golden raisins

1 teaspoon ground ginger or 1½ ounces peeled fresh gingerroot, finely shredded

1 teaspoon ground coriander

1 teaspoon mustard seed

¼ teaspoon ground nutmeg

1. In a large saucepan, combine all the ingredients, tossing well to distribute the spices. Bring to a boil over moderately high heat. Reduce the heat to moderately low and simmer for 20 to 25 minutes, until the liquid thickens to the consistency of a light sugar syrup; remove from the heat.

2. Carefully ladle the hot chutney into 5 hot pint canning jars to within ¼ inch of the rims. Cover with lids and tighten the screw bands to seal. Lower the jars onto a rack in a large pot of boiling water or into a water-bath canner; the tops should be covered by 1 to 2 inches of water. Return to a boil and process the jars for 15 minutes. Store on a cool, dark shelf.

Cranberry Chutney

MAKES ABOUT 2 CUPS

2 cups (8 ounces) fresh or frozen cranberries

½ cup granulated sugar

¼ cup (packed) light brown sugar

1 cinnamon stick

4 whole cloves

2 allspice berries

¼ cup raisins

1 small onion, chopped

¼ cup chopped celery

½ cup chopped unpeeled tart apple

1. In a medium saucepan, combine the cranberries, granulated sugar, brown sugar and ½ cup of water. Tie the cinnamon, cloves and allspice in cheesecloth and add to the pan. Bring to a boil over moderate heat, stirring to dissolve the sugar. Lower the heat and simmer, partially covered, until the cranberries begin to burst, about 10 minutes.

2. Stir in the raisins, onion, celery and apple. Simmer the chutney, uncovered, until the mixture thickens, about 20 minutes.

3. Remove from the heat and let cool to room temperature; discard the spice bag. Refrigerate the chutney, covered, for at least 24 hours before serving, or up to 2 weeks.

Strawberry Jam

MAKES 4 PINTS

2 quarts strawberries
¼ cup fresh lemon juice
7 cups sugar
1 pouch (3 ounces) liquid pectin

1. Rinse the strawberries in a bowl of cold water, drain well and dry them on paper towels. Remove the hulls.

2. Place the berries in a preserving pan or large saucepan and crush them with a potato masher or wooden spoon to release the juices. Add the lemon juice and sugar. Place over low heat, stirring occasionally, to allow the sugar to dissolve; this will take about 10 minutes.

3. Increase the heat to moderate and bring to a boil. Boil for 1 minute, stirring.

4. Remove from the heat and stir in the pectin all at once. Skim off the foam.

5. Immediately ladle into 8 clean, dry, hot half-pint jars to within ¼ inch of the top. Wipe the rims with a clean, damp cloth. Place lids on the jars and tighten the screw bands. Process in a boiling water bath for 15 minutes.

Peach and Raspberry Jam

MAKES 3 PINTS

7 large unblemished peaches—
   peeled, pitted and chopped
   (about 6 cups)
2 tablespoons fresh lemon juice
5 cups sugar
1 pint raspberries, rinsed and
   drained

1. Place the peaches, lemon juice and sugar into a heavy saucepan.

2. Slowly bring to a boil over low heat, stirring occasionally, until the sugar dissolves, 10 to 15 minutes.

3. Increase the heat to moderate and boil, stirring occasionally, for 20 minutes. Remove from the heat and add the raspberries. Return to the heat and boil, stirring, for 5 minutes. Skim off any foam.

4. Remove from the heat and test for thickness by dabbing about ½ teaspoon of the jam onto a chilled saucer and

placing it in the freezer for 3 minutes. Push the jam gently with your finger. If the surface wrinkles, the jam is ready for processing. If it does not, the jam is too thin: Return to the heat and boil for another 5 minutes, then retest.

5. When the jam is properly thickened, ladle into 6 clean, dry, hot half-pint jars to fill them within ¼ inch of the top. Wipe the rims with a clean, damp cloth. Place lids on the jars and tighten the screw bands. Process in a boiling water bath for 15 minutes.

Apple Cider Jelly

This is one of those recipes that's too easy to be true. By simply boiling down a gallon of apple cider, you're left with a naturally sweet, syrupy jelly. Absolutely nothing else is added; the natural sugars and pectin in the apples do all the work. Serve on top of toast, muffins or ice cream, with pancakes and waffles, or as a condiment with roast pork.

MAKES 2 CUPS

1 gallon unsweetened apple cider
   with no additives

In a large heavy pot, bring the apple cider to a boil over high heat. Reduce the heat to moderate and cook the cider at a low, rolling boil until it is reduced to 2 cups, about 2 hours. Pour the hot jelly into a clean, hot canning jar, close the lid and cool to room temperature. Refrigerate overnight before serving. Store in the refrigerator; the jelly will keep for months.

Homemade Golden Syrup

MAKES ABOUT ⅓ CUP

¼ cup sugar
½ teaspoon vinegar (distilled white,
   cider or white-wine)
⅓ cup light corn syrup

1. Place the sugar in a small heavy saucepan. Shake gently to form an even layer. Add the vinegar and 1 tablespoon of water. Cook, without stirring, over low heat for 5 minutes.

2. Increase the heat to moderate and cook for 5 minutes longer, or until the syrup has caramelized to a golden liquid. Immediately remove from the heat and pour in the corn syrup. The mixture will bubble up but do not stir. When all the bubbles have subsided, after 2 or 3 minutes, stir with a wooden spoon for a minute or so, until the caramel and corn syrup are thoroughly mixed.

3. Let cool to room temperature before using. If made ahead, store in a covered jar at room temperature.

Brandied Peaches

MAKES 4 PINTS

2 pounds sugar (4¼ cups)
2 tablespoons distilled white
   vinegar
2 tablespoons salt
4½ pounds small, unblemished
   ripe peaches, preferably
   freestone
1⅓ cups brandy

1. In a large noncorrodible saucepan or Dutch oven, combine the sugar with 3 cups of water. Bring to a simmer over moderate heat, stirring to dissolve the sugar. Continue to simmer the syrup for 2 minutes. Remove from the heat and set aside.

2. Fill a large bowl two-thirds full with cold water. Add the vinegar and salt.

3. Bring a large pot of water to a boil. Add the peaches and cook for 30 seconds to 1 minute, depending on the ripeness of the fruit. Drain into a colander and rinse under cold running water. Working with one peach at a time, slip off the skin, quarter the peach and discard the pit. As each peach is cut, drop it into the salted water to prevent discoloration.

4. Return the syrup to a simmer over moderate heat. Rinse the peaches under cold running water and add them to the syrup. Poach for 6 minutes. Remove with a slotted spoon and pack into 4 clean, dry, hot pint jars.

5. Boil the syrup over moderate heat for about 10 minutes, until it is reduced to 2½ cups. Pour ⅓ cup brandy into each jar. Ladle in enough of the syrup to fill the jars to within ½ inch of the top.

6. Tap the jars gently on the counter to release any air bubbles. Wipe the rims with a clean, damp cloth. Place lids on the jars and tighten the screw bands. Process in a boiling water bath for 10 minutes.

Hot Fruit Mustard

A tangy sauce that goes particularly well with pork, cold ham and other smoked meats.

<u>MAKES ABOUT 1 CUP</u>

2 tablespoons dry mustard
1 tablespoon white wine vinegar
1 cup marmalade, preferably three-fruit

Place the mustard and vinegar in a small bowl and mix to a smooth paste. Cover and let stand for 10 minutes. Stir in the marmalade.

Sweet Horseradish Mustard

Use as a condiment or as a base for other sauces and glazes.

<u>MAKES ABOUT 1⅓ CUPS</u>

½ cup yellow mustard seed
1 cup dry white wine
½ cup white wine vinegar
1 tablespoon drained prepared white horseradish
1½ teaspoons honey
½ teaspoon salt

1. In a small bowl, place the mustard seed, wine and vinegar. Cover and let soak at room temperature overnight.

2. Mix in a blender or food processor until creamy but still somewhat grainy, about 2 minutes.

3. Pour into a serving bowl and stir in the horseradish, honey and salt.

Quick Ketchup

This slightly spicy ketchup may become an instant staple in your kitchen. It is made in the blender without salt or sugar. If tightly covered and refrigerated, it will keep for months.

<u>MAKES ABOUT 1 CUP</u>

1 medium onion, chopped (about 1 cup)
½ garlic clove
5 tablespoons frozen apple juice concentrate
1 can (6 ounces) tomato paste
½ cup malt vinegar
½ teaspoon cayenne pepper
¼ teaspoon cinnamon
⅛ teaspoon ground cloves

Place the onion, garlic and apple juice in a blender and puree until smooth. Add the tomato paste, vinegar, cayenne, cinnamon and cloves and blend until smooth. Keep in an airtight bottle or jar and refrigerate.

Raspberry Vinegar

<u>MAKES 1 CUP</u>

1 cup white wine vinegar
1 cup fresh raspberries

1. Place the raspberries in a 3-cup glass or ceramic container and pour the vinegar over them. Cover the container and let it sit undisturbed at room temperature for 5 days, until the color and flavor have been extracted from the berries.

2. Strain the vinegar through a fine sieve; discard the raspberries. Pour the vinegar into a glass bottle, cover tightly and store in a cool, dry place.

Low-Sodium Mustard

If you read the label on a jar of prepared mustard, domestic or imported, you will notice that it is loaded with salt. This recipe combines mustard seeds with powdered mustard, herbs and other flavorings. The initial preparation must rest overnight, so plan accordingly.

<u>MAKES ABOUT ⅔ CUP</u>
(1.3 mg sodium per tablespoon)

3 tablespoons yellow mustard seeds
About 2 tablespoons powdered mustard
1½ teaspoons turmeric
1 teaspoon tarragon
¼ teaspoon cinnamon
¼ cup plus 2 teaspoons distilled white vinegar
¼ cup dry white wine
2 tablespoons sugar
2 tablespoons olive oil or other vegetable oil
1 garlic clove, minced

1. In a small, heavy, noncorrodible saucepan, combine the mustard seeds, 2 tablespoons of powdered mustard, the turmeric, tarragon and cinnamon; add ⅔ cup of water and stir to dissolve the mustard. Bring to a boil over high heat, stirring constantly. Remove from the heat, cover and let stand at room temperature for 8 hours or overnight.

2. Add ¼ cup of the vinegar, the wine, sugar, oil and garlic. Bring to a boil over high heat; reduce the heat to low and simmer, stirring frequently, for 5 minutes.

3. Puree the mustard in a food processor or blender, stopping occasionally to scrape down the sides. Transfer to a small bowl and let cool to room temperature. Stir in the remaining 2 teaspoons vinegar and taste the mustard. If you would like it a little hotter, stir in up to 1 additional teaspoon powdered mustard. Cover and refrigerate for as long as 2 weeks.

DIET MENUS

Low-Calorie Menu

Sweet Corn and Crab Meat Soup *(p. 31)*

Servings	9
Calories	73

Diet adaptation: Omit the sugar and reduce the cornstarch to 1 tablespoon. Allow ½ cup per serving.

Avocado Frittata *(p. 113)*

Servings	3
Calories	232

Diet adaptation: Use ¼ avocado and cut it into ½-inch chunks. substitute Neufchâtel cheese for the goat cheese.

Spaghetti Squash Provençal

Servings	8
Calories	52

Pierce a 2½-pound spaghetti squash all over with a fork. Cook it in boiling water, covered, until the sides start to give when pressed firmly, about 40 minutes. Halve the squash and scoop the "spaghetti" into a serving dish. Sauté a minced garlic clove, ¼ teaspoon basil, ¼ teaspoon thyme and ⅛ teaspoon oregano in 1½ teaspoons olive oil and 1½ teaspoons butter for 1 minute. Toss with the squash and season to taste with salt and pepper.

Poached Pears with Apricot Brandy

Servings	2
Calories	68

Place 1 peeled, halved and cored pear in a medium saucepan with 1 cup of water. Sprinkle each pear half with 1 teaspoon lemon juice; cover and bring to a boil. Reduce the heat to moderately high and cook for 10 minutes. Transfer the pear halves to dessert dishes and top each with 1½ teaspoons apricot brandy and the syrup remaining in the saucepan. Serve chilled or at room temperature.

Low-Calorie Menu

Steamed Mussels *(p. 21)* and Green Herb Sauce with Champagne *(p. 207)*

Servings	6
Calories	253

Diet adaptation: Prepare the mussels as directed. For the sauce, reduce the cream to ⅓ cup and the champagne to ¾ cup. Reduce the mayonnaise to ⅓ cup and use only spinach and watercress.

Green Beans with Beef Sauce

Servings	6
Calories	103

Diet adaptation: (Based on Stir-Fried Green Beans with Beef Sauce, p. 113). Steam the green beans instead of frying them, and use only 1 teaspoon of peanut oil in Step 3.

Coffee Anisette

Servings	6
Calories	97

Prepare 6 cups (4 ounces each) espresso coffee. Add 3 ounces (½ ounce per cup) anisette liqueur.

Low-Calorie Menu

Shredded Chicken Salad with Ginger and Sesame *(p. 156)*

Servings	6
Calories	220

Sesame Noodle Salad *(p. 160)*

Servings	8
Calories	139

Diet adaptation: Reduce the sesame oil to 2 tablespoons and the soy sauce to 1½ tablespoons.

Mango Sorbet

Servings	1
Calories	65

Scoop ⅓ cup of mango ice or sorbet (available at specialty food shops and some grocery stores) into a shallow dessert dish. Garnish with a lemon and/or lime slice.

Low-Calorie Menu

Summer Vegetable Salad *(p. 156)*

Servings	4
Calories	216

Diet adaptation: Omit the walnut oil and decrease the olive oil to 2 tablespoons.

Lemon-Parsley Biscuits *(p. 196)*

Servings	18
Calories	94

Diet adaptation: Prepare 3 dozen biscuits and allow 2 per serving.

Strawberries in Vermouth

Servings	4
Calories	41

Wash, hull and halve 2 cups of fresh strawberries. Toss the berries with ¼ cup sweet vermouth and chill. Serve in dessert dishes garnished with fresh mint and lemon zest.

Low-Calorie Menu

Salmon and Sorrel Soufflé *(p. 104)*

Servings	9
Calories	250

Diet adaptation: Omit the Maltaise sauce.

Herbed Carrots and Green Beans *(p. 116)*

Servings	6
Calories	71

Diet adaptation: Reduce the butter to 1 tablespoon and use a nonstick skillet.

Crêpes Pernod *(p. 195)*

Servings	20
Calories	39

Diet adaptation: Use skim milk. Omit the butter and add 2 extra tablespoons of club soda. Using a nonstick skillet, prepare 20 crêpes with 1½ tablespoons of batter per crêpe. Allow 1 crêpe per serving.

Fresh Fruit with Raspberry Sauce

Servings	8
Calories	59

Diet adaptation: (Based On Fruit Loaf with Raspberry Sauce, p. 187.) Prepare the Raspberry Sauce without the sugar. Combine the fruit listed for the loaf and divide it among 8 dessert dishes. Serve topped with the sauce.

Low-Calorie Menu

Veal Scallops with Basil (p. 47)

Servings	6
Calories	183

Diet adaptation: Add the shallots to the wine in Step 1; omit the cream and the sauce. Decrease the butter to 1 tablespoon and cook the scallops in a nonstick skillet. Serve the scallops garnished with the slivered basil.

Stuffed Mushrooms Véronique (p. 25)

Servings	9
Calories	60

Diet adaptation: Omit the butter. Decrease the Parmesan to 3 tablespoons and sprinkle it over the stuffed mushrooms before baking.

Broccoli with Pine Nuts and Raisins (p. 115)

Servings	6
Calories	73

Diet adaptation: Decrease the oil to 1 tablespoon and use a nonstick skillet. Reduce the pine nuts and raisins to 2 tablespoons each and omit the tomatoes.

Orange Popovers (p. 197)

Servings	8
Calories	115

Diet adaptation: Use skim milk. Dust the muffin cups lightly with granulated sugar before pouring in the batter.

Low-Calorie Menu

Watercress-Pork Soup (p. 42)

Servings	6
Calories	80

Diet adaptation: Substitute ½ pound chicken breast for the pork butt.

Braised Turkey Breast with Cider Sauce (p. 88)

Servings	20
Calories	250

Diet adaptation: Reduce the butter to 2 tablespoons. Omit the sauce. Instead, degrease and reduce the reserved broth; serve over the turkey slices.

Brussels Sprouts

Servings	5
Calories	38

Clean and steam 1 pound Brussels sprouts until tender. Garnish with basil or caraway seeds, if desired.

Pear-and-Walnut Relish (p. 216)

Servings	20
Calories	80

Honey Broiled Grapefruit

Servings	6
Calories	59

Halve 3 grapefruits, drizzle each half with ½ teaspoon honey. Broil 5 to 6 minutes, until golden.

Low-Calorie Menu

Marinated Mushrooms (p. 214)

Servings	8
Calories	75

Diet adaptation: Substitute 7 ounces defatted chicken broth and 2 tablespoons olive oil for the 1 cup olive oil.

Red Snapper Provençal (p. 98)

Servings	6
Calories	189

Diet adaptation: Reduce the olive oil to 1 tablespoon. Increase the court bouillon to ⅞ cup.

Bibb Lettuce with Herbs

Servings	2
Calories	14

Clean 1 head of Bibb lettuce and arrange the leaves on a plate. Sprinkle with ½ teaspoon basil, ½ teaspoon rosemary, 1 tablespoon lemon juice and freshly ground black pepper to taste.

Fresh Blueberries

Servings	4
Calories	45

Wash 2 cups of blueberries and allow ½ cup per serving.

Low-Calorie Menu

Potatoes with Three American Caviars (p. 24)

Servings	6
Calories	104

Diet adaptation: Substitute low-fat yogurt for the sour cream. Reduce the butter to 1 tablespoon and use a nonstick skillet. Use 1 ounce each of the caviars.

Panfried Tournedos (p. 68)

Servings	4
Calories	128

Diet adaptation: Omit the butter, reduce the olive oil to 1 teaspoon and use a nonstick skillet.

Glazed Carrots with Pearl Onions (p. 116)

Servings	6
Calories	97

Diet adaptation: Reduce the butter to 1 tablespoon and use a nonstick skillet. Decrease the sugar to 1 teaspoon.

Creamy Four-Fruit Sherbet (p. 190)

Servings	11
Calories	101

Diet adaptation: Substitute low-fat yogurt for the sour cream. Allow ½ cup per serving.

Low-Sodium Menu

Braised Mushrooms with Pine Nuts

Servings	4
Sodium	31 mg
Calories	273

Diet adaptation: (Based on Braised Mushrooms with Pancetta and Pine Nuts, p. 118). Omit the *pancetta* and added salt.

Shrimp-Garlic Risotto (p. 144)

Servings	4
Sodium	179 mg
Calories	542

Diet adaptation: Substitute low-sodium chicken broth for the clam juice and omit the added salt.

Peppers with Balsamic Vinegar and Fresh Herbs (p. 121)

Servings	8
Sodium	17 mg
Calories	92

Diet adaptation: Omit the added salt.

Iced Zabaglione

Servings	5
Sodium	54 mg
Calories	115

Over boiling water, whisk 4 egg yolks, ¼ cup Marsala, 2 tablespoons honey and ¼ teaspoon powdered ginger until at least doubled in bulk and thickened, about 5 minutes. In a separate bowl, beat 4 egg whites until stiff, and fold the yolk mixture into them. Spoon into 5 dessert dishes and freeze for 4 hours. Garnish with finely grated semisweet chocolate before serving.

Low-Sodium Menu

Gingered Honeydew

Servings	8
Sodium	14 mg
Calories	91

Slice a medium honeydew melon into 8 wedges and place on dessert plates. Drizzle each wedge with a teaspoon of syrup from preserved ginger (available at specialty food shops) and a teaspoon of lime juice. Garnish with lemon slices and parsley.

Papaya Golden Sole (p. 103)

Servings	4
Sodium	104 mg
Calories	496

Diet adaptation: Omit the salt.

Coriander Rice

Servings	4
Sodium	6 mg
Calories	209

Place 1 cup long-grain white rice and 1½ cups water in a medium saucepan. Bring to a boil over high heat; cover, reduce the heat to low and simmer until the rice is tender, about 20 minutes. Toss the rice with 1 tablespoon unsalted butter and 2 tablespoons chopped fresh coriander.

Three-Green Salad with Pears (p. 151)

Servings	6
Sodium	76 mg
Calories	275

Diet adaptation: Omit the salt.

Golden Delicious Apple Tart (p. 167)

Servings	6
Sodium	5 mg
Calories	408

Diet adaptation: Omit the salt.

Low-Sodium Menu

Pumpkin Seed Dip (p. 19)

Servings	6
Sodium	9 mg
Calories	299

Diet adaptation: Omit the salt. Use low-sodium chicken broth. Also add 2 tablespoons fresh chopped parsley. Serve with 1 medium yellow squash and zucchini, sliced into 3-by-¼-inch sticks, for dipping.

Fish Fillets with Rosemary (p. 102)

Servings	4
Sodium	192 mg
Calories	389

Diet adaptation: Omit the salt. Use low-sodium bread to make the bread crumbs. Use fresh parsley.

Carefree Potatoes (p. 121)

Servings	6
Sodium	5 mg
Calories	153

Pears Baked with Wine (p. 190)

Servings	4
Sodium	8 mg
Calories	160

Low-Sodium Menu

Honeydew and Green Grape Salad with Lime Vinaigrette (p. 151)

Servings	4
Sodium	24 mg
Calories	160

Diet adaptation: Omit the salt.

Gingered Veal with Three Mushrooms (p. 46)

Servings	6
Sodium	307 mg
Calories	664

Diet adaptation: Omit the salt and use low-sodium chicken broth.

Spinach Noodles

Servings	4
Sodium	11 mg
Calories	250

Add 10 ounces dried spinach noodles to 2 quarts boiling water. Cover and cook over moderate heat for 5 minutes. Drain and serve.

Filbert Torte (p. 183)

Servings	14
Sodium	54 mg
Calories	833

Diet adaptation: Use up to 1 tablespoon unsalted butter for the tube pan. Omit the salt.

Low-Sodium Menu

Vegetable Pâté (p. 126)

Servings	12
Sodium	68 mg
Calories	209

Diet adaptation: Use a salt substitute and unsalted butter. Substitute low-sodium mozzarella or Gouda for the Gruyère.

Lobster Custard (p. 110)

Servings	6
Sodium	121 mg
Calories	386

Diet adaptation: Omit the sherry in the sauce and substitute wine for sherry in the custard. Use diet-pack tomato paste, unsalted butter and low-sodium chicken broth.

Wild Rice

Servings	6
Sodium	3 mg
Calories	149

Allowing for ½ cup per serving, prepare the rice according to package instructions, but omit the salt.

Bananas with Orange Liqueur

Servings	4
Sodium	2 mg
Calories	132

Slice 4 small bananas into dessert dishes. Splash each serving with 1 tablespoon of orange liqueur.

Low-Sodium Menu

Triangles with Two-Mushroom Filling (p. 25)

Servings	21
Sodium	123 mg
Calories	96

Diet adaptation: Omit the salt. Prepare 64 small triangles and allow 3 per serving.

London Broil Marinated in Lemon and Pepper (p. 66)

Servings	5
Sodium	90 mg
Calories	370

Diet adaptation: Use a salt substitute.

Crispy Onion Rings (p. 119)

Servings	6
Sodium	6 mg
Calories	281

Diet adaptation: Use a salt substitute. Substitute 3 teaspoons low-sodium baking powder for the baking soda.

Broiled Tomatoes (p. 124)

Servings	4
Sodium	5 mg
Calories	132

Diet adaptation: Omit the bread crumbs. Omit the salt or use a salt substitute.

Apricot Almond Crêpes (p. 167)

Servings	4
Sodium	147 mg
Calories	692

Low-Sodium Menu

Soup Provençale with Poached Eggs (p. 37)

Servings	2
Sodium	54 mg
Calories	454

Diet adaptation: Substitute 2¼ pounds of fresh tomatoes for the canned. Omit the salt.

Fresh Boiled Lobster

Servings	2
Sodium	181 mg
Calories	378

Rinse two ¾-pound lobsters under cold water. Plunge the lobsters head first into a stockpot of boiling water. Bring the water back to a boil and cook for 5 minutes. Serve with the claws cracked and accompany with a sauce of ¼ cup clarified unsalted butter and 1 tablespoon lemon juice.

Spinach Rice (p. 147)

Servings	4
Sodium	123 mg
Calories	365

Diet adaptation: Use low-sodium milk. Omit the salt.

Grand Marnier Crème Caramel (p. 186)

Servings	10
Sodium	46 mg
Calories	382

Diet adaptation: Use low-sodium milk.

Low-Sodium Menu

Curried Turkey Salad with Grapes and Almonds (p. 158)

Servings	8
Sodium	88 mg
Calories	1026

Diet adaptation: Omit the salt. Use mayonnaise that is prepared without salt and that does not contain egg whites. Use a homemade unsalted chutney or substitute 2 tablespoons apricot preserves mixed with 2 teaspoons white vinegar for the chutney. Reduce the lemon juice to 1 tablespoon. Omit the watercress; serve the salad on individual lettuce beds (Boston or Bibb). Accompany with toast points made with low-sodium bread. Allow 1 slice per serving.

Pistachio Lace Cookies (p. 183)

Servings	9
Sodium	15 mg
Calories	327

Diet adaptation: Allow 4 cookies per serving. Use unsalted pistachios.

Low-Carbohydrate Menu

Lamb Chops with Bacon, Garlic and Onion

Servings	2
Carbohydrate	4.3 gm
Calories	340

Peel and mince 1 small onion and 6 garlic cloves. Place the onion and garlic on top of 2 lamb shoulder chops (about 8 ounces each), dividing evenly. Wrap each chop with 3 strips of bacon and secure with toothpicks. Broil the chops 4 minutes on each side 3 inches from the heat.

Sherried Mushrooms (p. 118)

Servings	3
Carbohydrate	3.9 gm
Calories	154

Tomatoes with Fresh Ricotta Cheese

Servings	8
Carbohydrate	8.1 gm
Calories	151

Diet adaptation: (Based on Fresh Ricotta Cheese, p. 28.) Spread 2 tablespoons of the ricotta on each of 8 large ½-inch-thick tomato slices. Garnish with chopped chives.

Ice Creamed Berries

Servings	4
Carbohydrate	13.2 gm
Calories	229

Place 1 cup unsweetened berries, ½ cup sour cream, ½ cup heavy cream and 2 tablespoons honey in a blender and blend thoroughly. Freeze in the blender container for 1 hour. Blend for 30 seconds and return to the freezer for another hour. Blend again for 30 seconds and freeze again for at least 2 more hours. Divide the mixture among 4 dessert dishes and top each portion with 2 tablespoons unsweetened whipped cream.

Low-Carbohydrate Menu

Fresh Salmon Steak Tartare (p. 105)

Servings	4
Carbohydrate	4 gm
Calories	342

Shredded Brussels Sprouts Sautéed in Cream (p. 115)

Servings	6
Carbohydrate	7 gm
Calories	149

World's Best Hamburger (p. 61)

Servings	3
Carbohydrate	0 gm
Calories	507

Diet adaptation: Omit the roll.

Orange-Ginger Whipped Cream with Candied Orange Peel

Servings	4
Carbohydrate	47 gm
Calories	383

Diet adaptation: (Based on Ginger Génoise with Whipped Cream and Candied Orange Peel, p. 181). Prepare the candied orange peel as directed. Serve over 2 cups prepared Orange-Ginger Whipped Cream (½ cup per person).

Low-Carbohydrate Menu

Egyptian Stuffed Game Hens (p. 77)

Servings	8
Carbohydrate	21.7 gm
Calories	414

Diet adaptation: Except for the chicken broth, reduce the stuffing recipe by half and substitute brown rice for bulgur. Cook the rice mixture until the liquid is absorbed, about 15 minutes, before stuffing into the hens. Strain the onions out of the marinade before basting the hens. Allow ½ hen per serving and serve with the cut-side down.

Spinach Salad with Warm Anchovy Dressing (p. 151)

Servings	10
Carbohydrate	3.7 gm
Calories	166

Frozen Ginger Soufflé (p. 192)

Servings	12
Carbohydrate	8.1 gm
Calories	209

Diet adaptation: Increase the powdered ginger to 1 teaspoon and omit the crystallized ginger. Reduce the sake and the sugar to ½ cup each. Garnish each serving with 2 tablespoons of unsweetened whipped cream.

Low-Carbohydrate Menu

Vegetable Consommé

Servings	12
Carbohydrate	0 gm
Calories	25

Diet adaptation: (Based on Vegetable Stock, p. 205.) Serve ½ cup hot vegetable stock per person.

Spontaneous Chicken in Mustard Sauce (p. 82)

Servings	4
Carbohydrate	5.5 gm
Calories	530

Swiss Chard with Chopped Tomatoes (p. 123)

Servings	4
Carbohydrate	9.2 gm
Calories	365

Narsai's Original Chocolate Decadence (p. 179)

Servings	12
Carbohydrate	18.6 gm
Calories	420

Diet adaptation: Use unsweetened frozen raspberries or 1½ cups fresh raspberries.

Low-Carbohydrate Menu

Chèvre Mousse (p. 27)

Servings	12
Carbohydrate	4 gm
Calories	177

Diet adaptation: Serve with cucumber slices, allowing ¼ cucumber per serving.

Roast Rack of Lamb (p. 48)

Servings	4
Carbohydrate	.8 gm
Calories	592

Lacy Artichoke Pancakes (p. 112)

Servings	4
Carbohydrate	12.2 gm
Calories	226

Diet adaptation: Omit the onion and applesauce.

Strawberries Splashed with Rum

Servings	1
Carbohydrate	12 gm
Calories	118

Wash and hull 1 cup fresh strawberries and splash with 1 tablespoon rum.

Low-Carbohydrate Menu

Iced Buttermilk Soup (p. 44)

Servings	6
Carbohydrate	10.8 gm
Calories	104

Grilled Flank Steak with Dill (p. 66)

Servings	4
Carbohydrate	.86 gm
Calories	252

Broccoli-Pepper Vinaigrette (p. 115)

Servings	6
Carbohydrate	9.5 gm
Calories	168

Pickled Onions (p. 214)

Servings	8
Carbohydrate	3.6 gm
Calories	19

Fresh Kiwi Fruit

Servings	1
Carbohydrate	8.4 gm
Calories	30

Allow 1 kiwi per serving.

Low-Carbohydrate Menu

Fresh Oysters in Spinach Leaves (p. 22)

Servings	6
Carbohydrate	4.4 gm
Calories	226

Boned Broiled Quail (p. 75)

Servings	6
Carbohydrate	1.1 gm
Calories	820

Jade Broccoli with Pecans (p. 114)

Servings	4
Carbohydrate	5.7 gm
Calories	208

Blueberry Flan (p. 185)

Servings	12
Carbohydrate	20.6 gm
Calories	178

Diet adaptation: Omit the crust. Reduce the sugar in the filling to ¼ cup. Serve in champagne glasses.

Low-Carbohydrate Menu

Spinach and Avocado Salad (p. 151)

Servings	4
Carbohydrate	7.7 gm
Calories	300

Pot-Roasted Brisket of Beef (p. 68)

Servings	9
Carbohydrate	3 gm
Calories	438

Diet adaptation: Use only lean brisket.

Tea-Flavored Bavarian Cream (p. 186)

Servings	8
Carbohydrate	14 gm
Calories	183

Diet adaptation: Reduce the honey to ⅓ cup.

Low-Carbohydrate Menu

Pickled Shrimp (p. 106)

Servings	12
Carbohydrate	4.4 gm
Calories	158

Sole and Salmon in Lettuce Leaves (p. 102)

Servings	6
Carbohydrate	5 gm
Calories	702

Sautéed Tomatoes with Cream (p. 123)

Servings	4
Carbohydrate	2 gm
Calories	74

Brandied Fresh Peaches

Servings	2
Carbohydrate	10.7 gm
Calories	96

Peel and slice 2 medium peaches and place in two dessert dishes. Splash 1 tablespoon of brandy over each.

Low-Cholesterol Menu

Artichoke Hearts with Mushrooms (p. 112)

Servings	6
Fat	3.0 gm
Saturated Fat	0.3 gm
Polyunsaturated Fat	0.2 gm
Cholesterol	0 mg
Calories	95

Diet adaptation: Use an additional ½ cup lemon juice to coat the artichoke hearts before adding them to the saucepan. Omit the vegetable oil and reduce the olive oil to 1 tablespoon. Omit the Parmesan cheese.

Chicken Breasts with Lime (p. 86)

Servings	5
Fat	1.3 gm
Saturated Fat	0.3 gm
Polyunsaturated Fat	0.3 gm
Cholesterol	54.4 mg
Calories	136

Diet adaptation: Omit the clarified butter and broil the chicken for 10 to 12 minutes instead of sautéing. Add the uncooked shallots to the broth and reduce to ½ cup. Omit the crème fraîche; thicken the sauce with 1½ teaspoons arrowroot before adding the lime juice. Omit the cold butter.

Panzanella (p. 153)

Servings	8
Fat	7.2 gm
Saturated Fat	0.5 gm
Polyunsaturated Fat	4.4 gm
Cholesterol	0 mg
Calories	245

Diet adaptation: Substitute safflower oil for the olive oil and use only 3 tablespoons.

Lemon Ice with Anisette

Servings	1
Fat	0.5 gm
Saturated Fat	0 gm
Polyunsaturated Fat	0 gm
Cholesterol	0 mg
Calories	193

Sprinkle a ½-cup scoop of lemon ice with 1 tablespon of anisette. Garnish with mint leaves.

Low-Cholesterol Menu

Steamer Clams with Wine

Servings	4
Fat	16 gm
Saturated Fat	0.5 gm
Polyunsaturated Fat	0.6 gm
Cholesterol	54 mg
Calories	136

Scrub 3 dozen steamer clams (about 4 quarts unshucked) under running water. Soak for 1 hour in a salt solution (1 gallon of water and 5 tablespoons salt). In a stockpot, place 1 cup white wine, 4 chopped scallions and 4 crushed garlic cloves; cover tightly and bring to a simmer over moderate heat. Rinse the clams and add them to the stockpot. Cover tightly and cook until they open, 5 to 8 minutes (discard any that do not open). Serve in a bowl with the broth.

Wild Rice with Mushrooms

Servings	4
Fat	1.4 gm
Saturated Fat	0.1 gm
Polyunsaturated Fat	1.7 gm
Cholesterol	0 mg
Calories	84

Diet adaptation: (Based on Wild Rice with Bacon and Mushrooms, p. 147). Substitute soft safflower margarine for the butter, decrease it to 1 teaspoon and use a nonstick skillet. Omit the bacon.

Dilled Vegetables

Servings	3
Fat	2.0 gm
Saturated Fat	0.1 gm
Polyunsaturated Fat	1.1 gm
Cholesterol	0 mg
Calories	51

Diet adaptation: (Based on Dilled Chicken and Vegetables in Pita Bread, p. 82.) Substitute safflower oil for the peanut oil and reduce it to 1 teaspoon. Using ½ teaspoon of the oil, prepare the vegetables as directed in Step 2; transfer to a serving dish and keep warm. Using the remaining oil, cook the mushrooms as directed in Step 3 until tender. Toss them with the other cooked vegetables, 2 tablespoons of the dill, the lemon juice, hot pepper sauce, salt and pepper. Prepare the tomatoes as directed in Step 5 and spoon them over the cooked vegetables.

Apricot Compote (p. 190)

Servings	6
Fat	0.3 gm
Saturated Fat	Trace
Polyunsaturated Fat	Trace
Cholesterol	0 mg
Calories	260

Diet adaptation: Omit the pine nuts.

Low-Cholesterol Menu

Six-Onion Soup (p. 39)

Servings	4
Fat	2.3 gm
Saturated Fat	0.5 gm
Polyunsaturated Fat	0.4 gm
Cholesterol	1.3 mg
Calories	201

Diet adaptation: Use low-fat chicken stock and increase it to 5 cups. Omit the butter; add the raw vegetables to the stock in Step 2. Use up to 1 cup dry croutons for garnish.

Poached Breast of Chicken with Autumn Vegetables (p. 86)

Servings	7
Fat	1.8 gm
Saturated Fat	0.3 gm
Polyunsaturated Fat	0.2 gm
Cholesterol	56 mg
Calories	264

Diet adaptation: Use skinless, boneless chicken breasts. Prepare 7 of each of the vegetables instead of 4.

Green Caper Sauce (p. 207)

Servings	8
Fat	2 gm
Saturated Fat	0.2 gm
Polyunsaturated Fat	0.1 gm
Cholesterol	0.6 mg
Calories	30

Diet adaptation: Substitute low-fat yogurt for the olive oil. Allow 2 tablespoons of the sauce per serving.

Pickled Strawberries (p. 189)

Servings	6
Fat	0.4 gm
Saturated Fat	Trace
Polyunsaturated Fat	0.2 gm
Cholesterol	0 mg
Calories	133

Low-Cholesterol Menu

Split Pea Soup with Herbed Croutons (p. 38)

Servings	8
Fat	8.1 gm
Saturated Fat	1 gm
Polyunsaturated Fat	5.5 gm
Cholesterol	2.6 mg
Calories	351

Diet adaptation: Substitute 2 tablespoons margarine for the butter. Use defatted chicken stock. Use 1-percent-fat milk.

Valentine Duck Salad (p. 157)

Servings	4
Fat	47.7 gm
Saturated Fat	3 gm
Polyunsaturated Fat	18 gm
Cholesterol	93 mg
Calories	828

Diet adaptation: Omit the duck skin.

Jigsaw Pears (p. 189)

Servings	6
Fat	3.4 gm
Saturated Fat	0.3 gm
Polyunsaturated Fat	1.9 gm
Cholesterol	0 mg
Calories	297

Low-Cholesterol Menu

Clear Mushroom Soup (p. 32)

Servings	6
Fat	.3 gm
Saturated Fat	.1 gm
Polyunsaturated Fat	.1 gm
Cholesterol	.3 mg
Calories	59

Broiled Bass with Endive Vinaigrette (p. 92)

Servings	4
Fat	26 gm
Saturated Fat	3.6 gm
Polyunsaturated Fat	14.6 gm
Cholesterol	61 mg
Calories	600

Diet adaptation: Reduce the bass to 1¼ pounds. Reduce the vinaigrette ingredients by half to make about ½ cup dressing.

Papaya Sherbet (p. 190)

Servings	4
Fat	0.4 gm
Saturated Fat	0.1 gm
Polyunsaturated Fat	0.1 gm
Cholesterol	0 mg
Calories	297

Low-Cholesterol Menu

Green Salad with Sesame Oil and Vinegar Dressing

Servings	4
Fat	28 gm
Saturated Fat	4 gm
Polyunsaturated Fat	24 gm
Cholesterol	0 mg
Calories	271

Prepare 1 head of leaf lettuce. Combine ½ cup sesame oil with 3 tablespoons vinegar.

Hot Sweet-and-Sour Borscht (p. 40)

Servings	6
Fat	1.8 gm
Saturated Fat	0.7 gm
Polyunsaturated Fat	0.1 gm
Cholesterol	2.3 mg
Calories	201

Diet adaptation: Omit the beef brisket from the stock and vegetable oil from the soup. Skip Step 3 and add the onion and garlic with the stock in Step 4. Substitute low-fat yogurt for the sour cream.

Smoked Trout (or Salmon) Niçoise (p. 160)

Servings	8
Fat	26.8 gm
Saturated Fat	3.4 gm
Polyunsaturated Fat	2.2 gm
Cholesterol	21.4 mg
Calories	400

Diet adaptation: Use brook trout only. Omit the egg yolks and use whites only.

Green Grapes and Walnuts

Servings	4
Fat	17 gm
Saturated Fat	1 gm
Polyunsaturated Fat	16 gm
Cholesterol	0 mg
Calories	150

Prepare and combine 1 pound seedless green grapes and ½ cup walnuts. Serve in dessert cups.

Low-Cholesterol Menu

Tequila Pear (p. 13)

Servings	1
Fat	0.7 gm
Saturated Fat	0.4 gm
Polyunsaturated Fat	0 gm
Cholesterol	0.7 mg
Calories	240

Diet adaptation: Use low-fat yogurt.

Chicken Quenelles with Mushroom Duxelles (p. 77)

Servings	8
Fat	5.7 gm
Saturated Fat	1.1 gm
Polyunsaturated Fat	2.6 gm
Cholesterol	34.1 mg
Calories	156

Diet adaptation: Substitute soft safflower margarine for the butter and decrease it to 3 tablespoons. Use low-fat yogurt instead of heavy cream and omit the Beurre Blanc.

Asparagus Bundles (p. 112)

Servings	2
Fat	10.5 gm
Saturated Fat	1.0 gm
Polyunsaturated Fat	5.3 gm
Cholesterol	0 mg
Calories	181

Diet adaptation: Substitute soft safflower margarine for the butter and reduce it to 1 tablespoon plus 2 teaspoons. Butter only the side of the phyllo dough that will touch the cookie sheet and do not butter the bundles again in Step 2. Allow 2 bundles per serving.

Raspberries and Oranges with Rosewater

Servings	1
Fat	0.7 gm
Saturated Fat	0.1 gm
Polyunsaturated Fat	0.3 gm
Cholesterol	0 mg
Calories	72

Peel and slice a chilled orange. Arrange the slices on a dessert plate, top with ½ cup fresh chilled raspberries and sprinkle with 10 drops (⅛ teaspoon) rosewater.

D-E-F

G-H-I

J-K-L

T-U-V

W-X-Y-Z

CONTRIBUTORS

In addition to the recipes developed by our test kitchen, we are pleased to include recipes from the following contributors to the magazine. The numbers and letters indicate page number and location of the contributors' recipes: **L** = Left, **M** = Middle, **R** = Right, **T** = Top, **B** = Bottom. Example: 42LT = on page 42, in the Lefthand column, at the Top.

Jean Anderson is the author of a number of cookbooks, including *Jean Anderson's New Processor Cooking* (Morrow) and *Jean Anderson Cooks* (Morrow), and is the co-author of *The Doubleday Cookbook*: 199M.

Nancy Arum is a cooking teacher, food writer and author of *Ice Cream & Ices* (Harper & Row) : 190RB.

Nancy Barr works with Julia Child on a number of projects, including a column in *Parade* magazine, the "Good Morning America" show, and the Chef's Company Cooking School in Providence, Rhode Island: 116LB, 118R, 121LT, 122M.

Melanie Barnard is a freelance food writer. 12M, 30LB, 154M, 216M.

Jo Bettoja runs Lo Scaldavivande cooking school in Rome and is co-author of *Italian Cooking in the Grand Tradition* (Doubleday): 52R.

Anna Teresa Callen is a cooking teacher (in New York City), food writer and author of *The Wonderful World of Quiches, Pizzas and Savory Pies* (Crown) and *The Anna Teresa Callen Pasta Menu Cookbook* (Crown): 87LB.

Dolores Casella is a cooking teacher (in Idaho Falls, Idaho), caterer and the author of a number of cookbooks, including *The New Book of Breads* (David White): 200R.

Elizabeth Schneider Colchie is a food writer and the author of *Ready When You Are: Made-Ahead Meals for Entertaining* (Crown) and co-author of *Better Than Store-Bought* (Harper & Row): 32LB, 67M, 72L, 137L, 148R, 161R, 190LB.

Carolyn Dille and Susan Belsinger, food writers and co-authors of *Cooking with Herbs* (CBI and Van Nostrand Reinhold), are currently working on a cable television series on cooking and gardening: 44MB, 154L.

Florence Fabricant is a regular contributor to *The New York Times* food section and is the author of *With the Grain* (Scribner's), scheduled for publication in 1985: 78R.

Jim Fobel, author of *Beautiful Food* (Van Nostrand Reinhold), was *Food & Wine*'s test kitchen director for years: 19R, 24R, 31LT, 31R, 42R, 43R, 50M, 62R, 81L, 81R, 116R, 122RB, 123R, 124L, 137LT, 137LB, 138M, 152L, 152R, 153R, 162M, 163LB, 167L, 178R, 183M, 190M, 190RT, 196M, 196R, 198M, 198R, 209RT, 210M, 211RB, 212L, 214LT, 218R.

Marcella Hazan is a cooking teacher (in Bologna and Venice) and the author of *The Classic Italian Cook Book* (Knopf) and *More Classic Italian Cooking* (Knopf). She is currently working on a third cookbook, scheduled for publication in 1985: 101L.

Madhur Jaffrey is an actress, cooking teacher, food writer and author of a number of books including *The World of the East Vegetarian Cooking* (Knopf) and *Indian Cooking* (Barron's). She is currently working on an international cookbook (Simon & Schuster): 49L.

Dora Jonassen is a Danish-born food stylist based in New York City: 22R.

Jane Helsel Joseph is a food writer based in Germany: 19M, 42L, 46L, 156R, 212MB.

Leslie Land writes a nationally syndicated newspaper column, "Good Food": 16L, 23L, 211RT.

Edna Lewis is the author of *The Taste of Country Cooking* (Knopf) and *The Edna Lewis Cookbook* (The Ecco Press): 197 LB.

Tom Maresca and Diane Darrow write frequently on the wine and food of southern Europe. Maresca is currently writing a book on wines, scheduled for publication in 1985: 141RB, 141L, 141M.

Perla Meyers is a cooking teacher, food writer and consultant, and the author of *The Seasonal Kitchen* (Vintage), *The Peasant Kitchen* (Vintage) and *From Market to Kitchen* (Harper & Row): 64R, 74R, 108L, 145M.

Marian Morash is the author of *The Victory Garden Cookbook* (Knopf), the featured chef on the PBS series "The Victory Garden" and executive chef for Julia Child's show "Dinner with Julia": 112L.

Jo Northrop writes a monthly food column for *Country Living* magazine: 24L, 196L.

Judith Olney is a food writer and the author of *Judith Olney's Entertainments* (Barron's) and *The Joy of Chocolate* (Barron's): 201R.

Shirley Sarvis is an entertaining and food writer and author of *Woman's Day Home Cooking Around the World* (Simon & Schuster). She also conducts weekly wine and food tastings in San Francisco and special-event wine and food dinners across the country: 80M, 97RT, 97RB, 103R, 107RT, 114R, 162R, 179M.

Joan Scobey is a food writer and editor: 86R, 141RT, 147L.

Martha Rose Shulman, who runs a catering firm in Paris, is the author of *The Vegetarian Feast* (Harper & Row) and *Fast Vegetarian Feasts* (Dial Press): 197R.

Ruth Spear is food editor for New York's *Avenue* magazine and the author of *Cooking Fish and Shellfish* (Doubleday) and the upcoming *The Classic Vegetable Cookbook* (Harper & Row), scheduled for publication in 1985: 30R, 40M, 180L.

Harvey Steiman is food and wine editor of the *San Francisco Examiner*, the host of a San Francisco radio talk show (KCBS Kitchen) and co-author of *Chinese Technique* (Simon & Schuster): 68R, 179M.

Martha Stewart is a caterer and the author of *Entertaining* (Clarkson Potter) and *Martha Stewart's Quick Cook* (Clarkson Potter): 75R, 99R, 212RT.

Barbara Tropp is the author of *The Modern Art of Chinese Cookery* (Morrow) and chef-owner of China Moon, a Chinese bistro in San Francisco: 100L, 140M, 191MB, 191R, 211 LB.

Michèle Urvater is the author of *Cooking Nouvelle Cuisine in America* (Workman), *Fine French Food Fast* (Irena Chalmers) and *Cookies and Candies for Christmas* (Irena Chalmers) and is working with the Culinary Institute of America on a cooking technique cookbook: 38R, 39M, 114L, 114MT, 148M.

Anne Walsh writes *Food & Wine*'s "Good Fast Food" column: 18RT, 37LT, 42MT, 48R, 66RT, 86L, 123MB, 151M, 151RT, 207RB.

Anne Willan, director of La Varenne cooking school in Paris, is the author of a number of books, including *French Regional Cooking* (Morrow) and *La Varenne Cooking Course* (Morrow): 84L, 101R, 158M.
Sallie Williams is a food consultant and writer and is the author of *The Art of Presenting Food* (Hearst). She was the director of La Varenne for two years: 24MB.
Paula Wolfert is a food writer, cooking teacher and the author of *The Cooking of South-West France* (Dial Press), *Mediterranean Cooking* (Quadrangle) and *Couscous and Other Good Food from Morocco* (Harper & Row): 98R, 187L.

And from the *Food & Wine* staff (past and present)—**Susan R Brennan:** 43M; **James W. Brown, Jr.:** 168R; **John S. Connors:** 15LT; **Anne Disrude:** 23M, 113MT, 163M, 208 LT; **Bette Duke:** 191L, 191MT, 211MT; **Kathy Gunst:** 117LB, 151LB; **Rosalee Harris:** 28M, 44MT, 47L, 146L, 182M, 189M, 201L, 216LB; **John Robert Massie:** 142R, 143 (all), 144LT, 207L, 208LB; **Anne H. Montgomery:** 147M; **Nancy Muzeck:** 15MT, 15MB; **Maria Piccolo:** 28M, 37LB, 44MT, 146L, 181R, 182M, 184R, 201L, 216LB; **W. Peter Prestcott:** 12LT, 12RB, 13LT, 13MT, 13MB, 13RB, 18LB, 19L, 20M, 20R, 25L, 25RT, 26R, 27M; 38LT, 44L, 52L, 72R, 80L, 82M, 82RT, 88L, 115LB, 121MT, 122LT, 125M, 138RB, 141L, 141M, 151RB, 157L, 158R, 160L, 161L, 166L, 167R, 189RB, 190LT, 196RB, 210LM; **William Rice:** 150M; **Shirley Rush:** 138RT; **Kate Slate:** 185L, 217MT; **Diana Sturgis:** 110M, 112M, 116M, 117LT, 184L, 184M, 212RB, 217MB.

Reynaldo Alejandro: 14LB; **Pepe Berg:** 92R; **Georges Blanc:** 85L, 105L, 107RB; **Henri and Gérard Charvet:** 120L; **Sally Darr:** 167L; **Andrea Zeeman Deane;** 216M; **Marcel Desaulniers:** 100R; **Mary Wilson Price Donleavy:** 183R; **Felicia Eppley:** 106L; **Lawrence Forgione:** 73L; **Pearl Byrd Foster:** 41MB; **Bobby Goldman:** 210RB; **Jean-Pierre Goyenvalle:** 98L; **James Haller:** 70R, 150LT; **James Heywood:** 65R; **Ken Hom:** 121LB, 146R, 210MB; **Marika Horodecki:** 18M; **Malcolm Hudson:** 150LB; **Judith Huxley:** 152MT; **Jon Kasky:** 118MT; **Bob Kinkead:** 207RT; **Dean Kolstad:** 200M; **Martha Kostyra:** 32M; **Jean-Paul Lacombe:** 22L; **Guy Legay:** 164L; **Sandy McAdams:** 106M; **Loretta Mayer:** 126R; **Dene Miller:** 125R; **Helen and Aaron Millman:** 128L, 153L, 183L; **Barry Morganstern:** 185R; **Madame Mourière:** 16M, 37M; **James and Helen Nassikas:** 70L, 123MT; **Bill Neal:** 99L, 99M; **Patrick O'Connell:** 102R; **Anne O'Hara:** 185M; **Janice Okun:** 20LB; **Pierre Orsi:** 147R; **Silvio Pinto:** 88R, 114MB, 115LT; **Christian Planchon:** 74L; **Walter Plendner:** 41L, 115MT, 117M; **Wolfgang Puck:** 24MT, 76L; **Seppi Renggli:** 145R; **Belle and Barney Rhodes:** 75M, 107L, 148L; **Jacques Robert:** 48L, 112RB, 214LM; **John Rudolph:** 92L; **Rick Sajbel:** 104M, 181L; **Jay Schaeffer:** 97L; **Jimmy Schmidt:** 139R; **Andrew Spahr:** 104L, **Betty Stofko:** 215M; **Peter Sussman:** 180M, 186M; **Bath Szerenyi:** 210LT; **Susan Tait:** 121R; **Ben and Jane Thompson:** 21R, 30LT, 47R, 120R; **John Tovey:** 41R, 43L; **Guy Tricon:** 38LB, 109R, 125L; **Ghislain and Cathérine deVogüé:** 126LB, 192R; **Alice Waters:** 28T; **Penny Winship:** 218MT.

Amandier de Mougins, Mougins, France: 86M, 118L, 207M; **The American Café,** Washington, D.C.: 160R; **Aubergine,** Camden, ME: 37R; **Beach Plum Inn,** Menemsha, MA: 14LT; **Box Tree Inn,** Purdys, NY: 42MB; **Café des Artistes,** New York City: 105M; **Citadel Grill,** Cairo, Egypt: 77L; **Dean & DeLuca,** New York City: 115MB; **Lavins,** New York City: 65L; **Mitchell Cobey Cuisine,** Chicago, IL: 156M; **The Oyster Bar,** near Bellingham, WA: 108M; **Proof of the Pudding,** Atlanta, GA: 154M; **Rex, Il Ristorante,** Los Angeles: 163 LT; **The Silver Palate,** New York City: 39R; **Staats ,** Aspen, CO: 31LB; **Stephenson's,** Kansas City, MO: 195 RT; **Wild Wind,** Naples, NY: 41MT.